Henry W. Blake

Quarter century edition of The paradise of childhood

A practical guide to kindergartners

Henry W. Blake

Quarter century edition of The paradise of childhood
A practical guide to kindergartners

ISBN/EAN: 9783337374020

Printed in Europe, USA, Canada, Australia, Japan

Cover: Foto ©Paul-Georg Meister /pixelio.de

More available books at **www.hansebooks.com**

QUARTER CENTURY EDITION

OF THE

PARADISE OF CHILDHOOD.

A PRACTICAL GUIDE TO KINDERGARTNERS,

BY

EDWARD WIEBÉ.

EDITED BY MILTON BRADLEY.

INCLUDING A

LIFE OF FRIEDRICH FROEBEL,

BY

HENRY W. BLAKE, A. M.

PROFUSELY ILLUSTRATED.

—

SPRINGFIELD, MASS.:
MILTON BRADLEY COMPANY.
1896.

Entered according to Act of Congress, in the year 1896,
BY
MILTON BRADLEY COMPANY,
In the Office of the Librarian of Congress, at Washington.
All rights reserved.

Registered at Stationers' Hall, London, England.
All rights reserved.

Entered according to Act of Congress, in the year 1869,
BY
MILTON BRADLEY & COMPANY,
In the Clerk's Office of the District Court of the District of Massachusetts.

Contents.

Editor's Preface,
Introduction to the Life of Froebel,
Map of Central Germany,
THE LIFE OF FROEBEL,
   In His Father's House,
   With His Guardian,
   The Forester's Apprentice,
   A Student at Jena,
   Becomes a Teacher,
   Relations with Pestalozzi,
   Final University Studies,
   A Soldier of the Legion,
   Curator at Berlin,
   Principal at Keilhau,
   In Switzerland,
   Blankenburg,
   Wanderings About Germany,
   Marienthal,
   Since Froebel's Death,
THE PARADISE OF CHILDHOOD,
   Author's Preface,
   Kindergarten Culture,
   Establishment of a Kindergarten,
   Means and Ways of Occupation,
   The First Gift,
      Editor's Notes: General Impression—Color—Form—Motion.
   The Second Gift,
      Editor's Notes: The Sphere—The Cube—The Cylinder.
   The Third Gift,
      The Presentation of the Third Gift—Preparation for Constructing Forms—Forms of Life—Forms of Knowledge—Forms of Beauty. Editor's Notes.
   The Fourth Gift,
      Preparation for Constructing Forms—Forms of Life—Forms of Knowledge—Forms of Beauty. Editor's Notes: Furniture Sequence—Baker Sequence—House Building and Furnishing Sequence.

CONTENTS.

The Fifth Gift, ... 119–135
    Cube, Twice Divided in Each Direction—Forms of Life—Forms of Knowledge—Forms of Beauty. Editor's Notes: First Sequence—Second Sequence—Third Sequence.

The Fifth Gift B, ... 136–138
    Forms of Life—Forms of Symmetry.

The Sixth Gift, ... 139–148
    Large Cube, Consisting of Double Divided Oblong Blocks—Forms of Life—Forms of Knowledge—Forms of Beauty. Editor's Notes: A Life Sequence—A Beauty Sequence.

The Seventh Gift, ... 149–168
    Square and Triangular Tablets for Laying of Figures—The Quadrangular Laying Tablets (Squares). Right-Angled Triangles—Forms of Life—Forms of Knowledge—Forms of Beauty. The Equilateral Triangle—Forms of Knowledge—Forms of Beauty. The Obtuse-Angled Triangle with Two Sides Alike—The Right-Angled Triangle with No Equal Sides. Editor's Notes.

The Eighth Gift, ... 169–176
    Sticks for Laying of Figures. Editor's Notes.

The Ninth Gift, ... 177–182
    Whole and Half Rings for Laying Figures. Editor's Notes.

The Tenth Gift, ... 183–211
    Material for Drawing The Vertical Line—The Horizontal Line—Combination of Vertical and Horizontal Lines—Oblique Lines—The Curved Line. Editor's Notes.

The Eleventh and Twelfth Gifts, ... 212–224
    Material for Perforating and Embroidering. Editor's Notes: Elementary Color Teaching.

The Thirteenth Gift, ... 225–234
    Material for Cutting Papers and Mounting Pieces to Produce Figures and Forms—Mounting the Figures. Editor's Notes.

The Fourteenth Gift, ... 235–241
    Material for Braiding or Weaving. Editor's Notes.

The Fifteenth Gift, ... 242–246
    The Interlacing Slats.

The Sixteenth Gift, ... 247–253
    The Slat with Many Links.

The Seventeenth Gift, ... 254–256
    Material for Intertwining. Editor's Notes.

The Eighteenth Gift, ... 257–263
    Material for Paper Folding. Editor's Notes.

The Nineteenth Gift, ... 264–267
    Material for Peas-Work. Editor's Notes.

The Twentieth Gift, ... 268–274
    Material for Modeling. Editor's Notes. The Kindergarten Games.

EDITOR'S PREFACE.

In the year 1868 the editor of the present edition was persuaded to publish "The Paradise of Childhood," by one of his neighbors, Mr. Edward Wiebe, and also to begin the manufacture of kindergarten material for use in America. Mr. Weibe, who came to Springfield a few years prior to that time, was a very intelligent and well educated man and was then engaged in teaching music, but had gained a knowledge of the kindergarten system through his association with the widow of Froebel before leaving Germany. He was anxious to introduce it in this country, and as soon as he became acquainted with the editor, who was at the head of a factory for making children's games and home amusements, began to urge his co-operation, both from an educational and a commercial standpoint. The editor knew nothing about the kindergarten and did not take any interest in it so long as Mr. Wiebe was its only advocate. Not many months later, however, he attended an exposition of kindergarten principles and aims by Miss Elizabeth P. Peabody, who had recently returned from a careful study of them in Germany and undertaken to convert America to the cause. To that single evening talk, given in a school-house near his home, the editor attributes whatever he has done in the name of the kindergarten during the last twenty-five years, and as an immediate result he yielded to Mr. Wiebe's entreaties to publish the manuscript of "The Paradise of Childhood," which had been prepared for a long time, and also began making the kindergarten material.

In those days all the kindergarten literature that had been published in this country was confined to a few newspaper and magazine articles. The first edition of "The Paradise of Childhood" contained what is here inserted as the Author's Preface, but was then called the introduction, a few preliminary explanations about establishing a kindergarten and the author's text on the twenty gifts and occupations. The illustrations were reprints from "Goldammer's Kindergarten," being lithographed on separate plates, in the back part of the book.

In subsequent editions the paper entitled "Kindergarten Culture," was added, and in 1878 the plates of "The Paradise of Childhood" were prefaced with a brief text and published in separate form as "A Hand-Book for the Kindergarten," the contents of which were afterwards incorporated with the "Paradise" during many editions. For a quarter of a century this work has been accepted as the only single book furnishing in brief an outline of both the theory and practice of the kindergarten. In 1876 it received honorable mention at the Philadelphia Centennial Exhibition as being the first illustrated guide to the kindergarten ever published in the English language.

At the end of twenty-five years the editor felt that the time had come to prepare an edition of the book which should in some respects differ radically from any yet published. It was, therefore, resolved to print again Mr. Wiebe's original text, with the paper on "Kindergarten Culture" as an introduction, putting the illustrations in the body of the book, instead of grouping them at the end, and adding such notes as the kindergarten knowledge of to-day would naturally approve. These notes include some suggestions regarding the use of color in the kindergarten, a matter to which the editor has given much special study, and a brief paper at the end of the book about the games. As a proper prelude to the study of the kindergarten

EDITOR'S PREFACE.

system a Life of Froebel has been made a part of this book, with a concluding chapter about the movement since his death, which will, it is hoped, prove helpful to such students as have not had the benefit of other biographical works relating to the founder of the kindergarten. This life is illustrated with pictures taken in Germany for that purpose and also a map of the section where Froebel lived and labored. The editor is, of course, aware that some leading kindergarten training teachers object to the use of all "guide books" by either the pupils or teachers of the system. He believes, however, that they still have their place in the educational world, although they may not be as essential as they were twenty-five years ago. When the first edition of "Paradise" was published, argument was in order to convince the public not only that the kindergarten was necessary but that it was possible. It now is usually acknowledged to be a good thing, but it is thought by some of those who manage the affairs of nations, states, cities and school districts, to be too expensive. Doubtless good things are usually more costly than those which are inferior, but it is not by any means certain that they are always most expensive in the long run, either to individuals or communities. The experimental stages of the kindergarten are now passed so far as the proof is necessary to determine the value to the world of the general truths first set forth by Froebel. It now remains for the friends of the work to devise the best means for fully carrying those principles to the masses. They must put forth every effort to rightly direct those who are to determine the nature of the education which is to be provided for the children of the coming generation.

While it is readily admitted that no single book nor even a library can furnish the instruction necessary to equip a kindergartner in the best sense, and that only personal contact with experienced kindergartners and practical experience with children can make a kindergartner, it is still maintained that there is a demand for the publication of a fairly full but concise statement of the theory and practice of the system of education which was evolved by the labors of Froebel, for the benefit of a large class in the community. For instance, those primary teachers who are to receive pupils from the kindergarten should have instruction in the details of the kindergarten system sufficient at least to enable them to go on with the instruction in such lines as to connect logically with the education already received. For this purpose there must come a connecting school between the kindergarten system and the primary school in which the teacher shall be fully informed as to the kindergarten course from which the child has graduated, and hence able to gradually and without friction induct him into the school system. If a child of average ability spends the years from four to six in a kindergarten, and then one year in a connecting school, he should afterwards require practically no more of the concrete than is always necessary in all education which relates to the more practical matters of life. It is evident that in all scientific and mathematical education the concrete illustrations must be continued in the form of experiments, and the kindergarten education enables the pupil to make the best use of them as they are required, but under the conditions named all the counting of blocks, folding of papers, cutting and pasting of mathematical and artistic forms will have merely prepared the way for clear mathematical thinking and artistic designing and drawing. Under such a condition of things each primary school teacher should at least have as much familiarity with the kindergarten methods as can be gained by a very careful study of this book, and such knowledge is fully as desirable on the part of every mother with young children.

At this point the editor desires a word of explanation regarding the paper which has so long been published under the name of "Kindergarten Culture." This résumé of the kindergarten system was originally prepared by Mr. Wiebe to be used as an address before some educational meetings in this country previous to the publication of "The Paradise of Childhood," and was at a much later date first printed as a pamphlet for advancing the kindergarten cause in America, with the title "Kindergarten Culture," and still later, long after Mr. Wiebe had left this country, was made a part of "The Paradise of Childhood," without any knowledge by the publishers of the source from which it was originally prepared, or any assertion by Mr. Wiebe that it was or was not original. Since its publication in connection with "The Paradise of Childhood," it has been criticised as being a translation of an article by Baroness von Marenholtz-Bulow, with the added inference that in presenting "The Paradise of Childhood" to the American public, Mr. Wiebe was guilty of plagiarism or deceit. In the light of subsequent research "Kindergarten Culture" proves to have been a paraphrase or a very free translation of an article written by the Baroness but which had never at that time been translated into English.

When the work on this new edition was begun the hope was entertained that it might be completed within twenty-five years of the first appearance of the book, but certain unavoidable delays have made the task a longer one than was at first anticipated. Doubtless some critics will feel that in the attempt to remodel the book too much has been done, while others will regret that too little is undertaken. The editor can but hope, however, that this edition, taken as a whole, will prove a help to many earnest students of Fræbel and the kindergarten system. In conclusion he desires to return sincere thanks to all his co-laborers in the kindergarten field who by counsel and suggestions have done so much to help him in his work.

Springfield, Mass., January 1, 1896.

INTRODUCTION TO THE LIFE OF FROEBEL.

One of the principal objects of studying any subject is to gain the power of thinking analytically about it. To do this it may be necessary to acquire many facts pertaining to that subject, but after all this preliminary work has been done the knowledge of those facts will prove of but comparatively little consequence unless we understand and appreciate their co-relation. Consequently the argument for a careful study of Froebel's life as essential to the understanding of the kindergarten system, both in its theory and practice, is based on the broad proposition that whoever aspires to understand any system of philosophy, ethics or education must be able to think analytically about it. While all earnest students of Froebel's system realize the more thoroughly they pursue it that they have a life work in hand, there are unquestionably certain methods of study that will become especially helpful when applied to this subject, just as there are in all lines of mental investigation. And now we come to the general principle that one cannot understand the philosophy of any man who is really great without becoming familiar with his career, with the procession of events which, taken together, have made up his life.

The author once had the pleasure of listening to an address by a distinguished judge regarding the aims and methods of Bible study in which he maintained that primary investigation of historical facts is essential to the successful comprehension of any principles, doctrines, or theories which pertain to those facts. If we wish to put ourselves in touch with the teachings of Christ so that they shall become a lamp to our feet and a guide to our path, we must make ourselves familiar with His life, so that, as far as is possible, we may live as He lived, and feel as He felt. And the same may be said of other great men for whom no claim of divinity has ever been made, but who have been pioneers in the fields of spiritual, mental or material activity.

It would seem, however, that this principle of facts before theories has not been the prevalent one on the part of students and teachers. The judge just quoted admitted that it took him many years in his private study of the Bible to discover that this method is the natural one, and there is reason to fear that the average teacher is very apt to give his pupils principles and theories without being careful to present to them the biographical facts which so often lie behind those principles and theories. In other words, we are encouraged and compelled to read Cæsar's commentaries, regardless of our previous acquaintance with Cæsar. Coming to the particular application of the argument, are we not forced to admit that the accurate acquaintance with the events of Froebel's life among students of the kindergarten system has been left somewhat to accident, such study being taken up at any time in the course when it was most convenient for the teacher, and not always with the systematic application which alone insures the best results?

Friedrich Froebel lived a peculiar life and inaugurated a peculiar educational system, and it is pre-eminently true that we must study that life in order to comprehend that system, to say nothing of acquiring the ability to teach it. If we admit the truth of this statement, it follows that the study of Froebel's life should begin at the opening of the kindergarten course.

If we are to undertake such study, the question arises, Into what periods does the life of Froebel naturally divide itself? Speaking in a general way, the answer is: Into three periods, Froebel as a Student, as a Teacher, as a Kindergartner. Of course these periods overlap each other in various ways. He was always a student, from the earliest hours of his conscious existence in the lonely parsonage of Oberweisbach to his dying days at Marienthal. He became a teacher long before his professional studies ended and continued teaching till his latest breath. The germ of the kindergarten idea came to him with the prattling speech of babyhood and to perfect it was the loving labor of the rest of his days. But for purposes of classification we may regard him as a student from his birth in 1782 to 1816; a teacher from 1816 to 1837; and a kindergartner from 1837 to 1852, a span which completes the seventy years of his life.

If the division named above is correct it gives us our point of view from which to study Froebel. We are to consider him as a student, as a teacher, as a kindergartner. We are to ask ourselves what his life in these different capacities contributed to the kindergarten, and the object of such an investigation is not to satisfy idle curiosity, but to put ourselves in a position where we can understand his educational system, otherwise we cannot make any just claim to comprehending it.

In compiling this work the author has consulted the common authorities within reach of the American student and also some that are out of the usual course. The translation of Froebel's autobiographical letter to the Duke of Meiningen by Miss Lucy Wheelock of Boston, as published in Dr. Barnard's "Kindergarten and Child Culture Papers," has been relied on to furnish the thread of the narrative from 1782 till 1815. The other translation of this letter by Emilie Michaelis and H. Keatley Moore, which forms a part of their "Autobiography of Friedrich Froebel," published by C. W. Bardeen of Syracuse, N. Y., has been found valuable in throwing light on this same period, particularly through the foot notes. This book also contains a long extract from another letter of Froebel, written to Friedrich Krause, the eminent philosopher, which is a review of his life from infancy down to the year 1828, so that by consulting these two letters we get an account in Froebel's own words of his career for forty-six years, or nearly till the time when he relinquished his principalship at Keilhau.

For what happened in Switzerland we are dependent on Barop's article on "Critical Moments in the Life of Froebel," a different translation of which appears in each of the books already named. Then for the intervening period between the establishment of the first kindergarten at Blankenburg and the residence at Liebenstein we depend largely on "Froebel's Letters," edited by Arnold H. Heinemann and published by Lee & Shepard of Boston, and "The Story of My Life" by Georg Ebers, translated by Mary J. Safford and published by D. Appleton & Co. of New York. These books do not give the continuous story of Froebel's wanderings and the gradual development of the one idea of his life from 1837 to 1849, but they do contain suggestions and pen-pictures by which it is possible to piece out the narrative so that it can be readily understood and appreciated.

There are other articles to be considered, most of them being translations from Dr. Wichard Lange's "For the Understanding of Froebel," reproduced in the Barnard book. From 1849 to the time of Froebel's death the world for the most part relies on "Reminiscences of Friedrich Froebel" by Baroness Von Marenholtz-Bulow, translated by Mrs. Horace Mann and published by Lee & Shepard, Boston. A little pamphlet "Reminiscences of Friedrich Froebel," by Frau Froebel, published by the Chicago Kindergarten College, is also very helpful in supplementing the account of the Baroness, and for an account of the last days of the great apostle of the new education we are indebted to the translation of a pamphlet published by Middendorf immediately after the death of his friend. "Froebel and Education by Self-Activity," by H. C. Bowen, published by Charles Scribner's Sons, New York, adds somewhat to the story, and so does "Friedrich Froebel, How He Became an Educator," by Frau Elsie Von Calcar. This book was originally written in Dutch and then translated into German, although no English translation has ever been published. In compiling the concluding pages regarding the progress of the kindergarten movement since Froebel's death the author is indebted to "The Pratt Institute Monthly," "The Kindergarten News" and "The Kindergarten Magazine" for data. To all authors and publishers who have helped him in any way he desires to make grateful acknowledgement.

The pictures illustrating the narrative were made expressly for this book. The portrait of Froebel is copied from a picture taken from the oil painting which hangs in the schoolhouse at Oberweisbach by H. Enders, a member of the Royal Academy at Dresden, who painted it from an engraving on steel. The copy of the portrait is known as the "jubilee picture," having been selected by a committee of gentlemen appointed to choose a picture to be published at the time of the celebration of Frœbel's one hundredth birthday, in 1882. It is regarded as an excellent likeness by those people in Germany most competent to judge. The picture of Frœbel's birthplace, of the village as seen from the top of the Memorial Tower, in which the church is such a prominent feature, and the view of the tower itself were taken by special representatives of the publishers of this book for reproduction here, and they give a clear and adequate idea of the surroundings of his early days.

The pictures of the house at Marienthal, where Frœbel died, of the monument in the little wood adjoining that house and of the tombstone over the grave at Schweina were also taken for exclusive use here. In regard to the tombstone picture it is proper to say that because the photographs and woodcuts which have previously been brought from Europe by kindergartners and other tourists have shown such unmistakable proofs that they were made from drawings, and not from the tombstone and its natural surroundings, the publishers forwarded one of them to their agent in Germany with an inquiry about its authenticity. As a result the picture was returned without comment, except the word "fantasm," penciled on the back. Concerning the picture here presented it is proper to say that owing to the crowded condition of the burying ground a photograph of the monument which is entirely satisfactory cannot be secured, and that in this direct front view the symbolical cylinder and cube necessarily appear like one shaft or two similar forms of the same size. This picture is doubtless as good as could be secured under the circumstances, and bears evidence that it is from an original photograph and not the copy of an imaginative drawing. The portrait of Frau Frœbel is from a photograph taken about a dozen years ago, while she was still in active service as a training teacher at Hamburg. It was presented to Miss Louise M. Steinweg, now of Pittsburg, Pa., when she graduated from the training class, and was loaned by her to the publishers. The map used to illustrate the theater of Frœbel's life has been redrawn to fit the limits of this book from German maps, which can be relied on for their accuracy.

So far as the author is aware this is the first biography of Frœbel undertaking to cover his whole life, single newspaper articles excepted, which has been published from the pen of an American. It is the outcome of a course of lectures delivered in the winter and spring of 1895, to the kindergarten departments of the Springfield (Mass). Industrial Institute and the State Normal School at New Britain, Conn. The author has aimed to tell the story as clearly as possible, so that the student can get a distinct idea of what Frœbel was doing during each year of his life, without any attempt to explain or inculcate the philosophy of the kindergarten. In putting together the record free use has been made of every authority within reach that could throw any possible light on the story as a whole, or in its details. Now that the work is supposed to be done no one has a keener sense of its defects than the author, nor can any other person appreciate how much better it could be accomplished were it to be done over again.

Doubtless the comprehensive, erudite, and enlightening biography of Frœbel for American readers, which they can thoroughly understand and delight in, is yet to be written. When it is published the world will have a story of absorbing interest and convincing power.

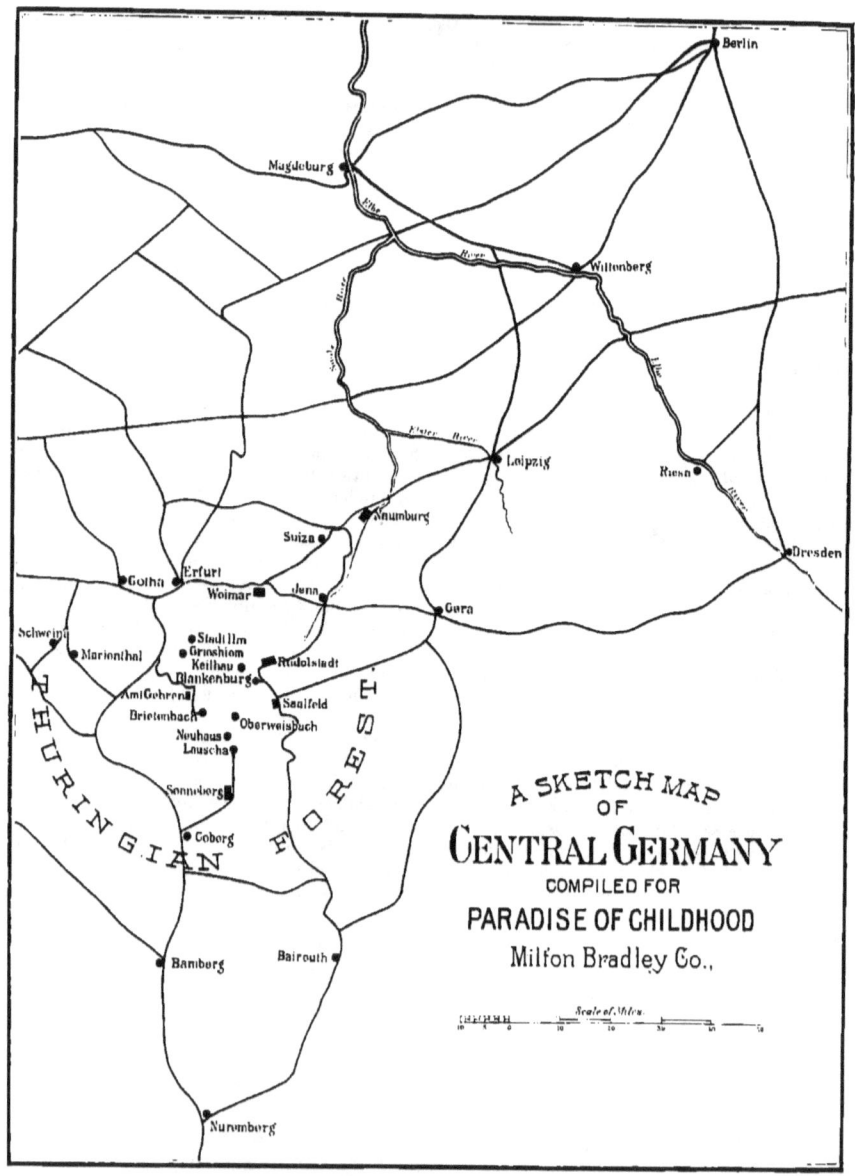

THE LIFE OF FROEBEL.
1782—1792—IN HIS FATHER'S HOUSE.

The story of Friedrich Froebel's life begins at the village of Oberweisbach in Central Germany, where he was born, April 21, 1782. It is located in what is commonly called the Thuringian Forest, a section of country which is triangular in shape, nearly one hundred miles on its longest side and from twenty-five to eighty in breadth. This region is not wholly a forest, as the name implies, but is a mountainous district within the borders of which there are many charming and romantic places; so lovely that the tourist is fully repaid for the trouble it takes to reach them. One such visitor tells us that the forest, although penetrated at various points by railroads, is for the most part accessible only by carriage roads and footpaths. The places are still picturesque, the ruins primitive and the life of the people simple and unspoiled. Within the "Forest" are mountains, some bare or tilled in patches, others covered with trees which form deep forests in which are found deer, wild boar and many other kinds of game. Again there are valleys large and small, villages and towns, castles and ruins, and all sorts and conditions of men. Within the limits of this territory Froebel spent most of his seventy years.

Oberweisbach is located in the southern part of this district, three thousand feet above the sea level, ten miles north of Lauscha, the nearest railroad station on the main line running through the Forest to Schwartzburg. It is a delightful place for a summer sojourn, but the winter weather is exceedingly cold and the neighboring mountain roads are often blockaded for weeks by snow. It has a population of nineteen hundred, and the history of the settlement runs back to 1540.

The house where Froebel was born is situated on the main street of the village, next to the "Golden Anchor," which is the principal hotel, and nearly opposite the church. It is of generous proportions, both the main structure and the L being two stories high, while the former is surmounted with a high gambrel roof containing a double row of dormer windows. Over the front door is a tablet giving the date of Froebel's birth and death. The house is still occupied by the village pastor, as it was a hundred years ago, who is president of the local Froebel society and who takes pleasure in showing to American visitors the room where the great educator was born, together with various Froebel relics.

To our minds the photograph of this house shows a substantial, cheerful home, with the gardens, village guide-board, watering-trough, telegraph poles, and lamp-post in the foreground. But Froebel's remembrance of it was very different. He describes it as being closely surrounded by other buildings, walls, hedges and fences, and also enclosed by a courtyard and by grass and vegetable gardens, his entrance to which was severely punished. The dwelling had no other outlook than right and left on houses, in front on a large church, and behind on the grassy base of a high mountain. Another writer describes Froebel's youthful environment in this way: "There was nothing in the dark lower part of the house, surrounded with buildings and walls, to captivate a child, and outside there was quite as little. There was no free prospect, which is so salutary for a child. In close proximity before the house stood the church, and behind the house the view over the little kitchen garden was obstructed by the steep rocky wall of a high hill. Only beyond the hill was a free outlook, and the boy did not fail to frequently raise his eyes to the blue heavens, which in the mountain regions are so clear and serene; and this sight and the rushing wind from the hills through the little high-walled garden sometimes caused in him a kind of ecstasy which he remembered through life."

Froebel's father was the village pastor, a learned, resolute, preoccupied, Lutheran clergyman. His mother, judging from the little that we can learn of her by inference, possessed a very mild and lovely character, rare insight, and sound, liberal views of life. He believed that he inherited from her his imaginative and artistic spirit. To these parents were born five sons, the eldest dying in infancy and the others growing to man's estate. Friedrich was the youngest, and after nursing him for nine months his invalid mother died. Writing of that event long after, the son says: "In that moment, when my dying mother kissed her highest benediction on brow and lips, the world took my tender being, so easily accessible to all influences, to lead me into the warfare of life, with all its misery, its corruption and its deformity; but the blessing of my dying mother remained with me, and the protecting angel who heard her last prayer walked by and with me."

It is a pathetic story of those infantile years, which Froebel tells himself, almost as much so as the early chapters of David Copperfield, in which Dickens is supposed to recount the tale of his early life. Shut up in the gloomy parsonage most of the time and left to the care of the single housemaid and his own devices, he seems to have lacked not only playfellows but also play-things. Thus was his life in its beginning set to the strains of a minor key, and the refrain of its after years contained but few livelier notes. But the solitude and want of companionship which fell to his lot during the time that he lived in his father's house developed and confirmed in him a habit of self-inspection and a yearning after better things which subsequently bore wonderful fruit. He tells us that at one time during this period of his life he became greatly interested in watching some workmen who were repairing the neighboring church, and that a strong desire took hold of him to undertake the building of a church, and that he began to collect sticks and stones as heavy as he could carry for such a structure. His impulse was to use such pieces of furniture or other objects as he could secure with which to imitate the real builders. But his efforts ended in utter failure, and in giving an account of his experiment he says he remembers very well that even at that early age he thought that children ought to have suitable material and somebody to show them how to go to work with it, so that they might attain better results. In relating this anecdote Madam Kriege adds: "Who can fail to see that in this incident, which made such a deep impression on the boy's mind, lay the germ of his endeavor, later in life, to devise the gifts and occupations of the kindergarten?"

In reviewing this condition of domestic affairs at the Froebel parsonage we must not blame the father too severely. His people numbered from three to five-thousand souls, located in half a dozen groups and scattered over an area of several miles; they had many pressing wants and the religious services which the pastor was called to attend were frequent and engrossing. It also happened that during Froebel's early childhood the associate charge of a large new church was given him in addition to his previous duties, so that he was necessarily away from home much of the time. But the chief trouble that cast a cloud over the first twenty years of Froebel's life lay in the fact that father and son were so differently constituted that the former never understood the latter. On this point Froebel says: "Although my father was a stirring, active man, seldom surpassed in his relations as country pastor, in education, learning and experience, yet I remained a stranger to him through his entire life, owing to these separations caused by early circumstances."

And yet Dr. Lange says that Froebel's father was "a man rich in insight, and truly religious, and that he turned his attention with the greatest solicitude to the early education of this youngest son of his beloved, departed wife. He understood how to unfold his heart and mind in the promising boy by a judicious training." While it is not for us to decide regarding the relative justice of the two quotations, we can easily see that the two essential elements which were lacking in the first decade of Froebel's life were mother love and helpful play, just those elements of child life which he afterwards strove so hard to develop and perpetuate in the kindergarten system. We are often told that in this imperfect world there is no glory except it is wrought out through suffering, and it is probable that if Friedrich Froebel had been born into a happy home he could never have felt the need of the kindergarten, and would therefore never have worked out the educational system which is the fruitage of a life filled with privation and self-sacrificing experiment.

Froebel's own testimony on this point, outlined in a speech which he made to the ladies of Hamburg, many years after, is worthy of note. In that speech he said: "Fate showed me the importance of an education conformable to nature by giving me bitter experiences and privations, while the early loss of my mother threw me upon self-education. What one has been obliged to contend with bitterly he wishes to soften to his fellow men. Thus the necessity of self-education led me to the education of my fellow men."

When Froebel was four years old a new element entered into the family life, that of the step-mother. Of this woman we are compelled to say that she fully lived up to the traditions of her position, proving herself the typical stepmother as that person is portrayed in books of fiction and brought out on the stage. What made matters worse than usual, however, was the apparent sincerity and love with which she treated the boy during the first few months after her marriage, only to repel him as soon as she had a son of her own, when she at once began to call him by an appelation commonly addressed to a servant. While he basked in the sunlight of her brief smile we are told that the household were surprised at the astonishing change that took place in the silent, taciturn child, who gained visibly every day in health, strength and activity. But scarcely had the young mother begun to fondle her own baby than it seemed to little Friedrich that she had become quite another person. His caresses were tiresome, his presence disagreeable. He must always go away, and if he remained she had neither ears nor eyes for him; she saw only her nursling and had no heart, no interest for the boy who still so greatly needed the tenderness of a cherishing mother.

The result was that Friedrich became what is usually called a bad boy. Nobody, says one writer, seemed to understand him or cared to understand him. Motives for his actions were attributed to him which he never had, and unfortunately all this distrust and want of harmony had finally the effect of altering his naturally good disposition. He often concealed facts and even told untruths, because he knew that he would be punished for things that were not wrong in themselves. As the years passed matters seemed to get from bad to worse, so that his father came to regard him as a very bad boy.

But the picture of his home life was not altogether a sad one. As soon as he was able to do anything he began to help his father in gardening and received in this way many lasting impressions. His observation was directed to what was near to him in nature, and the plant world became to him, so far as he could see and touch it, an object of his thoughtful contemplation. His habit of nature study clung to him through life, and was made an essential part of the kindergarten system when it came to be established. The parsonage household was a bustling, energetic one. We are told by Froebel himself that both husband and wife displayed great activity, loved order and sought in all imaginable ways to beautify their surroundings. The father believed in keeping up with the times, and for that purpose he took the latest publications and carefully considered all that was offered to him in them. This plan contributed not a little to the general Christian life that reigned in the household. All the members of it were assembled for devotions morning and evening each day of the week, and at such times the works of Zallikafer, Hermes, Marezoll, Sturm and others were read aloud for the inspiration, unfolding and elevation of the spiritual life of the family. "Thus," writes Froebel, "my life was early influenced by nature, by work and by religious perceptions, or as I prefer to say, the natural and primitive tendencies of every human being were nurtured in the germ."

All these things had their influence on the boy, and he tells us that he was often deeply stirred with the resolve to be truly noble and good. But he also adds: "As I hear from others, this firm resolution often contrasted with my outer life. I was full of youthful spirits and the joy of life, and did not always know how to moderate my activity, and through carelessness got into critical situations of all kinds, and in my thoughtlessness destroyed everything around me that I wished to investigate."

The father made some attempt to begin the boy's elementary education, but the results were not satisfactory and so he decided to send him to school. There were two schools in the village, one for the boys and the other for the girls. Both were connected with the church, and as its pastor the father could choose either for his son. He selected the girls' school, because he was not satisfied with the way the boys' teacher discharged his duties.

Probably the best idea of Froebel's first day at school can be given by quoting his own words in a letter written some sixty years later to Col. Von Arnswald:—

"It was a Monday when my father took me to school himself. I was placed on the seat of honor by the side of the teacher, for the reason, I suppose, that I was the son of the pastor, or, it may be, because I was reputed a mischievious boy that ought not to sit with the girls. The smallest girls on the first form were seated just in front of me. A verse from the Bible, treated in the sermon on the Sunday preceding, was spoken aloud by one of the older girls and repeated by all the small girls in front. On this first day of my attendance they repeated the words of the Lord: 'Seek ye first the kingdom of God and his righteousness, and all these things shall be added unto you.' The verse was explained to the older girls and also to me. But the little girls were not required to know it perfectly before Sunday. Meanwhile the verse was repeated in parts again and again, in the high pitch of their childish voices, in chorus, and in the old chanting manner of village schools. I heard this verse repeated for a long time every morning of the six days of the week, until the sounds, the words and the sense had produced so strong an impression upon me as to make this verse the motto of my life in the truest sense of the word; for it has resounded like the chant of a chorus of nuns in my ears all the days of my life. The older I grew the more thoroughly was I led to recognize the full importance and efficacy and the profound living truth of the maxim. It became the basis and the regulator of numerous understandings of mine, and proved its entire truthfulness." In his school Froebel read in the Bible with the older pupils and he also learned with them the sacred songs which were sung on Sundays in the church. Among these hymns he says there were two which shone on the clouded dawn of his early childhood like bright morning stars.

"They became," he adds, "to me as my life songs, because in them I saw mirrored my own little life, and their meaning touched my heart so deeply that in later years I have many a time been strengthened and refreshed by what they imparted to my soul." These songs were, "Rise my heart and soul," and "It costeth much to be a Christ." He mentions in this connection that he followed his father's Sunday sermons with great attention, sitting apart from the rest of the congregation, in the vestry.

During these years the problems of life sat heavily on those young shoulders and bewildered that youthful brain. For the most part he was kept closely at home, although he sometimes rode about the parish with his father while the latter was making pastoral calls. It was his delight to mount the high hill back of the house that he might enlarge his actual horizon and relieve his spirit from the depressing confines of the narrow valley. Tradition says that on the spot where the Memorial Tower now stands he spent many hours in watching the sunset and in boyish musing. Year by year he became enamoured of all the different phases of nature which came within his observation, and more fond of studying their development.

As he grew into boyhood we are told that his mind was moved most deeply not by the many admonitions and the pious instructions which he received, but by the many interviews between his father and members of the pastor's flock to which he listened. One writer states the case in this way: "A boy of between eight and eleven years, small and slight in stature, apparently busied with a book, or some kind of writing, seemed to the visitors at the parsonage no hindrance. They had come to open their hearts to the highly honored and spiritual teacher and to ask his counsel in their distressed circumstances. But the child listened with all the sharp attention of an inquisitive, penetrating mind, to which the world and all its complications was wholly strange. Each person served as a rent in the curtain which concealed life from him, a telescope through which he could study the world.

But it was the dark side of life that was thus revealed to him. It was the complaint of the sorely-tried mother over the ungrateful son, the acknowledgment of a hidden sin, a melancholy fall, it was the sting of conscience, fear, repent-

TOWER

VILLAGE

BIRTH HOUSE

ance, despair, which alternately had the word, while the earnest, yes, severe teacher, now through the inexorable precepts of the divine law, then with the consolations of mercy, strove to work on the dejected minds. These conversations and other influences of that time revealed to him the inner life of men, with its hidden springs and its concealed strife and pain, and he perceived more and more the connection between things and words and aims, without being able to discover in himself and around him anything satisfying, anything atoning, and although this fair soul had already felt an indefinable need of unity and harmony, yet he could no more unite them than he could the most incongruous opposites, the most irreconcilable enmities."

The boy was ten years old when his eldest brother, Christoph, a theological student at the University of Jena, came home for a visit, and great was his joy in seeing him. Together the brothers roamed the fields, the elder appearing to the younger an angel of consolation who understood him and was ready to protect him from unjust treatment, because he saw through all the youthful faults the glimmer of the beautiful side of his misapprehended and suppressed character. To him he unfolded some of his mental troubles, asking him why it was that God did not make all the people men or all women, so that there should be no quarreling, his idea being that most of the contention in the world arises from the difference which exists in the sexes. To direct his mind from the problem of human discord his brother showed him the processes of vegetation — the compensating nature of imperfections in male and female flowers, and how through the principle of growth harmonies of beauty and use are born out of the connection of opposites.

As the plants and flowers of the parsonage garden had until now been Friedrich's dearest playfellows, so the new revelation of the vegetable world which his brother disclosed to him in their talks attracted his interest and he besieged Christoph with all manner of questions.

Just then the beautiful purple threads of the blossoming hazel claimed a considerable share of their attention and threw the boy into raptures. His brother gave him careful instruction regarding the flowers and his visit proved a great and lasting benefit in calming the perturbed spirit of the child. But when he was gone the father's house seemed more desolate than ever to the little motherless boy who had a home there only in name, and a burning desire took possession of his soul to get away, as his brothers had done, to find some other abiding place with a more desirable environment and better means for helpful growth.

1792—1797—WITH HIS GUARDIAN.

A visitor came to the parsonage at Oberweissbach in the autumn of 1792 who took a deep interest in Friedrich Fræbel. It was Herr Hoffman, his mother's brother, who was pastor at Stadt Ilm, a market town north of Fræbel's home. This uncle resembled his sister in many ways and had never ceased to mourn her loss. He could not help noticing how unhappy and ill-suited to his surroundings Fræbel appeared, marking the contrast between the step-mother and her predecessor. The uncle and nephew were mutually drawn together, and we are told that when at a certain time during the visit Fræbel fixed upon Herr Hoffman his soft and melancholy eyes, as if with longing, it suddenly seemed to him as if he saw the mother in the face of the child; as if the soul of the loved sister had directed a prayer to him, through this glance, and he decided in his heart to give it a hearing. As a consequence, soon after returning home he made the father a proposition for the care and education of the boy, which was gladly and quickly accepted. In this way the uncle became Friedrich's guardian and he was also the custodian of certain funds left to Friedrich by his mother.

Life at Stadt Ilm was very different from what it had been at Oberwiesbach. The little city lies in a broad valley, by a clear but narrow stream. Herr Hoffman had lost his wife and child years before and his family consisted of himself and his aged mother-in-law. The parsonage was a spacious, airy house. There was a garden adjoining it where the boy spent many happy hours, and he was allowed to roam at will through the whole region, provided he never failed to be at home at the appointed time. Concerning these days he writes:—

"As austerity reigned in my father's house, so here kindness and benevolence. I saw there, in respect to myself, distrust; here, confidence; there I felt constraint, here, freedom. While there I had been hardly at all among boys of my own age; here I found certainly as many as forty fellow-pupils, for I entered the higher class in the town school." This last-mentioned fact would seem to indicate that Fraebel had made considerable progress in the school at Oberweisbach, although some of his biographers would have us think that the training received there was of little benefit to him. He says, in his autobiography, that in the new school reading, writing and arithmetic were well taught, and that the religious instruction was excellent. And he adds, "Mathematics lay near my nature. When I received private instruction in this branch my advance steps were so marked that they bordered on the height of knowledge and ability possessed by my teacher, which was by no means slight."

Our pupil also informs us that Latin was miserably taught and still more sparingly learned, but that the time which he spent on it was not entirely lost, because he learned to understand that a course of instruction so carried on can bring forth no fruit in the pupils. The recitations in geography were parrot-like, the boys being allowed to use many words without receiving any adequate knowledge of the subject or of its relations to the life of the world, although they could correctly name all the colored market towns and little boroughs on the local map. Fraebel was given private geographical lessons in regard to England, but as he could get no clear idea of its connection with his own country this special instruction did him but little good. There was also teaching in writing and spelling, and training in singing and piano-playing, but Fraebel's verdict, rendered many years later, was that they amounted to but very little. He says that the element of generalization was entirely lacking, and while he praises the arithmetical instruction he immediately adds that notwithstanding the training which he received he was very much surprised and mortified to find, when he was ten years older, that he could not solve the problems given out to the boys in Pestalozzi's school. What a pity it was that those instructors of Fraebel did not teach him how to write clearly, the art and habit of expressing himself with pen and speech so that the world, or at least the educational part of it, might understand his language without profound study and the intervention of many interpreters!

Nevertheless, the boy gained freedom of mind and bodily strength day by day, and "drank fresh courage in long draughts." He explains that in his efforts to put himself on common ground with the other boys the frequent reaction after play was often grievous, because his strength and activity were not developed according to his age, and his bold daring could never supply the quiet, vigorous strength and the knowledge of its limit which his companions enjoyed. He was regarded by them as being very peculiar and the more he exerted himself to win them to him, so much the more striking his awkwardness appeared to them. He was very anxious to do everything they did, but his movements were so stiff and his demeanor so wooden, says one of his biographers, that he would have been rejected by the band, had not one of the boys recognized his good qualities and resolved to give him aid and protection. For a time he could take no part in the games of the other boys, no matter how hard he tried, because the robust strength and activity of his companions, who had grown up in freedom, quickly overcame his despairing efforts. But eventually his perseverance conquered, and the air, the active movements, the better care and the joyousness assisted not a little to improve his elasticity and health, and after a hard probation he received permission of the boys to play with them.

He was much effected by the religious instruction given in the school and its representation of the character and the life of Christ. With all these occupations and diversions some four years and a half passed, the chief advantage being "that he became a child again in a youthful world whose joys could warm and cheer his soul so that his heart could resume its natural elasticity." He was a different boy even when he went back to the parsonage at Oberweisbach, where he spent his vacations, entering heartily into all the activities of the household and taking special pleasure in study.

ing the books and engravings in his father's library. Before leaving Stadt Ilm he was confirmed and admitted to the church by his uncle. Of this time he writes: "The earnest days of preparation and the holy solemnity might pass away, but deep and lasting were the impressions of those beautiful hours in which all the threads of my life were comprehended in a glorious center of peace and unity."

Thus ended the second period of his career. While it afforded him many advantages it did not secure for him the preparation for practical life which is so much to be desired in every boy who has his way to make in the world. His uncle lived in a kind of an ideal life and in all his generous efforts for Froebel's development it never for a moment occurred to him how little he was forming his pupil to become a useful citizen. On this point let us quote once more from Froebel's autobiography. "I was really as though placed in a garden where I could freely move about and where the glad sun shone on me and warmed me, but where there were fruits that were hard to reach, which hung on trees that, considering my undeveloped strength, were very hard to climb. In this meager way I was left to gather strength without leader or guide for an independent life—for work—for action. As my mind was satisfied only with the relative, the analogous, I received a very one-sided direction. I created a world for myself, which was very little like the world, and was comprehensible or intelligible only to me. I knew and understood very much for myself, but it was a heightened self-consciousness which had no value for others. I knew and comprehended absolutely nothing of the world, nothing of the social life for which I was destined."

1797–1799—THE FORESTER'S APPRENTICE.

In the spring of 1797, at the age of fifteen, we find Froebel back again in his father's house, with a great question confronting him and the rest of the family, the choice of an occupation for life. It had seemed to him that he would like to be a preacher, but he dared not let his thoughts dwell on such a thing, because, according to his step-mother it had been "distinctly understood" for years that he must not go to the University for the reason that his two brothers, Christoph and Traugott, were already there, and the other brother, Christian, was expecting to follow them. This woman said that to undertake to send the fourth son would certainly impoverish the family finances to an extent which would be unbearable, and, moreover, that Friedrich was too stupid to have any more time or money wasted on his education. It is said, however, that her scruples about spending more money at the University faded out of sight when her first-born son came to be old enough to enter it.

But it was determined that for Friedrich something commercial should be sought, and his father applied to a neighboring revenue officer for a clerkship, but without success. There was also some talk of his entering into the service of a wealthy family named Von Holzhausen, the same one in which he subsequently became a tutor, but he was very much opposed to this plan and tells in his subsequent writings "that he never felt in his heart such violent feelings of horror against anything as he did in the thought of having a position where he must brush clothes and shoes and serve at the table."

Then the father consulted the boy's wishes and he expressed a desire for an outdoor life, because of his love of nature. About this time the elder Froebel became acquainted with a surveyor and assessor living at Neuhaus, a place lying south of Oberweisbach, who had a special reputation for his knowledge of geometry. Of him one record says that he was "a noble and earnest man, in ecclesiastical matters a congenial spirit." But it was a record that fell far short of the mark in the case of Froebel, who was apprenticed to him for two years, to learn geometry, surveying, the method of assessing taxes and the care of forests. The master was well versed in the duties of his profession, but he did not understand the art of teaching and could therefore impart very little instruction to others. Neither did he have the time to do what he had promised for his apprentice, so engrossing were the demands of the practical work connected with his daily business. Moreover, he was often away from home for long periods, when the pupil was left entirely to himself with ample time to study the library of books belonging to the house. Froebel was not slow to improve this opportunity, giving much attention to works on geometry and forest affairs and the collecting and drying of plants, as well as the drawing of maps of the district. He also made the acquaintance of a physician in the neighboring market town who loaned him additional books on botany.

During these years we are told that he lived in peace and quiet, protected from evil, in an ideal world which he himself had created and that he obtained a closer knowledge of field, meadow and forest, for he saw nothing else but field, meadow and forest, through which he wandered by day and night. "He felt that in nature there must be a higher interest than to supply us with certain material advantages and facilities, and he began also to perceive that in order to represent the ideal farmer something else was necessary than merely the proper management of the various objects of husbandry. How greatly he wished that all men who thus lived from, with and in nature could look on her with other eyes, and not make her tributary as their slave—but accept her also as their friend, in a pure, beautiful and elevated, God-glorifying life." We are further told that in those days he was always dressed in green, the color of the fields, with yellow top-boots and a feather in his hat, and that no one who saw him wandering about the country could possibly have suspected the depth and earnestness of soul, thirsting for light and truth, which dwelt in this fantastic boy.

During the latter part of his stay at Neuhaus a company of strolling actors gave a series of plays in a neighboring castle. Froebel attended their first presentation and was so much moved by it that he came again and again to see and hear them. These dramas seemed to offer to his fancy the long deprived element of poetry, and touched his susceptible mind all the more deeply because he recalled and lived over again the scenes of each play during the long walk home, beneath the starry heavens, which followed every performance. He vividly remembered, in later years, the enthusiasm which was awakened in his breast by the rendering of such plays as "The Huntsmen" by Iffland. He invested all he saw and heard on that rural stage with lofty thoughts and purposes, and believed those actors happy who could, according to his view, work so powerfully for the improvement of mankind. He imagined that the profession of the stage was a noble calling and one that he would like well to follow. He wrote home to his father about his new aspirations and the latter replied by upbraiding him in good set terms. This letter was a matter of genuine grief to him, because he tells us that he had come to regard his patronage of the theater a matter to be as much commended as his best church attendance.

He even went so far, before receiving his father's letter, as to introduce himself to one of the actors that he might disclose his wish to join such a desirable profession. The biographer tells us that the peculiar interview ended in this way: "The actor listened earnestly to Friedrich, but a melancholy smile played around his mouth as he took his hand and answered him: 'You deceive yourself, young friend; our society is nothing of all that which you dream. We hold together only through hunger. Would to God that I had never trod the boards and could labor with my hands.' He then went on to depict all the misery of the life behind the curtain, particularly for one, who like himself belonged to a cultured family and had taken it up through necessity." This ended Froebel's theatrical aspirations, but in order to mollify his father's anger he wrote to his brother Christoph the whole story and begged his intercession with their father.

The apprenticeship with the surveyor or forester, as he is commonly called, came to an end in the summer of 1799, and Froebel and his master parted unpleasantly. He had proved himself valuable to this man, who on that account wanted to keep him another year. But the boy felt that he must have time to follow out his studies more systematically than he could possibly do by remaining, and therefore started for home on foot as soon as his time had expired. This action so enraged the surveyor that he sent a letter to Froebel's father complaining that the young man had been unfaithful in many ways and deserved censure. On his way home Froebel stopped at the village where his brother Christoph had located as a pastor and while the brothers were visiting together the forester's letter was forwarded to them from Oberweisbach. As a result Friedrich related to Christoph all that had happened during his stay at Neuhaus, naming the books he had studied, showing the maps he had drawn and his collections of botanical specimens. As a result Christoph stood perfectly amazed while he heard of such inexcusable neglect on the part of the forester, and at once began to reproach Friedrich because he had not informed his father of the great waste of time which had been going on during such an important apprenticeship. But in reply the younger brother reminded him of the sentence pronounced on him by the father when he went to Neuhaus: "We will not hear any complaints, we shall always consider you in the wrong." Christoph well knew the father's severity and was silent, but he took on himself at once the duty of pointing out to him the gross neglect of the forester and that Friedrich, considering the meager means at his command, had improved his time and made real progress in map drawing, mathematics and botany.

Nevertheless, his reception at home was little calculated to inspire a young man with courage and hope for the future. The step-mother had lent a willing ear to the forester's letter and was prepared to estimate it at face value, and she saw in the rich and excellent collection of plants, dried with the utmost care, nothing but foolery. The world looked particularly dark to Froebel just then, the question what to do next being more perplexing than ever. What the result would have been had not an accident helped shape his future course in life no one can predict. His brother Traugott, who was studying medicine at Jena, wrote home for money, and as the matter was urgent and as Friedrich had nothing to do it was decided to make him the messenger to take it there. And so to Jena he went in the summer of 1799, and being once there remained as a student, thereby fulfilling his highest ambition and accomplishing the day dreams of all his conscious years.

1799—1801—A STUDENT AT JENA.

When Froebel reached the University town he persuaded his brother to write home that his time could be profitably employed there for the eight remaining weeks of the term in the study of topographical and local drawing. The request was granted, the reason being, in all probability, that the step-mother had very little idea of what she could do with the boy if he came home. The brothers returned to Oberweisbach in September and Friedrich began at once to plead with his father for leave to become a regular student at Jena. The father said that he would gladly favor such a project, but that he did not see how the money could be provided for both Christian and Friedrich to take a prescribed course at the University, and that it would involve a good deal of sacrifice to carry Christian, who was two years the elder, through the studies which he had already begun. But he told Friedrich to talk the matter over with his brothers and his guardian, which he did. As a result his darling wish was secured by an act of generous self-renunciation on the part of Christian.

This brother was a young man of noble character; he loved Friedrich sincerely and understood how much harder it would be for him to give up the life and subsequent career of a student than it would be if he himself should choose some vocation in what we are accustomed to call practical life. It was evident that only one of the brothers could go to college and Christian resigned all his prospects in a professional way and decided to devote himself to manufacturing interests. In this new departure he was successful, securing in time a competency which he freely placed at the disposal of Friedrich in aid of educational schemes to which he also gave his personal service and that of his family for many years.

It was therefore decided that Christian's offer should be accepted and that Friedrich should take his brother's place at Jena, the uncle as guardian having consented to apply to the cost of his education there the money held in trust as a legacy from his mother. Consequently we find him back at Jena in the last months of 1799, registered as a student of philosophy.

This labeling was evidently the work of Froebel's father, rather than by the direction of the pupil himself, for he says that it appeared to him very strange, because he had only thought of practical knowledge as the object of his study. The lectures which he attended pertained to mathematics, arithmetic, algebra, geometry, mineralogy, botany, natural history, physics, chemistry, the science of finance, care of forest trees, architecture, building and surveying. He also continued topographical drawing, but we are told that he learned nothing of philosophy, except what was imparted to him through the conversation of his friends. But the fact that he had been registered in the department of philosophy, he tells us, made on his dreamy, easily-moved and susceptible life a very great impression, and gave his studies an unexpected, higher meaning. Concerning the mathematical lectures he says: "The lectures of my excellent teacher had not the same value that they might and would have had, if I had seen in the sequence of the instruction and in the progress of the same, more inner necessity and less arbitrariness."

He found more satisfaction in the teaching which he received in botany, zoology and natural history. In the handling of mineralogy, which he greatly loved, he discovered how little his eyes were opened and how feebly he had learned to see. He says that in the natural history branches he had a sensible, loving and benevolent teacher and that through him his insight into nature was essentially quickened and his love for observing it made more active.

It was this experience which led him in after life to give little children suitable directions and encouragement in acquiring habits of close observation.

Our young student lived very economically and in a secluded way at Jena, seldom appearing in public places and visiting few other students except his brother. But we are told that he did attract the attention of several naturalists because of his eagerness to advance in their line of study, and that he accepted their invitation to join two societies which they were forming at that time.

But here in Jena, being well started in his studies, he soon began to meet with fresh trouble, an element which was destined to enter into every period of his life. He had brought enough money with him to last for a considerable time but after awhile, at the request of his brother, he loaned him the greater part of his little store, on a promise that it would be repaid so that no inconvenience should result to him from the loan. This promise was not fulfilled, and some accounts say that Traugott, who was in his last year at the University, even departed from the city leaving the boy without support for the future or means to pay bills which were already over-due. At all events Friedrich found himself toward the end of his third half year, in the summer of 1801, in debt thirty thalers, a little less than $25, to a restaurant keeper, and having nothing to pay was thrown into the University prison where he languished for nine weeks.

There are some things about this narrative which seem incredible. Previous to his imprisonment the creditor had for a long time threatened to resort to extreme measures and had made a demand on the father, which the latter had met with a very positive denial. The reason for this refusal is said to be that the elder Froebel allowed himself to be wholly dominated in the matter by his wife. After his confinement had begun Friedrich wrote again to his father for help and also to his guardian, who still held a part of his money. But he received no aid from either quarter, the uncle declining succor because of some section of the city ordinances which prevented him from interfering in such an affair. It is supposed that he took this ground because he felt that the money he had already advanced had been misapplied and that, under the circumstances, it was the father's duty to take action and that by withholding help he could ultimately force his brother-in-law to meet the obligation and release his ward.

Meanwhile Froebel spent the nine weeks of his prison life in the study of Latin, in which he felt himself to be deficient. He was finally released by deciding to give a note of hand for the amount involved, as his father's heir. This note his father cashed, on condition that he renounce all further claim to the parental estate. Being at liberty, he went home at once, thus giving up his course after a residence at Jena of about eighteen months. It was in the springtime when he was just nineteen that he came back to the parsonage at Oberweisbach and he writes as follows: "Naturally I entered the house with a heavy heart, a troubled mind and an oppressed spirit." He now began to apply himself to literature and wished to make a close review of all that he had learned and treasured. Happy in this occupation he shut himself up in his little chamber day after day, with his books. The step-mother suggested to the father that it would be well to surprise him at his work, being suspicious that something was going on that ought to be stopped. And so the father entered the room suddenly one day, to find Friedrich writing at a table, with a pile of papers before him. He looked through several sheets and then angrily exclaimed: "Now what nonsense is this? What an aimless destruction of paper!" And the record adds: "No doubt all his papers would have been thrown into the fire and he banished from the place had not his brother Christoph been present and moderated the father's displeasure. A little later Friedrich went to an estate in Hildburg owned by a relative of his father, to become the steward's assistant, where he remained some months.

The weeks which he had spent at home had revealed to him in a stronger light than ever before his father's excellent qualities, and he deeply regretted the estrangement between them. Days and nights he tells us that he was busy in his mind planning how to write to his father in the warmest words what was passing within his heart, but when he sat down for that purpose his courage sank and the fear of arousing new and greater misapprehensions made him lay his pen aside.

A little later the father was taken sick and sent for Friedrich to help in regulating his affairs and correspondence. The old man died in February, 1802, and in writing of this event the son says: "My father carried his anxiety for my future in his heart till his last hour. May his glorified spirit, while I write this, look down on me with pleasure and benediction, and now be contented with the son who loved him so deeply." It was at Easter 1802, that the young man left the parsonage at Oberweisbach, once more to seek his future in the wide world, and there is no record that he ever returned there for any permanent stay. Henceforth he was the master of his own actions.

1802—1808—BECOMES A TEACHER.

FROM Oberweisbach Fræbel went first to the forest court near Bamberg, to take the place of court actuary or clerk. According to one translation this position was that of treasurer of the episcopal department of finance. He remained there for nearly a year and then went to Bamberg, which had meanwhile been ceded to Bavaria. He made the change because he thought that the projected land survey under the new government would give him employment. This change resulted in his doing some map drawing and surveying, but he did not get the government appointment for which he had hoped. Therefore he advertised in one of the papers for a position, at the same time sending the editor some of his architectural and geometrical work for use as illustrations. This advertisement brought him the offer of a private secretaryship to the president of Dewitz in Mecklenburg, who lived at Gross Milchow, which he accepted in February, 1804. His most important work there was to reduce to order, according to a plan laid out by the owner, some accounts that were badly tangled.

But this occupation became distasteful after a little and the young man resolved to supplement his mathematical attainments by studying architecture, so as to make it his life work, provided the means could be secured. He had a friend who was a private tutor at Frankfort, and he determined to join him there for the purpose just named. Consequently he wrote to his eldest brother asking for assistance. In due time the answer came, but Fræbel carried it around with him for hours without unsealing it, and for days he did not read it, because he felt, as he says, that there was little probability that his brother could help him in accomplishing the wish of his soul, and so feared to find in the letter the destruction of his life. And he adds: "When after some days of alternation between hope and doubt I finally opened the letter I was not a little astonished that in the beginning of it the most heartfelt sympathy was expressed. The further contents moved me deeply. It contained the news of my uncle's death and the announcement that a legacy had fallen to me."

As a result he established himself at Frankfort in the summer of 1805, expecting to devote all his energies to architecture. But this choice was not a lasting one. The student began to ask himself, "How can you work through architecture for the culture and ennobling of man?" In a few weeks he met the principal of a model or normal school which had lately been opened in the city. This man's name was Gruner and he urged Fraebel very strongly to give up the idea of being an architect and to at once become a teacher in his school, a proposition made on the first evening of their acquaintance, because Fraebel spoke so earnestly about the necessity of each person getting into the place in this world for which he is best fitted. We are told that in the midst of his spirited talk he felt the touch of a hand on his shoulder and that Dr. Gruner said: "My friend, you should not be an architect, you should be a schoolmaster. There is a place open in our school; if you agree to it the place is yours."

Fraebel accepted this summons as a call of Providence; in August, 1805, he went to Yverdun in Switzerland to see and hear Pestalozzi, who was then the great educational light of the day, the fountain-head of all new educational ideas. He tarried there as an observer for two weeks. He attended the recitations and wrote out the account of what he saw, so that he might report it on his return to Frankfort, which occurred in October. Then he began teaching in good earnest, according to the new plans, his branches being arithmetic, drawing, geometry and the German language. There were two hundred children in the school, with four regularly-appointed and nine private teachers. His first venture, he being then in his twenty-fourth year, was with a class of thirty or forty boys, between the ages of nine and eleven.

An extract from a letter written to his brother Christoph at this time shows conclusively the spirit with which he entered into the work: "I must tell you candidly that my duties in the school are prodigiously exacting. Even in the first hour they did not seem strange to me. It appeared to me as if I had already been a teacher and was born to it. I cannot sketch my strange observations in all their fullness. It is plain to me now that I was really fitted for no other calling, and yet I must tell you that never in my life had I thought to become a teacher. In the hours of instruction I feel myself as truly in my element as the fish in the water or the bird in the air. You cannot think how pleasantly the time passes. I love the children so heartily that I am continually longing to see them again. You should see me sometimes when I am busy; you would truly rejoice over my happiness. I have certainly this pure enjoyment of the consciousness of the high aims of my work, the cultivation of the human soul to thank, as well as the hearty love of the children with which they reward me."

At another time, speaking of those days, he said: "I was inexpressibly happy—from the first moment I felt complete consecration. What many-sided efforts! What abundant activity! I must give advice, explanation, interpretation, decision over so many things on which it had never been necessary for me to think definitely. I was alone in a strange city. I sought my answer therefore where I had so often found it, in my own mind, in life and in nature. And from them came voices which revealed to me how excellent for my own culture had been my toilsome development, for I received from out the depths of the mind, of life and of nature, answers which were not only satisfactory, but which also, through their simplicity and undoubted accuracy, possessed a youthful newness and vigor which produced a quickening and animating effect." While entertaining such ideas how could Fraebel torment his pupils with the system of teaching which had so vexed and tortured him when a boy? He was forced for himself and for them to break a new road, to create a new system of instruction. He was now in a position not only to make his experiments freely, but was under obligation to map out original pedagogical work.

One of his first suggestions to his fellow teachers along this line of new educational endeavor was that they should undertake weekly walks with the pupils, as a direct aid in pursuing the particular study which was under consideration at the time. One teacher should take his class out with reference to botany, another for the investigation of zoology and a third as a help in acquiring knowledge of geography or for gaining new lessons in horticulture. In many respects he adopted the plans already proposed by Pestalozzi, but with important variations. Pestalozzi held, for instance, that the study of geography need not in the least be associated with the child's observatious, but should have for its starting-point the bottom of the sea. But Frœbel first talked with his pupils about the house in which they found themselves, advancing from the house to the street and the city in general, and then out into the world at large. Regarding this method, he says: "I took everything according to nature and drew the picture immediately, diminished in size, on an even surface of ground or sand chosen for the purpose." Do we in these words catch the first suggestion of the sand modeling which forms such an important part of the geographical instruction of our day? By way of further explanation, Frœbel adds: "When the picture was firmly grasped and imprinted we drew it in school on a horizontal blackboard. It was first sketched by the teacher and pupil, then made an exercise for every scholar. Our representation of the earth's surface had at first a spherical form like the apparent horizon." His method won the approbation of the teachers associated with him and also of the children's parents, owing to the excellent results shown at the first public examination of the school.

In addition to his school duties he gave instruction for two hours to three children in a private family named Von Holzhausen, who lived on the plains near Frankfort, spending a good deal of his time with his pupils in the open air and in getting acquainted with the plant world.

In July, 1807, he left the school to become the regular teacher of the three boys just mentioned, under the contract which stipulated that he need never be obliged to live with his pupils in the city, and also that they should be committed to his care without reservation. Of this period he writes: "My life at first with my pupils was very circumscribed. It consisted of living and walking in the open air. Cut off from the influence of a city education, I did not yet venture to introduce the simple life of nature into the sphere of education. My younger pupils themselves taught me and guided me to that. In the following year this life with my pupils was especially roused and animated, when the father assigned them a piece of field for a garden, which we cultivated in common. Their highest joy was to give their parents and me fruits from their garden. Oh, how their eyes glistened when they could do it! Beautiful plants and little shrubs from the field, the great garden of God, were planted and cared for in the little gardens of the children."

"After that time my youthful life, as I mentally reviewed it, did not appear to me so entirely useless. I learned what a very different thing is the care of a plant, whether one has seen and watched its natural life at the different epochs of its unfolding or if he has always stood far from nature. A little child that freely and voluntarily seeks flowers and cherishes and cares for them in order to wind them into a bouquet for parents or teachers cannot be a bad child or become a bad man. Such a child can easily be led to the love and to a knowledge of his father, God, who gives him such gifts."

The above passage is worthy of a second reading, because it illustrates the fact that although Frœbel was at times very obscure in his attempts to give expression to his ideas he was, nevertheless, able on occasions to clothe his thought with a clearness and beauty which challenges admiration.

In those days which Frœbel spent with his pupils in the little country house that had been fitted up for them he sought always to combine labor with instruction and when the boys were busy with hatchet and spade, with oar or fishing tackle, he made every occupation serviceable to awaken their desire for knowledge. And we are told that the regular and moderate method of living which they followed banished all the indolence and helpless dependence of the children, so that in a short time they improved wonderfully in health and strength and the keenness with which they enjoyed life was greatly increased.

When, however, autumn approached, with its dark days, long evenings and bad weather, considerable time was given to the practice of music and drawing. But there were still unoccupied hours which in summer had been devoted to rural occupations. How could they be spent pleasantly and profitably? Referring to his experience at this time, Frœbel says: "When my pupils came to me with some new demand I asked myself, 'What did you do when a boy? What happened to you to quicken your impulse for activity and representation? By what means was this impulse at that age most fitly satisfied?' Then out of my earliest boyhood something came to me which gave to me at that moment all that I needed. It was the simple art of imprinting, on smooth paper, signs and forms by regular lines." He also remembered how he had tried to keep himself busy with all kinds of braided work from paper and binding twine, and he resolved to try this occupation with the boys.

In carrying out this plan he was brought at once to a realizing sense of the crudeness with which the unpracticed hand does its work, how poorly the will is master of the finger-ends under such circumstances, and how inaccurately the eye observes. Consequently he designed a few preparatory exercises for training the hand and eye, so that the boys could undertake their pasteboard work. He began with the folding and the separating and pasting of papers. He also let them work with twine, till they became experts in making nets and game bags. In these occupations they had to bring into practice what they had learned in drawing, arithmetic and geometry. Later in the season they did some work in wood.

Thus early in his career we catch the germ of the kindergarten thought which dominated Frœbel's life in after years. We are also told that the little house where he and his young people worked is still preserved as a token of remembrance and contains a room in which everything is left just as it appeared in those days. The mother of the three boys preserved every memorial of Frœbel with religious veneration during his lifetime, while he in turn held her in high esteem, so that for a long period a correspondence was kept up between them. After a year of this special work as a private tutor Frœbel became anxious to secure a wider development for himself and his pupils than country life afforded, and so, in the summer of 1808, he took them to Pestalozzi's school at Yverdun, where he remained with them for two years, acting meanwhile as pupil and teacher, being resolute in his determination to secure a pedagogical education.

1808—1810—RELATIONS WITH PESTALOZZI.

The records of Frœbel's life at Yverdun are meager, much being left to the reader's imagination. We know that he tried on his arrival to secure quarters for himself and his pupils in the main school building, or castle as it was sometimes called. Failing in this, the quartette obtained lodgings in an adjoining dwelling, taking their meals with the other students and sharing in their instruction. Frœbel tells us that during this period he was both teacher and scholar, educator and pupil. He made it his business to talk with Pestalozzi regarding every subject that came up from its first point of connection, so that he might understand it from the foundation. And he adds: "I soon felt the need of unity of endeavor in means and end. Therefore I sought to gain the highest insight into everything. I was pupil in all subjects, numbers, form, singing, reading, drawing, language, geography, natural science, dead languages, etc. In what was offered for youthful life, for comprehensive teaching, for higher instruction I missed that satisfying of the human being, the essence of the subject. Pestalozzi's views were very universal, and, as experience taught, only awakening to those already grounded in the right. In connection with the subjects taught, the instruction in language struck me first in its great imperfection, arbitrariness and lifelessness. During the time spent at Yverdun the discovery of a satisfying method of teaching the mother tongue occupied me especially.

I proceeded from the following considerations: Language is the image, the representation of a world, and is related to the outer world through articulately formed tones; if I wish properly to represent a thing I must know the original according to its character. The outer world has objects; I must also have a decided form, a decided word for the object. The objects, however, show qualities; language must, therefore, have quality words in its construction. These qualities are necessarily bound up with the objects; qualities of being, having and becoming."

Containing the story of his life at Yverdun, Frœbel says that he learned there to recognize boyish play in the free air, in its power, developing and strengthening spirit, disposition and body. In the plays which were there carried on and with what was connected with them, he discovered the chief source of the moral strength of the young people in the institution. He says that at that time the higher symbolical meaning of play had not yet been opened to him, so that he could only regard it as a moral power for body and mind. The walks which the students took had an equally good influence with the plays, particularly those taken in the company of Pestalozzi. In summing up the results secured by his stay at Yverdun Froebel writes: "There is no question that Pestalozzi's public and especially his evening reflections, in which he liked to exert himself to awaken and unfold the ideal of noble manhood and true human love, contributed most essentially to the development of the inner life. On the whole, I spent in Yverdun an inspiring, grand, and for my life, decisive time."

From another account of this period we get, first a clear idea of what Froebel hoped and expected to find in Pestalozzi's teachings, and then the particulars wherein he was disappointed. "If I comprehend what I sought and expected there," writes Froebel, referring to Yverdun, "it was a robust inner life, which should find utterance in many ways in creative acts; a healthy and strong life of child and youth that should answer all the requirements for the development of body and soul. I thought that Pestalozzi must be the arteries and central point of all this vitality and effort, and out from this focus in all directions the life of the youth, as of the teacher, must be penetrated. With such high-strung expectations I arrived at Yverdun, and I doubted not that I should find there the solution of all my questions."

In a certain sense, this same narrative adds, Froebel was not deceived in his expectations. Pestalozzi did indeed form the shining center of his circle and from his warm heart radiated light and life. But after a little Froebel, who had nothing to do but observe, investigate and examine what was being done, began to discover more and more weakness in the methods which were practical, methods that produced desirable results only through the inspiring mind of Pestalozzi, results that could have been reached by other means quite as well, and perhaps better. Meanwhile the strength of his love and self-sacrificing benevolence replaced in many respects the want of the clearness, discretion and firmness which he lacked.

As Froebel lingered at Yverdun month after month his aims became plainer to him and he gained a deeper insight of the early requirements and laws of the child's development than Pestalozzi possessed. This fact, however, did not prevent him from esteeming the country fortunate where such a man as Pestalozzi lived and worked, and he felt anxious to render him all the honor which was his due and also to sound his praise in public. But he became thoroughly convinced that the foundations of popular education for real life must be fixed on some basis more natural, more anthropological than any which Pestalozzi could offer.

When Froebel and his pupils left the school the management had reached a crisis, so that everything fell into disorder, and he was obliged to accept the conviction that the esteemed and amiable Pestalozzi was surrounded by false friends and badly supported, and that his work however excellent in itself, lacked a sufficiently healthful vitality to set forth and prove itself a permanent reform in popular education.

In dwelling on this part of Froebel's life we have taken pains to record as fully as possible his impressions of Pestalozzi which were gained through two years of daily intercourse with him, because many people of the present day, some of whom are regarded as eminent educators, persistently maintain that in publishing to the world the kindergarten system of infantile education Froebel really originated very little, and that all the ideas which he put forth that have since proved of any value were derived from Pestalozzi. While there is neither room nor disposition for us to argue this question here, we advise all students of the kindergarten system to undertake to settle it for themselves. Let them study, as they have opportunity, the philosophy of both men, as it is outlined in their writings, and trace out the results as they appear in the educational field to-day. Then each one will be competent to decide whether through native ability and the practical training of experience it was possible for Pestalozzi to transmit to Froebel anything on which he could evolve what the world calls in our day the kindergarten system.

The reader of these lines is asked always to bear in mind that the purpose of the present narrative is to give the well-accepted facts of Froebel's life in the order in which they occurred, with as little embellishment as possible. But if at this particular point we may be allowed an opinion as to what constitutes the radical and essential difference between the philosophy of Froebel and that of Pestalozzi, it is the difference between self-activity and imitation. The latter is always preaching what we may term the gospel of imitation, always teaching the child to imitate what the teacher has done; on the other hand the kindergarten system inculcates the gospel of originality by presenting certain basal principles which must be followed, but which when mastered by the pupil are sure to stimulate him to original work. Pestalozzi was helpful to Froebel at a time when he most needed pedagogical enlightenment, but to assert that Froebel is merely the interpreter of Pestalozzi is to make a claim which is not to be lightly accepted without analytical and conclusive proof.

Returning to Frankfort in 1810 Froebel continued his engagement as private tutor in the Von Holzhausen family for a year longer, and then resumed his University studies with much satisfaction to himself.

1811-1813—FINAL UNIVERSITY STUDIES.

In the summer of 1811, being twenty-nine years old, Froebel entered the University at Gottingen, more than ten years after he had relinquished student life at Jena. At Gottingen he at once devoted himself to the study of languages, beginning with Hebrew and Arabic, with a view of also paying some attention to the Indian and Persian. He also devoted a certain amount of time to Greek and dipped into the old favorites, physics, chemistry, mineralogy and natural history in general with renewed ardor, and also astronomy. He enjoyed himself greatly in the pursuit of knowledge under these new conditions and lived alone that nothing might interfere with his chosen work. It was his habit to walk about the beautiful suburbs of the city during the latter part of the afternoon, "in order to be greeted by the friendly rays of the sinking sun," and these rambles were sometimes extended till near midnight.

He had been at Gottingen but a few weeks, however, when his chronic lack of funds became once more a serious matter and he made up his mind that he must turn his attention to literary work as a help in his support. His apprehensions were relieved, however, by the receipt of a legacy from his mother's sister which made it possible for him to continue his studies without interruption. He was particularly interested in the lectures on mineralogy, which gave him an insight into the fundamental forms of crystals and other minerals. For us to trace the fruits of this study in the kindergarten system as Froebel has handed it down to us is not difficult.

What he learned at Gottingen stimulated his ambition to go to Berlin and continue his investigations of mineralogy, geology, crystallography and their laws, at the college of Prof. Weiss, who was a famous instructor in those branches. He also resolved to make the change because he hoped that Berlin would afford better opportunities for securing a place as tutor, as the legacy just mentioned would not support him for many months. Consequently he went to Berlin in October, 1812, at once devoting himself with undiminished enthusiasm to the subjects which he loved and at the same time becoming instructor in a distinguished private school.

The months of fall and winter passed quickly and in the early spring the throb of the war drum cut short, almost in the twinkling of an eye, his University course, as it has done that of many noble men in other lands and times.

Right here, if we stop for a moment to review the years which Froebel spent within college walls we must admit that he acquired a good education, although it was gained under difficulties. Eighteen months at Jena, a year at Gottingen, six months at Berlin, three University years in all, spread over a period of fourteen, this was his peculiar college course, supplemented with a good many months of professional study. As a result he was thoroughly grounded in mathematics, had an expert knowledge of natural history and a training in languages which was respectable. He seems to have been a faithful student, although there is little evidence that he was a brilliant scholar. In addition to the learning of the schools he also secured the practical experience of a draftsman and surveyor, and taken together, the circumstances of his life, as thus far recorded, particularly fitted him to be the founder of the kindergarten system.

In the spring of 1813, Freidrich Froebel, a student of the natural sciences in the University of Berlin, aged thirty-one, enlisted at Dresden as a private in the Lutzow corps of the German army, under a call of the king for the nation to take up arms against Napoleon. In writing of that time Georg Ebers, the novelist, says, "The snow drops which bloomed during the March days of 1813 ushered in the long-desired day of freedom, and the call 'to arms' found the loudest echo in the hearts of the students."

At this point in the narrative we may, perhaps, be pardoned for remarking that the critics of Froebel have always delighted to embellish certain allegations against him with such metaphors of ridicule and invective as they could command. One of the principal charges is that of effeminacy, which, it must be confessed, is somewhat borne out by several of his pictures which are on the market and certain characteristics of dress which he affected. While his admirers might be glad to eliminate these matters from his private history, if they could, it is nevertheless true that the world will forgive a man for parting his hair in the middle, if his thoughts and acts are such as to render him immortal.

That Froebel had a realizing sense of woman's wonderful possibilities in the training of young children, which amounted to an inspiration, is not to be denied. That he delighted in gathering the mothers about him in constant attempts to give them some inkling of those possibilities and that he spent the strength of his last years in forming what we now call kindergarten training classes is well-known to all who are familiar with his history. That the little children loved him and hung about him all his days is always admitted. But these things do not make a man effeminate. Some of them were characteristics of the Son of Man who dwelt in Palestine nearly two thousand years ago. There was no charge of effeminacy filed against Private Friedrich Froebel while he wore the uniform of the Lutzow Jagers or lay in the trenches and coolly calculated the velocity of the bullets whizzing over his head from the armies of Napoleon, as to how much faster those which came from the muskets were flying than those discharged from the flintlocks.

He put aside every ambition, took every risk of life and limb, health and happiness, for the honor of the flag which represented to him the head and front of civilization, the one country which was worth living or dying for, as destiny might decide. As to his motives in entering the army, he says: "It was the feeling and consciousness of the ideal Germany that I respected as something high and holy in my spirit. Moreover, the firmness with which I held to my educational career decided me. Although I could not really say that I had a fatherland, as I am not a Prussian, it must happen that every boy, that every child who should later be instructed by me would have a fatherland and that fatherland now demanded protection when the child himself could not defend it. I could not possibly think how a young man, capable of bearing arms, could become the teacher of children whose country he had not defended with his life blood. The summons to war appeared to me a sign of the common need of man, of the country, of the time in which I lived, and I felt that it would be unworthy and unmanly not to struggle for the common necessity of the people among whom one lives, not to bear a part toward repelling a common danger. Every consideration was secondary to these considerations, even that which grew out of my bodily constitution, too feeble for such a life." Truly sentiments like these have been regarded in all ages as belonging to "the stuff that heroes are made of."

Froebel joined the infantry division of the Lutzow corps, "Lutzow's Wild, Bold Troop," commonly known as the "Lutzow Jagers," and marched from Dresden, April 11, 1813. This volunteer organization had been formed during the previous month by Baron Von Lutzow, his instructions being "to harass the enemy by constant skirmishes and to encourage the smaller German states to rise against the tyrant Napoleon. The corps became celebrated for swift, dashing exploits in small bodies. Froebel seems to have been in the main body and to have seen but little of the more active duties of the regiment."

Owing to the seclusion of his life in the University his comrades were in the beginning of the campaign all strangers to him, although many of them were Berlin students. At the end of the first morning's march the sergeant introduced him to a divinity student named Heinrich Langethal, born at Erfurt, September 3, 1792. A little later Langethal in turn presented his friend, Wilhelm Middendorf, also a divinity student, and a life-long intimacy began between the three, then and there. Middendorf was a Thuringian, having been born in Westphalia, September 20, 1793. Aside from his connection with Froebel his history was not eventful. Of him Dr. Ebers writes:—

"The source of Middendorf's greatness in the sphere where life and his own choice had placed him may even be imputed to him as a fault. He, the most enthusiastic of all Froebel's disciples, remained to his life's end a lovable child, in whom the powers of a rich poetic soul surpassed those of the thoughtful, well-trained man. He would have been ill-adapted to any practical position, but no one could be better suited to enter into the soul-life of young human beings and to cherish and ennoble them."

Langethal finished his grammar school studies at Erfurt and then entered the University at Berlin, where he proved himself a scholar of unusual talent. Midway in his career there the elevation of the Prussian nation led him into the war. He was advised that he must not write home to his father of his intention, because if the letter should be intercepted his act would be regarded as high treason by the French authorities who held sway at Erfurt. When asked how he would procure the uniform of the black Jagers, he answered: "The cape of my coat will supply the trousers, I can have a red collar put on my cloak, my coat can be dyed black and turned into a uniform, and I have a hanger." He had a dauntless spirit that knew no such word as failure.

The first halt of the corps came at Meissen, at the close of a beautiful spring day, when the students who were in the command gathered together about a long table in an open space on the banks of the river Elbe, where they greeted and pledged each other with old Meissen wine. The three young men just named lingered at the table till midnight, laying the foundation of a friendship that has since become immortal, and the next morning they went together to examine the city's beautiful cathedral. To this circle Bauer, later an instructor in a Berlin grammar school, was subsequently admitted, and to those three men Froebel limited all intimate association during the campaign.

In the fragmentary autobiography which Froebel some years later prepared for the Duke of Meiningen he speaks of these days as follows: "My principal care was to improve myself in my present calling, and so one of my endeavors was to make clear to myself the inner necessity and the connection of demands of service and drill; it came to me very soon and easily from the mathematical, physical side, and strengthened me against many little reprimands which easily befell others when they thought this or that command could be omitted, as too trifling." Another writer puts the same idea in these words: "The peculiarly regular and orderly inclination of his mind made him so accurate in all points of his service that he never gave cause for the little unpleasantness which befell most raw recruits."

These extracts become of importance when considered in the light of some modern criticism which confidently asserts that Froebel could not have made a good soldier because he had no natural aptitude for such service. It is evident that he tried to adapt himself to the needs of the hour and his surroundings, no matter how great the personal inconvenience. That he was a good soldier, as a matter of fact, was fully attested by his promotion to be an officer in 1815, although he was not allowed the opportunity to act in such a capacity.

When the corps reached Havelburg there was a long halt, occasioned by an armistice, lasting from June 4 to August 10, during which the four friends sought to be together as much as possible. The life of the camp was especially pleasant to Froebel, he says, because it made many facts of history clear to him. He lived in nature as much as he could, and we are told that "on the march, under the hottest July sun, when most of the men were trying to get rid of everything which they could do without, so as to make their knapsacks lighter, Froebel collected all kinds of stones, plants and mosses for his study of nature and filled his knapsack with them. At the bivouac fire he brought out his treasures to serve as the subject of conversation on natural history."

There has always been some discussion as to how far Froebel shared in the hostilities of this campaign. Bowen in his biography says that of actual fighting his regiment saw nothing, a statement that is evidently without foundation. Froebel modestly speaks of the "few battles in which we took part." There can be no question, however, that Froebel found time for the active cultivation of the practical study of natural history and the cementing of a friendship with Middendorf, Langethal and Bauer. At times the four friends indulged in pedagogical and philosophical discussions which were greatly to their mutual edification. "In this way," writes Froebel, "we passed, at least I did, our war life as a dream. Now and then, at Leipzig, at Dalenburg, at Bremen, at Berlin, we seemed to wake up; but soon sank back into feeble dreaminess again."

The Lutzow corps marched through that section of Germany known as the Mark of Brandenburg, of which Berlin is a part, going in the latter part of August, 1813, through Priegnitz, Macklenburg, the districts of Bremen, Hamburg and Holstein, and coming to the Rhine in the last days of the year. Napoleon abdicated in the spring of 1814, went to Elba as an exile April 20, and the peace of Paris was proclaimed May 30. Meanwhile Froebel's regiment was stationed in the Netherlands till July, when all the volunteers who did not care to serve longer were honorably discharged.

Doubtless Froebel was a better man and a better kindergartner because of his military service. In later years he brought into the kindergarten the spirit of patriotism which will always be one of its prominent characteristics, wherever it is established. He also brought into it the stirring marches and lively music which the military camp suggests. And although the kindergarten must always be regarded as a mighty bulwark of the kingdom of peace, we may well ask what would it be worth with these things taken out of it?

1814–1816—CURATOR AT BERLIN.

When Froebel entered the army he received the promise of a position under the Prussian government at the close of the war, that of assistant in the mineralogical museum at Berlin under Prof. Weiss, who had been his instructor, a post that was offered him through the influence of friends. Consequently his first thought on quitting the army was to secure for himself this coveted place, and so he set his face toward Berlin, arriving there early in August, having stopped on the way at Lunen, Mainz, Frankfort and Rudolstadt, moved by a desire to visit once more the region of his birth.

He began his duties as curator in the museum at once. He was occupied most of each day in the care and arrangement of minerals in a room which was perfectly quiet and which he kept locked against all intruders. The investigation and explanation of crystals also formed a part of his duties. Regarding this period of his life, he writes: "While engaged in this work I continually proved to be true what had long been a presentiment with me that even in these so-called lifeless stones and fragments of rock, torn from their original bed, there lay germs of transforming, developing energy and activity. Amidst the diversity of forms around me, I recognized under all kinds of various modifications one law of development. Therefore my rocks and crystals served me as a mirror wherein I might descry mankind, and man's development and history. Geology and crystallography not only opened up for me a higher circle of knowledge and insight, but also showed me a higher good for my inquiry, my speculation and my endeavor."

These discoveries made Froebel think for a time that he would like to fit himself to teach in some University, but he soon gave up the idea, believing that he was "generally deficient in the preparatory studies necessary for the higher branches of natural science." Another reason why he relinquished the desire for such a career resulted from his reflection that the amount of interest shown in their work by the University students of his day was too little to attract him to a professorship. On this theme he remarks: "The opportunities I had of observing the natural history students of that time, their very slight knowledge of their subject, their deficiency of perceptive power, their still greater want of the true scientific spirit, warned me back from such a plan."

During his service as a curator he continued attending lectures on mineralogy, crystallography, and geology and also on the history of ancient philosophy. Those were months of marked development for the young man, who still had the work of life before him. They made up the one brief period of his career when he was prosperous and at peace with the world, unless we except a few months passed at Marienthal, thirty-five years later. They served to so perfect his studies of natural history that those studies bore excellent fruit when he came to present to the world the kindergarten system of education. No one who had not first made the forms of crystallography a profound study could have brought them into that system as an integral part of it in the way that Fræbel did.

During the last months of his term as a soldier Fræbel became separated from his friends, Langethal, Middendorf and Bauer, so that when he left the army he did not know where they were. All three of them, however, soon returned to Berlin, to resume their theological studies. Meanwhile Napoleon had ended his exile at Elba, resumed his former place as emperor of France and for a few short weeks menaced Europe as of old. A new war cloud hung over Germany in the spring of 1815, and the four friends re-enlisted. "On account of our previous service" says Fræbel, "and by royal favor, we were at once promoted to officer's rank and each one was appointed to a regiment. There was such a throng of volunteers, however, that it was not necessary for any state officials to leave their posts or for students to interrupt their studies, and we therefore received counter orders commanding us to stay at home."

Middendorf came to room with Fræbel, pending his expected departure for the war, and in this way the two were brought into close companionship for several months. About this time both Langethal and Middendorf became tutors in private families, to secure means for continuing their studies, and they appealed to Fræbel to instruct them for two hours a week in the best methods of teaching arithmetic, which he gladly did.

It was during his curatorship at Berlin that Fræbel first met Henrietta Wilhelmine Hoffmeister, whom he subsequently married. She was the daughter of an official of the Prussian war department, was born at Berlin, September 20, 1780, had been a pupil of Schleiermacher and Fichte and was highly cultured. She had previously married an official connected with the war office named Klepper, but had separated from him because of his misconduct. She came to the museum on one occasion and we are told that Fræbel "was wonderfully struck by her, especially because of the readiness with which she entered into his educational ideas." Langethal and Middendorf were well acquainted with the family and had often spoken to him about her.

Fræbel remained at Berlin till October, 1816, when he left suddenly and without giving his friends any definite idea of his future plans. He had, in 1815, declined the offer of a valuable post as mineralogist at Stockholm and he secured his discharge from the museum against the earnest remonstrance of Prof. Weiss.

The reason for his action soon became apparent, however. Christoph Fræbel, his well-beloved elder brother, who has been so often mentioned in these pages, died of typhus fever in 1813, while nursing French soldiers in the hospitals. He was settled as a clergyman at Griesheim and left a widow and three sons. The mother wrote to Friedrich Fræbel in 1816, expressing her anxiety regarding the proper education of the boys and appealing to him for advice. It was this letter that caused him to make the sudden resolve to give up his place in the museum. We are told that he had hardly finished reading it when his latent interest in the education of man suddenly manifested itself in all power and energy and pushed him irresistably forward to take up again his natural vocation and be a teacher. He determined to devote himself to the education of his nephews, and as a preliminary step he traveled from Berlin to Osterode, where his brother Christian had become a spinner and dyer of linen thread. There the brothers held a consultation and it was decided that Friedrich should open a school at Griesheim, the primary object being the training of Christoph's children, and that Christian should also send his two sons to this school. Friedrich took the latter with him, the elder being eight and his brother six years old, and began his teaching November 16, 1816, calling himself and the five pupils "The Universal German Educational Institute," although they were housed in a peasant's cottage.

CASTLE AT MARIENTHAL.

FRŒBEL tarried at Griesheim but a few months. In the summer of 1817 his sister-in-law, owing to the death of her father, decided to move her family to Keilhau, where she bought a small farm. The school went with her and was re-opened June 24. The hamlet of Keilhau lies on the mountain side about five miles south-west of Rudolstadt, guarded by nature on three sides with protecting walls, which keep the wind from entering the village.

It is one of the most attractive spots in the Thuringian Forest, which is not a region of great height, but famous for its beautiful valleys, offering a great variety of the most beautiful scenery to be found anywhere.

The primitive condition of the village of Keilhau, as late as 1815, seems strange enough to us. "Although not poor," says one writer, "the peasants had remained in the condition of the Middle Ages. Three houses retained the old form of Thuringian architecture and the date of 1532 was to be seen over the door of one of them. The church with its pretty tower was nevertheless more like a cellar than the house of God. In the midst of the village a water course marked the street and five springs kept the road wet all the time. There were only about one hundred inhabitants and the living of the peasants was very simple. As had been done five hundred years before, the mayor still counted off on a notched stick the number of measures of wheat which each man was bound to pay as corn tax or tithe. He also gave orally to the peasants any new regulations of the government, and in order to keep up a military appearance a day watchman paraded the village with a broad halberd over his shoulder. The dress of the old man was what he had worn in his youth, and that of the women descended from the mother to daughter."

The beginnings of the school at Keilhau were very humble. The teachers, Fræbel and Middendorf, during the summer of 1817, lived in a wretched little hut with neither door, flooring or stove, while Fræbel was building a school-house. The quarters assigned him had formerly served as a place for keeping hens. In July Langethal graduated from the University at Berlin with the highest honors and in September he visited Keilhau to see his old comrades and take his brother to Selesia, where he had an engagement as tutor to the young nobility. Fræbel received him with the utmost cordiality and the sight of the robust, merry boys who were lying on the floor that evening building forts and castles with the wooden blocks which Fræbel had made for them, according to his own plan, excited the keenest interest. He had come to take his brother away; but when he saw him among other happy companions of his own age complete the finest structure of all, a Gothic Cathedral, it seemed almost wrong to tear the child from this circle. The result of this visit was that Langethal decided to stay at Keilhau with his brother, so that there might be a trio of teachers, and a great gain he was to the institution, where his life work was done. More pupils arrived when he did and the new building was completed in November.

When Fræbel first came to Griesheim he told his sister-in-law that he wished to be a father to her orphaned children, a statement which she interpreted to suggest an ultimate marriage between him and herself. He, however, had never intended it in that sense, and after reaching Keilhau he offered himself by letter to Henrietta Hoffmeister of Berlin, asking that she would give her life to the advancement of those educational ideas in which she had shown so deep an interest during their interview in the museum. She received his proposal favorably, but her father made objection and refused to give her any dowry. The record says that "she had lived all her life in comfortably, almost affluent circumstances. But she relinquished everything, even the home of which she was the light and joy, a dear mother and greatly beloved father who adored her, to devote her whole life and being to the apostle of a new education, whose ideas and schemes had elevated her soul as with the light of divine inspiration." When the widow of Christolph Fræbel learned of the engagement she made over her property to Friedrich, and went to live at Valkstadt in June, 1818.

The wedding occurred September 20, the

bride being thirty-eight that day, and the groom two years younger. She brought with her to Keilhau an adopted daughter, Ernestine Chrispine. "Never," says one writer, "has man found a better helpmate than this woman was to Froebel. She devoted herself to the assistance of the Keilhau teachers and their educational mission with her whole being; made willingly any necessary sacrifice; submitted willingly to every privation; lived through days of most painful struggles with poverty and want, and did this all with a courage and devotion that was a shining example to all the women who have since devoted their lives to the realization of Froebel's ideas."

In order to do exact justice to Fran Froebel, who is so often and so deservedly praised, it may be necessary to add this quotation: "Froebel's wife was revered and beloved in the highest degree by the whole pedagogical group and by Froebel was ever treated with deepest tenderness and esteem. Eye witnesses assert, however, that although a very capable woman she was not perfectly qualified to guide the helm of so large and composite a household with sufficient circumspection and tact, and that in the idea of 'unity of life' which Froebel wished to realize there was at times something wanting, in spite of the poetic, yes idyllic character of the lives of these amiable and noble-minded idealists, who were ready to become martyrs to their philanthropic and pure principles."

What the privations endured during those years really were we can hardly conceive. Froebel says: "We had now a severe struggle for existence for the whole time, up to 1820. With all our efforts we never could get the school-house enlarged; other still more necessary buildings had to be erected first." As an illustration of the straits to which Froebel was subjected, it is stated by an associate, who had the incident from his own lips, that at one time during his early struggles to put the school on its feet he had to live for a week on two large loaves of bread, on which he first measured the daily portions with chalk marks, so that he should not cut off more than the allotted part. We are told, moreover, that he was not afraid of long journeys on foot for the benefit of the cause, from which he often returned with bleeding feet, and that many a night he slept in the open air to save traveling expenses and then gave the money to some poor child to support him in the school.

Shortly after Froebel's marriage the father of Middendorf died, and he, without any hesitation, devoted the whole of his inheritance to the institution. Early in the year 1820 Christian Froebel decided to give up his manufacturing business at Osterode and join the community with his wife and three daughters, the two sons being already members of the school. He also invested all his property in the venture. The completion of the schoolhouse was now pushed with zeal, a work that ended in 1822. The following year Johannas Arnold Barop, born at Dortmund in 1802, a nephew of Middendorf and a divinity student at Halle, visited Keilhau and decided to remain as a teacher, much to the disgust of his family. He eventually became the mainstay of the whole enterprise.

At this time the Keilhau family began to enjoy greater comforts in life. It was found that "the wonderful enthusiasm of the teachers and the wisdom of the educational methods employed, had, in a few years, made the average pupil of the Keilhau school so greatly superior to the average pupil of all other educational establishments of the country, that the number of pupils increased rapidly and money began to flow more freely into the households of all the teachers."

It was in the summer of 1826 that both Middendorf and Langethal were married, the former choosing for his wife Albertine, the eldest daughter of Christian Froebel, and his comrade taking Ernestine Chrispine, the adopted daughter of Friedrich Froebel's wife. Barop married Emilie, Christian Froebel's second daughter, in 1828, and the third one in due season wedded another of the teachers.

It will hardly be possible within the limits of this brief narrative to give the full history of Froebel's career as principal of the Keilhau school. But in order to get a glimpse of the institution during its most prosperous days under the leadership of its founder we must quote from the reminiscences of Col. Hermann Von Arnswald, who was a pupil there for three years about 1824–26, as found in the introduction of "Froebel's Letters." He says that when he reached the school Froebel took him immediately to the boys, with whom he was soon at home, so thoroughly, in fact, that it made his mother feel quite sad to see how cheerful her boy was at parting, when tears filled her own eyes.

The account goes on to explain that in the domestic life of the institution strict order had to be observed, and great care was taken to promote personal cleanliness, new comers being examined every morning before breakfast to see that there was no lack in this respect. And woe to the boy who was reckoned deficient, because his allowance of milk for breakfast was cut off, and he had to be content with only a piece of bread. This reduction of rations was almost the sole punishment that was deemed necessary. Whoever deserved correction was sure to find at dinner or supper a piece of bread on his plate, which indicated that he must pass by all other dishes without tasting them. On one occasion Von Arnswald yielded to the temptation of eating a strawberry, taken from the supper table before the meal was quite ready. Fræbel saw the act and as a consequence the ominous piece of bread was put on his plate. The boy who did any damage at Keilhau must see to its being repaired personally, and the colonel remembers one luckless fellow who having carelessly or mischievously broken a window had to take the frame on his back for five miles before he could get it mended.

During the three years of Col. Von Arnswald's stay at the school no doctor ever set foot there. The small injuries that occurred occasionally in the gymnasium were always cured by the boys' mutual helpfulness. One day when he was at the top of the climbing rope his strength gave out and he slid so fast to the bottom that his hands were badly blistered and he could not dress without help for a month. During that time his chum cared for the wounded members, but nobody else noticed the mishap. Another peculiarity of this school was the absence of all vacations. No pupil ever went home for a while and then returned. But a tramp through the woods extending over several days was repeatedly made during the summer season. On such occasions coffee and cakes were served, and the birthdays of the teachers joyfully remembered. Ordinarily the pupils drank nothing but milk and water.

The anniversary of the battle of Leipzig, the loss of which forced Napoleon to withdraw his armies from Germany, was always celebrated on the 18th of October, the national sentiment being powerfully developed. A big fire was lighted on the mountain top that evening, "and when the flames raised their golden tongues skyward, popular and patriotic songs were sung, and we listened to the inspiring words of our teachers, every one of whom had fought through the wars of deliverance as a volunteer, all having been faithful comrades in the service of the great fatherland."

When winter came it brought frequent sleigh rides on the ice, and the boys were sometimes called out of bed for this pastime. On Christmas eve they were treated to poppy soup, which made them sleep soundly till five o'clock in the morning, when they were summoned to a short religious service, gifts were distributed and they were taken to church. Col. Von Arnswald sums up his story with these significant words: "I lived at Keilhau for three years. At the end of that time I went home to the house of my parents healthy in soul and body. After a life so natural and so completely secluded from all the injurious impressions of the outside world there could not have been any other result than perfect health."

For fourteen years Fræbel was at the head of the Keilhau school. The highest number of pupils during that time seems to have been about sixty, and in 1829 it dwindled to five. As an educational experiment it was in great measure a real success, though it did not reach Fræbel's ideal. All mental requirements were richly provided for, and his own views of education carried out as far as time would allow, considering the imperative necessity of preparing the boys for the University; but the material wants were met with great difficulty and in the poorest fashion. "None of the noble men connected with the school had in the remotest degree," says one writer, "imagined what great sums were required for the founding and continuing of so extensive an institution as they had in view, and were expending little by little. It was very nearly true that they shared with each other, lovingly and trustingly, all they possessed, for it could be affirmed of them as of the first Christians 'No one said that anything was his own.'"

The account goes on to relate, "It was in vain that every item of income was devoted to the common use and that each one joyfully brought to the sacrifice all his goods and chattels, his inheritance and earnings." Froebel was too much of a philanthropist to derive very much gain from the pupils. He could not turn away an orphan or the child of a widow merely because only half could be paid to him, so that the school, well filled though it was, yielded too little profit to enable it to sustain itself." Moreover, as Emily Shirreff points out in her biographical sketch, Froebel was by nature a man in whose hands material interests could not prosper. He had no practical ability of any kind ; and being engrossed with the interest of carrying into effect the cherished views which had become a part of his very life, he was probably less fitted than ever to calculate and dwell upon prudential and economical considerations.

Barop had constantly hoped for support from his well-to-do family, but they had never approved of his connection with the school and finally withdrew from him altogether. Little by little all sources of help were exhausted, while the needs of the school continually grew. The credit of the managers began to sink, so that "malevolence followed in their track and suspicion stalked around them in all kinds of deformity."

Some of their troubles arose from political causes. Among the patriots who had fought in the war and the generation of University students which came after them there was much enthusiasm for German unity and liberty, and here and there not a little wild socialistic talk. The Keilhau community had adopted the German dress, and both teachers and pupils allowed their hair to grow long, and for these reasons the Prussian government became suspicious of the school and in September, 1824, induced the local prince to appoint Superintendent Zeh to investigate the institute and make a report regarding it.

This official came to the school November 23, and again March 1st, 1825, and the very favorable report which he made in detail is still preserved, and a part of it is worth quoting. "I found here," said the inspector, "what is never and nowhere shown in real life, a timely and closely united family of some sixty members, living in quiet harmony, all showing that they gladly perform the duties of their various positions ; a family in which, because it is held together by the strong hand of mutual confidence, and because every member seeks the good of the whole, everything, as of itself, thrives in happiness and love."

"With respect and hearty affection all turn to the principal ; the little five years' old children cling to his knees, while his friends and colleagues hear and honor his advice with the confidence which his insight and experience and his indefatigable zeal for the good of the whole deserve ; while he has bound himself to his fellow-workers, as the supports and pillars of his life work, which to him is truly a 'holy work.'

Self activity of mind is the first law of the institution ; therefore the kind of instruction given there does not make the young mind a strong box into which as early as possible all kinds of coin of the most different values and coinage, such as are now current in the world, are stuffed ; but slowly, continuously, gradually and always inwardly, that is according to a connection founded upon the nature of the human mind, the instruction steadily goes on, without any tricks, from the simple to the complex, from the concrete to the abstract, so well-adapted to the child and his needs that he goes as readily to his learning as to his play."

This report was made to the local prince of Schwarzburg-Rudolstadt, and of course he could make no move against the school after such a report, had he wished to do so. therefore he directed the community to dress like other people and cut their hair, a very Solomon's judgment, says Bowen, for there was nothing else the matter with them.

But the agitation which led to this report caused nearly all the patrons of the school to take their boys away from it. Moreover, for years trouble had been fermenting from within as well as without. One of the teachers, named Herzog, set himself in stubborn opposition to the principal and drew Froebel's sister-in-law and her sons to his side of the controversy ; the three nephews quarreled with their uncle and left in 1824 ; Herzog soon followed and industriously libelled the institute for some time.

All of these causes placed the school under a temporary cloud. In writing on the "Critical Moments of Froebel's Life" Barop describes the situation with a graphic pen. "The number of our pupils, he remarks, "had diminished to five or six, and consequently the vanishing little revenue increased the burden of debts to a height that made us dizzy. From all sides creditors rushed in, urged on by attorneys, who washed their hands in our misery. Froebel vanished through the back door to the mountain when the duns appeared and it was left to Middendorf to quiet most of them in a degree which only he can believe possible who has been acquainted with Middendorf's influence over man."

For a time relief from all these troubles was promised because of the expected help of the duke of Meiningen. Several influential friends of the Keilhau work called his attention to it and as a result he sent for Froebel to explain a scheme for an educational institute to include with the ordinary "literary" branches instruction in carpentery, weaving, bookbinding and tilling the ground. Half the school hours were to be devoted to study and the other half were to be occupied by some sort of handiwork. This plan was the work of all the Keilhau teachers and the duke was much pleased with it. He proposed to place the estate of Helba, with thirty acres of land and a yearly grant of some five hundred dollars, at Froebel's disposal, as an aid in carrying out the scheme. These negotiations began in 1827, and it was then that Froebel wrote out the story of his life previous to 1816, for the information of the duke. This record breaks off abruptly and probably was never presented to the duke. Secret influences were set at work to change the duke's purpose regarding the new educational plans and his right-hand man in such matters, fearing lest Froebel's influence should supplant his own, did all that he could to prevent the establishment of the industrial school. Consequently the duke proposed, in 1831, as a compromise, that Froebel begin with an experimental establishment of twenty-five pupils. Froebel felt that he had been betrayed and refused to except such an offer or to have anything more to do with the duke.

Meanwhile Froebel had formed a close friendship with the celebrated philosopher Carl Krause, under peculiar circumstances. In 1822 two articles by Froebel describing his work at Keilhau, which had been previously printed in another form, appeared in The "Isis," a noted scientific journal edited and published by Lorenz Oken. During the following year Krause contributed an article to the same periodical criticising in some particulars what Froebel had written. The latter was too much occupied with his regular work to give the matter much attention at the time, but five years later, under date of March 24, 1828, he wrote Krause a long letter in reply, which was followed by a trip to Gottingen by Froebel and Middendorf in the fall of that year that they might become personally acquainted with Krause. Long discussions on education took place during this celebrated meeting and Krause made Froebel familiar with the works of Comenius, "and introduced him to the whole learned society of Gottingen, where he made a great and somewhat peculiar impression." There can be no doubt but that his relations with Krause at this time had considerable to do in shaping Froebel's future course in respect to the kindergarten.

As soon as Froebel decided that he could no longer depend on the duke for any substantial help he went to Frankfort to discuss his difficulties with friends in that city and this step resulted in his practically relinquishing the control of affairs at Keilhau, although he spent many months of his subsequent life there.

A brief review of Froebel's writings while he was principal at Keilhau should naturally be included in the account of this period. His first published essay appeared in 1822, the title being, "On the Universal German Educational Institute of Rudolstadt," which was followed in 1823, by a "Continuation of the Account of the Universal German Educational Institute at Keilhau." The next year he printed a paper on "Christmas at Keilhau;" "A Christmas Gift to the Parents of the Pupils at Keilhau, to the Friends and Members of the Institute." In 1826 "The Education of Man" was brought out, the full title being as follows: "The Education of Man, The Art of Education, Instruction and Training Aimed At in the Educational Institute at Keilhau," written by its principal, F. W. A. Froebel, Volume I; "To the Beginning of Boyhood, Keilhau, 1826." Published by the Institute. Sold in commission at Leipzig by C. F. Doerffling, 497 pages. That same year Froebel undertook to edit and publish, at Leipzig and Keilhau, "The Family Weekly Journal of Education." In speaking of these writings one editor of Froebel's biography, Emilie Michaelis, says: "Froebel in his unbusinesslike way, published all these productions privately. They came out, of course, under every disadvantage, and could only reach the hands of learned persons, and those to whom they were really of interest by merely a chance. Further, Froebel, as has already abundantly appeared, was but a poor author. His stiff, turgid style makes his works in many places most difficult to understand, as the present translators have found to their cost, and he was therefore pratically unreadable to the general public. In his usual self-absorbed fashion he did not perceive these deficiences of his, nor could he be made to see the folly of private publication. Indeed, on the contrary, he dreamed of fabulous sums which one day he was to realize from the sale of his works. It is needless to add that the event proved very much the reverse."

Thus closes an important period of fourteen years in Froebel's life, a formative, educating period, like all those which had gone before. For him to found the Keilhau school, an institution which has to this day maintained an illustrious reputation, was indeed an honor. But Keilhau did more for him than he did for Keilhau, it disciplined him for the immortal work of later years. Had he been successful as its principal he would have been content with the place for the rest of his days, and consequently the world would never have heard of the kindergarten.

1831—1837—IN SWITZERLAND.

It was in the month of May, 1831, that Froebel went to Frankfort, and there he chanced to meet the noted musician and naturalist Zavier Schnyder of Wartensee, in the canton of Lucerne. He told this new acquaintance of what he had tried to do at Keilhau and how the work had resulted. He enlisted his sympathy and "exercised upon him that overpowering influence which is the peculiar property of creative minds." Schnyder appreciated the man and his efforts and we are told that he fairly begged Froebel to open a school in his castle at Wartensee. The offer was accepted without debate and Froebel at once departed for Switzerland, taking Ferdinand Froebel, the oldest son of his brother Christian, with him, Middendorf assuming the helm at Keilhau for the time being. The uncle and nephew located themselves in the castle so kindly placed at their disposal, with its splendid library, abundance of silver plate and elegant furniture, and began their school with a few peasant children from the immediate neighborhood.

But obstacles sprang up before these enthusiasts had really secured a foothold in their new quarters. The opposition of the local clergy against the "heretics" and foreigners was from the first pronounced and aggressive. It prevented pupils coming to them from any distance and from families who were well-to-do, and so limited their income by the narrowest bounds. It also caused the people about them to harbor the continual suspicion that they were ready to do something which would injure the community. Added to the hate of the priests, according to some writers, was the malevolence of Herzog, a native of that section, who had been deposed from his place as teacher at Keilhau some years previous, because he had shown himself to be a promoter of strife. Moreover, the teachers found their rooms in the castle very inconvenient for school purposes, but the owner would not consent to addition or alteration on any account.

Such was their condition at the end of a few months, when Barop joined them, having tramped there from Keilhau, where their friends had become concerned about them and appointed him a messenger to report how they were faring. He remained in Switzerland more than a year. Soon after his arrival the three friends were sitting in a hotel near Wartensee, talking about their difficulties with some strangers who happened to be there, and the conversation was overheard by some business men from the neighboring town of Willisau, who became much interested in what was said. They went home and reported what Froebel and his associates were trying to do in the interest of education, and soon an invitation came from twenty families in Willisau to remove the school to that place. An association was formed to support it and a building which resembled a castle was secured for it, by consent of the authorities of the canton. Some forty pupils entered the school as soon as it was relocated and for a time prosperity seemed assured.

But the fury of the priests blazed out afresh and the teachers went about in fear of their lives. On one occasion during a church festival a fanatical Capuchin monk made such a fierce speech against them that everybody present expected that a riot must result. While the tirade was going on Froebel stood in the crowd directly facing the monk, without moving a muscle or changing a feature, and his two associates appeared equally oblivious to their danger. Strange to relate, no hand was raised against the heretics, and after the monk had disappeared they passed quietly through the threatening mob.

Barop resolved to procure protection if it could be obtained, and laid the matter before the mayor, who advised that a public examination of the pupils be held, as a means of winning popular esteem. It occurred on a beautiful autumnal day, being attended by a great crowd from different cantons, and a number of officials. It began at seven in the morning and continued till seven in the evening, closing with games and gymnastic exercises by the whole school. It was a great success in every way, and as a result glowing speeches about the school were made in the council of the canton and that body voted to let the castle to Froebel and his associates at a low rate and to expel from the canton the monk who had attacked them. A little later, in 1833, Barop returned to Keilhau and became its principal. Gradually he raised the financial standing of the school, continuing there till his death, many years later, and handing it down to his son, the present principal.

Just before Barop decided to return to Keilhau a deputation of citizens came from Berne to invite Froebel to organize an orphanage at Burgdorf, in addition to his work at Willisau, and he accepted the task on condition that other pupils should be admitted besides orphans. Middendorf came from Keilhau to take the place of Barop, locating at Willisau with Ferdinand Froebel, while Friedrich Froebel and his wife took up the new enterprise at Burgdorf. In connection with the regular instruction given at the orphanage Froebel was required to conduct what was called a Repetitive Course for the teachers of the canton. They were given three months' leave of absence from their regular duties once in two years, during which time they were gathered at Burgdorf for special study. Concerning this period in Froebel's life Barop writes as follows: "Froebel had to preside over the debates and to conduct the studies which were pursued in common. His own observations and the remarks of the teachers brought to him a new conviction that all school education was as yet without a proper foundation, and, that until the education of the nursery was reformed, nothing solid and worthy could be attained. The necessity of training gifted, capable mothers occupied his soul, and the importance of the education of childhood's earliest years became more evident to him than ever. He determined to set forth fully his ideas on education, which the tyranny of a thousand opposing circumstances had always prevented him from working out in their completeness; or at all events to do this as regards the earliest years of man, and then to win over the world of women to the actual accomplishment of his plans."

After a stay of three years at Burgdorf the health of Frau Froebel broke down and the doctors ordered her to seek another climate. In June, 1836, she and her husband went to Berlin, the immediate cause of the journey being the death of her mother and the necessity of adjusting some matters pertaining to her inheritance. While he tarried at Berlin the fundamental thought of all his educational efforts made a deeper impress than ever before on Froebel's mind. There it was that his hours of musing were occupied with the plan which was taking shape for the early education of little children. It was now clear to him that the earliest childhood is the most important time for human development, and that in the child's behalf play as his first activity, must be spiritualized and systematically treated.

He naturally felt that his native Germany was the country in which to work out these ideas and he never returned to Switzerland. Langethal went from Keilhau to take Froebel's place, and for a time he and Ferdinand Froebel were directors of the Burgdorf school. Then Langethal left it to take charge of a girls' school at Berne, and not long after Ferdinand Froebel died, being sincerely mourned by the whole community. The Willisan institute was given up also. Middendorf returning to his family at Keilhau, and thus it happened that the educational experiment in Switzerland lasted only a few years and met with but limited success, compared with the mental and physical effort that it cost.

After a few months, in 1837, Froebel and his wife came to Keilhau once more, and there the idea of the kindergarten burst upon him. He wrote at once to Berlin for his first materials for the plays and occupations, and selected, with the help of his friend Barop, who was the principal of the Keilhau school, the neighboring village of Blankenburg, a little south-west of Keilhau, for the launching of his new enterprise, a place which he felt, on account of its healthy location, would make the best home for his invalid wife.

In giving an account of these days Barop writes as follows: "When Froebel came back from Berlin the idea of an institution for little children was fully formed in him. I rented him a locality in the neighboring Blankenburg. For a long time he could find no name for his cause. Middendorf and I were one day walking to Blankenburg with him over the Steiger Pass. He kept on repeating, 'Oh, if I could only find a name for my youngest child.' Blankenburg lay at our feet and he walked moodily toward it. Suddenly he stood still as if riveted to the spot, and his eyes grew wonderfully bright. Then he shouted to the mountain so that it echoed to the four winds, 'Eureka, Kindergarten shall the institution be called.'" This was literally a "mountain moment" in his life, a brief period of inspiration which counted for more than months of every-day existence. After finding the right name Froebel determined to make an effort to put the whole establishment at Blankenburg on a satisfactory financial basis and include in it a training college in which women teachers should be shown how to deal with little children up to the age of seven.

The house where Froebel lived and labored at Blankenburg remains to-day as it appeared then, a large, unattractive, three-story structure on the hillside. It is still used for school purposes and bears on the front a tablet of black and gold with these words: "Friedrich Froebel Established His First Kindergarten Here on the 28th of June, 1840." This date is chosen because it was a festival day in all that region, commemorating the four hundredth anniversary of the discovery of printing, which was celebrated in common by the schools of Blankenburg and Keilhau, Froebel being the orator of the day. As a matter of fact, however, he began the kindergarten work soon after locating at Blankenburg.

To Col. Von Arnswald we are indebted for a glimpse of the Blankenburg kindergarten as it appeared in 1839. "Arriving at the place," he writes, "I found my Middendorf seated by the pump in the market-place, surrounded by a crowd of little children. Going near them I saw that he was engaged in mending the jacket of a boy. By his side sat a little girl busy with thread and needle upon another piece of clothing; one boy had his feet in a bucket of water washing them carefully; other girls and boys were standing around attentively looking upon the strange pictures of real life before them, and waiting for something to turn up to interest them personally. Our meeting was of the most cordial kind, but Middendorf did not interrupt the business in which he was engaged. 'Come, children,' he cried, 'let us go into the garden,' and with loud cries of joy the crowd of little men followed the splendid looking, tall man with willing feet, running all around him."

"The garden was not a garden, however, but a barn with a small room and an entrance hall. In the entrance Middendorf welcomed the children and played with them an all-round game, ending in the flight of the little ones into the room where every one of them sat down in his place on the bench and took hold of his gift box. Then for half an hour they were all very busy with their blocks, and then the summons came, 'Come, children, let us spring and spring,' and when the game was finished they went away full of joy and life, every one passing by his dear friend and teacher and giving him his little hand for a grateful goodbye." And then the colonel adds: "I shall never forget this image of the first kindergarten, so lovable and cheerful. I preserved it all in my memory and used it all as a pattern, when in time I had occasion to establish an educational garden in my own home."

Nevertheless, Froebel and Middendorf had the greatest difficulty in persuading the Blankenburg people to merely allow them to have any intercourse with the little children, because the parents thought that the teaching a child to play would help to make him a sluggard and a loafer. But the two earnest pioneers persisted in their labor of love, and succeeded in overcoming the local prejudice to a certain extent. Froebel had begun the publication of a Sunday paper the year before which he called "Seeds, Buds and Fruits out of Life, for the Education of United Families." It bore the motto, "Come, let us live with our children." But he did not confine his work to Blankenburg or the immediate neighborhood. In January, 1839, we find him giving a kindergarten address at Dresden, where the Queen of Saxony was present, and a month later he gave another at Leipsig. Soon after he was called to Dresden to further explain the system and Middendorf and Adolf Frankenberg went with him. The visit evidently lasted some time and resulted in the establishment of a kindergarten in that city, which was taught by Frau Frankenberg, who thus became the first woman kindergartener, so far as we can learn.

While Froebel was at Dresden his wife died, May 13, 1839. She was one of those rare women who served an idea at the greatest possible sacrifice, that of her life. Although mourning her loss sincerely he did not pause in his work, but soon after, at Hamburg, repeated what he had said at Dresden. Month by month the idea of the kindergarten grew clearer in Froebel's mind, so that in 1840, at the Guttenburg festival, which the schools of Blackenburg and Keilhau celebrated in common, he was able to present a new and more comprehensive plan than any which he had previously entertained, one which he hoped to carry out with the help of his fellow countrymen. On the first day of May he issued an appeal to the public to help him to establish a kindergarten training school, the special feature of his scheme being the proposition that each person interested in the enterprise should take one or more shares in it, each share having the value of ten dollars. His address at the festival of June 28th was largely devoted to advocating the plan and was directed chiefly to the ladies who were present on that occasion.

Some idea of this speech can be gained by the closing words: "Therefore, I dare," said he, "confidently to invite you who are here present, honorable, noble and discreet matrons and maidens, and through you and with you all women, young and old of our fatherland, to assist in your subscription in the founding of an educational system for the nurture of little children, which shall be named Kindergarten, on account of its inner life and aim, and German Kindergarten on account of its spirit. Do not be alarmed at the apparent cost of the shares; for if in your housekeeping or by your industry you can spare only five pennies daily, from the presumptive time of the first payment until the end, the ten dollars is paid at the last payment. Do not let yourself be kept from the actual claims of the plan by the contemptible objection 'Of what use to us is it all?'

Already the idea of furthering the proper education of the child through appropriate fostering of the instinct of activity, acts like light and warmth, imperceptibly and beneficently, on the well-being of families and citizens; for good is not like a heavy stone which only acts and is perceived when it is pressed; no, it is like water, air and light, which invisibly flows from one place to another, awakening, watering, fertilizing, nourishing what is concealed from the searching eye of man—even slumbers in our own breasts, unsuspected by ourselves. Good is like a spark which shines far and points out the way. Therefore, let us all, each in his own way, advance what our hearts recognize as good, the care of young children.

Do you ask for the profits of your investment, the dividends on your shares? Open your eyes impartially, your hearts also; there is more in it than we have represented in the plan of the undertaking. Oh, is the beautiful any the less a gift and a real value in our life because it passes away easily? Is the true any the less a gift because it is unseen and only the spirit observes it? And shall we count for nothing the reaction on the family and the happiness of the children in joy of heart and peace of mind? You can enjoy these great gifts in full measure; for they are the fruit of your co-operation, the fruits of the garden which you establish and care for, the fruits of your property. Besides, is it not almost more than this to take the lead and stand as models for a whole country, to advance the happiness of childhood and the well-being of families, of the whole nation?" We are told that as a result of this speech Froebel's hearers were greatly moved and that they did not separate without pledging a goodly soon to advance the spread of the German Kindergarten.

This success was only temporary, for while Froebel and Middendorf were able to overcome in a measure the local prejudice against their system of education for young children the parents kept insisting that they were doing the educators a great favor in allowing them to spend their time on the children, and were far from thinking that kindergartners ought to be paid for the services rendered. Froebel was able to get the municipality to grant him the free use of a place in which to do work. But it soon became evident to him that he must seek a broader field and take up the task of educating the public sentiment in favor of the new educational system. Consequently the institution at Blankenburg was given up in 1844 and Froebel determined to travel about Germany and expound his views, taking with him his faithful and eloquent friend Middendorf. In order to kindle the sparks of appreciation glimmering here and there into a clear flame by the breath of his own never-failing enthusiasm, he proposed to visit all the large cities. But before setting out on this pilgrimage, in 1843, he published the "Mutter Und Kose-Lieder," a book which was destined to become the most popular of all his works, the song and picture book for mothers and little children. "Traveling through the country," says Elizabeth Harrison, "Froebel listened to the cradle songs and stories which the German housewives told to their children. He noticed how the little children are constantly in motion, how they delight in movement, how they use their senses, how quickly they observe and how they invent and contrive. And he said to himself, 'I can convert the children's activities, energies, amusements, occupations, all that goes by the name of play, instrumental for my purpose, and transfer play into work. This work will be education in the true sense of the term. The conception I have gained from the children themselves; they have taught me how I am to teach them.'"

1844—1849—WANDERINGS ABOUT GERMANY.

In the summer of 1844 Froebel and Middendorf started out on their missionary tours for the propagation of the kindergarten, which were destined to continue a number of years and extend over a considerable area. They visited in succession Frankfort, Heidleberg, Darmstadt, Cologne, Carlsruhe, and Stuttgart. During the following year Froebel became acquainted with Louise Levin, who subsequently became his second wife. The history of this woman is an interesting story to all who are in any way attracted to the kindergarten or its literature. Louise Levin was born at Marienvorstadt, a suburb of Osterode, in the Harz mountains, April 15, 1815. Her father was a tanner and across the street from his house lived Christian Froebel, brother of Friedrich, a spinner and dyer of linen thread and the owner of a factory. His children were the first playmates of little Louise, outside of her own household.

In her later years Frau Froebel has written a pamphlet entitled "Reminiscences of Friedrich Froebel," which includes an outline of the story of her early life. She says that Christian Froebel was a busy man in those days, but that he found time for mental culture as well as an earnest and loving discharge of his duties as husband and father. Also that he had suffered from the want of a thorough education and that it was his great desire to procure more for his children in that respect than he himself had enjoyed. Friedrich always had great influence in his brother's family, and the narrative relates that his nephews and nieces, as well as the older brothers and sisters of Louise, looked forward to his visits as a treat. It was at the house of his brother, in 1816, when she was eighteen months old, that Froebel first met her. He had recently resigned his position as assistant superintendent of the mineralogical museum at Berlin, and resolved to open a school at Griesheim. But he wanted more pupils than this one family afforded and so visited his brother at Osterode, to persuade him to let his two sons join their cousins at Griesheim. A little later the school was moved to Keilhau, and in 1820 Christian Froebel and his family went there to live.

Concerning this change Frau Froebel writes: "I was five years old when our dear, faithful friends removed from our neighborhood. Well do I remember my brothers' and sisters' sorrow at departing; my grief was more speedily as sauged by a legacy of all the toys left in the forsaken nursery over the way." She soon began to exchange letters with Elsie Froebel, who was two years older, although at first her baby hand had to be guided by that of a more mature sister. We are told that they sent flowers to each other, exchanged garden seeds, and in similar ways kept alive the friendship of former years. In due time the boys of the Froebel family paid a visit to the Levins, and Louise was much attracted to them, as they appeared greatly to be preferred to her ordinary boy playmates. Then her brothers were allowed an outing at Keilhau, and on their return they were constantly talking about the happy life of the boys who were at school there, and of the kindness of "Uncle Froebel," meaning Friedrich, to them. They also brought back with them many things which the pupils there had given them as samples of their own handiwork, models of toys, furniture and machines, cut out from wood or cardboard and pasted together.

Louise Levin endured many hardships in her early days. Her father died when she was thirteen, her two brothers were left widowers with children to care for within a few years after they were married, and her eldest sister lost her husband in the prime of life. All of these families looked to her for help in the midst of their troubles, and it was not till she was thirty years old that she was at liberty, to leave the home circle. As for her education, she tells us that it was "neither better nor worse than that of most girls at that time, the chief female accomplishment of that day being skill in various domestic arts."

Finding herself no longer indispensable to her relatives Louise Levin felt that she must make herself indispensable to some one, to fill a breach and have an object in life. Frau Middendorf had lately been visiting her and invited her to come to Keilhau. With the words of invitation ringing in her ears she wrote a letter offering her services to the community and received an immediate answer urging her to lose no time, but to at once become a working member of the household. This was in June, 1845, and when Louise joined the family it included three daughters of Christian Froebel, Frau Middendorf, Frau Barop and Fraulein Elsie Froebel, her former correspondent. Froebel himself was then living in the neighborhood, but did not make his home in the school building. But he called to see Louise soon after her arrival, and gave her much friendly counsel, which she remembered well and rendered useful in her relations and duties to those around her.

In 1846 Froebel and Middendorf made a journey similar to the one undertaken the previous year, but it was apparently barren of results, just as the former trip had been. Discouraged with the reception he met with from men and professional teachers in general, Froebel henceforth more than ever addressed himself to women, mothers and teachers, with increasing enthusiasm. In the summer of 1847 he gave an exhibition of games at a meeting at Quetz near Halle. As a result of this meeting one of his converts decided to add a kindergarten to her high school for girls at Hamburg and to employ Middendorf's daughter Alvine as the kindergartner. But before this plan could be carried out it was deemed best for her to take a course with Froebel, and Louise Levin determined to join his training class at the same time. Consequently both of them became his pupils during the winter of 1847-1848.

About this time Froebel drew up the prospectus of an institution which he proposed to form for the training of the masses and the educators of children. In this prospectus he says: "It is very desirable that young maidens entering the institution should have a good school education. They ought to be more than fifteen years old and healthy and full grown. The age from seventeen to twenty odd years seems best for this training. More important than school education, however, is the girlish love of childhood, an ability to occupy herself with children, as well as a serene and joyful view of life in general. There ought also to be a love of play and occupation, a love and capacity for singing. It goes without saying that purity of intentions and a lovely, womanly disposition are essential requisites. The fuller the educational accomplishments of a lady all the more rapid and satisfactory will be her progress in the science."

"The means at the disposal of those willing to take the course are generally so limited as to compel a curtailment of the time of study to six months. Nothing but inexorable necessity could have enforced such a reduction of time, rendering next to impossible the acquisition of even such knowledge as is absolutely indispensable. Every part of the course must be shortened too much in order to render it possible to reach the end at all. The entire scheme is made up with a consciousness that the pupils themselves must fill the gaps in their development and by incessant industry and spontaneous labor work out and perfect the ideas and principles mentioned in the course. There is no possibility of reaching the goal desired in so short a time unless a pupil will give her whole mind, and give it determinedly and perseveringly, to study.

But this is not sufficient unless the pupil has also learned to observe and study the phenomena of her own life and activity, and thereby learned to observe and guide the life and activity of children. In this direction the study of the kindergarten ought to be continuous. A complete education for bringing up and educating children ought to make the pupil theoretically and practically conversant with all the requirements of the child concerning its bodily (dietetic) and mental (pedagogic) needs from the cradle to school age. But this is not enough. The normal school pupil ought also to be enabled to impart a good preparation for the first grade of the elementary classes in the public schools. It is not possible, however, to include this branch in a short course of only six months. A second course is necessary to give time enough for that kind of teaching. In either case, however, success cannot be completed, unless the pupil on entering the normal school is sufficiently prepared as regards her school education, her maturity of character and good judgment. Such efficient preliminary preparation will alone enable the pupil to avail herself of all the suggestions offered during the course, and, after leaving the school, to continue the study, reflect and labor for the purpose of finishing her own education."

The idea of Fræbel suggesting the possibility of taking the kindergarten course in six months will doubtless seem an absurdity to many kindergarteners to-day. But their adverse judgment will be somewhat modified when we come to review the proposed daily schedule given in the prospectus of his training school, which laid out work for the whole day, from seven in the morning until bedtime. First came the morning service and a religious lesson which attempted to trace the evolution of religious ideas in the child and thereby to indicate a method of awakening truly religious sentiments in the little ones. At nine o'clock the regular school day opened. The hour from nine to ten o'clock was spent in teaching "the science of the phenomena and laws of the evolution of the child; of the essential nature of the child and the requirements of his nursing and his education." During the two hours from ten to twelve o'clock the principles which had been taught theoretically the preceding hour were practically demonstrated. These demonstrations were supposed to embrace practical exercises in personal intercourse, appropriate language in talking with the children, accompanying the singing with the appropriate practice of the sense and limbs." The specific relations between these exercises and the unfolding of the soul life of the child as an individual and as a member of the social whole were successfully pointed out. The Mutter Und Kose-Lieder served as a text book in these lessons.

The afternoon lesson began at two o'clock. Till four o'clock the gifts and occupations were handled. Seven small text books were used, and it was Fræbel's intention to make clear at every point the manifold relations between the occupations and his gifts and the labors of man in contact with the circumstances of nature and events in life. The hour from six until seven was spent in practicing the occupations and games that had been taken up during the day with the children who came to the school for that purpose. After supper the pupils gave further attention to any of the day's exercises which they felt they had not mastered, being helped by Fræbel and his assistants.

Such was the prospectus for the normal kindergarten, as laid out on paper in 1847. The criticisms which its announcement caused resulted in some modifications, but in many respects it was the scheme actually carried out a little later. During the six months of the course Fræbel devoted his whole time and energy to his pupils, from seven o'clock in the morning until bedtime, never wearying of explaining, lecturing, laboring and playing with them. And what the reader naturally asks, was the compensation required for all this trial? Half a thaler each week, that is, about, thirty-seven cents for each pupil.

During all these years Fræbel's schemes were many, one being to found an institution for the support and education of orphans, with a model kindergarten and a normal institute for children's nurses and kindergartners. Meanwhile he kept up his travels, with head-quarters at Keilhau. Wherever a festival could be arranged in commemoration of Christmas or some other event, there was Froebel to plan and lead the kindergarten games as a special attraction.

We may not find it out of place right here to ask ourselves, How did Froebel look at this time in his life? The most definite description yet published occurs in the "Story of My Life" by Georg Ebers, the eminent novelist, as translated by Mary J. Safford. Dr. Ebers was eleven years old when he entered the Keilhau school, in the spring of 1848, and he gives this pen picture of Froebel: "When I came to Keilhau he was already sixty-six years old, a man of lofty stature, with a face that seemed to be carved with a dull knife, out of brown wood. His long nose, strong chin, and large ears, behind which the long locks parted in the middle, were smoothly brushed, and would have rendered him positively ugly had not his, Come let us live with our children, beamed so invitingly from his clear eyes.

People did not think whether he was handsome or not ; his features bore the impress of his intellectual power so distinctly, that the first glance revealed the presence of a remarkable man. Yet I must confess—and his portrait agrees with my memory—that his face by no means suggested the idealist and man of feeling ; it seemed rather expressive of shrewdness, and to have been lined and worn by several conflicts concerning the most diverse interests. But his voice and his glance were generally winning and his power over the heart of the child was limitless. A few words were sufficient to win the shyest boy whom he desired to attract ; and thus it happened that even when he had been with us only a few weeks he was never seen crossing the courtyard without having a group of the younger pupils hanging to his coat tails and clasping his hands and arms. Usually they were persuading him to tell stories and when he consented to do so the older pupils were sure to flock around him, and what fire, what animation the old man had retained!"

This whole story is everywhere dotted with dark spots indicating privation on the part of Froebel. At one time he sold all of his household furniture at public auction at Rudolstadt to help him in the cause to which he was so thoroughly devoted. "When he was in these difficulties," writes Frau Froebel, "he seemed to shrink within himself, he was so silent ; he no doubt felt the hardship of being without a settled home after all these years of toil." At Keilhau he lived in the most modest style ; he endured physical discomfort with absolute indifference, absorbed in one object. "New Year's eve" Frau Froebel continues, "was always kept as a beautiful traditional festival at Keilhau. During the early part of the evening old and young joined in all kinds of games and home amusements and then a simple prayer was offered, with a retrospect of the year, followed by a general shaking of hands and mutual good wishes for the New Year, as the bells rang out from the village church. At this moment, in the year 1848, Froebel appeared on the scene, and great was the joy of the assembled household that he had kept his promise. A table covered with Christmas gifts was quickly arranged for him in the blue room, and I remember him chatting pleasantly about his recent wanderings ; telling those in Keilhau about the increased support his kindergarten cause was receiving in different places in Thuringia, describing new acquaintances he had made, until he at length withdrew in the early hours of the first morning of the New Year. Retiring to his own rooms he sat up until breakfast time inditing a letter 'To Womanhood,' as he afterwards told us."

During the winter of 1848 Froebel went to Schalkau, in company with Louise Levin, who helped him in the direction of the games. He lived at the schoolhouse and she was hospitably entertained by a neighbor. The afternoons were occupied with rehearsals and in the evening the schoolmasters of that section used to gather around Froebel to hear more about his educational views and talk over the arrangements for the festival which it was proposed to hold, some months later, but which was, however, forbidden by the authorities. A similar visit was made to Brunn, where the two kindergarten missionaries were guests of the vicar.

In the summer of 1848 Middendorf published his book entitled "The Kindergarten" and dedicated it to the German parliament, which had just assembled at Frankfort, hoping to secure their earnest attention to the system. Froebel helped him in correcting the proof sheets of this book and meanwhile busied himself in preparing for a public gathering at Rudolstadt, issuing invitations to many schoolmasters and other prominent people from all parts of Germany. Places of entertainment had to be provided for those who came from a distance and the children of the neighborhood were practiced in the games and taught paper folding, paper cutting and the lath interlacing by Fraulein Levin, at the little Eichfeld schoolhouse. Meantime Froebel attended a meeting at Oschatz, where a resolution was unanimously passed "That the governments of Saxony and Meiningen be respectfully urged to make the support of kindergartens obligatory in every parish within their dominions, as the best possible foundation upon which to rear any system of public instruction."

The Rudolstadt meeting came in June and lasted three days. Several members of the national legislature were present, having been sent there to inquire into Froebel's methods, as well as representatives of reigning families in the Thuringian states. Many distinguished men took part in the debates, which waxed warm. There was a strong element of opposition in the assembly and Froebel and his friends were often challenged. But they were able to defend their position with energy and skill, and on the whole their cause was greatly benefited. In speaking of this meeting Hanschmann says: "Although some people might have retained intellectual doubts about some details of his method, no one went away from that meeting without warmly sympathizing with his work as a whole. No one could wring from him the undoubted honor of having brought to light some neglected truths respecting child-nature and of giving fresh means for its development."

After the Rudolstadt meeting Froebel's correspondence increased greatly and expressions of sympathy flowed in upon him from every quarter and greatly encouraged him in the belief that a better day was about to dawn. He spent the following winter at Dresden, giving a course of lectures for kindergartners and using the kindergarten of Adolph Frankenberg and his wife as practice ground. He also gave a second course to ladies and gentlemen interested in his system, being guaranteed an adequate salary for his work. Meanwhile Fraulein Levin had accepted a position as governess in a family at Rendsburg and they met at Bergedorf during the Christmas holidays, 1848, where they and Alvine Middendorf happened to be visiting.

About this time Froebel became attracted to the village of Liebenstein as a promising location for a permanent training school and during the Easter vacation he went there from Dresden to look for a house. Liebenstein is a summer resort for strangers who come from all parts of the country to drink the waters and he felt that it would be a good place from which to extend his cause. He returned there in May, "with a view," says Frau Froebel, "to obtaining a lease of the country house,'Marienthal' from the Duke of Meiningen."

1849—1852—MARIENTHAL.

Froebel secured rooms in a Liebenstein farmhouse through the kindness of Frau Muller, and he began to live there with his pupils and his grand-niece, Henrietta Breymann, (Frau Schrader) as housekeeper. She also helped teach some of the children who were beyond the kindergarten age. We come now to the period in Froebel's life when he ceased to fight his educational battles single-handed and in obscurity and was thereafter seconded in some measure by the rich and the powerful. But for the aid of Baroness B. Von Marenholtz-Bulow and her friends it is doubtful if the name of Friedrich Froebel would have come down to this generation as being of any importance. All of the reforms in this world are brought about by visible means, and most of them have to make use of help from the influential and the wealthy before lasting success is secured. How could Columbus have carried out his darling scheme and thereby changed the world's history if Isabel had not pledged her jewels in his favor? And how could Washington, notwithstanding the valor and self sacrifice of his countrymen, have brought the American Revolution to a triumphant issue in the way that he did if the standard of France had not been joined with the flag of our infant republic? In this case it was not altogether because the Baroness secured for Froebel and his training school a delightful home at Marienthal for the rest of his life and furthered his plans in every possible way among the nobility and scientific men of the day, or even because she gave her life with rare devotion and lack of selfishness to advancing the kindergarten cause in different European nations that her alliance proved of such great importance to him. There was another service which she did for Froebel, she became his interpreter. By reading her "Reminiscences" one gets a clear and minute account of the last three years of his life, which serves as a key to the whole. Her account covers what in many respects is the most interesting part of his career.

It was at the end of May, 1849, that the Baroness reached the village, where she had sojourned during previous summers. After the usual salutations and her question as to what was happening in the place that season she was told by her landlady that a few weeks before a man had settled down on a small farm near the springs and danced and played with the children and for that reason was called "the old fool." Going out to walk some days later she met him and she described his appearance on that occasion as follows: "A tall, spare man with long gray hair, was leading a group of children between the ages of three and eight, most of them barefooted and scantily clothed, who marched two and two up a hill, where having marshalled them for play, he practiced with them a song belonging to it. The loving patience and abandon with which he did this, the whole bearing of the man while the children played various games under his direction were so moving that tears came into my companions eyes as well as my own."

An acquaintance followed which soon ripened into friendship, and through the intercession of the Baroness, Froebel obtained a lease of the castle of Marienthal as a seminary for his normal classes. How this arrangement came to be made the Baroness explains as follows: "On a walk which I once took with him, we came to the neighborhood of Liebenstein, charmingly elevated among the green fields. Froebel stood still and said: 'Look around you, Frau Marenholtz. This would be a beautiful place for our institution, and even the name would suit it so well, Marienthal, the vale of the Marys, whom he wished to bring up as the mothers of humanity, as the first Mary brought up the Saviour of the world.' I remarked that he might petition the duke to grant him the building, which was standing unused, and that I would try to help him through the Duchess Ida. By means of the continued promptings of her brother on the part of the duchess this end was reached at the end of some months. And I had the pleasure of surprising Froebel with the official permission after he had almost given up all hope."

In the month of July Diesterweg, a distinguished German educator, came to Liebenstein and was introduced to Froebel by the Baroness. He became much interested in the principles which lie at the foundation of Froebel's system and with the Baroness devoted considerable time during the summer to studying them. It was also in July, that Fraulein Levin secured a release from her engagement at Rendsburg and came to Liebenstein, where for a short time she shared with Fraulein Breymann the duties of housekeeping and instructing the pupils, but the latter soon went to her home, being in delicate health. When Louise Levin arrived, to use Froebel's words to the Baroness, "she gave to his institution the stamp of family life," which in his view was of the highest importance to an enterprise of that kind. During the month of September Middendorf came from Keilhau to visit his friend, and while he was at Liebenstein a sufficient sum was raised, chiefly from among the nobility, to establish a local kindergarten. A little later he was invited, through the influence of the Baroness to deliver two lectures before the court at Weimar, which materially advanced the kindergarten cause. In October Froebel went to Hamburg for the winter, and Fraulein Levin remained at Liebenstein to continue training the pupils and to receive new ones, also taking charge of the kindergarten as a practice field for the pupils.

"Froebel passed a busy winter in Hamburg, by the invitation of the Women's Union, where society was much divided on the subject of the 'higher education of women,'" says Frau Froebel, "and where he undoubtedly overtaxed his strength. On the other hand, he felt strengthened and upheld by the sympathy and interest his views met with during his lectures. With many aspects of the woman question agitating the public mind at that time Froebel had but little sympathy, but he had the great satisfaction of seeing the first Burger-kindergarten opened under his fostering care, as well as many private kindergartens." During the Christmas holidays he came back to Liebenstein and addressed the parents of the kindergarten children, also joining with the little ones in the customary celebration. While he was there the negotiations for the lease of Marienthal were completed and he began the return journey to Hamburg New Year's eve. Just as he was finishing his lectures there Louise Levin moved the school from the farmhouse, where it had been quartered for a year, to Marienthal, and Froebel himself went directly from Hamburg to Keilhau, to talk with his friends there about his intended marriage with Louise Levin. This plan met with opposition because he could not give the required proof that he had sufficient means to support a widow, in the event of his death. He also visited Blankenburg and was presented with the title of honorary citizen, but when he asked that this might be transferred to his future wife the people refused to grant the request. Frau Froebel says that he accepted this rebuff with his customary patience under trial and then went to Marienthal to resume his place in the school.

He reached there with the first awakening touches of spring, and, to quote once more Frau Froebel, "We gaily decorated every doorway with an archway of green leaves to bid him welcome. I was painfully aware of the expression of weariness on his face. 'Oh! I shall quickly recover in this beautiful place' was his cheerful answer, 'city life with its excitements has worn me out, but in the rural seclusion of this place and the simplicity of life at home I am sure to get well again.'"

At this point, in order that we may get some idea of Marienthal and its surroundings, the reader will be interested in a description of that section as it appeared to an American kindergartner two or three summers ago: "We finally come out to the light again refreshed by our temporary absence from the outside world, and drive on to Liebenstein. Here we see the place that Madam Von Bulow has made famous; here Fraulein Heevort shows us the dining-room of the hotel where she once, as a child, met Froebel. The house and hotel border the long narrow street, with the baths and springs at the upper end. We drink the sparkling water, which is delicious, and think of this as another spot in the Thuringian Forest, where time might be pleasantly spent. We imagine Froebel walking through this village with the children at his heels, and Madam Von Bulow's account makes us wish we, too, could have followed them up to the lawn where they played their games. We refresh ourselves with some delicious German coffee, and drive to Marienthal. The path Froebel and his friend often walked lies across the fields besides us, and as we stop in front of the house we feel the reality of the life so devoted to an idea that the roots were firmly fixed in that lifetime. Through the courtesy of the owner of Marienthal we see the house. Two stories and a roof of tiles, a middle doorway, and rows of windows face one. A square garden extends to the road from the house, and stretches to the right and around to the back. To the left is a courtyard, surrounded on three sides by barns and outhouses, the fourth side being open to the house. Many a primitive scene is being enacted here. All kinds of beasts and birds are within the enclosure. Threshing is going on, and the bright dress of the peasants at work enlivens the scene. We speak of Froebel's 'Song of the Barnyard Gate,' and wonder if he got his inspiration here. We go inside and see the room where Froebel's second marriage took place and the room where he passed out of the life where 'we behold but darkly,' into one of light."

In the year 1850, Liebenstein was one of the most fashionable resorts of Central Germany and many noted visitors came to Marienthal, Froebel being the wonder and talk of the town. The Baroness gives this description of one such visit, when she piloted a party of which Dr. Gustav, editor of "The Europa," was a member:—

"We had now arrived at the gate of Marienthal and heard the voices of the children singing in the kindergarten, whom Froebel himself led in the afternoon, in order to give to his pupils instruction in the manner of conducting the movement plays. He was in the midst of the troop of little ones when we entered. 'This then, is the house of the prophet,' said some one in our party, as we entered the great courtyard of the Marienthal house, which stood back, two stories high, looking more like the dwelling house of a farm than like a castle, but pleasant and homelike in the midst of the old green trees that surrounded it. In the large

MONUMENT NEAR MARIENTHAL.

square before the house door, to which stone steps led up, was a grass plot upon which was planted some shrubbery, and on one side were very beautiful old lindens, which in flowering time spread their fragrance far and wide. In their shade were some benches and tables on which in good summer weather Froebel was accustomed to give his morning lessons.

At the moment when we entered he stood in the midst of the courtyard surrounded by his pupils and a troop of little children, who had wound themselves around him as their central point in the play 'Little thread, little thread, like a little wheel,' and were just beginning to unwind their skein again. With glowing face and eyes beaming with happiness Froebel greeted the company, immediately asking whether they would like to see some of the movement plays before going up into the hall. The guests were quite willing. With truly childish delight he again conducted some of those ingenious plays, the first gymnastics of the childish limbs. These he copied from the traditional plays of children and the people, leaving out their rougher features in order to make them serve his educational idea; partly to make children represent, somewhat dramatically, facts out of the life of nature and man."

A long discussion relative to the principles involved in the play followed, and when it was ended and the children had sung their closing song they were led to the door by the young ladies who were playing with them. Froebel then invited the company to follow him into the upper story of the house, where he lived. He crossed the great hall, situated in the midst of the rooms, the four windows of which commanded a view of delightful landscape extending to the distant mountains of the Rhone. In the midst of the hall stood a long table covered with Froebel's "gifts for play" and many specimens of children's work from various kindergartens.

Early in August, 1850, a notable play festival was held at Marienthal, conducted by Froebel and Middendorf, in which three hundred children from all the surrounding villages participated, with their teachers. The multitude of spectators was ranged outside the square, in the shadow of the surrounding woods. A concluding address was given by Middendorf and the whole affair made a profound impression on the community. In writing about it afterwards Froebel said: "Yes, it was a festival of the union of nature, man and God, and God's blessing rests on such a day, as the old peasant expressed it. How easily might such child and youth festivals be exalted to a universal people's festival! Should we not do everything to call such festivals into life, that so we may at last reach what the hearts of all desire, an all-sided 'unity of life?'"

In this way the summer was spent. "Froebel loved to teach," says his widow, "even whilst in the act of walking; here he drew our attention to the stratification of the rocks, there to a tuft of moss, or to some other plant struggling for life upon a barren stone, steadily expanding by virtue of a principle of life within." His first lessons were generally given out of doors in the morning, as well as the first lesson in the afternoon during the summer months. Toward evening groups of children put in an appearance in front of the house; they came from the neighboring village of Schweina." The last daylight hours were passed in the games with these children and all of Froebel's time when he was not teaching was taken up with visitors. Consequently he overtaxed his strength with the work of the year and doubtless shortened his days. But according to the Baroness he was well preserved, for she writes that no one who did not know the fact could believe that his age was sixty-eight. "The youth and freshness of intellect, which was so remarkable in him prevented one from thinking of his actual age, whose infirmities had not yet appeared."

The course of training ended in November and new pupils were immediately received. About this time Dr. Wichard Lange, who afterwards married Middendorf's daughter, came to Marienthal and a long discussion occurred between him and Froebel regarding the carrying on of the latter's work in the future. Froebel maintained that Dr. Lange was the best fitted person living, to take up his work when he should leave it and hand it down to coming generations. But Lange felt that no man could succeed Froebel and that the chief apostles of the kindergarten must thereafter be women, and that he himself, while in hearty sympathy with Froebel and his system, must devote his faculties to teaching in the higher grades. This decision was a great disappointment to Froebel, although in all probability a wise one on the part of Lange, who subsequently did the world and the cause a valuable service by publishing a book on "The Understanding of Friedrich Fræbel."

The winter which followed was a quiet one. On Christmas eve the pupils decorated Fræbel's study, making it look as though the whole forest had moved in. Each member of the family was assigned a separate table covered with gifts and "Fræbel's fatherly words seemed to endow these presents with a higher meaning for us all." On New Year's eve the family was invited to Liebenstein to enjoy private theatricals.

Fraulein Levin remained at Marienthal for two years as Fræbel's assistant, and they were married July 9th, 1851. The groom was then at the height of his popularity as an educator, and success as a kindergarten teacher, being sixty-nine years old. The Baroness thus describes her meeting with him a few days before the wedding: "I found Fræbel at his writing table in his study. He greeted me with an expression of the profoundest satisfaction. It was clear how truly happy and pleased he was made by the new-found home which had already formed a cultivated family circle of young, bright pupils, in quiet undisturbed domesticity. The battle of life lay behind him, he had parted from the world which did not understand him, and whose applause he had never sought. He now found himself in rural surroundings, which he had always desired, and he could give himself up, unmolested by opposition and obstacles, to the further development of his idea and the improvement of the practical meaning of it, and could sow the seeds of his doctrine in the receptive minds of his female pupils. He was assisted and well taken care of by her whom he had chosen to be the companion of his last days. After a life of labors and cares, trouble and combat, he could to all appearances, reckon on a beautiful, peaceful evening of life, which would allow him to look with increasing clearness upon the development of his cause and fill up the gaps still existing in it."

The wedding was a gay affair, in spite of the advanced age of the groom. On the previous evening the pupils brought their presents, with all kinds of play, songs, original poems and allegorical representations. The rooms were adorned with flowers, and Fræbel himself led off in some of the kindergarten plays, all present taking part. The next day the bride and groom stood at a flower-decked altar while Pastor Ruckert, a brother of the poet, united them, taking occasion to speak in deep recognition of Fræbel's blessed work. Middendorf was groomsman and the Baroness bridesmaid. When the ceremony was over we are told that Fræbel met the congratulations of his friends with streaming eyes and was as gay and as happy as a child, joining in the dancing until late in the evening, as did Middendorf, regardless of their advanced age. As the company dispersed he said: "Now we will go to work with new power," and the next morning he met his classes as usual.

Frau Fræbel speaks of her feelings at this time as follows: "I was at rest and happy in my work for him and for the object he had in view. In childlike veneration I had first of all tried to approach him in thought; and in his ineffable goodness of heart for the weak Fræbel had drawn out my trust; at length there was on both sides a desire to be legally linked by the closest tie. His age did not trouble me at all; in mine eyes he was the greatest and best of men, and I only marveled how he could condescend to care for a woman so much beneath his level in every respect. My one anxiety was to make sure that the rather unusual step of marriage at his age would not do harm to his work in the world. The wedding day was truly a high festival of the soul for me. We called together a few friends and in their presence and that of our pupils Pastor Ruckert asked a blessing on our union. His words seemed as though they had been spoken out of mine own heart. We did not keep a honeymoon, we were so happy every day of our lives that we did not wish for anything more."

The number of pupils was large that summer and a gala day was observed, when the kindergarten children assembled from all the neighboring villages on the grounds of the castle Altenstein, where Frau Fræbel gave special instruction to the children of the ducal family. But early in August a blow was dealt the kindergarten cause by the Prussian government which ultimately caused the death of its founder. This was an edict prohibiting all public kindergartens throughout the country, occasioned by the published utterances of Karl Fræbel, nephew of Friedrich, which were regarded as socialistic and even atheistic. Strenuous efforts were made by Frœbel and all his friends to convince the minister of state that a mistake had been made in confounding uncle and nephew. But these efforts were unavailing, although Frœbel sent copies to Berlin of every book and pamphlet he had ever written and the Baroness gave Frœbel's petition to the king personally. The government was obdurate and the edict was not revoked until 1860.

In September a teachers' convention was held in the hall of the Liebenstein Baths, which was largely attended by the friends of Frœbel. It began on the morning of the 27th, with Diesterweg in the chair. After he had welcomed the company reports were given of the different kindergartens in the country, in which Frœbel and Middendorf joined. In the afternoon Frœbel presented a statement regarding his work "with the most peculiar vividness and impressiveness and deepest conviction of its value, which made a universal impression and called out great unanimity of opinion. This statement dealt chiefly with the practical part of the kindergarten system—the early use of the child's powers for manipulation and productive activity." The next morning Counsellor Peter opened the convention as chairman and the statement was thoroughly discussed, the debate pertaining for the most part to the practical application of Frœbel's methods, without entering into the fundamental idea of the scheme. In the afternoon the company witnessed the plays of the Liebenstein children with much enthusiasm and frequent applause, much to Frœbel's delight. The games were also played in the evening, under the lead of Frau Frœbel, many of the visitors participating. On the third morning the convention passed a "Declaration" of its views concerning Frœbel's ideas which was favorable to the kindergarten.

It was also proposed by this gathering that Frœbel should write an essay on his system, publish "A Kindergarten Guide" for teachers, and also establish a new periodical to further the cause. All these things he promised to undertake, but he was not spared to do any of them. Many discussions followed on this the last day of the convention. The Baroness says that a warm and lively sympathy prevailed and that every individual present was intent upon expressing recognition of Frœbel and making him forget the injustice of the government prohibition of kindergartens. But according to Frau Frœbel's Reminiscences he was much disappointed in the failure of the convention to enter into the real spirit of his plans and to adopt measures for their intelligent advancement. She puts it in this way: "Frœbel himself was much more mortified by the refusal of an investigation of his work than by the prohibition on the part of the Prussian government."

It was about this time that Frœbel exerted himself to have Middendorf leave Keilhau and live at Marienthal, in the hope that they might work together for the rest of their days. But the Keilhau community could not spare him, much to Frœbel's regret. Late in the autumn the Baroness left Liebenstein for her winter home in Berlin, having first arranged to live during the next summer in the upper story of the kindergarten building, that she might more closely study the kindergarten children. Regarding her departure she writes: "The picture of idyllic rural and domestic repose which Marienthal afforded at that time and the protection and care in which I left Frœbel, in view of the watchfulness and fidelity of his wife, made the parting easy and free from any presentiments that it would be for the last time." After she reached Berlin Frœbel sent her a short statement of his theories which was an explanation of symbolism and which is often referred to as "Frœbel's last words." She speaks of it as a "short and pregnant statement, in spite of its abstract subject, written with great clearness." She did not feel justified, however, in publishing it, and now that she is dead there is but little prospect of finding any trace of it.

During the winter which followed, owing to the obstacles which stood between him and the carrying out of his plans, Frœbel seriously entertained the project of immigrating to this country. His wife had a brother living in Philadelphia and a scheme for establishing a kindergarten training school in that city was sent to him. Years before Frœbel had entertained the same idea and even made some arrangements to immigrate with a friend who finally came here without him. It is doubtful, however, if Frœbel could have made any substantial progress with his system if he had lived to set foot in the United States. Of course he might have found an interpreter here who would have advanced his cause, but his own efforts, it is safe to predict, would have been futile. There is no evidence that he ever paid any attention to the English language and his personal appearance at that time of life would have told heavily against him in a foreign land. He would have been regarded as an ideal enthusiast, as an intense specimen of the "crank," with greater positiveness here than he was in Germany. It was better by far that Froebel remained at home; that the Baroness became his biographer and representative in Europe and that on Elizabeth Peabody was laid the burden and the glory of transplanting the kindergarten to America.

During the winter which followed the Baroness received occasional letters from Froebel and his wife expressing great content with their surroundings. Occasionally mention was made of his being slightly ill and temporarily suspending work, but for the most part his usual duties were uninterrupted. In a letter to a friend in America, dated May 2, 1895, Frau Froebel writes as follows regarding that time in her life:—

"Faithful labor for the true welfare of others is sure to add to our own welfare, to our peace of mind. I have experienced this in my paternal home as well as by the side of my noble husband. With my mind's eye I see him clearly now as he used to put down his pen late in the evening, after a long day passed in teaching his disciples and conversing with visitors, and to turn to me with an expression of serenest joy in his countenance and to speak in a clear and restful voice words showing that he had written some educational thesis in order to recover his own self, his individual consciousness from within the maze of foreign impressions left behind by the experiences of the day. This wonderful power and love of work the Almighty had bestowed on him that through it vast multitudes should be blessed. And now I hope and trust that there are great many actively engaged in singleness of purpose to continue to erect the edifice of which Froebel laid the foundation, the edifice of the natural education of man."

The idea of observing the seventieth birthday of Froebel with a notable celebration originated with Middendorf, who knew that Froebel regarded his seventieth year as the most important period of life, the time for the complete survey of one's own as well as of human life in general. At sunrise, on the morning of April 21, 1852, Froebel was awakened by the festal song of his pupils and he spake to them briefly in recognition of the day. The Baroness could not be present because of sickness, but Middendorf told her the full story of the day, and she describes it in detail. To her we are indebted for this picture: "As Froebel stepped out of his chamber into the lecture-room he stood still on the threshold, taken by surprise, admiring, with his eyes beaming with joy, the beautiful decoration of the room, which was adorned with flowers in flower-pots, festoons and wreaths, and the table richly covered with presents of all kinds. Again the song burst out from the semicircle of scholars dressed in white holiday garments, ornamented with green wreaths, which expressed the meaning of the ornamentation and pointed to the blessing which would go forth to the world of childhood out of Froebel's work. Then Madam Froebel handed out her birthday present and the scholars followed with an orange tree bearing flowers and fruit, which Froebel had often pointed out to them as a symbol of the united ages of man in leaves, buds, flowers and fruit borne at the same time, representing childhood, youth, manhood and old age."

Among the presents was a picture of Pestalozzi, an illustrated Bible and an engraving of Raphael's Madonna, together with tokens from the neighboring kindergarten children and those at Keilhau. In the afternoon the children came from Salzung and Liebenstein to sing him a song and play their games, while at sunset the postman brought a bag of letters "from the Lower Rhine to the Baltic" testifying to the powerful influence of Froebel's teachings and the honor and esteem in which he was held. In the evening Pastor Ruckert and his family were visitors at Marienthal and the pupils acted a dramatic farce, which was followed by kindergarten games. Then the company sang a song composed for the occasion and a green wreath was placed on Froebel's head by one of the pupils. Writing about this day Frau Froebel says: "He was in the best of spirits, but I noticed that his strength failed him occasionally. He was, nevertheless, the life and soul of our party and until late in the evening he was seen distributing trifles as gifts to friends."

According to Middendorf Froebel's life immediately after the celebration was happier and more tranquil than ever before, and he enjoyed his existence like a child. But very soon a new cause for disturbance arose because there appeared a number of letters in the daily papers from the contending religious parties of the day with claims from each of them that he sympathized with its particular views. His own understanding of Christianity was far clearer than any opinions held by them and he could only regard their assertions concerning him as false. Therefore he undertook to formulate a statement of his religious views for publication and sent it to the Baroness at Berlin. But his bodily weakness and agitated mind prevented him from putting forth an effort worthy of himself, and she wrote him that it would be better not to print the manuscript and he accordingly requested her to return it to him.

Shortly after the birthday celebration, during Whitsuntide, there was a large gathering of teachers at Gotha and Froebel was invited to be present. He and his wife left Marienthal very early in the morning, a carriage drive being necessary before taking the trip by rail. When he entered the hall, in the midst of the exercises, the whole assembly rose to do him honor. At the end of the speech that was in progress when he came in the president gave him a hearty welcome, which was followed by three cheers from the whole company. Froebel thanked them in a few simple words and then took up the discussion of the subject in hand, "Instruction in the Natural Sciences," and was heard with profound attention. After the convention he was made especially happy in the garden of a friend who lived in Gotha, where he examined almost every group of flowers and gratefully acknowledged all the good things which were offered him. He also visited the local kindergarten and explained the intellectual significance of some of his occupations and material.

In the evening he took part in a reunion of the friends of his cause, speaking of the importance of the kindergarten for women and the duty of teachers to learn to understand it on its own theory, and prepare for its introduction into the schools. But the strain of this effort was too much for him and he urged his wife to leave at an early hour. "During our drive home," she writes, "the weather being fine, he stopped the carriage at the crest of the hill and we got out and walked up the slope of the neighboring summit, 'der Gloekli,' as we called it. There we had often spent happy hours together, but I noticed then the difficulty he had in walking and unutterable fears filled my mind. Arrived at the top of the hill, he said: 'I should somehow like my name to be placed here when I am gone.' On our return to Marienthal we found the whole house garlanded with evergreens by the pupils. Visitors called and Froebel again became animated by their presence, but his strength was ebbing fast."

Up to this time there is no evidence that Froebel was ever seriously sick. For seventy years he had been a constant worker, devoting but little time to recreation save as he found it in his daily work with the children, and sparing himself no physical exertion or privation which seemed necessary for the advancement of the cause. Although never robust, he must have possessed a strong constitution, when we consider his record as a soldier and the long journeys he took on foot, even in the later years of life. His last illness began June 6, and appears to have been caused by a general breaking down of the system, resulting doubtless more from long continued overwork and the deferred hope which "maketh the heart sick" than from an acute attack of disease. We are told that when this sickness began he thought he saw in it a crisis which would lead to recovery. From day to day he retained his repose and cheerfulness and was very grateful for whatever was done for him, especially when flowers were brought him. For the particulars of this last sickness and the funeral we are indebted to a pamphlet written by Middendorf and published at Liebenstein that same year. To those who stood by the bedside of the dying man it was evident that "the highest peace, the most cheerful resignation were expressed not only in his words but in his face. The former anxious care to be active in his life-task resolved itself into trust in Providence and his spirit looked joyfully in advance for the fulfillment of his life's idea."

This is the testimony of the physician who attended Froebel, as related to the Baroness a few weeks later: "I have seen many men die, but never anyone who looked into the face of death so cheerfully and so calmly as Froebel. One day he asked me what I thought of his condition and whether he could live a little longer. I thought I ought to speak the real truth and was able to do so to him. I advised him not to postpone his last directions, since the failing of his powers left slight hope of recovery. He took my words with the greatest calmness and I did not notice the least change in his countenance. When I went to him on the following noon they told me that he had added some directions to his will that morning. At the door of his chamber I heard a low singing, like the chirping of the birds which were singing out of doors, and when I entered I found Froebel sitting up in the bed, which was pushed up to the open window, looking with glorified joy on the landscape before him and singing softly to himself. To my remark, 'You appear to be better and more cheerful,' he replied, 'Why should I not? I enjoy beautiful nature even in my last moments.' I never found him, on my visits, impatient, complaining or even discontented.

On the Sunday before his death a favorite child brought him flowers and he received her with great delight. With difficulty he reached out his hand and drew her hand to his lips. In his last hours he asked for flowers and said, "Take care of my flowers and spare my weeds; I have learned much from them." He wanted the windows open frequently and often repeated the words, "Pure, vigorous nature." To Barop who had come from Keilhau to be with him, he said, "Remain true to God." And then he asked them to read the letter written by his godfather when he was baptized and which contained the confession of Christian faith. During the reading he often exclaimed, "My credentials! My credentials, Barop!" He called it his letter of credit for heaven and repeated again and again the words used in the letter, "The Saviour shall henceforth hold immediate communion with him in justice, grace and mercy." He said that he had labored to make Christianity a reality and he repeated many times with great emphasis that he was "A Christian man."

At midnight, June 21, 1852, the final moment approached. He was in a sitting posture and his eyes were partially open. Middendorf says that his last words were, "God, Father, Son and Holy Ghost." His breathing continued to grow shorter and "at half-past six in the morning he drew two long breaths and all was still." To those who were standing about him his departure seemed like the death of a beloved child.

At the burial service the bier was adorned with flowers and a crown of laurel, made by his wife and pupils, and stood in the spot lately occupied by his bed. After all present had gathered about the body to look for the last time on that beloved countenance from which all trace of pain had been effaced the casket was carried through his study and then through the sitting-room and placed in the wide vestibule, to be strewn with wreaths and flowers by many children, all of whom, even the smallest, tried to show their gratitude for him once more. The mourning company included numerous friends from a distance, with not a few whom he had helped. The teachers sang a funeral hymn and then the procession started for the churchyard at Schweina. A heavy shower fell on the way and the people were compelled to stand under shelter for a long time, which led the clergyman to remark, "Even his last journey is through storm and tempest." As the funeral train moved on the bells of the village church began to toll and at the cemetery the teachers took the bier on their shoulders, to carry it to the grave.

Although the rain still continued a large part of the community, young and old, had gathered to honor him. The hymn, "Jerusalem, thou lofty city" was sung and then Pastor Ruckert began his remarks, just as the rain stopped. When he had finished the teachers sang, "Rest softly" and the casket was lowered into the grave, which had been lined with flowers. Then Middendorf made a short address, after which a song which he had written, beginning "Rise again, thou shalt rise again," was sung. As the pastor threw a handful of earth into the grave he said, "May God grant to each of us such an end as that of this just man." Then the scholars threw flowers upon flowers into the grave, one of them snatching the bouquet from her breast to throw in, and Middendorf cast in the manuscript of his song.

Concerning the surroundings of the grave, Middendorf wrote as follows : "The newly laid out churchyard, situated outside the village upon an eminence, has a singularly beautiful location. The town lies half-concealed in verdure, at the foot of the tower which rises up alone, like a finger-post pointing to heaven; the whole glorious country lies spread out before the eye like a living picture. At the left

Altenstein, with the summer dwellings of the ducal family stretches out its high hand with noble grace, showing by its act that it truly reverences the cross which is erected in memory of Bonifacius, the earliest promulgator of Christianity here. Directly in front stands the old castle of Liebenstein whose name has a good sound near and far for its healing springs; and on the right, shaded with lofty poplars and surrounded by green meadows and waving fields of grain, with the murmur of clear waters streaming from the rock of Altenstein, the quiet, lovely Marienthal, the seat of peace, of untiring work for the worthiness and the unity of life, consecrated by him who has now come to this spot for undisturbed peace and harmony."

Thus died Friedrich Froebel. But although more than forty summers have passed over his grave at Schweina we cannot admit that Froebel is dead, but must rather remember that he said in the course of his last sickness, "I am not going away, I shall hover around in the midst of you." How true was this prophecy! Who of us would care to deny that his loving spirit is with us to-day and with the little children who gather about us in the kindergarten circle for the morning talk, or nestle in our arms at the home fireside when the shadows of the night rest upon us, and plead for "one more story" before it is time to say the evening prayer? Has there ever been a time when he was more truly alive than at the present hour? The world is just beginning to reap the first fruits of his life and labors. The fame which belongs to him to-day is but a faint rushlight compared with the beacon which will shine out in the future when generations yet unborn shall rise up and call him blessed.

1852—1895—SINCE FROEBEL'S DEATH.

It seems fitting to close this sketch of the founder of the kindergarten with a brief review of what has been done to advance his ideas since the time of his death. The sickness of the Baroness and domestic matters kept her in Berlin later than usual in the summer of 1852, and the notice of the loss of her friend did not reach her in time for the funeral. She arrived at Liebenstein July 2, and the first question she asked on meeting Middendorf was, "What will now become of the cause?" His answer was, "We will work with all our powers; truth is not lost." This watchword became their motto for the rest of their lives. The instruction of the training class continued at Marienthal through that summer, Middendorf giving all his time to teaching the kindergarten theory and Frau Froebel undertaking the work of teaching the occupations. Of her the Baroness writes: "Although deeply afflicted by the sad, irreparable loss of her husband after only one year's married life, she fulfilled the task, now become so much more difficult, with the greatest conscientiousness, firmly resolved to devote her whole strength to it in order to preserve and promote the work already begun. At the same time she remained an affectionate, motherly friend and guardian of the pupils."

The season was a quiet one for the kindergarten community and they mingled but little with the summer visitors. The class was continued at Marienthal through the autumn, but early in 1853 Middendorf and Frau Froebel removed their work to Keilhau. The former came by invitation to Liebenstein in May to represent the kindergarten movement at the general convention of German teachers and the Baroness also gave a demonstration in connection with a similar gathering held at Gera. She went to Keilhau in July to see how the work was progressing and gives a glowing account in the closing pages of the "Reminiscences" of the community as it appeared at that time, using these words: "But now one saw, instead of Froebel's little farmhouse where he and his pupils had to struggle at first with the greatest privations, several stately buildings which inclosed a large courtyard, surrounded by the steep mountains and beautiful woods of the rather narrow valley. There were beautiful spacious apartments and schoolrooms, and a large hall in the main building. Exemplary order and care for the bodily and mental needs of the pupils was evident. The watchful guidance, the sharp practical oversight and the somewhat strict discipline, but at the same time loving care of the director, Barop, were everywhere apparent."

The Baroness spent some weeks in the neighborhood and occasionally took Middendorf's place as instructor in the training class, because he showed increasing signs of failing health. She returned to Berlin in the autumn and soon received news of his death, which occurred from brain troubles, November 26, 1853, without previous sickness, at the age of sixty. The loss of Middendorf compelled Frau Froebel to leave Keilhau and she accepted an invitation to take charge of a training class in a Dresden school. This arrangement was but temporary, and in 1854 she went to Hamburg to accept the directorship of the free public kindergarten, and for many years was at the head of a training class which has furnished Germany and other countries with kindergartners.

In "Froebel Letters" we have this pen picture of Frau Froebel, as she appeared while visiting a German kindergarten in 1871: "I was charmed with her striking appearance. Her figure was tall, erect, and remarkably well-proportioned. Her carriage and movements were elastic and graceful. Her face had an expression of freshness, I would have said of youthfulness, but for the grayish tint of the hair, indicating her advanced age, and forming a striking frame for a countenance beaming with a charming vivacity, producing a conviction that her soul had perservered a youthfulness much greater than her gray hair seemed to indicate for her body. Her beautiful blue eyes bespoke an unusual development of loving kindness. At her request the games and occupations and the musical exercises were gone through with in the usual way. She went to and fro, observing everything and every now and then actively interfering or directing with the hand and word of a thorough master. She was greatly pleased with the questions and remarks, and her winning ways proved as powerful an attraction for the little folks as for the grown up people."

In writing about Frau Froebel at a later period one of her pupils says: "It was indeed a pleasure to see her walking through her kindergarten department in the morning. This stately, erect figure, this noble bearing, this kind smile on her lips, all these qualities combined inspired us who were her students with the greatest respect and devotion for her. She reproached and blamed us very little; in fact, she was very silent and thoughtful, but she observed everything, and the expression of her face was enough to both teach and direct us.

I remember that one morning I had a little talk with her about her kindergarten, and when I told her how charmed I was to see her still in her old age so loving and child-like, her own words to me were: 'I am old, but my heart will ever remain young.' She was particularly fond of teaching us the 'Mother and Cossett Songs,' in her training class, and liked to mention many happy hours which she had spent with Froebel.

When she resigned from her work no other town but Hamburg offered her a home to rest, and she has always been loyal to that city. In summer it has been her habit to travel to those places in Thuringen, where she spent so many delightful months in eager work with Froebel for the welfare of the young."

In the later years of her life Frau Froebel enjoys a serene old age, receiving an allowance large enough to satisfy all her legitimate desires, with something left to give to the numerous charities and needy kindergarten institutes with which her active life of benevolence has brought her in contact. In writing about her in September, 1895, A. H. Heinmann, editor of "Froebel Letters" says:—

"I could select hundreds from the pile of letters written by Frau Froebel to her friend at Chicago, all of which prove that her mind is as sound and clear as it ever was. At her age, eighty years and five months, her strength is failing, which is perfectly natural. Her letters prove that she is still the same clear-headed and public spirited disciple of Friedrich Froebel that she was when her husband died forty-three years ago."

The Baroness lived to be nearly eighty and died at Dresden, January 9, 1893. She was born at Brunswick, March 15, 1816, her father being president of the ducal chamber in the duchy of Brunswick and her mother the Countess von Wartenslehen, of the Mark of Brandenburg. She was married while yet in her teens to Baron Von Marenholtz, a member of the privy council and later court marshal of Hanover. She had one son and during the twenty years of his life she devoted herself to his education and the care of the children of her husband by a former marriage. Possessed of excellent advantages in her youth, she was always a student of the best methods of education, and at the time of her first meeting with Froebel her mind was well prepared for the reception and adoption of the kindergarten gos-

TOMBSTONE AT SCHWEINA.

pel. As we have already seen, she began at once to proclaim that gospel from the public platform and by using her pen and the printing press, while Froebel yet lived.

In 1854 she went to England to establish the kindergarten system there and published a pamphlet on "Infant Gardens," in English. A little later we hear of her performing a similar service in France, for in 1857 A. Guyard, a French author, wrote her from Paris as follows: "The more I listen to you in regard to Froebel's method, the more my interest increases, and the deeper grows my conviction that by this means a basis is laid for a new way to educate humanity. He is great, perhaps the greatest philosopher of our time, and has found in you what all philosophers need, that is, a woman who understands him, who clothes him with flesh and blood and makes him alive." In 1858 the Baroness was urged by Abbe Muraud, a learned Italian author, to travel through Italy for the advancement of kindergarten education and in 1871 the minister of public instruction invited her to come to Florence to found a school for the instruction of teachers.

Notwithstanding her work in foreign lands, the service which the Baroness rendered the world was mostly performed in her native Germany. In 1861 she was instrumental in starting a journal called "The Education of the Future," edited by Dr. Carl Schmidt, in which she published the essays on "The Child and Child Nature" which have since been revised and issued in a book by that name. The translation of her "Reminiscences of Friedrich Froebel" by Mrs. Horace Mann first appeared in this country in 1877. An American kindergartner who visited the Baroness in 1869 says that on a certain occasion when the representative educators of several nationalities were dining together she conversed with each and all of them with equal ease and freedom in their own language. The account adds: "Her manners were unaffected, simple yet gracious, and her thoughtful attention toward her guests won their personal admiration, while her animation and earnestness aroused the interest of all. Wherever the world will hear of Friedrich Froebel's discovery of the kindergarten philosophy, the name of Bertha Von Marenholtz-Bulow will arouse an equal amount of love and reverence in the hearts of those who love humanity and to whom the well being of childhood is dear. Her quick intuitive interpretation of the hidden meaning of his words made her work and instructions of the greatest value to the world."

Another American kindergartner who visited the Baroness ten years later, in 1879, writes: "The value of her work for the kindergarten can never be estimated; her heart and her house were always open to those who were in search for more knowledge in regard to Froebel and the kindergarten. Intellectually she seemed to grasp the length and breadth of his science of development, and she was devoted to the idea that to her was the highest. She cherished many things that Froebel had made with his knife while developing his gifts. The tablets of the Seventh Gift were his latest work and much experimented upon; and these experimented tablets she kept and showed with deep interest. Intellectually we can hardly realize how we could have had the kindergarten as at present, without the very help which the Baroness Marenholtz-Bulow gave, and the value of her work will be more appreciated as the years go on."

The one connecting link between the present and the past, so far as active service in the German kindergarten field is concerned, is Frau Henrietta Schrader, who is still at the head of the Pestalozzi-Froebel house in Berlin. She is a grand-niece of Froebel, studied with him and helped him carry on his work in Dresden and other places. She also was associated with the Baroness in Berlin and has been identified with the cause in that city for more than a generation. She married a railroad magnate, a man of high social and educational standing, and they are still leaders in society, in spite of their advanced age. Frau Schrader has in her possession many manuscript papers of Froebel, which have never yet been published, a part of them having been given her by Frau Froebel. Some of them are illustrated with pencil sketches. She speaks and writes English with ease.

Regarding the German kindergartens of the present day about all that needs to be said here is that they are found in all the large cities, with occasionally one in the smaller places. The leaders there say that they are still hampered in their work by the government regulations and for that reason the hope for the best development of the kindergarten rests with this country, just as it did in Froebel's mind. An American training teacher sums up the differences between the two countries as follows, in a recently published article:—

"And now I anticipate the question generally asked, how does the work in Germany compare with the American work? It seems to me the two can hardly be compared, because of the difference in environments and aim. In the work with the children we have much to learn from each other. If we could give them a little of the sunshine which emanates from light walls with their pictures, from the snowy white apron, which is so prominent a feature in the American kindergarten, if we could enclose them with the lightness of our singing, the grace and alertness of our motions, the real play-spirit of our games, if we could give them some of the sentiment, (of which we could spare a goodly amount,) and have breathed upon us in return their whole-souled interest, their practical common sense, their devotion in meeting all the needs of the child, we should both come nearer the ideal.

There is still less ground for comparison when we consider the training classes. Our requirements for admission to the training class are much greater than theirs, our standard higher. Many of the girls received there without detriment to the class as a whole, would be a most dangerous element in an American training class, because of that sense of 'free and equal' in our atmosphere which would lead them to expect positions for which they were unfitted.

Here special classes with special aims are needed and I hope the day is not far distant when our college and kindergarten settlements may open their doors to these girls of fifteen or sixteen years whose advantages have been few, and give them a special training which shall fit them to go out as children's nurses, in place of the ignorant women so generally employed to-day, who are not only ignorant of every law of child nature, of any need beyond those of food and clothing, but also of the English language."

Considerable has been done by his fellow countrymen to honor the memory of Froebel. On the hundredth anniversary of his birth, April 21, 1882, the monument which stands over the grave at Schweina was dedicated. It is a modification of the design originally suggested by Middendorf of the cube, cylinder and sphere, with ornamental additions and a medallion of Froebel. On it is inscribed the motto, "Come let us live with our children," with the dates of the birth and death and the statement that this monument has been erected as an expression of thankfulness for the great friend of childhood and mankind. It is surrounded by an iron fence, and mounted on a substantial stone base. There is also another monument in the grove near Marienthal, which follows Middendorf's design more strictly and bears the same motto and dates, and a third one at Blakenburg, placed there by contributors from different parts of the world.

Aside from the institute at Keilhau, presided over by the younger Barop, the most elaborate memorial of Froebel's life and work is the tower located on the hill at Oberweisbach, overlooking the birthhouse, on the spot where it is said he was wont to linger to watch the setting of the sun. It is of limestone, about one hundred and twenty feet high, and was built in 1889 by the Thuringia Verein, at a cost of thirty thousand marks or about seven thousand dollars. There are tablets on the house at Oberweisbach and at Blankenburg and there is a kindergarten maintained in a building attached to the parsonage property at the former place. The house is still occupied by the village pastor, as it was in Froebel's day. He is president of the local society, and in a letter written to an American counsul living in that vicinity, a few months since, he says: "We would be grateful if you would kindly tell your trans-Atlantic constituents that now, here in Oberweisbach, the room where Froebel was born is identified and is willingly shown at any time, together with sundry Froebel relics." And yet travelers who have gone over that whole section on foot tell us that there are not a few people living within ten miles of that village who have never heard of Friedrich Froebel.

The prescribed limits of this book will not allow us to devote much space to recounting the progress of the kindergarten in European countries outside of Germany. We are told that the kindergarten system was introduced into England in 1854 by Miss Praetorius, who opened a kindergarten at Fitzroy Square, London, and that about the same time Madam Ronge began her work at Manchester, which subsequently resulted in the formation of the Manchester Kindergarten Association. That same year, as has been previously mentioned, the Baroness made a lecturing tour to England in behalf of the cause. Five years later Fraulein Eleanor Herrwart, a pupil of Frau Froebel and Middendorf, and the Baroness Adele Von Partugall, pupil of Baroness B. Von Marenholtz-Bulow and Frau Schrader, both came to Manchester and were given positions in different kindergartens. In 1866 Fraulein Herrwart went to Dublin to found a kindergarten of her own. In 1874 Emilie Michaelis went to England to promote the kindergarten, lecturing before the schoolboard teachers at Croydon. The following year she founded the Croydon kindergarten. It was in 1875 that the Froebel Society of London was organized, Miss Doreck being the first president, with which many prominent English kindergartners have been connected.

In 1879 the London society founded the London Kindergarten Training College, which was maintained till 1883. In 1880 Frau Michaelis became head mistress of the work undertaken by the Croyden Kindergarten Company, and a similar organization was formed at Bedford in 1883, with Miss Sims as chief kindergartner. That same year Fraulein Herrwart went to Blankenburg to open a memorial kindergarten, with funds raised for that purpose in London. In 1884 an education conference was held in connection with the Industrial Exhibition at South Kensington, the section devoted to Infant Education being largely taken up with discussions regarding Froebel's principles, representatives from other nations joining in the debate. At this time the British and Foreign Society organized a complete exhibition of work and material, all the leading kindergartners in London being contributors. In this connection most of them gave lessons to classes of children to show the practical application of the kindergarten methods.

In these latter days the cause has advanced in England, and there are some kindergartens supported at the public expense. Fraulein Herrwart, although her home is at Eisenach, Germany, has direction of all the examinations in the public kindergartens, visiting England for two summer months of each year for that purpose. Frau Michaelis is principal of the new Froebel Educational Institute at West Kensington. The English kindergarten periodical, a monthly magazine, is called "Hand and Eye," being edited by G. Brockleburst, and is published in London by O. Newman & Co.

At a meeting held in London, June 5, 1895, M. H. C. Bowen, author of a book entitled "Froebel and Education Through Self-activity" made an address in which he said that the people who are interested in the kindergarten have been working many years to get Froebelian methods rightly understood, and, if possible, adopted in England. He closed his remarks as follows:—

"We are to have a Training College, which we hope will be of value not only to those who mean to be professional teachers, but also to those who need to know more about children than they do—I mean *parents*—to whom the Institute will be useful both directly and indirectly. We hope that it will give an opportunity to those who have the charge of little children to learn how to develop and train their powers. There is nothing so pathetic, I think, as a young mother, who because she loves her child very dearly, thinks that this love alone will suffice as a guide to action. Something more is wanted, some knowledge, some little experience; and that, we hope, may be gained in our Training College. Those who go there will not necessarily be those who intend to become teachers, but those who have to do with children in any way whatever. In fact, we desire to help the public as a whole; and we think one of the best ways of doing so is to show them how best to deal with little children."

A conference of the Froebel Society of Great Britain and Ireland was held at the College of Perceptors, Bloomsburg Square, London, September 12, 1895, when Frau Michaelis read a paper on "The Kindergarten Occupations in Their Relation to Manual Work."

Passing beyond Germany and England we find the kindergarten in almost every quarter. Speaking of the spread of the kindergarten movement throughout the world, a writer in the "Pratt Institute Monthly" for November, 1895, says:—

"If Froebel were to come back to us to-day he would be astonished to see the growth of the idea that found birth in the little cottage at Blankenburg in the Thuringian Forest in Germany. That little spark of divine fire has spread over all the world, and to-day the word kindergarten is familiar in almost every country in the world. When not recognized by the government of a country kindergartens have often been introduced through Christian missions. Missionaries find the kindergarten most helpful in reaching the children and through them the homes of those whom they wish to benefit. In a letter from China we are told that Froebel's method must be valuable, as it is so entirely the opposite of the artificial methods of the Chinese. In Japan, in India, in the Sandwich Islands, in Austria, in Turkey, in Russia, France, Switzerland, Norway and Sweden, has the kindergarten found a home. In Italy, England and Belgium it is recognized by the government, and in the latter country is a part of the school system."

Coming now to the rise and progress of the kindergarten in America we must confine ourselves to narrow limits, although there is much that it would be a pleasant task to write. "If without the Baroness Marenholtz-Bulow, Froebel lacked a clear interpreter in Europe, certainly without Miss Peabody and her sister, Mrs. Horace Mann, the kindergarten cause in America would not stand where it does to-day." This is the verdict of one of the leading kindergartners in this country who is thoroughly conversant with Miss Peabody's work. Elizabeth Palmer Peabody was born at Billerica, Mass., May 16, 1804. Her sister Sophia married Nathaniel Hawthorne and her sister Mary became the wife of Horace Mann. Miss Peabody was a teacher, a lecturer, and an author, devoting her life to educational and philanthropic matters. Her attention was first directed to the kindergarten in 1859, because of the peculiar brightness of a little boy of her acquaintance, the son of Carl Schurz, whose family were then living at Roxbury, Mass., and who, she was told, had been taught in a German kindergarten. Miss Peabody began at once to study the writings of Froebel and in 1860 she opened a kindergarten at No. 15 Pinckney street, Boston, in company with Miss Margaret D. Corlees.

This experiment was carried on for several years, but was finally given up by Miss Peabody, for reasons which were afterwards explained by herself as follows:—

"I felt that my kindergarten was not the right thing, for, although very popular, I found that it failed to produce the results promised by Froebel, which I had seen exemplified in the little Schurz child, and so, after a time, I gave it up to my partner, telling her to go on with it till I could go over to Europe and find out about it. This I did in 1867, taking eleven hundred dollars in gold which I had made by giving my course of lectures on the philosophy of history. I stayed a year and three months, saw the real kindergarten, and came back to devote myself to its introduction into America."

Returning to this country Miss Peabody resolved to leave the practical work of establishing kindergartens to others and devote her time to lecturing and writing on the subject, in the hope of creating a general public sentiment in America favorable to the kindergarten. While she was absent in Europe Madame Matilda H. Kriege, and her daughter, Alma Kriege, undertook to carry on the kindergarten department of a German school in New York, but after a few months they were persuaded by Mrs. Mann, the sister of Miss Peabody, to remove their work to Boston. So it happened in September, 1868, that the kindergarten which Miss Peabody and Miss Corlees had maintained for some years was transferred to Madame Kriege and her daughter, a new location being secured on Charles Street and a training school opened in connection with it.

Both teachers had received their training from the Baroness in Berlin and the elder one was a personal friend of Froebel. Both of them had lived for some years in this country before taking their training and were therefore thoroughly familiar with English. Madame Kriege brought with her from Germany kindergarten material and also a hand machine for cutting the weaving mats. While in New York she induced Mr. E. Steiger to begin importing material, and on reaching Boston she sold the machine to Mr. J. L. Hammett, a dealer in school supplies, and led him to begin manufacturing the building gifts in a limited way. Thus it was that the kindergarten gained a foothold in New England, for although the first normal class taught by the Krieges graduated but two women, the seed was sown for an abundant harvest in the future.

When Miss Peabody started out to conquer the country for the kindergarten she made Springfield, Mass., one of her first stopping-places, giving an evening lecture on the new education in the hall of the Elm Street School building. Mr. Milton Bradley was present on that occasion, and having heard Miss Peabody's presentation of the case, was subsequently, persuaded by Mr. Edward Wiebe to publish

"The Paradise of Childhood," which first appeared in 1869, and begin in his factory the making of kindergarten material on a larger scale than Mr. Hammett had found possible as a merchant.

At this point in the narrative mention should be made of Dr. Henry Barnard, for many years secretary of the Connecticut Board of Education and editor of "The Connecticut Common School" and "The American Journal of Education." In 1854 the General Assembly of Connecticut sent him to the International Educational Exposition and Congress, held at St. Martin's Hall, London, at which he was the sole representative from this country. He was then so impressed with Mr. Hoffman's exhibit of the apparatus devised by Froebel and the kindergarten conducted by Madame Ronge that he commended both in his official report to the governor of Connecticut and also wrote an article on "Froebel's System of Infant Gardens" for "The American Journal of Education" of July, 1856, which it is said contained the first mention of the kindergarten that ever appeared in an American periodical. From that time for a series of years Dr. Barnard continued to explain and agitate the kindergarten system, and in 1868 and 1870, as national commissioner of education, he recommended to Congress that in establishing a system of public schools for the District of Columbia the kindergarten should be given an important place. As soon as Miss Peabody took up the cause Dr. Barnard became a co-laborer with her, and has never ceased to do what he could for its advancement. In 1881 he published "Kindergarten and Child Culture Papers" in a book of eight hundred pages, and at the present time, 1895, he is still living in serene old age at Hartford. Conn.

In 1870 Miss Peabody succeeded in getting the city of Boston to establish a public kindergarten, which was maintained for seven years with growing interest, and then given up because the committee felt that it would cost too much to meet the demand which had sprung up for kindergartens in other parts of the city, and that to continue supporting a single one would be unfair. Meanwhile, in 1872, Madam Kriege and her daughter had gone back to Germany, although they afterwards returned to New York and had a kindergarten in connection with a private school, ultimately settling once more in the land of Froebel, where they still reside. Madame Kriege made a free rendering of "The Child, Its Nature and Relations," by the Baroness, and Miss Kriege compiled "Rhymes and Tales for the Kindergarten and the Nursery," both being valuable additions to the very limited kindergarten literature of that day to be found in this country. Miss Mary J. Garland was one of the earliest graduates from the Kriege school and she became the pioneer American training teacher for Boston and New England, being for many years associated with Miss Rebecca J. Weston, who died in 1895.

In 1877 Mrs. Quincy A. Shaw opened a summer kindergarten at Brookline and another at Jamaica Plain at her own cost, continuing them through the year. Others were soon added, Miss L. B. Pingree was made director, and in 1883 Mrs. Shaw supported thirty-one kindergartens in Boston and vicinity. Afterwards the number was reduced to fourteen and in 1892 the city assumed the whole responsibility of the work, till then so liberally sustained by Mrs. Shaw. During the later years of her life Miss Peabody was obliged to withdraw from active service because of failing health, and she died at Jamaica Plain, January 3, 1894.

Before leaving the New England record it is well to note that Mrs. Louise Pollock, who lived at Weston, Mass., became interested in the kindergarten as early as 1861, through her mother in Berlin, who sent her whatever had been published in Germany on that subject, and began to write about it in the newspapers. In 1862 she carried on a kindergarten at West Newton, in connection with the Classical Institute of which Mr. N. T. Allen was principal. In 1873 her daughter, Susan P. Pollock, who had meanwhile taken the training in Berlin, was appointed to teach a public kindergarten at Brighton. Shortly after that mother and daughter removed to Washington, D. C., the former having previously spent some months of study in Germany.

As has already been indicated, the movement in New York began among the Germans. It was in 1872 that Miss Maria Boelte opened the first English kindergarten in that city, and the next year, in connection with Prof. John Kraus, whom she married, began a training school, which has been continued until now. They have also published an elaborate work called "The Kindergarten Guide." In 1878 Prof. Felix Adler and Rev. Dr. Heber Newton undertook to bring the children of the working people under the kindergarten influence. Prof. Adler established a free kindergarten in January, which became the foundation for a full course up to fourteen years, the principles of the kindergarten being preserved throughout all the grades. In March Dr. Newton opened the first mission kindergarten, which was connected with his church on Madison avenue, and has since been a model for similar church work all over the country.

About this time the city started a public kindergarten at the Normal College, which soon developed into a training department, and the Hebrew Free School Association also took up the work. Some years later the Teachers College was established, and this institution from the outset made the kindergarten the basis of its work and in 1890 was influential in forming the New York Kindergarten Association, which maintains several free kindergartens. The Children's Aid Society has a kindergarten attached to each of its schools and there are a few supported by the school board. The names of Miss Angeline Brooks and Miss Caroline T. Haven are always prominently mentioned in connection with the New York work, the former having been for a long time connected with the Teachers College and the latter with the Workingman's School. The same can be said of Miss Alice E. Fitts, and Miss Hannah D. Mowry in reference to Brooklyn, because their influence in behalf of the kindergarten in Pratt Institute and through the city has been potent for years.

The city of St. Louis was early in the field in behalf of the kindergarten. About 1873 Miss Susan E. Blow petitioned the school board for a room in which to make the first local experiment, and she very soon opened a training school, giving her services without salary, which was continued for twelve years. Such beginnings stimulated the growth of public kindergartens, which was judiciously fostered by Dr. William T. Harris, who was then superintendent of city schools. Aside from the public kindergartens there have been for a long time a number connected with private schools and some that are free to children below the school age, the latter being supported by charitable organizations.

The Chicago Froebel Association grew out of a small mother's class that was formed in 1873, and some months later Mrs. John Ogden came there from Columbus, O., spending a year in the city conducting a kindergarten and training class. Mrs. Alice H. Putnam, Miss Sara Eddy and Miss Josephine Jarvis took up the work where she left it. The first free kindergarten was opened at the Moody Chapel, on Chicago avenue, by Mrs. E. W. Blatchford. In 1891 the school board voted to adopt all the kindergartens of the association which were located in the public school buildings as a part of the regular school system.

A distinctive feature of the Chicago work for a long time has been along the lines of the college settlement idea, a beginning having been made at Hull House, which was opened by two young women who knew about the Toynbee Hall enterprise in London and who felt "that the mere foothold of a house easily accessible, ample in space, hospitable and tolerant in spirit, situated in the midst of the large foreign colonies which so easily isolate themselves in the large American cities, would in itself be a serviceable thing for the community."

The Chicago Free Kindergarten Association, with headquarters at Armour Institute and Miss Eva B. Whitmore as superintendent and Miss Anna E. Bryan principal of the training class, supports twenty-five kindergartens and the tuition is free. The Chicago Kindergarten College, of which Miss Elizabeth Harrison is principal, and Mrs. J. N. Crouse director, is an influential factor in whatever pertains to kindergarten interests in the vicinity of Chicago and so is the Kindergarten Institute, of which Mrs. Mary Boomer Page is the principal.

Coming to the Pacific coast, the first name to be mentioned is that of Miss Emma Marwedel. She was one of the German kindergartners who were persuaded by Miss Peabody to transfer their work to this country. She graduated from the normal school at Berlin, went to Washington, D. C., in 1872 to open a training school, removing to Los Angeles, Cal., in 1876 for the same purpose. At the latter place Kate Douglas Wiggin was her first pupil. Two years later Miss Marwedel went to Oakland, where she was instrumental in founding the Central kindergarten. She devoted the rest of her life to teaching and lecturing at the Berkeley University, Oakland,

PARADISE OF CHILDHOOD.

and at Palo Alto. She wrote "Conscious Motherhood" and an "Illustrated Botany," and died at San Francisco, November 17, 1893, at the age of seventy-five.

The kindergarten movement in San Francisco begun in the Bible class of Mrs. Sarah B. Cooper, in October, 1879, the first one being opened on the "Barbary Coast" which is the "Five Points" of that city. Mrs. Cooper was able to influence public sentiment powerfully in favor of the cause by writing a series of articles for the leading newspapers. Subscriptions poured in, the Golden Gate Association was formed, and a wonderful work begun. The California record of Kate Douglass Wiggin and her sister Nora Archibald Smith, two of the most brilliant contributors to kindergarten literature that America can boast, in connection with the Silver Street kindergarten and training class, is too well-known to need extended review here.

The prescribed limits of this book will not admit of a more extended notice of the kindergarten movement in America, outside of the centers already mentioned. In Philadelphia the work was begun by the Sub-primary School Society which was maintaining thirty-three kindergartens when they were turned over to the school board, Miss Constance Mackenzie becoming the first public supervisor. Mrs. M. L. Van Kirk has maintained a training class there for many years, sending out a multitude of graduates throughout the country. At Baltimore the Free Association supports a number of kindergartens and provides a training class for the young women of that vicinity.

At Washington Mrs. Louise Pollock and her daughter, Miss Susan P. Pollock, begun to hold up the kindergarten banner in 1873, and many others have since joined in the campaign, including Mrs. Louisa Mann, who is the wife of a nephew of Miss Peabody, and Mrs. Eudora L. Hailmann, wife of the national superintendent of Indian schools. Favorable mention should also be made of Cincinnati, Louisville, Albany, Buffalo, Columbus, Indianapolis, Detroit, Milwaukee and Minneapolis, because of their associations and training classes. The kindergarten is also very influential in some parts of Canada, particularly in the city of Toronto, under the lead of Inspector James L. Hughes, who is ably assisted by his wife, Mrs. Ada Marean Hughes, who took her training with Madame Kraus-Boelte and Miss Blow.

There are two well-recognized periodicals in this country, "The Kindergarten Magazine," established in 1888 and published by the Kindergarten Literature Company, Chicago, and "The Kindergarten News," started in 1891 and published by Milton Bradley Company, Springfield, Mass.

The kindergarten department of the National Educational Association is one of the most popular and best attended of all those which are connected with the annual July meetings of that body. There is also a very practical organization called the International Kindergarten Union that meets annually in February and has branches in all parts of the country and some in other countries.

Here the record must close, an attempt having been made merely to outline the American work. To include the names of all earnest workers would require many pages. Only a beginning has yet been made toward establishing kindergartens throughout the world, but the outlook for the future is certainly promising.

FRAU LOUISE FROEBEL.

PARADISE OF CHILDHOOD.

WIEBÉ'S ORIGINAL TEXT

WITH EDITOR'S NOTES.

AUTHOR'S PREFACE.

UNTIL a recent period, but little interest has been felt by people in this country, with regard to the Kindergarten method of instruction, for the simple reason that a correct knowledge of the system has never been fully promulgated here. However the lectures of Miss E. P. Peabody of Cambridge, Mass., have awakened some degree of enthusiasm upon the subject in different localities, and the establishment of a few Kindergarten schools has served to call forth a more general inquiry concerning its merits.

We claim that everyone who believes in rational education, will become deeply interested in the peculiar features of the work, after having become acquainted with Froebel's principles and plan; and that all that is needed to enlist the popular sentiment in its favor is the establishment of institutions of this kind, in this country, upon the right basis.

With such an object in view, we propose to present an outline of the Kindergarten plan as developed by its originator in Germany, and to a considerable extent by his followers in France and England.

But as Froebel's is a system which must be carried out faithfully in all its important features, to insure success, we must adopt his plan as a whole and carry it out with such modifications of secondary minutiæ only, as the individual case may require without violating its fundamental principles. If this cannot be accomplished, it were better not to attempt the task at all.

The present work is entitled a *Manual for Self-Instruction and a Practical Guide for Kindergartners.* Those who design to use it for either of these purposes, must not expect to find in it all that they ought to know in order to instruct the young successfully according to Froebel's principles. No book can ever be written which is able to make a perfect Kindergartner; this requires the training of an able teacher actively engaged in the work at the moment. "Kindergarten Culture," says Miss Peabody, in the preface to her "Moral Culture of Infancy," "is the adult mind entering into the child's world and appreciating nature's intention as displayed in every impulse of spontaneous life, so directing it that the joy of success may be ensured at every step, and artistic things be actually produced, which gives the self-reliance and conscious intelligence that ought to discriminate human power from blind force."

With this thought constantly present in his mind, the reader will find, in this book, all that is indispensably necessary for him to know, from the first establishment of the Kindergarten through all its various degrees of development, including the use of the materials and the engagement in such occupations as are peculiar to the system. There is much more, however, that can be learned only by individual observation. The fact, that here and there, persons, presuming upon the slight knowledge which they may have gained of Froebel and his educational principles, from books, have established schools called Kindergartens, which in reality had nothing in common with the legitimate Kindergarten but the name, has caused distrust and even opposition, in many minds toward everything that pertains to this method of instruction. In discriminating between the spurious and the real, as is the design of this work, the author would mention with special commendation, the Educational Institute conducted by Mrs. and Miss Kriege in Boston. It connects with the Kindergarten proper, a Training School for ladies, and any one who wishes to be instructed in the correct method, will there be able to acquire the desired knowledge.

Besides the institute just mentioned, there is one in Springfield, Mass., under the supervision of the writer, designed not only for the instruction of classes of children in accordance with these principles, but also for imparting information to those who are desirous to become Kindergartners. From this source, the method has already been acquired in several instances, and as one result, it has been introduced into two of the schools connected with the State Institution at Monson, Mass.

The writer was in early life acquainted with Froebel; and his subsequent experience as a teacher has only served to confirm the favorable opinion of the system, which he then derived from a personal knowledge of its inventor. A desire to promote the interests of true education, has led him to undertake this work of interpretation and explanation.

Without claiming for it perfection, he believes that, as a guide, it will stand favorably in comparison with any publication upon the subject in the English or the French language.

The German of Marenholtz, Goldammer, Morgenstern and Froebel have been made use of in its preparation, and though new features have, in rare cases only been added to the original plan, several changes have been made in minor details, so as to adapt this mode of instruction more readily to the American mind. This has been done, however, without omitting aught of that German thoroughness, which characterizes so strongly every feature of Froebel's system.

The plates accompanying this work are reprints from "Goldammer's Kindergarten," a book recently published in Germany.

EDWARD WIEBE.

Springfield, Mass., 1869.

KINDERGARTEN CULTURE.

The fundamental principle of the Kindergarten system of education, so clearly laid down in his writings, and so successfully carried out in practice by Friedrich Fræbel, is expressed in the axiom, that, before ideas can be defined, perceptions must have preceded; objects must have been presented to the senses, and by their examination experiences acquired of their being, quality and action, of which definite ideas are the logical results, with which they are therefore inseparably connected. It is not claimed that this principle originated with the inventor of the Kindergarten; for long before him it was said that: "Nihil est in intellectu, quod antea non fuerit in sensu," but in the Kindergarten system, he has furnished all material to begin the education of mankind on this logical basis.

Definite ideas are to originate as abstractions from perceptions, (*Anschauungen*, as the Germans say, meaning literally *the looking at or into things*.) If they do not originate in such manner they are not the product of one's own mental activity, but simply the consent of the understanding to the ideas of others. By far the greatest part of all acquired knowledge with the mass of the people, is of this kind. Every one, however, even the least gifted, may acquire a stock of fundamental perceptions, which shall serve as points of relation in the process of thinking. Indefinite or confused fundamental or elementary perceptions prevent understanding words with precision, which is necessary to reflecting on the ideas and thoughts of others with clearness, and appropriating them to one's self. In the fact that a large majority of persons are lacking in clear and distinct fundamental perceptions, we find cause for the existence of so many confused heads, full of the most absurd notions. The period of life in which the first fundamental perceptions are formed must necessarily be our earliest childhood. They can form only during this state of, as it were, mental unconsciousness, because the impressions on the senses can best be fixed lastingly upon the soul, when this process is least disturbed by reflection; and impressions of objects of the world without upon our senses, are made more or less clearly and distinctly, according to the nature of these objects themselves. A mere acquisition of perceptions, however, is not sufficient. As in the development of all organism in nature, a certain, peculiar series of events takes place, which always must be the same, or at least take place in accordance with the same law, to reach the same aim, or produce the same form; so, also, in mental development, a peculiar process, a natural series of events must take place without disturbing occurrences, to successfully reach the corresponding idea in the mind. This series of events in the mind and heart, connected with the process of thinking, is in philosophy explained to consist of: 1st. A general or total impression. 2d. A perception or looking on a single thing. 3d. Observation of qualities and relations. 4th. Comparison. 5th. Judging. 6th. Conclusion. Although a right selection of objects, and their proper succession, are of the first importance, adherence to these two conditions is not yet sufficient to prepare and accustom the mind to logical thinking; these means should be applied or presented in a systematic, methodical way, also. A system of education in perfect accordance with the laws of nature is only possible, therefore, when the *modus operandi* of the natural functions of the soul, during their development, is fully understood, and the exact means are discovered to assist these functions in a corresponding manner from without. As long as this is not done, the education of the human race is left to be the result of chance, and at the mercy of mere educational instinct. We claim that the significance of Fræbel's educational system consists mainly in a perfect understanding of the natural process of mental development. This understanding guided him in preparing certain means of education, or play, all following the same course as the mental development which they are intended to promote. No man has ever looked so deeply as Friedrich Fraebel into the secret workshop of a child's soul, and so successfully discovered the means and their methodical application for a development of the young mind in accordance with nature's own laws. To be certain that the natural course of development be not interrupted but logically assisted, the child's instinct should have free choice within appointed limits, and still be obliged to receive the objects as they are presented to it for the first perceptions. The means to obtain this, Fraebel has found in allowing the child to manipulate the things destined for the production of changes according to his own choice. Thereby the child will be led to devote attention to the objects formed, because he looks upon them as his own work, and rejoices in what he is able *to do*. That free unrestricted activity of the child, which we call play, alone can comply with these conditions; anything else *forced* upon the child, can never be successfully employed for this purpose. A desire of acquiring knowledge of things is an innate faculty of the soul, hence there is no need of *forcing* the child into making acquaintance with the things given him to play with. We have only to select for his playthings the fundamental forms, which, like the typical formations in nature, offer, as it were, a fundamental scheme for an acquaintance with the large multitude of things. Knowledge of things can be acquired only by acquisition of a knowledge of their qualities. We then have to provide objects in which the general qualities of things are shown in perfect distinctness, in order to produce thereby clear and lasting perceptions in the mind of the child. These objects should be such that they may be easily manipulated by the limited strength of the child, that he may become acquainted with them by their use, and become enabled thereby to gather experiences in regard to events and facts in the physical world, and may, so to say, serve him for the first physical experiments. Examining the list of Fraebel's Kindergarten occupation material, we find it to consist of the following:

1. Six soft balls of various colors.
2. Sphere, cube, and cylinder, made of wood.
3. Large cube, divided into eight small cubes.
4. Large cube, divided into eight oblong blocks.
5. Large cube, consisting of 24 whole, 6 half and 12 quarter cubes.
6. Large cube, consisting of 18 whole oblongs with 3 divided lengthwise and 6 divided breadthwise.
7. Quadrangular, and various triangular tablets for laying figures.
8. Sticks or wands for laying figures.
9. Whole and half wire rings for laying figures.
10. Material for drawing.
11. Material for perforating.
12. Material for embroidering.
13. Material for paper cutting and combining the parts into symmetrical figures.
14. Material for weaving or braiding.
15. Slats for interlacing.
16. Slats with 4, 6, 8 and 16 links.
17. Paper strips for lacing.
18. Material for paper folding.
19. Material for peas work.
20. Material for modeling.

The list begins with the *ball*, an object, comprising in itself, in the simplest manner, the general qualities of all things. As the starting point of form—the spherical—it gives the first impression of form, and being the most easily moved of all forms, is symbolical of life. It becomes the first known object, with which all other objects for the child's play are brought into relation. Beside teaching form, the balls are also intended to teach *color*, hence their number of six, representing three primary and three secondary colors. The principle of combining, uniting, or bringing into the relation of *opposites*, which is a governing law throughout all occupations in the Kindergarten, is applied here to discriminating primary and secondary colors, the latter being produced by a combination of two of the former.*

For the purpose of acquiring clear and distinct, correct idea of things around us, it is indispensably necessary to become acquainted with them in all respects and relations. The balls are made the object of a great variety of plays or occupations, to make the child become well acquainted with its uses, and to

---

*The old Brewster theory of color here stated is wholly at variance with the modern ideas on that subject which are elsewhere outlined in this book.

enable him to handle it gracefully. Then, for the purpose of comparison, the second Gift is introduced, consisting of *sphere*, *cube* and *cylinder*. We can here, certainly not yet speak of a rational comparison on the part of the young child, but simply of an immediate, sensual perception or observation of the similarities and differences existing in the things presented. The child will find by looking at the three new objects exhibited to him that the sphere is just like the ball, except in its material. The first impression, that of roundness, made upon the child by the many colored, soft balls, finds here its further development by the fact that this quality is found in this wooden ball, or *the sphere*, as he may be led to name it, learning a new word. To facilitate the process of comparison, the objects to be compared should first be as different as possible, *opposites* in a certain sense. The opposition between sphere and cube relates to their form. Together with the oppositional, or difference in objects, their similarity should in the meantime be made prominent, for comparison demands to detect equality and similarity of things as well as their distinction by inequality and dissimilarity. The cylinder introduced as the mediatory between the opposites in form, given here, is the simplest and immediately suggested mediative form, because it combines the qualities of both *cube* and *sphere* in itself.

These three *whole* bodies, introduced as fundamental or normal forms or shapes, in which all qualities of whole bodies in general are demonstrated, and which serve to convey the idea of an impression of the *whole*, are followed by the introduction of *curiously divided* solid bodies. Without a division of the whole, observation and recognition, *i. e.*, knowledge of it, is next to impossible. The rational investigation, the dissecting and dividing by the mind, in short, *the analysis* should be preceded by a like process in real objects, if the mind is calculated to reflect upon nature. Division performed at random, however, can never give clear ideas of the whole or its parts, but a regular division, in accordance with certain laws, is always needed. Nature gives us also here the best instruction. She performs all her divisions according to mathematical laws.

The orders in the vegetable kingdom are distinguished according to form and number of parts. Fraebel here, also, borrowed from nature a guide which led him in systematizing the means of development of the young mind in the Kindergarten.

As the first *divided* body, a large cube is introduced, consisting of eight small cubes of the same size each, as its parts. The large cube is divided once in each direction of space, lengthwise, breadthwise and heightwise. The form of the *parts* is here like the form of the *whole*, and only their relation as to volume is different. In shape, alike, they differ in size, which fact becomes more apparent by a variety of combinations of a different number of the parts. Thus the relation of number is here introduced to the observation of the child, together with that of form and magnitude. A clear and distinct idea of these relations could hardly be attained unless presented in this manner. In the following Gift, diversity of form in the whole and its parts, is made apparent, preceding the introduction of the relations of the plane. The logical connection with the preceding Gifts consists in the same form of the whole, the cube, and the same manner of division; the 5th and 6th being divided twice, whereas the 3rd and 4th were divided only once in all directions of space. The variety of forms gained, by this division of the cube, gives the widest scope to the invention and production of combined forms, without ever leading to an indefinite, unlimited, unrestrained activity. The logical combination of parts to a whole, which is required in using these blocks, renders it a preparatory occupation for succeeding combinations of thought, for, also the construction of parts into a whole follows certain laws, thereby forming a serial connection, which, in nature, is represented by the membering or linking of all organisms. As nature, in the organic world, begins to form by agglomeration, so the child in its first occupations commences with mere accumulation of parts. Order, however, is requisite to lead to the beautiful in the visible world, as logic is indispensable in the world of thought for the formation of clear ideas; and Fraebel's law *to link opposites*, affords the simplest and most reliable guide to this end.

For example, in the building occupation this law is applied in relation to the joining of blocks according to their *form*, or the different position of the parts in relation to a common center. If I join sides and sides, or edges and edges of the blocks, I have formed *opposites*; side and edge or edge and side joined, are considered as links or mediation. Thus below and above are opposites in relation to which the right and left side of form or figure built, serve as mediative parts. Carrying out this principle, we have established a most admirable order, by which even the youngest pupil, frequently unknowingly, produces the most charming regular forms and figures. This regular and serial constructing of the *parts* to a *whole*, according to a determinate law, is followed by connecting various wholes with one another, to produce orders and series as we find them in all the natural kingdoms, just as we are in need of categories in the process of thinking. Therefore we produce in the Kindergarten, by means of our occupation material, *different series* of forms and figures from common *elementary forms*, which we call either *forms of life*, *forms of knowledge*, or *forms of beauty*. The first are representations of objects actually existing and coming under our common observation, as the works of human skill and art.

The second are such as afford instruction relative to *number, order, proportion*, etc. The third are figures representing only *ideal* forms, yet so regularly constructed as to present perfect models of symmetry and order in arrangement of parts. By occupation with these differently, yet always regularly constructed bodies, the child will make observations of the greatest variety, which, by immediate use of the objects by manipulation and experiment, make a real experience. The observations, for example, of the vertical and horizontal, of the right angled, of the directions of up and downward, of under, above and next one another; of regularity, of equipoise, the relation of circumference and center, of multiplication and division, of all that produces harmony in construction, etc., impress themselves, as it were, indelibly upon the child's mind almost at every step. The first knowledge, or rather idea of the qualities of matter, and the first experiences of its use, are obtained thus in the simplest manner and delightfully. Thus the lawful shaping, logical development and methodical application of the material, is, as it were, the logic of nature imitated, whose representation is found in the forms of crystallization. It is natural that the works of God should reflect the logic of the great Creator's mind, and thereby be made the teachers of mankind. What can man do better in educating the human mind, than imitate these means, for the purpose of unfolding and strengthening the germ of logic, implanted in the mind of every human being, created in the image of his God.

A condition of indisputable importance for the acquisition of knowledge of things, is the knowledge of the material of which they consist, and their qualities, and this should be introduced in right succession. From the 2d to 6th Gifts, the objects consist of *wood*, and they are in the meantime solid bodies.

The next step in the use of matter as the representation of mind, is the transition to the plane, Froebel's Tablets for laying figures. In them, the simple mathematic fundamental forms are given as embodied planes, beginning with the square, which is followed successively by the right-angled triangle with two equal sides (the half square); the right-angled triangle with unequal sides; the obtuse-angled triangle, and the equilateral triangle.

The *slats* given for the play of interlacing form the transition from the *plane* to the *line*, resembling the latter, although, owing to their width, still occupying space as a plane. They represent in one respect a progress beyond the sticks, because they may be joined for the purpose of representing lasting forms.

The sticks, representing the embodied line, facilitate the elements of drawing, serving as movable outlines of planes. They are to be looked upon as the divided plane in order to adhere to their connections and relation with the form from which we started. By means of the sticks, numerical relation first is made more prominent and evident by the introduction of figures. The application of the law of opposites relates in all previous occupations to the *form* and *direction* of parts.

In the so-called *peas-work* the sticks or wires are united by *points*, represented by peas, demonstrating that it is union which produces lasting formation of matter.

Here closes the first section of Froebel's embodied alphabet, intended to give the elemental images for the succeeding recognition of complex form, magnitude and numerical relations. Thus the child has been guided in a logical manner from the *solid body* through its *divisions* and through the embodied plane, line and point, in matter and by matter, to the borders of the abstract, without going over into abstraction, which is a later process, to be postponed to the school that succeeds to the Kindergarten. To *reduce* or *"lead back"* mathematical perception (abstract thinking) to appearances in the material world, no more appropriate means and method could have been devised. All abstractions are drawn—*abstracted*, according to the original meaning of the word—from manifestations of the visible world. Although further final conclusions (which may be continued ad infinitum) shall remove them from their origin, elevate them to their loftiest heights of thought, their roots are ever to be looked for in the material world. The assertion that ideas are founded and defined by perceptions only, is either entirely erroneous and not to be proved, or there must exist such a connection, such an analogy, between the things of the material world and the objects of thought, as has been indicated here. And if it can be proved that such a course of development of the human mind necessarily takes place in some degree without our assistance, as a natural process, then education should not dare to prescribe any other one; then this is the only true method of developing the mind, because it operates with nature's laws, although it does not exclude all assistance on our part, but invokes it. We have often opportunity to notice how easily the mind, without human assistance grows in *wrong* directions, like the young tree that never felt the effect of the pruning knife.

In the following occupations of the Kindergarten we shall notice the progress from the solid *body* or *object itself* to the representation of its *image* by drawing. Planes and lines, the various forms of the triangle and other geometric figures, occur also here, but they are produced by different material. The touching or handling of the solid body, the most important means of acquiring knowledge during the first years of a child's life, during the state of its rational unconsciousness, is now entirely changed to a looking at objects presented to its observation; and the image of the body, so to say, takes the place of the body itself. Drawing with pencil is of such paramount importance because the child is enabled by it to reproduce quickly and easily the images imparted to its mind by their own visible representation, whereby they become truly objective and are only then fully understood. Instruction in writing should never precede instruction in drawing.

In the development of the human race, the body unmistakably precedes its image or representation, as the drawn image preceded the written sign or letter. In the incipient stages of civilization, these signs for things were images, as we see in all hieroglyphic inscriptions. Our modern letters occupy the highest step in the scale of the language of signs (which we should not forget).

Fræbel's method of instruction in drawing is as ingenious as it is simple. The same course as pursued in the study of things, according to their form, size and number, and mathematical proportions is also here adhered to. The various forms which have previously occupied the child in their existence as bodies, appear here in drawn pictures, and are multiplied ad infinitum. The progression from the simplest rudiment to the more complicated, the great multiplicity of series, determined by the various directions of the lines and the geometric fundamental forms, the logical progression from the straight to the curved lines, render drawing—not considering here its immediate artistic significance—one of the most efficient means for disciplining the mind of the young pupil. It is the first step for the child to a future careful observation of the general connection of things from the smallest to the largest, as parts as well as wholes.

In the following occupations, the material of which is a more refined one, color is introduced in connection with multiplication of form, and the products of the children's work are constantly approaching real artistic creations. In the *braiding* or *weaving* the thought of *number* is predominating because the opposites of odd and even are combined by alternately employing both. In the *paper-folding*, opposites are formed by the oppositional directions of the lines, (horizontal or perpendicular) originating in the folding of the paper, and these opposites are connected by the mediative oblique line. In like manner this law is applied to angles, acute and obtuse as opposites, the right angle serving as a mediatory. This is repeated in the occupation of *perforating* and *embroidering*. The *cutting of paper*, also, especially affords a perfect view of all the mathematical elements for the purpose of plastic representation.

Thus we find everywhere the same logical chain of perception, and subsequent representation and experimental knowledge resulting from both, and thus all parts and sections of this system of occupation are logically united with one another, serving the child's mind as a faithful reflector of its own internal development at each and every step. And well may the matured mind, developed according to these principles, in future days retrace with facility its conceiving and thinking to the clear and sharply defined, as it were, typical images of this reflector, as their very origin, for such experiences surely can never be effaced.

It has been charged by those who have only a superficial knowledge of Froebel's educational system, that by it the faculties of the young mind are too soon awakened, which should not be taxed at so early an age. To this accusation we invite the most careful investigation, the result of which, we doubt not, will be a conviction that just the opposite is the case.

Manual occupation, performed in connection with all means of occupation in the Kindergarten, continual representation of objects, plastic formation and production, are all attractive to the nature of the child and touch the springs of spontaneity in its very core. All observations which appeal to the understanding and prepare mathematical conceptions occur, as it were, as accessories only, and to such an extent as the child's desire calls for them. Nothing is ever *forced* upon the pupil's mind. It cannot even be said that teaching is prominent, but rather practical occupation, individually-intended production, on the part of the children; which give rise to most of the remarks required to be made on the part of the Kindergartner. The element of *working*, which every child's nature craves is predominating. Activity of the hand is the fundamental condition of all development in the child, as it is also the fundamental condition for the acquisition of *knowledge*, and the subjection of matter. Mechanical ability, technical dexterity, education of all human senses require under all circumstances manual occupation. However, if this side of Froebel's educational system is mentioned, another class of opponents is ready to object, that the child should not begin with work, but that first its mind should be developed. We understand these various objections to mean that the child's powers should not be employed in mechanical occupation exclusively, nor be entirely deprived of it, but that a harmonious development of body and mind should be the task of education. This is in perfect accordance with Froebel's principles, which, if carried out rightly, will accomplish this in the fullest meaning of the word. No occupation in the Kindergarten is merely mechanical, it is one of the most important rules that the mere mechanical, as contrary to the child's nature, should studiously be avoided.

Nothing is plainer to the careful observer of the child's nature than the desire of the little mind to observe and imbibe *all* its surroundings with *all* its senses *simultaneously*. It wishes to see, to hear, to feel, all beautiful, joyful, and pleasant things, and then strives to reproduce them as *far* as its limited faculties will admit. To receive and give back, is life, life in all its directions, with all its powers. This is what the child desires, what it should be led to accomplish with a view to its own development. Eyes and ears seek the beautiful, the sense of taste and smell enjoy the agreeable, and the impression which this beautiful and agreeable make upon the child's mind calls forth in the child's innermost soul, the desire, nay, the necessity of production, representation, or formation. If we should neglect providing the means to gratify such desire, a full development of the heart of the individual, a higher taste for the ideal in it, never could be the result. We believe that this desire cannot be assisted more perfectly and appropriately than by accomplishment in *form*, *color*, and *tone*, each expressing and representing in its own manner, the feeling of the beautiful and agreeable. The earlier such accomplishment is begun, the more perfectly the heart or aesthetic sentiment in man will be developed, the more surely a foundation for the moral development of the individual be laid. Aptness in formation and production conditions the development of the hand, simultaneously with the development of the senses. It conditions, also, knowledge and subjection of matter and the proper material for the yet weak and unskilled hand of children. Formation itself furthermore conditions observation of the various relations of form, size, and number, as shown in connection with the gifts, employed for the preparatory development of the perceptive faculties. Mathematical forms and figures are, as it were, the skeleton of the beautiful in form, which, in its perfection always requires the curved line. Images of ancient peoples, as we find them, in the Egyptian temples, for example, are straight-lined, hence are geometrical figures. The curved line, the true line of beauty, we find subsequently, when the artistic feeling had become more fully developed. The forms of *beauty* alternating in all branches of Kindergarten occupation, with those of life and knowledge, afford the most appropriate means for the development of a sense of art as well as of aptness in art, in the meantime preventing a one-sided prevalence of a mere cold understanding.

The faculties of the soul are not yet distinctly separated in the young child, the understanding, feeling and will, act in union with one another and every one is developed through and with the others. The combinations of the power of representation in formation serve also as the preliminary exercise for that combination of thought; and what the hand produces strengthens the will and energy of the young mind in the meantime affording gratification to the heart. All work of man, be it common manual work, or a work of art, or purely mental labor is always the uniting of parts to a whole, *i. e.*, *organizing* in the highest sense of the word. The more we are conscious of aim, means, manner and method connected with our work, the more the mind is active in it, the higher and nobler the result will be. The lowest step of human labor is formed by mechanical imitation, the highest is free formation or production, according to one's own conception. Between these two points we find the whole scale by which the crudest kind of labor mounts to a free production in art and science and on which invention stands uppermost as the gradual triumphant result from simplest imitation. It is this scale *en miniature* through which the child's mind is conducted by means of Froebel's occupation material. From the first immediate impression, received from objects and forms of the visible world, it rises *to art*, or creation according to its own idea, which is its own production, a self-willed formation. For this purpose nature implanted in the human mind a strong desire to produce form, which, if correctly guided, becomes the most useful faculty of the soul. Simply by this desire of formation the images of perception attain the necessary perfect distinctness and clearness, the power of observation, its keenness and experience, its proofs, all of which are requisite, to afford to the working of the human mind a sure foundation. Free invention, creating, is the culminating point of mental independence. We lead the child to this eminence by degrees. Sometimes accident has led to invention and production of the new, but Froebel has provided a systematically graded method by which infancy may at once start upon the road to this eminent aim of inventing.

If the full consciousness, the clear conception of its aim is at first wanting, it is prepared by every step onward. The objects presented and the material employed, afford the child, under the guidance of a mature mind, the alphabet of art, as well as that of knowledge, and it is worth while here to remark that history shows that art comes before science in all human development.

THE PARADISE OF CHILDHOOD:

A GUIDE TO KINDERGARTNERS.

ESTABLISHMENT OF A KINDERGARTEN.

THE requisites for the establishment of a "Kindergarten" are the following:

1. A house, containing at least one large room, spacious enough to allow the children, not only to engage in all their occupations, both sitting and standing, but also to practice their movement plays, which, during inclement seasons, must be done indoors.
2. Adjoining the large room, one or two smaller rooms for sundry purposes.
3. A number of tables, according to the size of the school, each table affording a smooth surface ten feet long and four feet wide, resting on movable frames from eighteen to twenty-four inches high. The table should be divided into ten equal squares, to accommodate as many pupils; and each square subdivided into smaller squares of one inch, to guide the children in many of their occupations. On either side of the tables should be settees with folding seats, or small chairs ten to fifteen inches high. The tables and settees should not be fastened to the floor, as they will need to be removed at times to make room for occupations in which they are not used.
4. A piano-forte for gymnastic and musical exercises—the latter being an important feature of the plan, since all the occupations are interspersed with, and many of them accompanied by singing.
5. Various closets for keeping the apparatus and work of the children—a wardrobe, washstand, chairs, teacher's table, etc.

The house should be pleasantly located, removed from the bustle of a thoroughfare, and its rooms arranged with strict regard to hygienic principles. A garden should surround or, at least adjoin the building, for frequent outdoor exercises, and for gardening purposes. A small plot is assigned to each child, in which he sows the seeds and cultivates the plants, receiving, in due time, the flowers or fruits, as the result of his industry and care.

When a Training School is connected with the Kindergarten, the children of the "Garten" are divided into groups of five or ten—each group being assisted in its occupations by one of the lady pupils attending the Training School.

Should there be a greater number of such assistants than can be conveniently occupied in the Kindergarten, they may take turns with each other. In a Training School of this kind, under the charge of a competent director, ladies are enabled to acquire a thorough and practical knowledge of the system. They should bind themselves, however, to remain connected with the institution a specified time, and to follow out the details of the method patiently, if they aim to fit themselves to conduct a Kindergarten with success.

In any establishment of more than twenty children, a nurse should be in constant attendance. It should be her duty also to preserve order and cleanliness in the rooms, and to act as janitrix to the institution.

MEANS AND WAYS OF OCCUPATION
IN THE KINDERGARTEN.

BEFORE entering into a description of the various means of occupation in the Kindergarten, it will be proper to state that Friedrich Fræbel, the inventor of this system of education, calls *all occupations* in the Kindergarten *"plays"* and the materials for occupation *"gifts."* In these systematically-arranged plays, Fræbel starts from the fundamental idea that all education should begin with a development of the *desire for activity innate in the child*; and he has been, as is universally acknowledged, eminently successful in this part of his important work. Each step in the course of training is a logical sequence of the preceding one; and the various means of occupation are developed, one from another, in a perfectly natural order, beginning with the simplest and concluding with the most difficult features in all the varieties of occupation. Together they satisfy *all the demands* of the child's nature in respect both to mental and physical culture, and lay the surest foundation for all subsequent education in school and in life.

The *time of occupation* in the Kindergarten is three or four hours on each week day, usually from 9 to 12 or 1 o'clock; and the time allotted to each separate occupation, including the changes from one to another, is from twenty to thirty minutes. *Movement* plays, so-called, in which the children imitate the flying of birds, swimming of fish, the motions of sowing, mowing, threshing, etc., in connection with light gymnastics and vocal exercises, alternate with the plays performed in a sitting posture. All occupations that can be engaged in out of doors, are carried on in the garden whenever the season and weather permit.

For the reason that the various occupations, as previously stated, are so intimately connected, growing, as it were, out of each other, they are introduced very gradually, so as to afford each child ample time to become sufficiently prepared for the next step, without interfering, however, with the rapid progress of such as are of a more advanced age, or endowed with stronger or better developed faculties.

The following is a list of the *gifts* or material and means of occupation in the Kindergarten, each of which will be specified and described separately hereafter.

There are altogether twenty *gifts*, according to Fræbel's general definition of the term, although the first six only are usually designated by this name. We choose to follow the classification and nomenclature of the great inventor of the system.

LIST OF FRŒBEL'S GIFTS.

1. Six rubber balls, covered with a net work of twine or worsted of various colors.
2. Sphere, cube and cylinder, made of wood.
3. Large cube, consisting of eight small cubes.
4. Large cube, consisting of eight oblong parts.
5. Large cube, consisting of whole, half, and quarter cubes.
6. Large cube consisting of doubly divided oblongs.

[The third, fourth, fifth and sixth gifts serve for building purposes.]

7. Square and triangular tablets for laying of figures.
8. Sticks for laying of figures.
9. Whole and half rings for laying of figures.
10. Material for drawing.
11. Material for perforating.
12. Material for embroidering.
13. Material for cutting of paper and combining pieces.
14. Material for braiding.
15. Slats for interlacing.
16. The slat with many links.
17. Material for intertwining.
18. Material for paper folding.
19. Material for peas-work.
20. Material for modeling.

THE FIRST GIFT.

The First Gift, which consists of six rubber balls, over-wrought with worsted, for the purpose of representing the three fundamental and three mixed colors, is introduced in this manner:—

The children are made to stand in one or two rows, with heads erect, and feet upon a given line, or spots marked on the floor. The teacher then gives directions like the following:—

"Lift up your *right* hands as high as you can raise them."

"Take them down."

"Lift up your *left* hands." "Down."

"Lift up both your hands." "Down."

"Stretch forward your right hands, that I may give each of you something that I have in my box."

The teacher then places a ball in the hand of each child, and asks:—

"Who can tell me the name of what you have received?" Questions may follow about the *color, material, shape,* and other qualities of the ball, which will call forth the replies, *blue, yellow, rubber, round, light, soft,* etc.

The children are then required to repeat sentences pronounced by the teacher, as—"The *ball is round;*" "*My ball is green;*" "All these balls are made of *rubber,*" etc. They are then required to return all, except the *blue* balls, those who give up theirs being allowed to select from the box a *blue* ball in exchange; so that in the end each child has a ball of that color. The teacher then says: "Each of you has now a *blue, rubber ball,* which is *round, soft* and *light;* and these balls will be your balls to play with. I will give you another ball to-morrow, and the next day another, and so on, until you have quite a number of balls, all of which will be of *rubber,* but no two of the same color."

The six differently colored balls are to be used, one on each day of the week, which assists the children in recollecting the days of the week, and the colors. After distributing the balls, the same questions may be asked as at the beginning, and the children taught to raise and drop their hands with the balls in them; and if there is time, they may make a few attempts to throw and catch the balls. This is enough for the first lesson; and it will be sure to awaken enthusiasm and delight in the children.

The object of the first occupation is to teach the children to distinguish between the *right* and the *left* hand, and to name the various colors. It may serve also to develop their vocal organs, and instruct them in the rules of politeness. How the latter may be accomplished, even with such simple occupation as playing with balls, may be seen from the following:—

In presenting the balls, pains should be taken to make each child extend the right hand, and do it gracefully. The teacher, in putting the ball into the little outstretched hand, says:—

"Charles, I place this red, (green, yellow, etc.,) ball into your right hand." The child is taught to reply:—

"I thank you, sir."

After the play is over, and the balls are to be replaced, each one says, in returning his ball:—

"I place this red (green, yellow, etc..) ball, with my right hand into the box."

When the children have acquired some knowledge of the different colors, they may be asked at the commencement:—

"With which ball would you like to play this morning—the green, red, or blue one?" The child will reply:—

"With the blue one, if you please;" or one of such other color as may be preferred.

It may appear rather monotonous to some to have each child repeat the same phrase; but it is only by constant repetition and patient drill that anything can be learned accurately; and it is certainly important that these youthful minds, in their formative state, should be taught at once the beauty of order and the necessity of rules. So the *left* hand should never be employed when the *right* hand is required; and all mistakes should be carefully noticed and corrected by the teacher. One important feature of this system is the inculcation of habits of precision.

The children's knowledge of color may be improved by asking them what other things are similar to the different balls, in respect to color. After naming several objects, they may be made to repeat sentences like the following:—

"My ball is green, like a leaf." "My ball is yellow, like a lemon." "And mine is red, like blood," etc.

Whatever is pronounced in these conversational lessons should be articulated very distinctly and accurately, so as to develop the organs of speech, and to correct any defect of utterance, whether constitutional or the result of neglect. Opportunities for phonetic and elocutionary practice are here afforded. Let no one consider the infant period as too early for such exercises. If children learn to *speak* well before they learn to *read*, they never need special instruction in the art of reading with expression.

For a second play with the balls, the class forms a circle, after the children have received the balls in the usual manner. They need to stand far enough apart, so that each, with arms extended, can just touch his neighbor's hand. Standing in this position, and having the balls in their right hands, the children pass them into the left hands of their neighbors. In this way, each one gives and receives a ball at the same time, and the left hands should, therefore, be held in such a manner that the balls can be readily placed in them. The arms are then raised over the head, and the balls passed from the left into the right hand, and the arms again extended into the first position. This process is repeated until the balls make the complete circuit, and return into the right hands of the original owners. The balls are then passed to the left in the same way, everything being done in an opposite direction. This exercise should be continued until it can be done rapidly and, at the same time, gracefully.

Simple as this performance may appear to those who have never tried it, it is, nevertheless, not easily done by very young children without frequent mistakes and interruptions.

It is better that the children should not turn their heads, so as to watch their hands during the changes, but be guided solely by the sense of touch; and to accomplish this with more certainty, they may be required to close their eyes. It is advisable not to introduce this play or any of the following, until expertness is acquired in the first and simpler form.

In the third play, the children form in two rows fronting each other. Those of one row only receive balls. These they toss to the opposite row: first, one by one; then two by two; finally, the whole row at once, always to the counting of the teacher—"one, two, throw."

Again forming four rows, the children in the first row toss up and catch, then throw to the second row, then to the third, then to the fourth, accompanying the exercise with counting as before, or with *singing*, as soon as this can be done.

For a further variety, the balls are thrown upon the floor, and caught, as they rebound, with the *right* hand or the *left* hand, or with the hand inverted, or they may be sent back to the floor several times before catching.

Throwing the balls against the wall, tossing them into the air and many other exercises may be introduced whenever the balls are used, and will always serve to interest the children. Care should be taken to have every movement performed in perfect order, and that every child take part in all the exercises in its turn.

At the close of every ball play, the children occupy their original places marked on the floor, the balls are collected by one or two of the older pupils, and after this has been done, each child takes the hand of its opposite neighbor, and bowing, says, "good morning," when they march by twos, accompanied by music, once or twice through the hall, and then to their seats for other occupation.

EDITOR'S NOTES.

FROEBEL originally intended this gift for use in the nursery when the little one was under the direct guidance of his mother, and for such use it is admirably adapted. It is probably for this reason that so little was made of this gift by Prof. Wiebe, who was writing for children of older years, such as were supposed to be in the American kindergartens twenty-five years ago; but at the present time very much more is made of it, and its possibilities are great. As a part of the system it has its place in the kindergarten of to-day, being invaluable, inasmuch as it teaches color, form and motion. While from the following series of exercises we can only hint at the endless variety of games and songs that may be given to the children in making relations with this gift, the ingenuity of the kindergartner will suggest much by which the six soft balls of the first gift may be introduced as preliminary to the solid forms of the second gift. If the child has had no nursery training with the balls, only one should be given at a time, red being usually chosen. When the red ball has been fully introduced and the child has played with it in a rhythmical way until perfect sympathy is established between him and his plaything, another may be given, and so on.

GENERAL IMPRESSION.

The kindergartner shows the ball and introduces her observations with some fitting words, as:—

How pretty is the ball,
Now please look at it all!

While she distributes the balls to the children, who hold both hands to receive one, she sings:—

First open hands and take the ball,
Then close the little fingers all.

Then let each child open his hands and place the ball before him on the table; call attention to it by saying:—

This ball of bright and colored wool,
It looks so very beautiful,
Examine it, how neat, how clean,
So should a child be ever seen.

Ask the children if they can tell you anything about the ball. One will answer, "It is soft;" "it is rough;" "it is elastic;" "it will roll," etc. Then there is something to tell them about the rubber tree and an experience to gain with every moment during which the balls are used.

Ask the children to rock their balls to sleep, making a cradle of the hands, and singing:—

Our balls are going to Bye-low-land,
Going to sleep in each child's hand,
Rock them so gently to and fro,
Our little balls to sleep must go.

—or—

A little ball is lying here
So quietly asleep,
And as I rock it to and fro
A loving watch I'll keep.

Then, if it is not yet time to put the balls away, sing:—

It likes now to be moving,
Moving, roving, moving, roving,
Moving, roving so.

Accompany the song by passing the ball from one hand to the other, keeping time to the music, which should always be strongly marked for young children. Nothing is more harmonious or helpful in a kindergarten than to get hands and feet accustomed to rhythmical motions. In distributing, if preferred, the balls may be called flowers, as:—

These flowers are so bright and fair,
Please handle them with tender care;
And as I pass them to you all,
Take care they do not break or fall.

The balls may be flowers that are sleeping, and the children's hands the covers; let some child go around to awaken the flowers. Then the balls may be leaves on the trees and drop quietly down, the children using their arms held above their heads for the branches. Again, they may be birds, frogs, fishes, fruit, snowballs to be made and thrown up and caught; also gifts and decorations for a Christmas tree, some child representing the tree.

These are but a few suggestions as to the various purposes for which the balls are used. When it is time to put the balls away, sing:—

My ball lies in its little bed,
So quiet and so still;
I'll gently rock it to and fro,
And hush it well, I will.

COLOR.

Hold up the ball and ask the children what color it is, then to find something in the room or upon themselves of the same color, and when they have found several red things, give the name red; but do not give the name until they have watched the color and proved that they have experienced the sensation. In teaching the other prismatic colors in these exercises, observe the same caution—let the sensation come before the name. Children in private kindergartens usually know the names of the colors.

"Do you remember what we played in the ring? 'Johnny likes to wander.' Now we will let the red balls wander just as Johnny did." Give a red ball to each child next to you, and after it has passed two or three children start another, and so on. Sing:—

The red ball loves to wander
From one child to another,
And to each one will say 'Good Day.'
(repeat last line.)

"When Mr. Red Ball is tired we will gently place him on the table and let him rest, while we bring from the box one of his brothers. It is the color of a round, juicy fruit. Yes, it is the color of the orange, and we will let the orange balls wander." Compare real oranges with it, and let the children find orange-colored objects to match the orange ball.

After each game let the children do just what the ball has done. At the end of any regular exercise let the children choose any of the games they have played. It is well to let them glue red autumn leaves or red kindergarten papers on a circular piece of cardboard, either white or black, twelve or fourteen inches in diameter. A clearer impression of form as well as of color will be made if the form is varied with the color, using for instance, a round chart for red, square for orange, oblong for yellow, triangular for green, pentagonal for blue, hexagonal for violet and octagonal for all the colors. These can be fastened upon the wall in prismatic order.

Give each child two round papers of the same color. Let the children come one by one and find a ball like their papers. Pin the papers on the balls for wings, then let the children watch to see which bird flies up from the teacher's lap, and direct those who have the same color, to let theirs fly at the same time, singing:—

"Up, up in the sky."

Down goes the little bird out of sight and a new bird flies into the air. "Now take off the wings of your bird and they will be little balls again. Roll them to me, and we will let the yellow balls wander. Find other yellow things about the room. What have you seen that is yellow? Count the yellow balls."

If in private work the kindergartner finds herself with children five years old it may be better to use the more mature game of fruit selling. A bunch of balls is held up and the children allowed to name each one, as, red cherries, yellow lemons, green apples, etc., these answers being drawn from the children. Then a child goes down between the tables or around the circle to sell the fruit, singing alone or with the teacher:

Cherries ripe, cherries ripe,
Who will buy my cherries ripe?

and is answered by the children singing:—

Cherries ripe, cherries ripe,
We will buy your cherries ripe.

Meanwhile they hold out their hands to receive the ball, which the child gives to any one he pleases; the one who receives the ball holds it up and then puts it out of sight. An orange ball is sold by another child in the same way as he sings:—

Oranges ripe, oranges ripe,
Who will buy my oranges ripe?

A yellow ball can represent lemons, with the song, "Lemons ripe," etc., a green ball being used for apples, while the group is singing "Apples green," and so on. Then some child is sent to ask for the red ball, another for the orange, another for the yellow, etc. This exercise trains the attention and memory and teaches the children to make comparisons. For example: The red ball is like the cherry, the orange ball is like an orange, the yellow like a bird, the green like the leaves.

Repeat these games and let each child have several counters for money, and come and buy a ball of the same color as the money. Or for an occupation to develop color, hold the balls before the children and let them each select the color they like best. After making a choice give them a piece of paper of that color, also a needle and thread. Ask them to hold the bright face of the paper toward them and put the needle right through the middle; then give each child a straw and tell them to put their needle through the hole, then through another piece of paper, and so on until a long chain is made. These may be used for necklaces, or decorations for the room, etc.

For the older children the balls may be placed in a circle on the table and a game of hiding the balls played. Let some child close his eyes, and when a ball is taken away, have the children sing:—

Now tell little playmate,
Who has gone from our ring;
And if you guess rightly,
We'll clap as we sing.

If the child can tell on opening his eyes which ball is missing, whether the red, orange, violet, etc., the children clap their hands, at the same time singing, la-la-la. This game can be introduced by playing with a group of six children instead of six balls, and is afterward played with all the children in the ring.

The balls may be different flowers and the table a garden. Interest the children by showing them some real flowers, and talking about them. Ask the children if they can name the flowers, then suggest the idea that they use the balls for flowers, and the table for a garden and have just such pretty flowers growing in their beds.

Gather the balls in a bunch and holding them up ask which they will use for geraniums, which for marigolds, which for yellow roses, green buds, forget-me-nots and violets, letting each child pick out the flower and the ball corresponding to it in color.

Give each child the choice of the flower which he would like in his garden and if the smaller children cannot tell it by the name, have them point it out among the real flowers. Let their hands be used as a cover for the flowers and when they have placed them on the table with the palms downward, suggest that they go to sleep, as the little flowers when planted in their beds will want to sleep soundly until it is warm enough to throw off their covers and creep out. The children may then see if they have in their garden the kind of flower which they have chosen.

When all eyes are closed place the ball which is the color of the flower chosen under their hands. While the little plants are kept snug and warm have the children make a little rain shower with the other hand. Down the raindrops gently patter, whispering to the sleeping flowers that it is time to awaken from their long nap. "Let us see if the violets in our gardens have heard the gentle call of the rain drops and are going to creep out." Hold up the real violet that the sense impression of violet may accompany the words. And presently the violet balls begin to throw off their covers and peep out and with the string held close to the ball are slowly raised while the teacher sings:—

    Oh, lovely little violet,
      I pray you, tell me, dear,
    Why you appear so early,
      Ere other flowers are here.

The children with the violet balls answer:—

    Because I am so tiny,
      In early May come I,
    If I come with the others,
      I fear you'd pass me by.
        (Miss Jenks "Song and Games.")

When all the violets are in bloom let them bend and nod and whisper to each other, while the sunbeams speak to the other flowers.

Some child is chosen for the sunbeam, and flits from flower to flower, touching them softly and as they awaken one by one, the real flowers are held up that the balls may peep out and grow up in the same way as before. If some are still sleeping another child is chosen for the sunbeam, and when the garden is full of flowers ask the children if they would like to make them into bouquets. Have one child take his violet and find all its little sisters and make a bouquet of violets. Another child is chosen to secure a bunch of marigolds; and when the roses, buds, geraniums, and forget-me-nots are all gathered the game may be repeated. This time, however, have all the flowers bloom out together, and as they are growing up, sing the second verse of "The Little Plant" from Emilie Poulsson's Finger Plays.

Choose different children to gather the flowers this time, and make them into a wreath. Ask the children for the different flowers and as the balls are handed to you one by one, open the double string and loop it over the next ball and so on until the wreath is complete. One advantage of introducing more than one game is that of giving the children the favor of choosing. This should be done impartially and the dull, inactive children should be drawn out in the same way. The teacher should gently insist on their choosing, and the feeling that their choice guides the play of the others draws them out of their isolation into the sunshine of companionship. These little things in the hands of a skilled kindergartner who is working from the standpoint of the child to develop his whole being, may prevent much that is morbid and harmful. The ball is to him a bird, a flower, sometimes it tells one story to the child and sometimes another; it is a living, cherished playfellow, and gradually its qualities are mastered and found in other things. Thus the ball becomes a starting point for a vigorous and wholesome exercise of memory and imagination, and the insight of the child is quickened and extended.

FORM.

Call attention to the roundness of the ball by saying:—

    Look at the ball from left to right,
      You'll see the same appearance quite;
    'Tis round, and turn it as you will
      You'll see the same appearance still.

Have the children go through the movements and then ask them to name other round objects. A suitable story or song may be brought in. The ball being an unseparated whole, conveys the idea of unity, and may represent the world, an apple, a wheel, bird's nest, etc.

Although form is very little emphasized in this gift, the child's observation is gained by calling attention to its shape and color, and his activity called forth by simple exercises, while his moral faculty is being developed, and his intelligence opened to comprehend the law underlying all life as it exists externally, namely, that all the diversity of external phenomena returns to and rests in that which is itself a complete whole.

MOTION.

No other quality appeals more strongly to young children than motion, which is one of the chief characteristics of this gift. While every muscle receives exercise and strength, force and energy are developed, and with the abundance of matter which comes under the notice of the kindergartner it will be easy for her to introduce new observations. Wind the string around the ball and roll one to each child and let the children tell the color as the ball rolls. "What did the balls do?" They rolled. "Would you like to hear a song about rolling?"

  Roll over, come back here
  So merry and free,
  My playfellow dear
  Who shares in my glee.

Let the children on one side roll to the children on the other or place the hands a foot and a half apart and throw the ball from one to the other, singing:—

  The ball desires to wander,
  To fly across to yonder
  Right, left—right, left.

Regulate the rolling by the motion of the hand or by the rhythm of the song. At the end of the exercise let the children play the balls are marbles and roll down the length of the table, telling the color of the one they hit. Roll again, this time at word of command: "One, two, three, roll!" Vary the counting in order to exercise and develop attention, and let each child roll to counting, as this exercise results in training the hand and eye, and also develops color as well as attention.

Let the child take the ball in both hands and drop it into the hands of the next child, held together to receive it. Sing from Miss Jenk's book:—

  Little ball, pass along,
  Slyly on your way;
  While we sing a merry song,
  You must never stay,
  Till at last the song is done,
  Then we'll try to find
  In what pair of little hands,
  You've been left behind.

Older children may pass the ball by taking it in one hand, passing it to the other and from that placing it in the nearest hand of the next child, who repeats the same movements. These movements require care and attention and provide good exercise, but are too hard for very young children; for if they are attempted they should be done exactly right, as indeed should every exercise in the kindergarten. Accuracy rightly developed does not interfere with the spirit of play which should be kept. Children love to do things accurately if the requirement is suited to their capacity, and the kindergartner has the right spirit. This exactness in little things lays the foundation for habits that are of great value.

Let the balls hop from one hand (the nest) upon the table and sing, "Hopping Birds." Teach direction by showing how we make the ball sink and rise. "How does it go?" Ask the children to tell something that moves up and down, as elevator, window, curtain, etc., and sing:—

  Ball is sinking downward,
  Rising up again,
  Sinking, rising,
  See how the ball sinks and rises.
  —or—
  My ball comes up to meet me,
  Then down it goes so fleetly
  In the air, oh, hurrah!
  In the air, oh, hurrah!

Hold the ball in one hand, so that the string makes a vertical line. Notice things in the room whose position is upright, legs of piano, edge of door, etc.

Tell the children about carrier pigeons, how they carry letters tied under their wings. Not a whole bag full, like the postman, but just one. Some one ties it under the wing and then they fly up high and go a long way and take it to the right place. Before this exercise let the children play "See our pretty birdie fly," in the ring and let them now play this with their balls. Let the ball fly in the air and then alight on the table before them. "What kind of a bird is it?" Robin Redbreast, Oriole, Canary, Parrot, Bluebird, according to color. Sing: "Little bird, you are welcome." Let the balls of all colors fly up and then come to rest. Make a nest with both hands and sing:—

  Up, up in the sky the little birds fly.
  Down, down in the nest, the little birds rest.
  With a wing on the left and a wing on the right,
  These dear little birdies are all safe for the night.

Recall songs of previous exercises, and let the children choose which they like. Notice what they choose and develop conversation through songs and games. Ask the children how else or in what other direction the balls move. Introduce back and front movement, singing "The Pendulum," and let the children play it. Ask them to show you with their balls how the clock goes. "What does it say?" Tick, tack. "Would you like to sing about the clock?" Teach and sing: "Come and see" or "To and Fro," the children singing "tick, tack," only, if they cannot sing words readily. "Can you make your arms go like the pendulum? Let us make our arms go to the right, tick—to the left, tack, etc. Now make the balls swing right, left, tick, tack. Hold the string from left to right. How does the edge of the table go?" Left to right. Froebel says: "Direction should be rooted in motion." That is, the vertical movement should precede the vertical line and the horizontal movement the horizontal line.

Now bring out front and back movement and sing:—

Now ball swing to and fro,
More gently, soft and slow,
But far away, you cannot stay
While swinging to and fro.
—or—
Bim bom, bim bom,
So the bells swing in the steeple,
Call to church the kind good people.
Bim bom, bim bom, bim bom.

Let the children merely sing "Bim, bom." "Can you make your arm go like the bell? What kind of bells have you heard? What do the great church bells say?" Hold the ball in one hand and the end of the string in the other. "How does the string go?" Back and front.

Ask the children if they would like their balls to go round and round. Sing "Round and round it goes," repeating the first line of the mill wheel in Mrs. Hubbard's book and swing the ball round and round by the string, playing the balls are mill wheels. If the time has come to put the balls away sing:—

And now 'tis time to rest,
You've done your very best.

Go sleep dear ball till next I call!
For now 'tis time to rest.

As the ball swings round and round it may represent the windmill. And in this way the kindergartner may bring in the action of the wind. Ask the children to show with the balls and their hands the kind of work which the wind does.

Let them represent the trees, with the hands raised above the head and a swaying motion of arms and hands for the branches, which wave and bend as the wind blows.

Suggest that they show how the wind rocks the bird's nest, which may be built high up in the tree-tops where the little birds may come. Let them choose which kind of a bird they would like in their nest, then with the fingers curved upward to form the nest swing the balls one by one into their hands; then let the wind gently rock the tree-tops from side to side by a swaying movement of the hand from right to left, the ball being held in the center of one hand while singing from Mrs. Hailmann's songs:—

In the tall branch of the tree-top
There's a nest snug and warm.
In it lies a little birdie,
Safe in sunshine and in storm, etc.

Let them show how the wind plays with the leaves, how it moves the boats across the water when the waves are high, how it sails the kites, how it blows the clothes on the line, representing each movement with the ball held in the hand. When acting in unison, the children will feel the harmony of a movement more strongly, then when acting separately; then they enjoy rolling the ball from one to the other, throwing it up in the air, against the ground or wall and catching it, or by throwing it backward and forward to each other. These few hints will suffice to enable one to invent new plays and make suitable variations of those here given.

THE SECOND GIFT.

The Second Gift consists of a *sphere*, a *cube* and a *cylinder*. These the teacher places upon the table, together with a rubber ball, and asks:—

"Which of these three objects looks most like the ball?"

The children will certainly point out the sphere, but, of course, without giving its name.

"Of what is it made?" the teacher asks, placing it in the hand of some pupil or rolling it across the table.

The answer will doubtless be, "Of wood." "So we might call the object a *wooden ball*. But we will give it another name. We will call it a *sphere*."

Each child must here be taught to pronounce the word, enunciating each sound very distinctly. The ball and sphere are then further compared with each other as to material, color, weight, etc., to find their similarities and dissimilarities. Both are *round*; both *roll*. The ball is *soft*; the sphere is *hard*. The ball is *light*; the sphere is *heavy*. The sphere makes a *louder* noise when it falls from the table than the ball. The ball rebounds when it is thrown upon the floor; the sphere does not. All these answers are drawn out from the pupils by suitable experiments and questions and everyone is required to repeat each sentence when fully explained.

The children then form a circle, and the teacher rolls the sphere to one of them, asking the child to stop it with both his feet. This child then takes his place in the center, and rolls the sphere to another one, who again stops it with his feet, and so on, until all the children have in turn taken their place in the center of the circle. At another time, the children may sit in two rows upon the floor, facing each other. A white and a black sphere are then given to the heads of the rows who exchange by rolling them across to each other. Then the spheres are rolled across obliquely to the second individuals in the rows. These exchange as before, and then roll the spheres to those who sit third, and so on until they have passed throughout the lines and back again to the head. Both spheres should be rolling at the same instant, which can be effected only by counting or when time is kept to accompanying music.

Another variety of play in the use of this gift consists in placing the rubber ball at a distance on the floor, and letting each child, in turn, attempt to hit it with the sphere.

For the purpose of further instruction, the sphere, cube, and cylinder are again placed upon the table, and the children are asked to discover and designate the points of resemblance and difference in the first two. They will find, on examination, that both are made of wood, and of the same color; but the sphere can roll, while the cube cannot. Inquire the cause for this difference, and the answer will, most likely, be either, "The sphere is round," or "The cube has corners."

"How many corners has the cube?" The children count them, and reply, "Eight."

"If I put my finger on one of these corners, and let it glide down to the corner below it, (thus,) my finger has passed along an *edge* of the cube. How many such edges can we count on this cube? I will let my finger glide over the edges, one after the other, and you may count."

"One, two, three,——————12."

"Our cube, then, has eight corners, and twelve edges. I will now show you four corners and four edges, and say that this part of the cube, which is contained between these four corners and four edges, is called a *side* of the cube. Count how many sides the cube has."

"One, two, three, four, five, six."

"Are these sides all alike, or is one small and another large?" "They are all alike."

"Then we may say that our cube has six sides, all alike, and that each side has four edges, all alike. Each of these sides of the cube is called a *square*."

To explain the cylinder, a conversation like the following may take place. It will be observed that instruction is here given mainly by comparison, which is, in fact, the only philosophical method.

The sphere, cube, and cylinder are placed together as before, in the presence of the children. They readily recognize and name the first two, but are in doubt about the third, whether it is a barrel or a wheel. They may be suffered to indulge their fancy for awhile in finding a name for it, but are, at last, told that it is a *cylinder*, and are taught to pronounce the word distinctly and accurately.

"What do you see on the cylinder which you also see on the cube?" "The cylinder has two sides." "Are the sides square, like those of the cube?" "They are not."

"But the cylinder can *stand* on these sides just as the cube can. Let us see if it cannot *roll*, too, as the sphere does. Yes! it rolls; but not like the sphere, for it can roll only in two ways, while the sphere can roll any way. So, you see, the sphere, cube, and cylinder are alike in some respects, and different in others. Can you tell me in what respects they are just alike?"

"They are made of wood; are smooth; are of the same color; are heavy; make a loud noise when they fall on the floor."

These answers must be drawn out by experiments with the objects, and by questions, logically put, so as to lead to these results as natural conclusions. The exercise may be continued, if desirable, by asking the children to name objects which look like the sphere, cube, or cylinder. The edge of a cube may also be explained as representing a *straight line*. The point where two or three lines or edges meet is called a *corner*; the inner point of a corner is an *angle*, of which each side, or square, of the cube has four. To sum up what has already been taught: The cube has six sides, or squares, all alike; eight corners and twelve edges; and each side of the cube has four edges, all alike; four corners, and four angles.

The sphere, cube, and cylinder, when suspended by a double thread, can be made to rotate around themselves, for the purpose of showing that the sphere appears the same in form in whatever manner we look at it; that the cube when rotating, (suspended at the center of one of its sides,) shows the form of the cylinder; and that the cylinder, when rotating, (suspended at the center of its round side,) presents the appearance of a sphere.

Thus, there is, as it were, an inner trinity in these three objects—sphere contained in cylinder, and cylinder in cube, the cylinder forming the mediation between the two others, or the transition from one to the other. Although the child may not be told, the teacher may think, in this connection, of the natural law, according to which the fruit is contained in the flower, the flower is hidden in the bud.

Suspended at other points, cylinder and cube present other forms, all of which are interesting for the children to look at, and can be made instructive to their young minds, if accompanied by apt conversation on the part of the teacher.

EDITOR'S NOTES.

THE second gift consists of a box containing a sphere, a cube with staples, and a cylinder, together with sticks and an additional perfectly plain cube. It fulfills a varied and valuable office in child education and has an individuality we did not find in the first gift, since each form is distinct from and unlike the others.

Its strongest educational value consists in the fact that it represents the fundamental forms of the universe. The ball is the symbol of the earth, the sun, the moon and all the heavenly bodies. The cube symbolizes the mineral kingdom, and connecting these is the cylinder, which is the prevailing type of animal and vegetable life.

We find the sphere of this gift resembles the soft ball in form, and in many things which the ball can do, but it has additional powers; it can speak to us and is permanent in form and material.

Of this gift every child should have a full set, and as the sphere, cube and cylinder form a whole, they should be presented as a whole to the child, though in the beginning they may be given to him singly. The ball is first offered him. The child recognizes his old playfellow and his first thought will be that he has another ball, because the similar form will attract his attention.

This is right and will be found to be one of the principles in Frœbel's system. A similarity with the previous steps may always be observed, and this gives each new step the claim of an old friend, enlisting feeling as well as thought, while presenting something in advance.

The child will at once perceive, however, that the sphere looks, feels and sounds differently; that it resists his grasp although the woolen ball yielded to it. Immediately he begins to make comparisons. The new ball will be found, unlike the previous one, to be capable of making a noise on the table, and this should not be repressed too much. Children like to hear sounds, as they like to see and handle things; and although we have learned to discriminate between noise and music, we must remember that children delight in noise for its own sake until they are led through it to rhythmical sounds and later to music; so a little noise on the table with the sphere is legitimate if it is not aimless.

THE SPHERE.

The gift may be introduced by asking the children to close their eyes and placing a sphere in each child's hand; ask for a description before they open their eyes. "What is it like?" "How does it feel?" Give them a ball of the first gift and let them tell about both without opening the eyes. Then ask them to open their eyes and tell what they see. "Why! that is a ball, too." True enough, but not like the other ball, so let us find out what the difference is.

Lead the children to experiment with the sphere, play with it and tell you what they discover. They will tell you that the sphere will roll, toss, swing, and that it does not easily stand still. Give them hard and soft spheres, smooth and rough spheres, spheres of different sizes and colors and draw out their comparisons.

After the children have made their discoveries and comparisons let them look about the room for similar forms, and also ask them to bring similar forms from home. These lessons on solid forms give scope for much general information. Little talks about the wood, where it comes from, etc., may become a part of the work, suggesting many pretty songs.

If the three forms are brought out at one time they may be called three little friends who live together in a long, brown house, which is just large enough for them to get inside, each in his own place and close the door.

Ask questions to develop the children's ideas; who these people are, what they are like, what they can do, and so on. Then bring the sphere from the box. The first thing the children will want to do is to pound or make a noise. Do not restrain the action but as one kindergartner suggests, play concert, be their bandmaster and count for them. "All lift up the balls, one—two—knock; one—two—three—knock." and so on, putting a definite thought into an indefinite action.

Ask the children what they have played with the soft balls. Repeat the games as the children name them, until they have thought of what they played, and play these games with the sphere.

Their imagination changes the sphere into many new things. It is the carpenter's hammer or the blacksmith's sledge. It is a swift horse or a capering dog; not now so often the tiny bird, but something with more strength and vigor, yet still full of life and activity.

Let a sphere run to Robbie; now one to Mary. Bring out the fact that it goes over and over and rolls because it is round. After having given frequent illustrations of the roundness of the ball the name sphere is introduced. Ask the children to name something that goes round and round, and let them spin, roll and swing the sphere. Notice that "in every place, it always shows its one curved face." Let the sphere swing from left to right, repeating the exercise the children had with the ball of the first gift.

Give spheres to the children who are sitting of one side of the table to roll to those on the other side, while they all sing, "Roll over, come back here, so merry and free;" or "One, two, three, roll." Repeat the songs, letting some have the hard and some have the soft balls, exchanging them so that each may have both kinds. At the end of the exercise compare the two, thus bringing out the quality of sonorousness.

They find in this gift something that speaks to them, for after the motion of an object the sound which it makes is next noticed and it is this quality which gives its special charm to the sphere. To bring out sound especially, tap the soft ball on the table and let some child answer good morning to it and guess who it is; then tap the hard ball and let another child answer this time, and guess who it is; knock in different parts of the room, on different articles.

To connect the two gifts sing, while holding the soft ball by the string:—

Here's a little kitty,
  Going round and round;
  She has cushions on her feet,
  And never makes a sound.
With the hard ball sing:—
  Here's a little pony,
  Trotting round and round;
  He has hoofs upon his feet,
  And stamps upon the ground.

Let the children roll in turn a soft ball and the sphere to hit another ball at the end of the table. It will be enough for very little children to get an experience of the difference in the rolling of the two balls. Older children should be led to see and tell you that it is because the sphere is hard that it rolls better than the ball. This will make a foundation for the understanding of resistance when they study physics. Let the children come to you and roll the sphere in a plate. Sing for them "Round I roll when in a plate," then let them roll it along the length of the table and sing:—
  Now along the table straight,
  When I rest, or roll or fall,
  Always I'm your little ball.

The spheres can be nuts for the tree and so connected with the winter fireside or the Christmas time. A little skill keeps up the connection with the special season of the year and with the previous work.

In playing the "Fruit Game" substitute nuts for the fruit, as:—
  "Who will buy, who will buy,
  Who will buy our walnuts ripe?"

Let the children sell different kinds of nuts, and then try to find the buyer, which gives a test of memory, with no color to aid, although the children seldom fail to find them all. Repeat the games with ball and sphere sufficiently often to keep the connection. The number of times and amount of pleasure given by them will be in proportion to the interest and resources of the kindergartner.

THE CUBE.

After you have taught all you can from the sphere give each child the cube. Some one asks, "Why not the cylinder, as it is more like the ball?" Because it is similar is just the reason it is not presented next. All knowledge is based on comparison, but a comparison is not possible without differences and contrasts. The simplicity and unity which characterize the sphere are replaced by variety and multiplicity in the cube, and the decided contrast between the two will give the child a clearer impression, so that when he receives the cube he will again make comparisons.

Call for similarities first, differences afterward. Both are hard, smooth, made of wood, and of the same color. Let each child try to roll the cube, and he will see it will stand firmly but cannot roll, although the sphere readily obeyed the slightest impulse to move. The cube, standing solidly on one face refusing to roll or to yield to anything but force, opens a new world to him. It suggests big stones, and foundations for ground work. It is the type of the mineral world and possesses solidity and security. Hence in piling up the forms the child almost invariably places the cube at the bottom, needing no suggestion as to its proper position.

In comparing the two, the child finds that the sphere has one round face, while the cube has many faces; that the cube has edges and corners, which the ball has not; the ball gives the idea of motion and the cube of rest; the ball may be placed in a stationary position at any point, the cube will only rest on its faces.

Place a cube before each child near the front of the table, and ask the children how many faces they see; of course they can only see the one directly under their eyes. Move the cube back and ask again. They will see two faces. Let them turn their heads a little and hold perfectly still. Ask once more and they will say three faces. Lead them to realize that they can only see three faces at one time. A large paper cube suspended in the room with opposite faces of different colors will help the children to appreciate this fact. Ask them to bring things into the kindergarten which are like the cube in form.

Give each child six parquetry papers, two of one color; for instance, two red, two orange, two green. Make the face of the cube quite wet with a camel's hair brush and water, and let each child put on a red paper. Let him find the opposite side and put on the other red paper. Put on the orange and green in the same way, taking the faces in twos; the upper and lower first, then the front and back, then the right and left. If the child is too young to count the faces he will get an experience of many and opposite faces. The older children can count the faces without confusion, with the help of the opposite color, or they can roll the sphere and mark with chalk each one of the six square, flat faces, as they find and count them.

Let each child roll one sphere in turn and try to strike the cube at the other end of the table. "On what does the cube stand?" On one of its faces. Give the older children the name flat face and curved face. "How many faces has the cube?" Six. "How many faces has the sphere?" One. "What kind of faces has the cube?" "What kind of a face has the sphere?" Let each child come to you in turn and shutting his eyes, tell by feeling whether it is a curved or a flat face he is touching.

In the games the peculiar characteristics of the sphere and cube may be brought out by their movableness and steadfastness. The directions indicated through motion in the first gift are here found to be permanent in the faces and edges of the cube, and are easily recognized.

The cube may be a little house and the sphere a little boy who lives in it. Let the sphere run to this side of the house and knock, and now at this, and then this, and this, (four sides). Now we will put him on the top of the house. Then take the boy away and lift up the house to find one more side. Count the sides as you strike them. "What else can we find on the cube?" Bring out corners and edges by letting each child make a little dent on his hand with the corner of the cube, and a little crease with the edge. Ask the children if they can dent or crease their hands with the sphere. Ask them to show you all the corners and edges they can without counting. If the children are very young or very backward give them a clear idea of corners by letting a child stand in the corner of the room, and give each child a little seed to put in the corner of his cube, then one for the opposite corner, and so on. The six sides, eight corners and twelve edges appear a world of study to the children and give the foundation for number work.

Thus far the child has seen the cube in a state of rest. It will cause him more lively pleasure to note the peculiarities of its free motions. Suspend the cube and ask how many faces the cube has. If one child can answer, let him come up and spin the cube while the others sing to the air of "Be quiet dear cube," in Mrs. Hubbard's book :—

My six, square, flat faces are running away,
And chasing each other around in their play.
Come back little faces, come back and stand still,
And now you may run off again if you will.

The children call this singing the cube, and the desire to come up and spin the cube stimulates them to make an effort to remember the number of faces. If there is time finish with a rolling exercise. This dialogue between the cube and the child may be sung for many exercises until the number and kind of faces are firmly fixed. Those children who do not spin the cube may roll two spheres along the table to hit the cube.

When the number of faces are fixed, the corners may be sung to the same tune :—
My eight little corners are running away,
And chasing each other around in their play.
Come back little corners, come back and stand still,
And then you may run off again if you will.

This rolling may be used for several lessons until the children are sure of the number of corners, then the edges may be brought out by singing, "My twelve little edges are running away," etc.

While the sphere always presents one and the same appearance, the cube shows a marked difference of form with each movement. If a string is fastened to one corner or the middle of any edge and the cube is twirled, it has the appearance, viewed from the side, of a double, cone, or, as the children would call it, a top. When looked down upon, its edges and corners seem to slip away and we see a point in the center surrounded by a circle. When whirled from the center of a face the cylindrical form is shown, with a shadowy circle outside. All these peculiarities will be brought out under the child's notice while playing with the cube.

THE CYLINDER.

When the wonder and pleasure of the cube have been indulged in long enough, add the cylinder, or as the children call it, the "roller." "What can the sphere do?" "What can the cube do?" "Did you ever see anything that could roll and stand too?" Bring out the cylinder. It may be introduced as a cousin. Roll one to each child and let him tell wherein the cylinder resembles its cousins. This form will also make a noise and is in color like the sphere and cube. It will roll like the ball because it has one round face; it will stand or rest like the cube because it has flat faces. While the ball rests on a point, and the cube on a face, the cylinder can rest either on a face or a line. The cylinder has two curved edges, but no corners. Let the children show faces and edges. Roll it and then let it stand. Count one, two, three, and let each child roll his cylinder to you. Notice flat and curved faces. Let the children show you a flat face—a curved face. "How many flat faces are there?" "How many curved faces?" "Can you put your finger along a line on the curved face?" The outlines of the flat faces form circles. If the finger is passed around the curved face a circle is made, but by passing it up and down we get a straight line.

Let each child have a sphere to compare with the cylinder. "Can you find a straight line on the sphere's curved face?" Suggest that he close his eyes, and taking his finger see if he can tell whether he is touching the sphere's curved face, or the cylinder's curved face. Let each child in turn roll the cylinder and ball to hit the cube. Ask the children to bring things from home like the cylinder, and to tell all the reasons why it is a cylinder; also when they bring anything like the sphere and cube to tell why it is a sphere or a cube.

Let the children come to you and find things among those they have brought, or that you have collected, that look like the sphere, the cube or the cylinder; also let the older children tell you what they can see from the window that is like either of these forms.

As soon as the child becomes familiar with these forms they will become to him types of the life around him. He is very quick to observe how everything can be classified under one of these three forms; thus the trinne law of all growth is revealed to him, until gradually it dawns upon him that these objects are connected by having properties in common, and out of this feeling develops the perception of unity in the midst of diversity. As the cylinder seems to have been left in a somewhat isolated position, it is well to attract as much attention as possible to this object, a more extensive use of which, will be brought out in the fifth gift B.

The forms of the second gift are provided with staples in which strings may be inserted, and the object suspended by holding the ends of the string between the thumb and fingers. Twist the string, and let the child hold it while it revolves; he will be delighted to see one form merge into another, and finally come back to the first form. By holding an end in each hand, and skillfully pulling them apart, revolving the form as the string untwists, and then allowing the impetus of the form to twist the string as it is slackened, so that by repeating the operation a rapid rotary motion may be produced, first in one direction and then in the other, curious semi-transparent shapes may be seen which will create an interest in geometrical forms. The cube seems to change into a cylinder, a double cone, or a cylinder and wheel; the cylinder is a sphere within a sphere or a double cone in a sphere and wheel, and thus the child learns that things in motion seem very different from what they really are. Suspend a cube from its face with a double string and spin it. "How does the cube look now?" Like a cylinder or roller. "Now that it stops what does it look like?" Like the cube. "Now it spins again; what does it look like?" Sing to the tune of "Buy a broom":—

Oh, say Mr. Cube what now are you hiding,
What now are you hiding this morning from me?
I'll let you go flying, and then I'll be spying,
What it is you are hiding this morning from me.
'Tis the roller! 'Tis the roller!
'Tis the roller you are hiding this morning from me.

Let two children come up and spin the ball, singing, "Round goes the ball, but in every place." Let two more come and spin the cube, singing, "Oh, say Mr. Cube what are you hiding?" Let two more come and see what the roller hides. Sing:—

Here the roller comes with its faces three,
la-la-la-la-la.
He is just as sober as he can be,
la-la-la-la-la.
But when he is whirling, his faces grow thin,
And show the little hard ball within,
la-la-la-la-la-la-la-la-la-la.

(This may be sung to "Vive la Compance," a college song.)

If the cylinder is twirled from the middle of a curved face, a ball is seen with a shadowy rim around it. If twirled from the middle of a flat face, a double cone appears, when viewed from the side; when looked down upon, a ball flattened at the top, accompanied by a shadowy rim is seen. If twirled from the edge of a flat face a cone appears from the side, a ball from above. Thus the ball is seen in the cylinder, the cylinder in the cube, and the double cone in both cube and cylinder. This finding of one form within another brings out the unity of the second gift.

Instead of using the double string a rod may be passed through the holes in the cylinder and cube. Have the rod bluntly pointed at both ends, and with one end on the table, hold the top end with the finger resting on it, and impart a rotary motion to the form by impulses from the finger of the other hand. Several of these forms are shown in Figs. 1–5.

Fig. 1, represents the cube with the axis through the center of opposite faces.

Fig. 2, the cube with the axis through diagonally opposite corners.

This gift proves most instructive if the sphere, cylinder and cube are given all at once. They may be placed side by side, or as in Fig. 6, producing a column, which arrangement is embodied in the two Froebel memorial stones.

Fig. 1.   Fig. 2.   Fig. 3.

Fig. 6.

Fig. 3, the cube as rotated on an axis passing through the centers of two diagonally opposite edges.

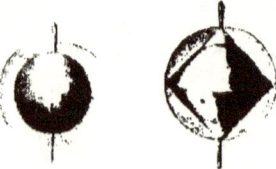

Fig. 4.   Fig. 5.

Fig. 4, shows the cylinder as being rotated on a rod perpendicular to the center of its natural axis.

Fig. 5, represents the rotating cylinder with the axis diagonally through from edge to edge. An interest in form inspired in this way, may lead to later investigation into the mysteries of the sciences, results of which eternity alone can measure. Do not make the child weary with this gift. Rolling the ball and cylinder may always be brought in to relieve monotony if necessary.

A sequence of lessons on bread-making may be given, after the child has become familiar with various seeds and the processes of ploughing, planting, reaping, etc., until finally the baker makes the bread; the sphere, cube and cylinder playing their part as raindrops, storehouse, seeds, plough, mill wheels, flour barrel, rolling pin and other well-known forms.

After the three forms have been enjoyed together place them in the box which may be given to the children and much pleasure derived from its examination. The shape of the box will be noticed, and the different ways of placing it, so that the length will be from back to front, from right to left, and up and down. But the height of joy is in the possession of such treasures as lie in the box. The friends he has known so intimately lie there together, the ball always at the "door end," as he calls it, of the box, which should always be placed at the right hand, the cube at the left and the roller in the middle. The other cube with "something the matter with its corners" and its edges is such a study; but it does not take the average child long to find that the little rattan in the box will just fit in the holes through the cube, or to notice that if he only had a string he could put it through the little "rings" that he sees. He makes one discovery after another, and when he finds that the two round sticks fit into the holes (which were before a mystery) in the lid of the box, and that the square stick goes on the top of these, a new world is surely discovered by each little Columbus. The box may be fitted up with paper sails for a boat, loaded with cylinders for barrels, cubes for boxes of freight and spheres for fruit, or it may be loaded with different things, as seeds, plants, vegetables, etc., according to the season.

The boxes may be turned down on the side as ovens, and the lids placed on the table as kneading boards; the perforated cube can be used for a stove, with a stick for the pipe; the plain cube for the kitchen table; the cylinder for a barrel of flour; or by putting a round stick through the hole it may be used for a rolling pin; the sphere may be a turkey or apple dumplings; other cubes may be used for bread, and cylinders for jelly rolls; then when all are ready, put them in the oven for baking.

In using the same form to represent different things in a play, do not fear that there will be any incongruity, provided the suggestion comes from the children, and the objects symbolized are closely related in thought, for the child's imagination is so free that he can clothe and re-clothe the same form with new life. The sense impressions which come from tracing resemblances and differences, experimenting and handling, will give a familiarity with the forms and their relation to each other, which no abstract lesson on surfaces, edges and corners could afford. The windmills, water-wheels, steamboats, wagons, and engines conceived and run by unconscious inventors and master workmen—especially when one little fellow finds out something new he can do with his treasures, and imparts it to the eager group—are a marvel and joy to any real kindergartner. No such wealth of resources to cultivate imagination and inspire confidence is found in any other gift as in this, which was an especial favorite with Frœbel, and is so invaluable that no kindergartner who has once shared the delight of the children in this gift for one year in the kindergarten course, will ever be willing to do without a box for each child.

This consists of a *cube* divided into *eight smaller one-inch cubes.*

A prominent desire in the mind of every child is to *divide* things, in order to examine the parts of which they consist. This natural instinct is observable at a very early period. The little one tries to change its toy by breaking it, desirous of looking at its inside, and is sadly disappointed in finding itself incapable of reconstructing the fragments. Froebel's Third Gift is founded on this observation. In it the child receives a *whole*, whose *parts* he can easily *separate*, and *put together again at pleasure*. Thus he is able to do that which he could not in the case of the toys—restore to its original form that which was broken—making a perfect whole. And not only this—he can use the parts also for the construction of other *wholes*.

The child's first plaything, or means of occupation, was the *ball*. Next came the *sphere*, similar to, yet so different from the ball. Then followed *cube* and *cylinder*, both, in some points resembling the sphere, yet each having its own peculiarities, which distinguish it from the sphere and ball. The pupil, in receiving the cube, divisible into eight smaller cubes, meets with friends, and is delighted at the multiplicity of the gift. Each of the eight parts is precisely like the whole, except in point of size, and the child is immediately struck with this quality of his first toy for *building purposes*. By simply looking at this gift, the pupil receives the ideas of *whole* and *part*—of *form* and *comparative size*; and by dividing the cube, is impressed with the relation of one part to another in regard to position and order of movements, thus learning readily to comprehend the use of such terms as *above*, *below*, *before*, *behind*, *right*, *left*, etc., etc.

With this and all the following gifts, we produce what Froebel calls *forms of life*, *forms of knowledge*, and *forms of beauty*.

The first are representations of objects which actually *exist*, and which come under our common observation, as the works of human skill and art. The second are such as afford instruction relative to *number*, *order*, *proportion*, etc. The third are figures representing only *ideal forms*, yet so regularly constructed as to present perfect models of *symmetry* and *order* in the arrangement of the parts. Thus in the occupations connected with the use of these simple building blocks, the child is led into the living world—there first to take notice of objects by comparison; then to learn something of their properties by induction, and lastly, to gather into his soul a love and desire for the beautiful by the contemplation of those forms which are regular and symmetrical.

THE PRESENTATION OF THE THIRD GIFT.

The children having taken their usual seats, the teacher addresses them as follows :—

"To-day, we have something new to play with."

Opening the package and displaying the box, he does not at once gratify their curiosity by showing them what it contains, but commences by asking the question :—

"Which one of the three objects we played with yesterday does this box look like?"

They answer readily, "The cube."

"Describe the box as the cube has been described, with regard to its sides, edges, corners, etc."

When this has been satisfactorily done, the box is placed inverted upon the table and the cover removed by drawing it out, which will allow the cubes to stand on the table. Lifting the box carefully, so that the contents may remain entire as in Fig. 1, the teacher asks :—

"What do you see now?"

The answer is as before, "A cube."

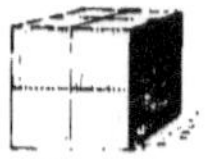

Fig. 1.

One of the scholars is told to push it across the table. In so doing, the parts will be likely to become separated, and that which was previously whole will lie before them in fragments. The children are permitted to examine the small cubes; and after each one of them has had one in his hand, the eight cubes are returned to the teacher who remarks :—

"Children, as we have broken the thing, we must try to *mend* it. Let us see if we can put it together as it was before."

This having been done, the boxes are then distributed among the children, and they are practiced in removing the covers, and taking out the cube without destroying its unity. They will find it difficult at first, and there will be many failures. But let them continue to try until some, at least, have succeeded, and then proceed to another occupation.

PREPARATION FOR CONSTRUCTING FORMS.

The surface of the tables is covered with a net work of lines, forming squares of one-inch. A space including a definite number of squares is allotted to each pupil. In these first conversational lessons, the children must be taught to point out the right upper corner of their table space, the left upper, the right and left lower, the upper and lower edges, the right and left edges, and the center. With little staffs, or sticks cut at convenient lengths, they may indicate direction, by laying them upon the table in a line from left to right, covering the center of the space, or extending them from the right upper to the left lower edge covering the center; then from the middle of the upper edge to the middle of the lower edge, and so on. The teacher must be careful to use terms that can be easily comprehended, and avoid changing them in such a way as to produce any ambiguity in the mind of the child.

Here, as in the more advanced exercises, everything should be done with a great deal of precision. The children must understand that order and regularity in all the performances are of the utmost importance. The following will serve as an illustration of the method: The children having received the boxes, they are required to place them exactly in the center of their spaces, so as to cover four squares. Then take hold of the box with the right hand and inverting it upon the table remove the cover with the left hand by drawing it out from beneath. The right hand is used to raise the box carefully from its place and eight small cubes will stand in the center of the space forming one large cube. Lastly the cover is placed in the box and the box placed in the upper corner of the space allotted to the child.

At the close of any play, when the materials are to be returned to the teacher, the same minuteness of detail must be observed as follows:—

Replace the box over the cubes, and draw toward the edge of the table; then slip the cover beneath, reverse the box and replace the cover.

These are processes which must be repeated many times before the scholar can acquire expertness.

FORMS OF LIFE.

The boxes being opened as directed, and the cubes upon the center squares—in each space— the question is asked:—

"How many little cubes are there?" "Eight."

"Count them, placing them in a row from left to right," (or from right to left).

"What is that?" "A row of cubes."

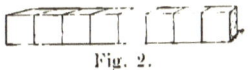

Fig. 2.

It may bear any appropriate name which the children give it—as "a train of cars," "a company of soldiers," "a fence," etc.

"Now count your cubes once more, placing them one upon another. What have you there?"

"An upright row of eight cubes."

"Have you ever seen anything standing like this upright row of cubes?"

"A chimney." "A steeple."

"Take down your cubes, and build two upright rows of them—one square apart. What have you now?"

"Two little steeples," or "two chimneys."

Fig. 3. Thus, with these eight cubes, many forms of life can be built under the guidance of the teacher. It is an important rule in this occupation, that nothing should be rudely destroyed which has been constructed, but each new form is to be produced by slight change of the preceding one.

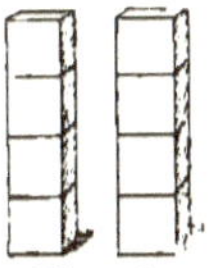

Fig. 4.

A number of these forms are given below. They are designated by Froebel as follows:—

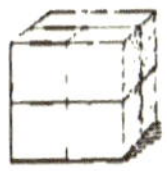

Fig. 5.

Cube or Kitchen Table.

QUARTER CENTURY EDITION

Fig. 6.

Fireplace.

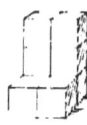

Fig. 7.

Grandpa's Chair.

Fig. 8.

Grandpa's and Grandma's Chairs.

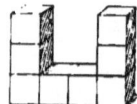

Fig. 9.

A Castle with two towers.

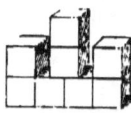

Fig. 10.

A Stronghold.

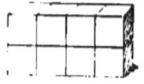

Fig. 11.

A Wall.

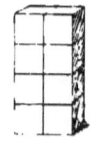

Fig. 12.

A High Wall.

Fig. 13.

Two Columns.

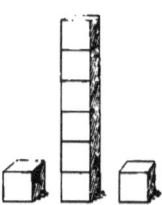

Fig. 14.

A Large Column, with two memorial stones.

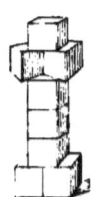

Fig. 15.

Signpost.

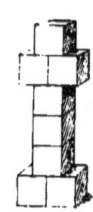

Fig. 16.

Cross.

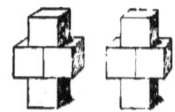

Fig. 17.

Two Crosses.

PARADISE OF CHILDHOOD.

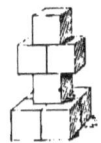

Fig. 18.

Cross, with pedestal.

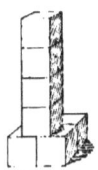

Fig. 19.

Monument.

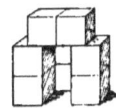

Fig. 20.

Sentry-box.

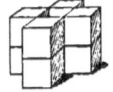

Fig. 21.

A Well.

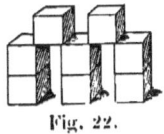

Fig. 22.

City Gate.

Fig. 23.

Triumphal Arch.

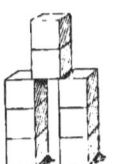

Fig. 24.

City Gate, with tower.

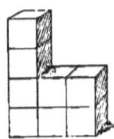

Fig. 25.

Church.

Fig. 26.

City Hall.

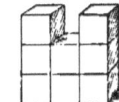

Fig. 27.

Castle.

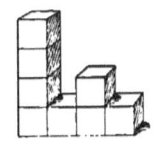

Fig. 28.

A Locomotive.

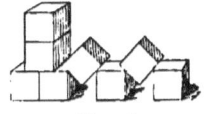

Fig. 29.

Ruin.

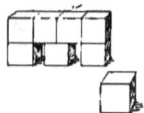

Fig. 30.
Bridge with Keeper's House.

Fig. 31.
Two Rows of Trees.

Fig. 32.
Two Long Logs of Wood.

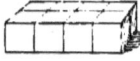

Fig. 33.
A Platform

Fig. 34.
Two Small Logs of Wood.

Fig. 35.
Four Garden Benches.

Fig. 36.
Stairs.

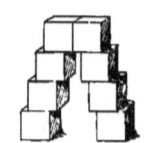

Fig. 37.
Double Ladder.

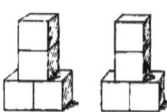

Fig. 38.
Two Columns on pedestals.

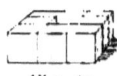

Fig. 39.
Well-trough.

Fig. 40.
Bath.

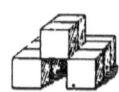

Fig. 41.
A Tunnel.

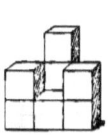

Fig. 42.
Easy Chair.

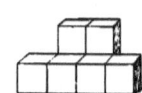

Fig. 43.
Bench with back.

Fig. 44.
Cube.

Several of the names in this list represent objects which, being more specifically German, will not be recognized by the children. Ruins, castles, sentry-boxes, signposts, perhaps they have never seen; but it is easy to tell them something about these objects which will interest them. They will listen with pleasure to short stories, narrated by way of explanation, and thus associating the story with the form, be able, at another time, to reconstruct the latter while they repeat the former in their own words. It is not to be expected, however, that teachers in this country should adhere closely to the list of Fræbel. They may, with advantage, vary the forms, and if they choose, affix other names to those given in these pages. It is well sometimes to adopt such designations as are suggested by the children themselves. They will be found to be quite apt in tracing resemblances between their structures and the objects with which they are familiar.

In order to make the occupation still more useful, they should be required also to point out the dissimilarities existing between the form and that which it represents.

It is proper to allow the child, at times, to *invent* forms, the teacher assisting the fantasy of the little builder in the work of constructing, and in assigning names to the structure. When a figure has been found and named, the child should be required to take the blocks apart, and build the same several times in succession. Older and more advanced scholars suggest to younger and less able ones, and the latter will be found to appreciate such help.

It is a common observation, that the younger children in a family develop more rapidly than the older ones, since the former are assisted in their mental growth by companionship with the latter. This benefit of association is seen more fully in the Kindergarten, under the judicious guidance of a teacher who knows how to encourage what is right, and check what is wrong, in the disposition of the children.

It should be remarked, in connection with these directions, that in the use of this and the succeeding gift it is essential that *all* the blocks should be used in the building of each figure, in order to accustom the child to look upon things as mutually related. There is nothing which has not its appointed place, and each part is needed to constitute the whole. For example, the well-trough (Fig. 39) may be built of six cubes, but the remaining two should represent two pails with which the water is conveyed to the trough.

FORMS OF KNOWLEDGE.

These do not represent objects, either real or ideal. They instruct the pupil concerning the properties and relations of numbers, by a particular arranging and grouping of the blocks. Strictly speaking, the first effort to count, by laying them on the table one after another, is to be classed under this head. The form thus produced, though varied at each trial, is one of the forms of knowledge, and by it the child receives its first lesson in arithmetic.

Proceeding further, he is taught to add, always by using the cubes to illustrate the successive steps. Thus, having placed two of the blocks at a little distance from each other on the table, he is caused to repeat, "One and one are two." Then placing another upon the table, he repeats, "One and two are three," and so on, until all the blocks are added.

Subtraction is taught in a similar manner. Having placed all the cubes upon the table, the scholar commences taking them off, one at a time, repeating, as he does this, "One from eight leaves seven;" "One from seven leaves six," and so on.

According to circumstances, of which the Kindergartner, of course, will be the best judge, these exercises may be continued further, by adding and subtracting two, three and so on; but care should always be taken that no new step be made until all that has gone before is perfectly understood.

With the more advanced classes, exercises in multiplication and division may be tried, by grouping the blocks.

The division of the large cube, to illustrate the principles of proportion, is an interesting and instructive occupation; and we will here proceed to give the method in detail.

The children have their cube of eight before them on the table.

Fig. 45.

The teacher is also furnished with one and lifting the upper half asks:—

Fig. 46.

"Did I take the whole of my cube in my hand, or did I leave some of it on the table?"

"You left some on the table."

"Do I hold in my hand more of my cube than I left on the table, or are both parts alike?"

"Both are alike."

"If things are alike, we call them *equal*. So I divided my cube into two equal parts, and each of these equal parts I call a *half*.

Where are the two halves of my cube?"

"One is in your hand; the other is on the table."

"So I have two *half* cubes. I will now place the half which I have in my hand upon the half standing on the table. What have I now?"

"A whole cube."

The teacher, then separating the cube again into halves, by drawing four of the smaller cubes to the right and four to the left asks :—

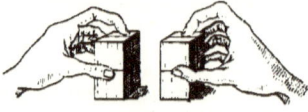

Fig. 47.

"What have I now before me?"

"Two half cubes."

"Before, I had an upper and a lower half. Now, I have a right and a left half. Uniting the halves again I have once more a whole."

The scholars are taught to repeat as follows, while the teacher divides and unites the cubes in both ways, also as represented in Fig. 48 :—

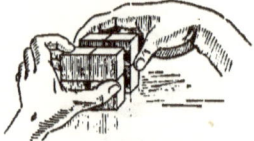

Fig. 48.

"One whole—two halves."

"Two halves—one whole."

Again, *each half* is divided, as shown in Figs. 49, 50 and 51. The children are required to repeat during these occupations :—

Fig. 49.

Fig. 50.

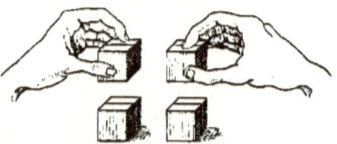

Fig. 51.

"One whole—two halves."

"One half—two quarters (or fourths)."

"Two quarters—one half."

"Two halves—one whole."

After these processes are fully explained and the principles well understood by the scholars, they are to try their hand at dividing of the cube—first, individually then all together. If they succeed, they may then be taught to separate it into eighths. It is not advisable in all cases, to proceed thus far.

Fig. 52.

Children under four years of age should be restricted, for the most part to the use of the cubes for practical building purposes, and for simpler forms of knowledge.

FORMS OF BEAUTY.

Starting with a few simple arrangements, or positions, of the blocks, we are able to develop the forms contained in this class by means of a fixed law, viz., that every change of position is to be accompanied by a corresponding movement on the opposite side. In this way symmetrical figures are constructed in infinite variety, representing no real objects, yet, by their regularity of outline, adapted to please the eye, and minister to a correct artistic taste. The love of the beautiful cannot fail to be awakened in the youthful mind by such an occupation as this, and with this emotion will be associated, to some extent, the love of the good, for they are inseparable.

The works of God are characterized by perfect order and symmetry, and his goodness is commensurate with the beauty manifest everywhere in the fruits of his creative power. The construction of forms of beauty with the building blocks will prepare the child to appreciate, by and by, the order that rules the universe.

These forms are of only one block's height, and, consequently, represent outlines of surfaces. It is necessary that the children should be guided, in their construction, by an easily recognizable center. Around this visible point all the separate parts of the form to be created must be arranged, just as in working out the highest destiny of man, all his thoughts and acts need to be regulated by an invisible center, around which he is to construct a harmonious and beautiful whole.

In order to produce the varied forms of beauty with the simple material placed in the hands of the scholar, he must first learn in what ways two cubes may be brought in contact with each other. Four positions are shown in Figs. 53 to 56. The blocks may be arranged either—side by side, as in Fig. 53; edge to edge, as in Fig. 54; or edge to side, and side to edge, as in Figs. 55 and 56. Figs. 53 and 55 are the opposites to Figs. 54 and 56. Other changes of position may be made. For example, in Fig. 53 the block marked *a* may be placed above or to the right or to the left of the block marked *b*. The cubes may also be placed in certain relations to each other on the table, without being in actual contact. These positions should be practiced perseveringly at the outset, so as to furnish a foundation for the processes of construction which are to follow. It is one of the important features of Froebel's system, that it enables the child readily to discover, and critically to observe, all relations which objects sustain to one another. Thoroughness, therefore, is required in all the details of these occupations.

We start from any fundamental form that may present itself to our mind. Take, for illustration, Fig. 57. Four cubes are here united side to side, constituting a square surface, and the outline is completed by placing the four remaining cubes, severally side to side with this middle square. In Fig. 58, edge touches edge; in Fig. 59, side touches edge, and in Fig. 60, edge touches side midway. Another mode of development is shown in Figs. 61-67.

The four outside cubes move toward the right by a half cube's length, until the original form reappears in Fig. 67.

Now, the four outside cubes occupy the *opposite* position. Fig. 68, edges touch sides. They are moved as before by a half cube's length, until, in Fig. 71, the form with which we started, is regained.

We now extract the inside cubes (*b*). Fig. 75, and each of them travels around its neighbor cube (*a*), until a standing, hollow square is developed, as in Fig. 81.

Now cube *a* again is set in motion. (Fig. 82). It assumes a slanting direction to the remaining cubes, and, pursuing its course around them, the form reappears in Fig. 88.

Next *b* is drawn out, (Fig. 89) and *a* pushed in, until a standing cross is formed, (Fig. 90) *b*, constantly traveling by a half cube's length, until all cubes are united in a large square, (Fig. 95) and *b* again begins traveling, by a cube's length, turning side to side and edge to edge. In Fig. 100, *b* performs as *a* has done.

But with more developed children we may proceed on other principles, Fig. 101, introducing changes only on two instead of four sides, and thus arriving successively at the forms found in Figs. 102-112.

After each occupation, the scholars should replace their cubes in the boxes, as heretofore described, and the material should be returned to the closet where it is kept, before commencing any other play.

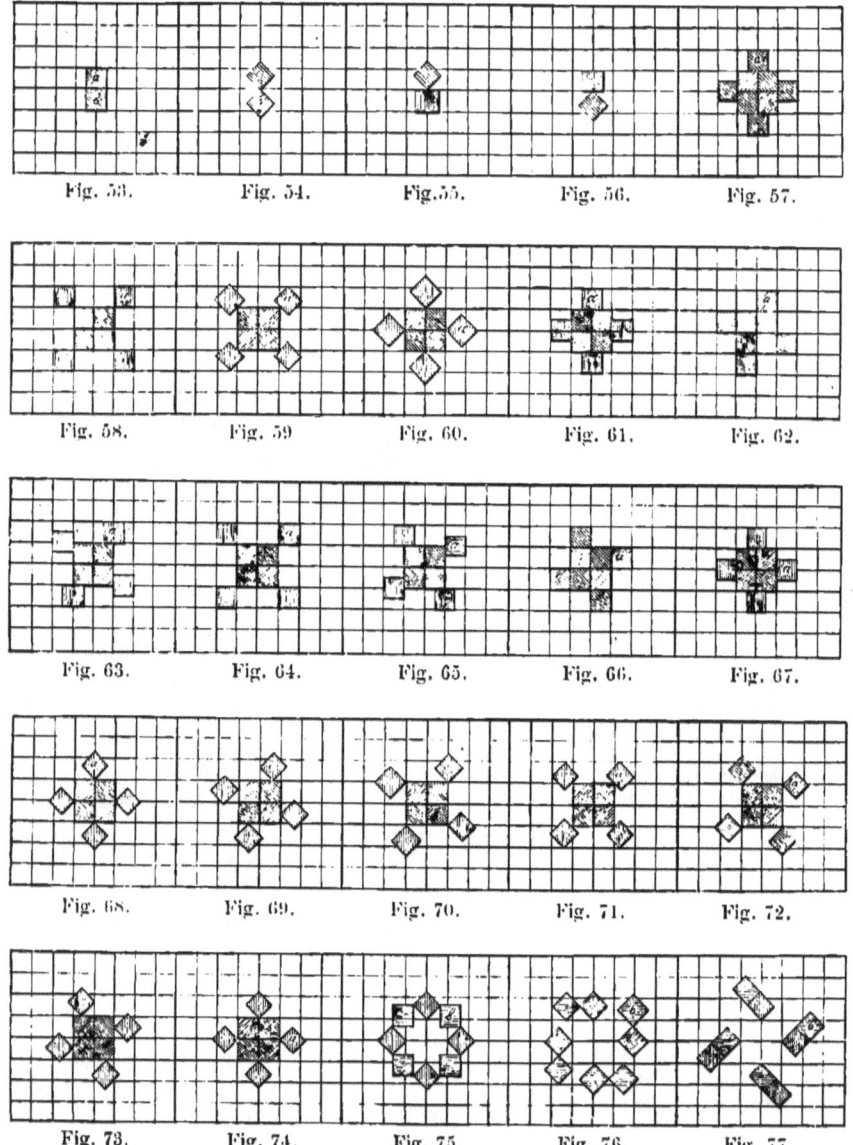

PARADISE OF CHILDHOOD. 103

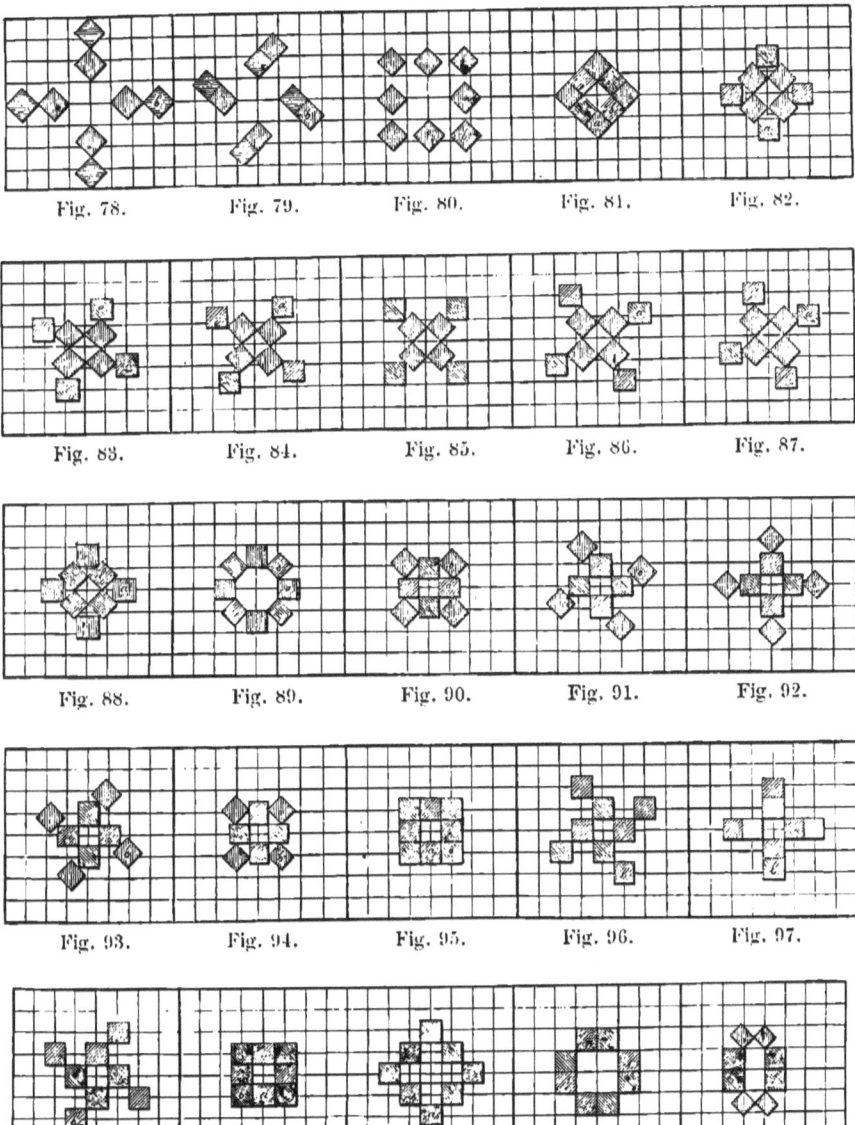

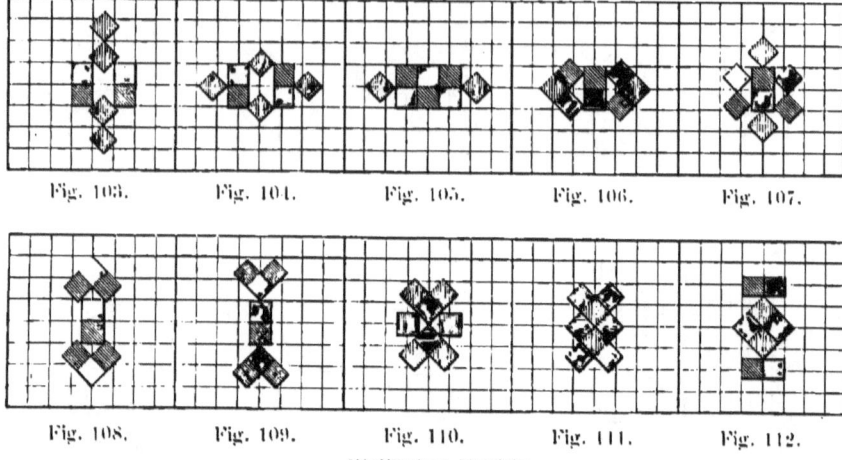

Fig. 103.   Fig. 104.   Fig. 105.   Fig. 106.   Fig. 107.

Fig. 108.   Fig. 109.   Fig. 110.   Fig. 111.   Fig. 112.

EDITOR'S NOTES.

As the best knowledge cannot be attained without division or analysis of a whole, the divided solids follow those which give the impression of wholes. An arbitrary division cannot give clear ideas, so a regular division, according to certain laws, is necessary.

Prominent features of this gift are the likeness of each part of the cube to the whole, and the contrast of size between the cube and its parts. The chief object of the gift is to develop the creative power of the child; so that he is encouraged to follow his instinctive wish to see the construction of things, and begins his investigation of particular phenomena. He divides the cube to find its component parts and examines the pieces. He finds that each part is like the whole, only smaller, so that the impression of this particular form is deepened; he can create many forms and by re-arranging discover new qualities and uses.

The material allows the child to express outwardly his inner conceptions, which is one of the first demands of life. The desire to look at the interior of things is the germ of the fullest development, the beginning of the formation of the scientific mind.

While this gift is similar to the cube of the second in size and material, and interests the child because of this likeness, it is the contrast between the two cubes that holds his attention. Thus he is taken from what he already knows, into a wider field of knowledge.

Let the child compare the two gifts in regard to faces, corners, edges, direction and element of rest; in this way test his memory and lead him to commence a classification of objects by deciding that all bodies of similar proportions and qualities must be cubical in form.

The harmony of the child's development through this gift rests chiefly on the method with which he begins and ends his play with it. If he takes the cube from the box as a whole, it stands before him a type of the unity he would learn about; and if after the play he reconstructs the typical whole, his inner nature is satisfied, for he has proceeded from unity, through his play to unity again; but if he takes the parts out one by one all is confusion, appealing only to the external side of his nature.

In playing, every part should be used, otherwise the material is wasted. The child should early learn that nothing is isolated and unconnected, nothing without its purpose and its appointed use. If all the given material is used the relation of the part to the whole is kept constantly before the mind and eye of the child; each part being of value only as it helps to make the whole complete.

Details in small things are of great importance, and the kindergartner should carefully impress on the child the idea of order and neatness in the taking out and putting away of the cube. As soon as the box containing this gift is given out the child recognizes it as another cube, and the kindergartner should call attention to the paper upon it, compare it with the other boxes, and talk about it. Then placing the box four inches from the front of the table reverse it so that it rests upon the top, draw out the cover, lift the box so as not to disturb the cubes, place the lid diagonally inside and remove the box to give free play for the work. This simple operation gives the child an example of order.

In this first presentation of the divided cube, lead the child to see it as a whole that can be divided into parts, so that he shall get a definite idea of the whole, its parts, of form and comparative size and of the relations of number and position, learning readily to comprehend the use of such terms as front, back, top, bottom, right and left. Review the naming of opposites and the directions of the different lines. Divide the cube in all its various ways, so that it has top and bottom halves, front and back halves and right and left halves; give a simple sequence with a short story, thus: Move the right half of the cube two inches to the right, to make the road which little Mary takes on her way to grandma's in the country. Place the halves together again, and move the left half two inches to the left (the brook which runs by the foot of the meadow where she sails her tiny boat and watches the fishes play). Put the parts together again and remove the top-half, placing it two inches to the back, (two lunch tables in the grove back of the house).

As from the whole to the half, so also proceed from the half to the quarter-cubes by dividing the halves into halves, then to the eighth of the whole cube, by dividing the quarters into halves. Show that two-fourths and four-eighths equal one-half, that two-eighths equal one-quarter, that eight-eighths equal the whole, etc. Of course these progressive steps can only be taken slowly and in accordance with the child's comprehension, the kindergartner making sure that each point is understood, before another is given. For the division of the gift sing the following song to the tune of "All for Baby," in Miss Poulsson's Finger Plays:—

(Whole cube).
    Here is mamma's kitchen,
    Built so close and tight;
(Place the top half on the table against the right of the lower half).
    Here's the breakfast table,
    Which we'll dress in white.
(Draw right-half one inch to the right).
    Now we will divide it,
    See! we have two more;
(Separate these halves right and left).
    Again we will divide it,
    Now we each have four.

    Push back all the back ones,
    Each one from its mate.
    Now if we should count them
    We'll find that we have eight.

    Push them up together
    As they were before.
    One and one are two, and
    Two and two are four.

    Lift the right half up,
    And place it on the top;
    Now our cube is whole
    And, it's time to stop.

The children find pleasure in dividing the cube into its parts, examining each separate piece, and in arranging and re-arranging the eight parts in different ways.

To bring out the number and position of the faces, call the cube a barn; let a little bird fly from the top, another from the front, one from the back, from the right side and from the left. Show the edges and their directions by building walls, platforms and columns of different heights and lengths in different directions, bringing the square faces of the cube so constantly before the child that his concept of a square becomes a true one.

In the use of the building material allow the little children much freedom. Check from the beginning any tendency to knock down any of the forms which they make, and lead them to change one form into another related to it by slight alterations. Keep this up until the child acquires the habit of following this plan. Have them build neatly and accurately according to the measurements of the squared table, as this brings the play building of the child under the fundamental law of all building and its beauty as well as its practicability is soon seen.

To increase the interest of the child, and draw out involuntary freedom, connect the building with his own experiences; connect the forms in his play by a simple story or let a child tell of something he has seen, and illustrate by building the object. Show the different ways cubes may touch each other, as face to face (direction front and back, or right and left); edge to edge, with the corners front, faces front right and left, or front and back; edge to face at the front, back, right and left. To add interest let the children invent and tell a story about the object. They are delighted to see their cube grow into a table, a chair for grandpa, a bed, a church, a bridge, a lighthouse to guide the sailors. These objects they clothe with life, developing their imagination and originality. Thus through this gift the formative and expressed powers of the child are exercised, his judgment and reason are developed and he gains a love of all that is beautiful and harmonious.

THE FOURTH GIFT.

The preceding gift consisted of cubical blocks, all of their three dimensions being the same. In the Fourth Gift, we have greater variety for purposes of construction, since each of the parts of the large cube is an oblong block, whose length is twice its width, and four times its thickness. The dimensions bear the same proportion to each other as those of an ordinary brick; and hence these blocks are sometimes called bricks. They are useful in teaching the child difference in regard to length, breadth, and height. This difference enables him to construct a greater variety of forms than he could by means of the third gift. By these he is made to understand, more distinctly, the meaning of the terms vertical and horizontal. And if the teacher sees fit to pursue the course of experiment sufficiently far, many philosophical truths will be developed; as, for instance, the law of equilibrium, shown by laying one block across another, or the phenomenon of continuous motion, exhibited in the movement of a row of the blocks, set on end, and gently pushed from one direction.

PREPARATION FOR CONSTRUCTING FORMS.

This gift is introduced to the children in a manner similar to the presentation of the third gift. The box is reversed upon the table and the cover is removed. Lifting the box carefully, the cube remains entire. The children are made to observe that, when whole, its size is the same as that of the previous one. Its parts, however, are very different in form, though their number is the same. There are still eight blocks. Let the scholars compare one of the small cubes of the third gift with one of the oblong blocks in this gift; note the similarities and the differences; then, if they can comprehend, that notwithstanding, they are so unlike in *form*, their *solid contents* is the same, since it takes just eight of each to make the same sized cube, an important lesson will have been learned. If told to name objects that resemble the oblong blocks, they will readily designate a *brick, table, piano, closet etc.*, and if allowed to invent forms of life, will doubtless construct *boxes, benches, etc.*

The same precision should be observed in all the details of opening and closing the plays with this gift as in those previously described.

FORMS OF LIFE.

The following is a list of Froebel's forms. If the names do not appear quite striking, or to the point, the teacher may try to substitute better ones:—

Fig. 1.

The Cube.

Fig. 2.

Part of a Floor, or Top of a Table.

Fig. 3.

Two Large Boards.

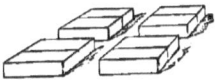

Fig. 4.

Four Small Boards.

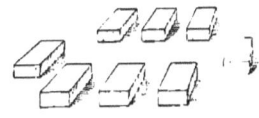

Fig. 5.

Eight Building Blocks.

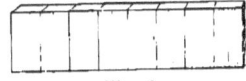

Fig. 6.

A Long Garden Wall.

108 QUARTER CENTURY EDITION

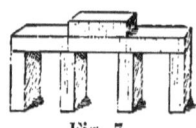

Fig. 7.

A City Gate.

Fig. 8.

Another City Gate.

Fig. 9.

A Bee Stand.

Fig. 10.

A Colonnade.

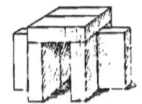

Fig. 11.

A Passage.

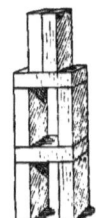

Fig. 12.

Bell Tower.

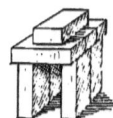

Fig. 13.

Open Garden House.

Fig. 14.

Garden House, with doors.

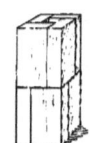

Fig. 15.

A Shaft.

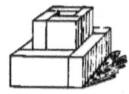

Fig. 16.

Shaft.

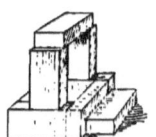

Fig. 17.

A Well, with cover.

PARADISE OF CHILDHOOD.

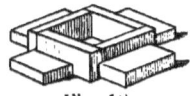

Fig. 18.
A Fountain.

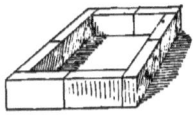

Fig. 19.
Closed Garden Wall.

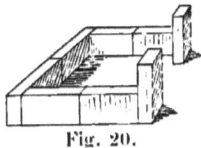

Fig. 20.
An Open Garden.

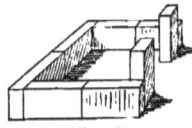

Fig. 21.
An Open Garden.

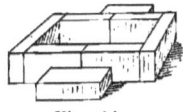

Fig. 22.
Watering Trough.

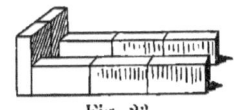

Fig. 23.
Shooting Stand.

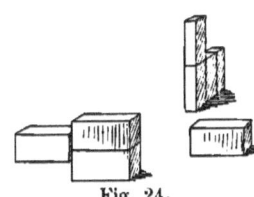

Fig. 24.
Village.

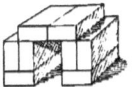

Fig. 25.
Triumphal Arch.

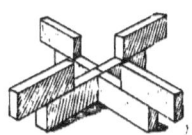

Fig. 26.
Merry-go-round.

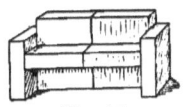

Fig. 27.
Large Garden Settee.

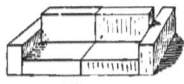

Fig. 28.
Seat.

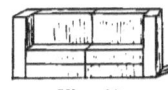

Fig. 29.
Settee.

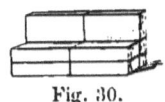

Fig. 30.
Sofa.

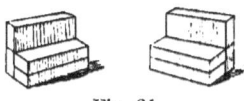

Fig. 31.
Two Chairs.

Fig. 32.
Garden Table and Chairs.

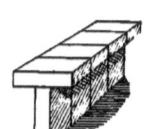

Fig. 33.
Children's Table.

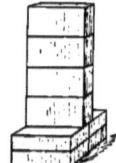

Fig. 34.
Tombstone.

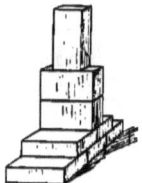

Fig. 35.
Tombstone.

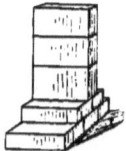

Fig. 36.
Tombstone.

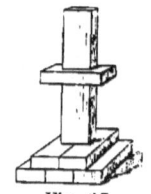

Fig. 37.
Monument.

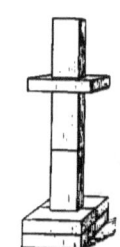

Fig. 38.
Monument.

Fig. 39.
Winding Stairs.

Fig. 40.
Broader Stairs.

Fig. 41.
Stalls.

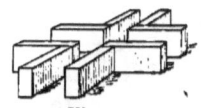

Fig. 42.
A Cross Road.

PARADISE OF CHILDHOOD. 111

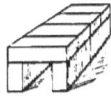

Fig. 43.

Tunnel.

Fig. 44.

Pyramid.

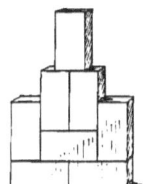

Fig. 45.

Shooting Stand.

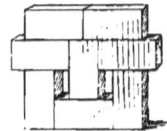

Fig. 46.

Front of a House.

Fig. 47.

Chair, with Footstool.

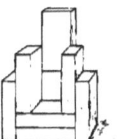

Fig. 48.

A Throne.

Fig. 49.

Fig. 50.

Figs. 49 and 50 are illustrations of Continuous Motion.

Here as in the use of the previous gift, one form is produced from another by slight changes, accompanied by explanations on the part of the teacher. Thus, Fig. 30 is easily changed to Figs. 31, 32, and 33, and Fig. 34 may be changed to Figs. 35, 36, and 37. In every case, all the blocks are to be employed in constructing a figure.

FORMS OF KNOWLEDGE.

This gift like the preceding, is used to communicate ideas of divisibility. Here, however,

Fig. 51.   Fig. 52.

on account of the particular form of the parts, the processes are adapted to illustrate the division of a surface, as well as of a solid body.

Fig. 53.

The cube is arranged so that one vertical and three horizontal cuts appear, (Fig. 51) and the child is then requested to separate it into

Fig. 54.

halves, (Fig. 52) these halves into quarters, (Fig. 53) and these quarters into eighths, (Fig. 54). Each of the latter will be found to be one of the oblong blocks, and this for the time may be made the subject of conversation.
"Of what material is this block made?"
"What is the color?"
"What objects resemble it in form?"
"How many sides has it?"
"Which is the largest side?"
"Which is the smallest side?"
"Is there a side larger than the smallest and smaller than the largest?"

In this way, the scholars learn that there are three kinds of sides, symmetrically arranged in pairs. The upper and lower, the right and left, the front and back, are respectively equal to and like each other.

By questions, or by direct explanation, facts like the following, may be made apparent to the minds of children. "The upper and lower sides of the block are twice as large as the two long sides, or the front and back, as they may be called. Again, the front and back are twice as large as the right and left, or the two short sides of the block. Consequently, the two largest sides are four times as large as the two smallest sides." This can be demonstrated in a very interesting way, by placing several of the blocks side by side, in a variety of positions, and in all these operations the children should be allowed to experiment for themselves. The small cubes of the preceding gift may also with propriety be brought in comparison with the oblong blocks of this gift, and the differences observed.

Fig. 55.

When the single block has been employed to advantage, through several lessons, the whole cube may then be made use of, for the representation of forms of knowledge.

Construct a tablet or plane as in Fig. 55. In order to show the relations of dimension, divide this plane into halves, either by a vertical or horizontal cut, (Figs. 56 and 57). These two forms will give rise to instructive observations and remarks by asking:—
"What was the form of the original tablet?"
"What is the form of its halves?"
"How many times larger is their breadth than their height?"

So with regard to the position of the oblong halves; the one may be said to be *lying* (Fig. 56) while the other is *standing*, (Fig. 57).

Fig. 56.   Fig. 57.

"Change a lying to a standing oblong block." In order to do this, the child will move the first so as to describe a quarter of a circle to the right or left.

Fig. 58.

Unite two blocks by joining their small sides. You then have a large lying oblong block, (Fig. 58).

Fig. 59.

"Separate again (Fig. 59) and divide each part into halves, (Figs. 60 and 61). You have now four parts called quarters, and these are squares, in their surface form."

Fig. 60.

Each of these quarters may be subdivided, and the children taught the method of division

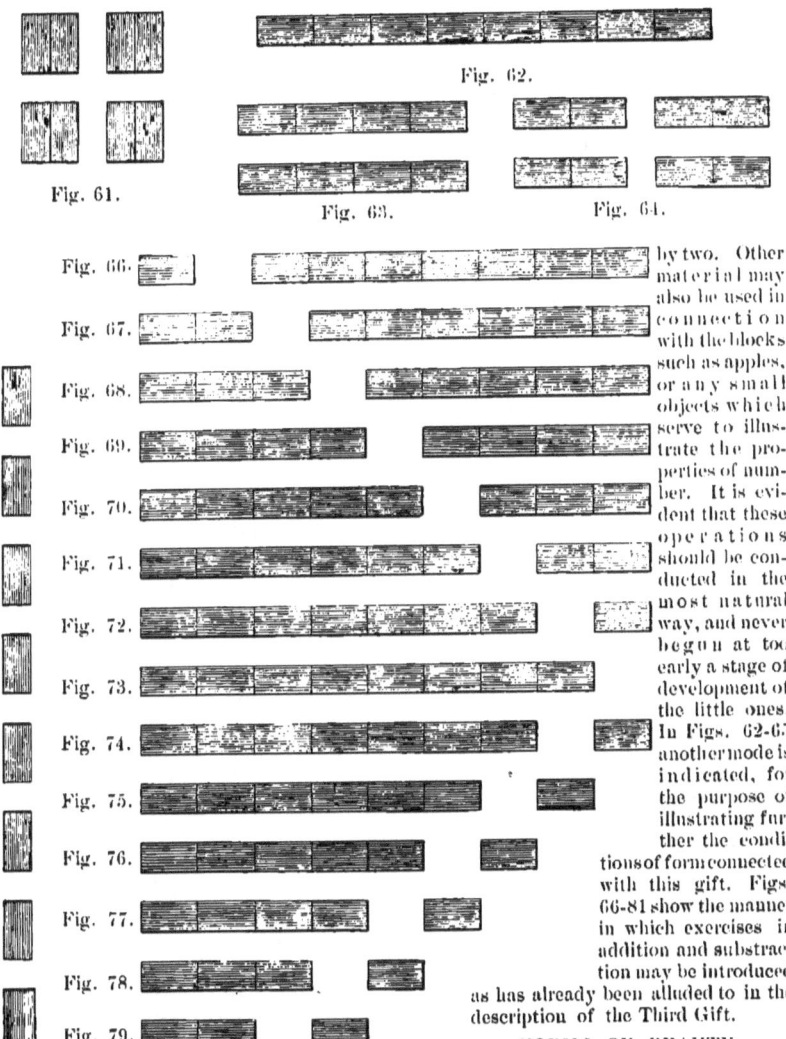

Fig. 62. Fig. 61. Fig. 63. Fig. 64.

Fig. 66. Fig. 67. Fig. 68. Fig. 69. Fig. 70. Fig. 71. Fig. 72. Fig. 73. Fig. 74. Fig. 75. Fig. 76. Fig. 77. Fig. 78. Fig. 79. Fig. 80. Fig. 81.

Fig. 65.

by two. Other material may also be used in connection with the blocks such as apples, or any small objects which serve to illustrate the properties of number. It is evident that these operations should be conducted in the most natural way, and never begun at too early a stage of development of the little ones. In Figs. 62-65 another mode is indicated, for the purpose of illustrating further the conditions of form connected with this gift. Figs. 66-81 show the manner in which exercises in addition and substraction may be introduced as has already been alluded to in the description of the Third Gift.

FORMS OF BEAUTY.

We first ascertain, as in the case of the cubes, the various modes in which the oblong blocks can be brought in relation to each other. These are much more numerous than in the

Third Gift, because of the greater variety in the dimensions of the parts. In the following designs a number of forms of beauty are shown derivable from the original form, (Fig. 82). Each two blocks form a separate group, which four groups touching in the center, form a large square. The outside blocks (*a*) move in Figs. 83-90, around the stationary middle.

The inside blocks (*b*) are now drawn out (Fig. 91) then the blocks (*a*) united to form a hollow square (Fig. 92) around which *b* moves gradually (Figs 93 and 94).

Now *b* is combined into a cross with open center, *a* goes out (Fig. 95) and moves in an opposite direction until Fig. 98 appears.

By extricating *b* the eight-rayed star (Fig. 99) is formed. In Fig. 100 *a* revolves, *b* is drawn out until edge touches edge and thus the form of a flower appears (Fig. 101).

Now *b* is turned (Fig. 102) and in Fig. 103, a wreath is shown. In Fig. 103 the inside edges touch each other; in Fig. 104, inside and outside; in Fig. 105 edges with sides, and *b* is united to a large hollow square, around which *a* commences a regular moving. In Fig. 110, *a* is finally united to a lying cross, and thereby another starting-point gained for a new series of developments.

Each of these figures can be subjected to a variety of changes by simply placing the blocks on their long or short sides, or as the children will say, by letting them *stand up* or *lie down*. The network of lines on the table is to be the constant guide, in the construction of forms. In inventing a new series, place a block above, below, at the right or left of the center; and a second opposite and equidistant. A third and a fourth are placed at the right and left of these, but in the same position relative to the center. The remaining four are placed symmetrically about those first laid. By moving the *a*'s or *b*'s regularly in either direction, a variety of figures may be formed.

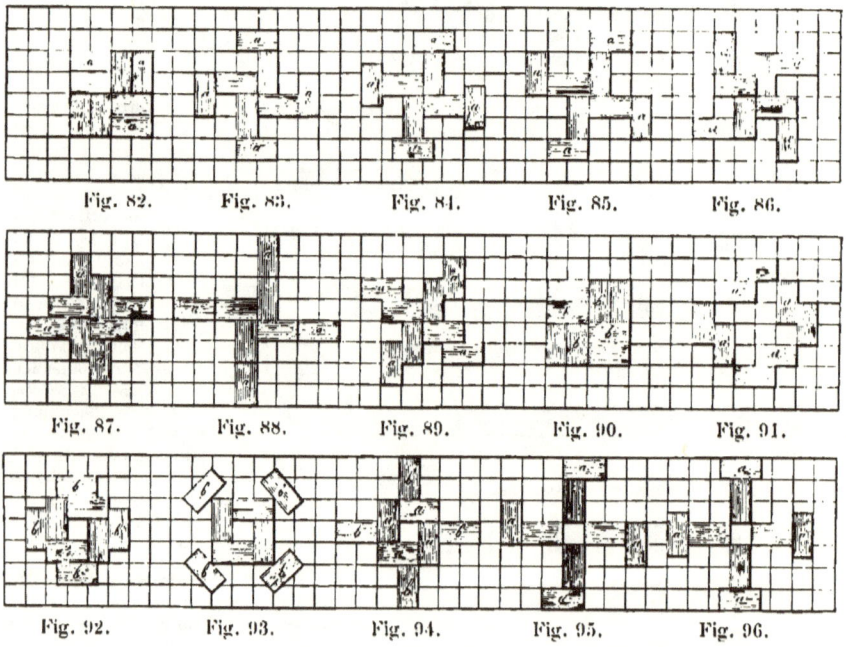

Fig. 82. Fig. 83. Fig. 84. Fig. 85. Fig. 86.

Fig. 87. Fig. 88. Fig. 89. Fig. 90. Fig. 91.

Fig. 92. Fig. 93. Fig. 94. Fig. 95. Fig. 96.

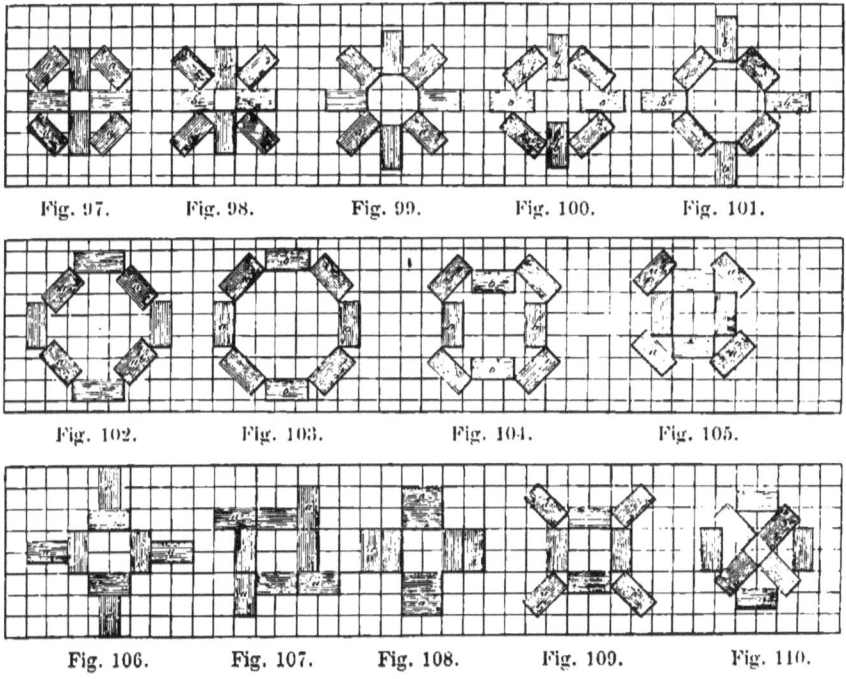

Fig. 97. Fig. 98. Fig. 99. Fig. 100. Fig. 101.
Fig. 102. Fig. 103. Fig. 104. Fig. 105.
Fig. 106. Fig. 107. Fig. 108. Fig. 109. Fig. 110.

EDITOR'S NOTES.

While we find that the eight equal parts of the third gift are of the same form as the whole, this gift shows eight parts in the form of parallelopipeds–solids, with three unequal dimensions, which constitute the chief characteristic of the gift, and adds to both gift and play a new and original importance.

In this as in all the building gifts, every part should be used, and when the boxes have been distributed they should be opened in such a way that the cube stands before the child as a whole, so that he may begin his work as a whole. Call attention to its being divided according to a new plan, and to the form of the component parts, which the child easily recognizes as being that of a brick.

Let a cube of the third gift be handed to the children so that they may compare it with the oblong brick of this gift; ask for similarities and differences; the unequal dimensions in these bricks make it necessary for the child to proceed with more reflection, to compare, and to experiment, in order to produce a symmetrical result. If two cubes are given, the children will readily see that two bricks laid one above the other are just as large as two cubes laid side by side, and in this way the truth is made evident that the solid contents are the same.

While in the third gift the solid appears most prominently, in this gift the idea of surface is suggested. Every face is an oblong, and the variety of size makes more clear the form itself, so the child gains as true a concept of an oblong as of a square.

To impress on the child the differences of position which each brick can occupy, let the bricks stand, as soldiers, sit or lie flat, as if asleep. Give the child a cube, and ask him to do the same with that. He finds it always remains the same on whichever of its faces it may rest; thus new lessons are taught him, and he is made to understand length and breadth more clearly. The different dimensions in the bricks make the variety and number of possible figures with this gift almost incalculable. Many philosophical truths may be illustrated, as the law of equilibrium—when a narrow face has to support a broader one; or continuous motion—by setting a row of blocks on end, and pushing the first one against the other, causing the whole row to fall.

As an exercise in the relation of size, let the children separate the cube into halves, which may be done by a vertical or horizontal division, and gives rise to suggestive questions and instructive observations; these halves may be separated again and divided into quarters, and again into eighths; in this manner the children are brought to comprehend successive divisions by two. These exercises admit of many variations.

Let the pupils find the different ways in which two bricks may be placed with regard to each other, and build forms while the teacher talks with them about the objects represented, so as to awaken thought within them.

Let the children work out for themselves with the blocks, a sequence of moves illustrating a story, or a sequence of thought given by the teacher. In this way they come to know the form as regards dimensions, faces and relation of parts to the whole.

A fresh delight comes to the child when he discovers how one object may be transformed into another, and particularly when there is some connection between each new figure and the child himself, who must have a clear insight into the most simple and natural relations of things, that the sight of things more complicated may not confuse him and hinder his development. The following sequences are suggestive and render it easy to find such connections.

FURNITURE SEQUENCE.

BUREAU.—Cube, with cut running right and left. Draw the front half away. Let a brick stand at either end of the back half touching it by the broad face. Join the two remaining bricks by their long narrow faces and place on top for a mirror, Fig. 111.

WASHSTAND.—Let the two bricks which formed the mirror stand directly back of the lying bricks, touching them by their broad faces. Let the top brick sit on the standing back bricks, Fig. 112.

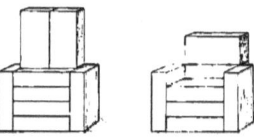

Fig. 111.   Fig. 112.

WRITING-DESK.—Lift sitting brick in the right hand, and the two bricks below it in the left hand. Let the two bricks lie on the remaining pile, projecting an inch in front, the cut running front and back. Let the remaining brick sit on them at the back, so its broad face coincides with their short faces, Fig. 113.

HAT-RACK.—Lift the three bricks just placed. Let two stand at the back as before. Lift the top brick, join it to the remaining brick by long narrow faces, and let them sit on the back bricks, Fig. 114.

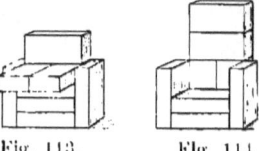

Fig. 113.   Fig. 114.

CHAIR AND TABLE.—Join right and left bricks by their broad faces. Let them lie, right and left, two inches in front of form. Lift the two top bricks and let them lie across the two front bricks, the cut running front and back, Fig. 115.

TWO CHAIRS.—Make a chair of the front bricks, facing and similar to the chair of the four back bricks, Fig. 116.

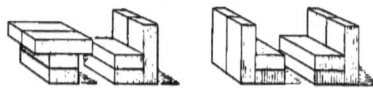

Fig. 115.   Fig. 116.

BED.—Remove the back of the front chair. Place the top brick in the back chair cushion, so that it touches the standing bricks by its broad face. Place the top front brick so that its

PARADISE OF CHILDHOOD. 117

broad face coincides with the narrow front face of the brick below it. Fit in the remaining

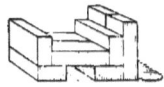

Fig. 117.

bricks for a mattress, the cut running front and back, Fig. 117. Then comes the orderly building of the cube.

BAKER SEQUENCE.

SHOP.—Cube, cut running right and left, Fig. 118.

EIGHT DRAWERS.—Remove the front half, placing it one inch to the right of the back half, in similar position, Fig. 119.

 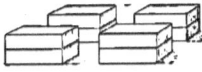

Fig. 118.   Fig. 119.

TWO COUNTERS.—Let the right and left bricks touch by their short faces. Place the top half two inches in front of the lower half, running right and left, Fig. 120.

FOUR LOAVES.—Draw the two back right bricks one inch to the right. The front bricks the same, Fig. 121.

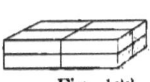 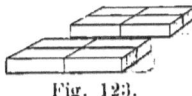

Fig. 120.   Fig. 121.

TABLE.—Push the bricks together forming a prism 4 x 1 x 1, Fig. 122.

BAKING SHEETS.—Place the top half two inches back of the lower half, Fig. 123.

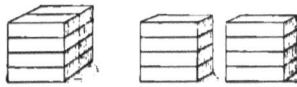

Fig. 122.   Fig. 123.

MOLDING BOARD.—Push the front and back halves together, Fig. 124.

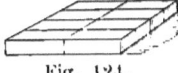

Fig. 124.

ROLLING PIN.—Place the two front right bricks at the right of and touching the back right bricks by their short faces. Place front left brick at the right of those just placed, the short faces just touching. Place the remaining brick at the left in a similar position, Fig. 125.

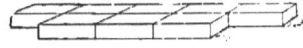

Fig. 125.

MIXING TROUGH.—Join the two end bricks by their short faces and let them sit back of the four left hand bricks touching by broad faces. Let the two front left bricks sit opposite those just placed. Take one of the right hand bricks in each hand, and let them sit at either end of the trough, closing the opening, Fig. 126.

FLOUR SCOOPS.—Draw the right half, one inch to the right, Fig 127.

Fig. 126.   Fig. 127.

WAGON.—Place the left-hand brick directly at the left of the right half, so that it shall touch it with the broad face. Remove the brick lying at the left between the two sitting bricks, and place it front and back across the middle of the wagon. The two remaining left bricks serve as horses, Fig. 128.

Fig. 128.   Fig. 129.

MONEY CHEST.—Lift one of the left hand bricks in each hand, place one right and left of the wagon seat, touching it by long narrow faces. This lid may be raised or lowered at will, Fig. 129. Return to cube.

HOUSE BUILDING AND FURNISHING SEQUENCE.

HOUSE.—Cube with the cutting right and left, Fig. 130.

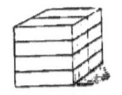 

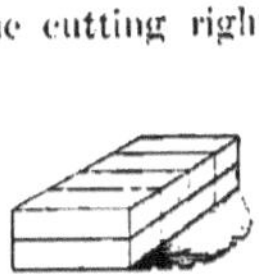

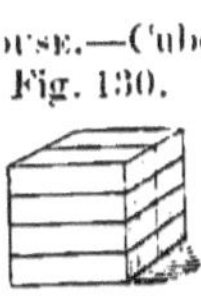

Fig. 130.   Fig. 131.

PIAZZA.—Lift the top half, place it directly in front of and touching the lower half, cut running right and left, Fig. 131.

OPEN DOOR.—Lift the two front bricks, and let them stand on the back brick, one inch apart, with the long narrow faces in front. Lift the top front brick and let it lie across the standing bricks, Fig. 132.

FOUR TABLES.—Move the five back bricks one inch back, move the front brick one inch front. Place the brick which forms the top of the door on the front brick, touching it by the broad face. Join the standing bricks by broad faces and let them lie one inch back of the back bricks, Fig. 133.

 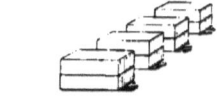

Fig. 132.   Fig. 133.

CAR-SEATS.—Let the upper back brick sit directly behind the lower back brick. Arrange remaining bricks in like manner, Fig. 134.

TWO LONG SEATS.—Lift the back seat, placing it beside the seat directly in front of it, so that they will touch by short faces. Join the two remaining seats in like manner, Fig. 135.

 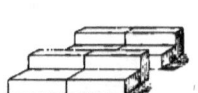

Fig. 134.   Fig. 135.

SOFA, WITH ARMS AND TABLE.—Remove the front, sitting bricks, and let one sit at either end of the back seat touching it by broad faces, the short faces being in front. Let two front bricks touch one another by broad faces, forming the table, Fig. 136.

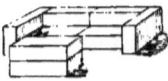

Fig. 136.

TWO SEATS WITH ARMS.—Draw three right hand bricks, two inches to the right. Let the brick which forms the top of the table, sit at the left hand end of the bricks just moved, touching them by broad faces. Left hand section the same, Fig. 137.

Fig. 137.

TWO MARBLE BASINS.—Draw out the brick which forms the right-hand seat, and let it sit one inch in front of the back brick, similar position. Left hand section the same, Fig. 138.

TWO WINDOWS.—Holding the right-hand bricks firmly together, place them in an upright

Fig. 138.

position, so that the bricks which were right and left, form the top and bottom of a window. Same with the left bricks, Fig. 139.

HIGH WINDOW.—Place the left-hand window on top of the right-hand window, Fig. 140.

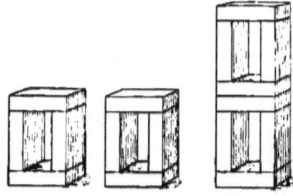

Fig. 139.   Fig. 140.

VESTIBULE.—Place the top half of the window directly in front of and touching the lower half, Fig. 141.

BAND STAND.—Let the two top bricks lie directly in front of and touching the lower bricks. Remove the standing bricks. Let one lie right and left across the cut between the two front bricks, another across the cut between the two back bricks. Let the two remaining bricks lie across the opening front and back, Fig. 142. Return to cube.

Fig. 141.   Fig. 142.

The children take pleasure in uniting, and building with this gift ; also, with the third and fourth combined, when they have become sufficiently acquainted with each separately ; combining the gifts gives them an opportunity of comparing the cube and brick more closely, and so learn their properties and peculiarities better, than by the use of each separately.

One will build a church, another a stove, a shop or house, and so a group of children will have a unity of purpose which is harmonizing in its effects.

THE FIFTH GIFT.

CUBE, TWICE DIVIDED IN EACH DIRECTION.

ALL gifts used as occupation material in the Kindergarten develop, as previously stated, one from another. The Fifth Gift, like that of the Third and Fourth Gifts, consists of a cube again, although larger than the previous ones. The cube of the Third Gift was divided *once* in all directions. The natural progress from 1 is to 2; hence the cube of the Fifth Gift is divided *twice* in all directions; consequently, in *three equal parts*, each consisting of *nine* smaller cubes of *equal size*. But as this division would only have multiplied, not diversified, the occupation material, it was necessary to introduce a new element, by sub-dividing some of the cubes in a slanting direction.

We have heretofore introduced only vertical and horizontal lines. These opposites, however, require their mediate element, and this mediation was already indicated in the forms of life and of beauty of the Third and Fourth Gifts, when side and edge, or edge and side, were brought to touch each other. The slanting direction appearing there transitionally—occasionally—here, becomes permanent by introducing the slanting line, separated by the division of the body, as a bodily reality.

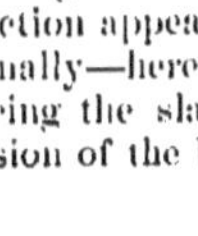

Fig. 1.

Three of the part cubes of the Fifth Gift are divided into half cubes, three others into quarter cubes, so that there are left twenty-one whole cubes of the twenty-seven, produced by the division of the cube mentioned before, and the whole Gift consists of thirty-nine single pieces.

It is most convenient to pack them in the box, so as to have all half and quarter cubes and three whole cubes in the bottom row, as in Fig. 1, which only admits of separating the whole cube in the various ways required hereafter, as it will also assist in placing the cube upon the table, which is done in the same manner as described with the previous Gifts.

The first practice with this Gift is like that with others introduced thus far. Led by the question of the teacher, the pupils state that this cube is larger than their other cubes; and the manner in which it is divided will next attract their attention. They state how many times the cube is divided in each direction, how many parts we have if we separate it according to these various divisions, and carrying out what we say gives them the necessary assistance for answering these questions correctly. In Fig. 2 the three parts of the cube have been separated and laid side by side.

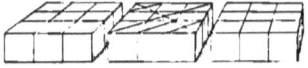

Fig. 2.

These three squares we can again divide in three parts, and these latter again in three, so that then we shall have twenty-seven parts, which teaches the pupil that 3×3=9, 3×9 =27.

To some, the repetition of the apparently simple exercises may appear superfluous; but repetition alone, in this simple manner, will assist children to remember, and it is always interesting, as they have not to deal with abstractions, but have real things to look at for the formation of their conclusions.

But, again I say, do not continue these occupations any longer than you can command the attention of your pupils by them. As soon as signs of fatigue or lack of interest become manifest, drop the subject at once, and leave the Gift to the pupils for their own amusement. If you act according to this advice, your pupils never will overexert themselves, and will always come with enlivened interest to the same occupation whenever it is again taken up.

After the children have become acquainted with the manner of division of their new large cube, and have exercised with it in the above-mentioned way, their attention is drawn to the shape of the divided half and quarter cubes.

They are divided by means of *slanting lines*, which should be made particularly prominent, and the pupils are then asked to point out, on the whole cubes, in what manner they were divided in order to form half and quarter cubes. The pupils also point out horizontal, vertical and slanting lines which they observe in things in the room or other near objects.

Take the two halves of your cube apart and say, "How many corners and angles can you count on the upper and lower sides of these two half cubes?" "Three." Three corners and three angles, which latter, you recollect, are the insides of corners. We call therefore, the upper and lower side of the half cube a triangle, which simply means a side or plane with *three* angles. The child has now enriched its knowledge of lines by the introduction of the oblique or slanting line, in addition to the horizontal and vertical lines, and of sides or planes by the introduction of the triangle, in addition to the square and oblong previously introduced. With the introduction of the triangle, a great treasure for the development of forms is added, on account of its frequent occurrence as elementary forms in all the many formations of regular objects.

The child is expected to know this Gift now sufficiently to employ it for the production of the various forms of life and beauty to be introduced.

FORMS OF LIFE.

The main condition here, as always, is that for each representation the whole of the occupation material be employed; not that only one object should always be built, but in such manner that remaining pieces be always used to represent accessory parts, although apart from, yet in a certain relation to the main position actively and effectively in relation to some greater whole.

Nor should it be forgotten that nothing should be destroyed, but everything produced by rebuilding. It is advisable always to start with the figure of the cube.

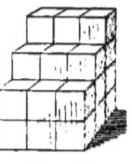

Fig. 4.

Flower-stand.

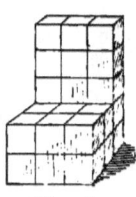

Fig. 5.

Large Chair.

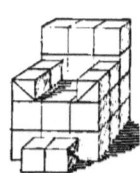

Fig. 6.

Easy Chair, with Foot Bench.

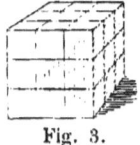

Fig. 3.

Cube.

figure. The child should, again and again, be reminded that nothing belonging to a whole is, or could be, allowed to be superfluous, but that each individual part is destined to fill its

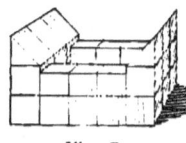

Fig. 7.

A Bed. Lowest row, fifteen whole cubes; second row, six whole and six half cubes composed of twelve quarter cubes; third row, six half cubes.

PARADISE OF CHILDHOOD.   121

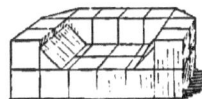

Fig. 8.

Sofa. First row, sixteen whole and two half cubes.

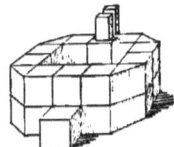

Fig. 9.

A Well.

Fig. 10.

House, with Yard. First row, twelve whole cubes; second row, nine whole and six half cubes; roof, twelve quarter cubes.

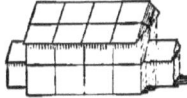

Fig. 11.

A Peasant's House. First row, ten whole cubes; second row, eight whole and two half cubes; roof, three whole, four half and twelve quarter cubes.

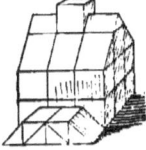

Fig. 12.

Schoolhouse. First row, nine whole and six quarter cubes; second row, nine whole cubes; third row, three whole and six half cubes; fourth row, six quarter cubes.

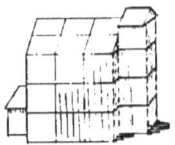

Fig. 13.

Church. Building itself, eighteen whole cubes; roof, twelve quarter cubes; steeple, three whole cubes, and three half cubes; vestry three half cubes.

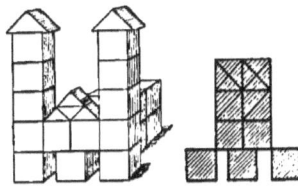

Fig. 14.   Fig. 15.

Body of Church. Eight whole, four half and eight quarter cubes; steeples, twice five whole and two half cubes; between steeples, three whole and four quarter cubes. Fig. 15, ground plan.

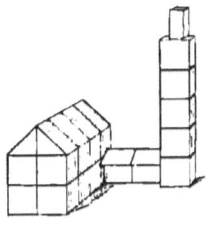

Fig. 16.

Factory, with Chimney and Boiler-house. Factory, sixteen whole cubes; roof, six half and four quarter cubes; chimney, five whole and two quarter cubes; boiler-house, four quarter cubes; roof, two quarter cubes.

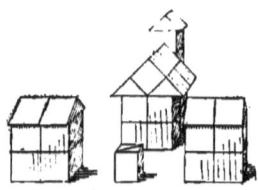

Fig. 17.

Chapel, with Hermitage.

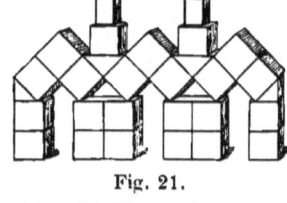

Fig. 21.

City Gate, with Three Entrances.

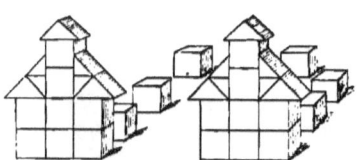

Fig. 18.

Two Garden Houses, with Rows of Trees.

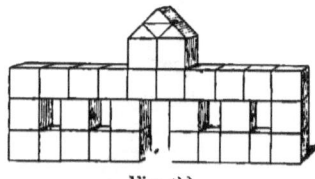

Fig. 22.

Arsenal.

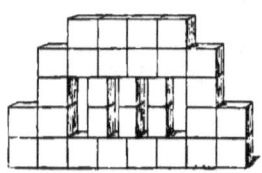

Fig. 19.

A Castle.

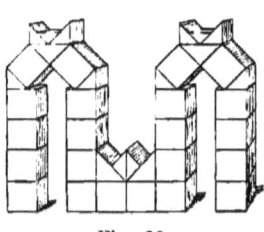

Fig. 20.

Cloister in Ruins.

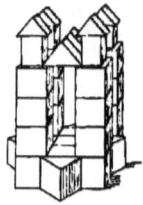

Fig. 24.

A Monument. First row, nine whole and four half cubes; second to fourth row, each, four whole cubes; on either side, two quarter cubes, united to a square column, and to unite the four columns, two half cubes.

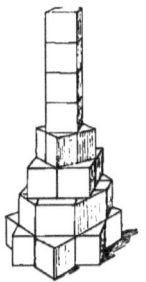

Fig. 25.

A Monument. First row, nine whole and four quarter cubes; second row, five whole and four half cubes; third row, four whole cubes; fourth row, two half and four quarter cubes.

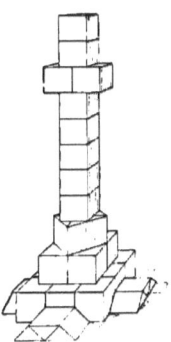

Fig. 26.

A Large Cross. First row, nine whole and four times three quarter cubes; second row, four whole cubes; third row, four half cubes.

Tables, chairs, sofas and beds, are the first objects the child builds. They are the objects with which he is most familiar. Then the child builds a house, in which he lives, speaking of kitchen, sleeping-room, parlor, and eating-room, when representing it. Soon the realm of his ideas widens. It roves into garden, street, etc., It builds the church, the schoolhouse, where the older brothers and sisters are instructed; the factory, and arsenal, from which, at noon and after the days's work is over, so many laborers walk out to their homes to eat their dinner and supper, to rest from their work, and to play with their little children. The ideas which the children receive of all these objects by this occupation, grow more correct by studying them in their details, where they meet with them in reality. In all this they are, as a matter of course, to be assisted by the instructive conversation of the teacher. It is not to be forgotten that the teacher may influence the minds of the children very favorably, by relating short stories about things and persons in connection with the object represented. Not their minds alone are to be disciplined; their hearts are to be developed, and each beautiful and noble feeling encouraged and strengthened.

Be it remembered again that it is not necessary that the teacher should always follow the course of development shown in the figures on our pages. Every course is acceptable, if only destruction is prevented and rebuilding adhered to. Some of the figures may not be familiar to some of the children. The one has never seen a castle or a city gate, a well or a monument. Short descriptive stories about such objects will introduce the child into a new sphere of ideas, and stimulate the desire to see and hear more and more, thus adding daily and hourly, to the stock of knowledge of which he is already possessed. Thus, these plays will not only cultivate the manual dexterity of the child, develop his eye, excite his fantasy, strengthen his power of invention, but the accompanying oral illustrations will also instruct him, and create in him a love for the good, the noble, the beautiful.

The Fifth Gift is used with children from five to six years old, who are expected to be in their third year in the Kindergarten.

A box, with its contents stands on the table before each child. They empty the box as heretofore described, so that the bottom row of the cube, containing the half and quarter cubes, is made the top row.

"What have you now?"

"A cube."

"We will build a church. Take off all quarter and half cubes, and place them on the table before you in good order. Move the three whole cubes of the upper row together, so that they are all to the left of the other cubes. Take three more whole cubes from the right side, and put them beside the three cubes which were left of the upper row. Take the three remaining cubes, which were on the right side, and add them to the quarter and half cubes. What have you now?"

"A house without roof, three cubes high, three cubes long and two cubes broad."

"We will now make the roof. Place on each of the six upper cubes a quarter cube with its largest side. Fill up the space between each two quarter cubes with another quarter cube, and place another quarter cube on top of it. What have you now?"

"A house with roof."

"How many cubes are yet remaining?"

"Three whole and six half cubes."

"Take the whole cubes, and place them one on top of the other, before the house. Add another cube, made of two half cubes, and cover the top with half a cube for a roof. What have you now?"

"A steeple."

"We will employ the remaining three half cubes to build the entrance. Take two of the half cubes, form a whole cube of them, and place it on the other side of the house, opposite the steeple, and lay upon it the last half cube as a roof. What have we built now?"

"A church with steeple and entrance." (Fig. 13).

FORMS OF KNOWLEDGE.

The representation of the forms of knowledge, to which the Fifth Gift offers opportunity, is of great advantage for the development of the child. To superficial observers, it is true, it may appear as if Frœbel not only ascribed too much importance to the mathematical element to the disadvantage of others, but that mathematics necessarily require a greater maturity of understanding than could be found with children of the Kindergarten age. But who thinks of introducing mathematics as a science? Many a child, five or six years of age, has heard that the moon revolves around the earth, that a locomotive is propelled by steam, and that lightning is the effect of electricity. These astronomical, dynamic and physical facts have been presented to him as mathematical facts are presented to his observation in Frœbel's Gifts. Most assuredly it would be folly, if one would introduce in the Kindergarten, mathematical problems in the usual abstract manner. In the Kindergarten, the child beholds the bodily representation of an expressed truth, recognizes the same, receives it without difficulty, without overtaxing its developing mind in any manner whatsoever. Whatever would be difficult for the child to derive from the mere word, nay, which might under certain circumstances be hurtful to the young mind, is taught naturally and in an easy manner by the forms of knowledge, which thus become the best means of exercising the child's power of observation, reasoning, and judging. Beware of all problems and abstractions. The child builds, forms, sees, observes, compares, and then expresses the truth it has ascertained. By repetition, these truths, acquired by the observation of facts, become the child's mental property, and this is not to be done hurriedly, but during the last two years in the Kindergarten and afterwards in the Primary Department.

The first seven forms of knowledge (Figs. 27-33) show the regular divisions of the cube in three, nine and twenty-seven parts. In either case, a whole cube was employed, and yet the forms produced by division are different. This shows that the contents may be equal, when forms are different. (Figs. 28, 29, 30, 31 and 32).

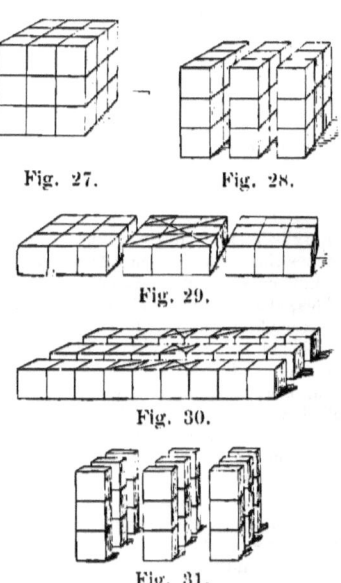

Fig. 27.   Fig. 28.

Fig. 29.

Fig. 30.

Fig. 31.

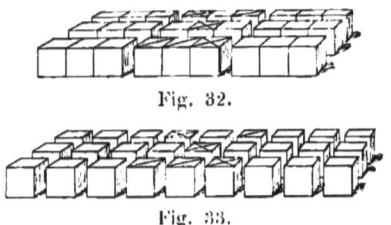

Fig. 32.

Fig. 33.

This difference becomes still more obvious if the three parts of Fig. 28 are united to a standing oblong, or those of Fig. 29 to a lying oblong, or if a single long beam is formed of Fig. 30.

"Take a cube children, place it before you, and also a cube divided in two halves, and place the two halves with their triangular planes or sides, one upon another."

These two halves united are just as large as the whole cube.

But the two halves may be united, also, in other ways. They may touch each other with their quadratic and right angular planes.

Represent these different ways of uniting the two halves of the cube simultaneously. Notwithstanding the difference in the forms, the contents of mass of matter remained the same.

In a still more multiform manner, this fact may be illustrated with the cubes divided in four parts. Similar exercises follow now with the whole Gift, and the children are led to find out all possible divisions in two, three, four, five, nine and twelve equal parts. (Figs. 34-44).

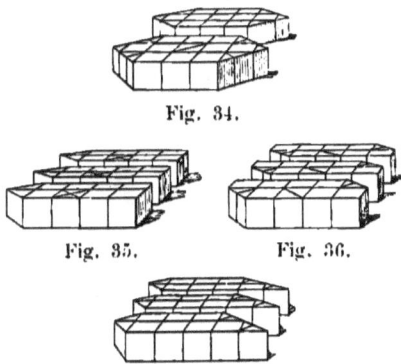

Fig. 34.

Fig. 35.   Fig. 36.

Fig. 37.

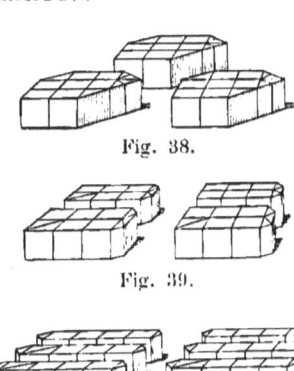

Fig. 38.

Fig. 39.

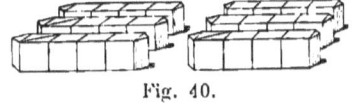

Fig. 40.

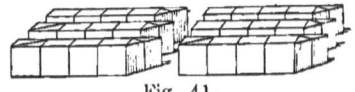

Fig. 41.

Fig. 42.

Fig. 43.

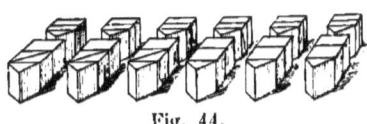

Fig. 44.

After each such division the equal parts are to be placed one upon another, for dividing and separating are always to be followed by a process of combining and reuniting. The child thus receives every time, a transformation of the whole cube, representing the same amount of matter in various forms. (Figs. 45-48).

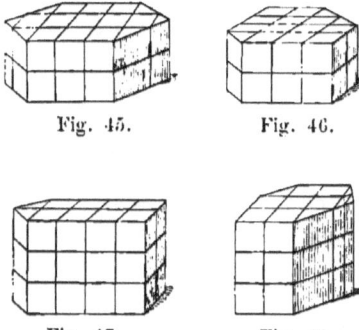

Fig. 45.   Fig. 46.

Fig. 47.   Fig. 48.

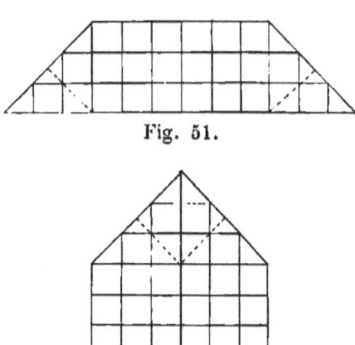

Fig. 51.

Fig. 52.

The child should also be allowed to compare with each other the various thirds, quarters, or sixths, into which whole cubes can be divided, as shown in Figs. 35, 36, 37, 38, or 40, 41 and 42.

It is understood that all these exercises should be accompanied by the living word of the teacher; for thereby, only, will the child become perfectly conscious of the ideas received from perception, and the opportunity is offered to perfect and multiply them. The teacher should, however, be careful not to speak too much, for it is only necessary to keep the attention of the pupil to the object represented, and to render impressions more vivid.

The divisions introduced heretofore, are followed by representations of regular mathematical figures, (planes), as shown in Figs. 49-52. The manner in which one is formed from the preceding one is easily seen from the figures themselves.

As mentioned before, part of the occupation described in the preceding pages, is to be introduced in the Primary Department only, where it is combined with other interesting but more complicated exercises. Simply to indicate how advantageously this Gift may be used for instruction in geometry in later years, we have added Fig. 56, the representation of which shows the child the visible proof of the well-known Pythagorean axiom, by which the theoretical, abstract solution of the same, certainly, can alone be facilitated.

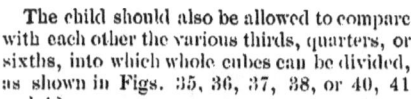

Fig. 49.

Fig. 50.

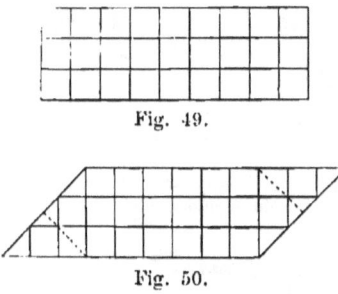

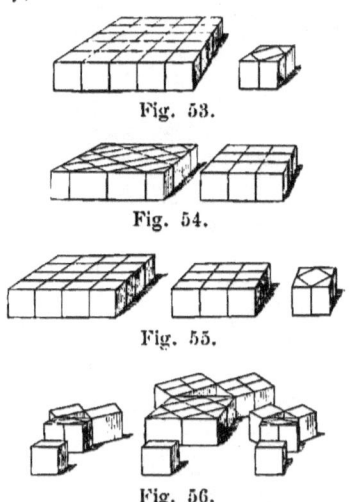

Fig. 53.

Fig. 54.

Fig. 55.

Fig. 56.

For the continuation of the exercises in arithmetic, begun with the previous Gifts, the cubes of the present one are of great use. Exercises in addition and subtraction are continued more extensively, and by the use of these means, the child will be enabled to learn, what is usually called the multiplication table, in a much shorter time and in a much more rational way than it could ever be accomplished by mere memorizing, without visible objects.

FORMS OF BEAUTY.

If we consider that the Fifth Gift is put into the hands of pupils when they have reached the fifth year, with whom, consequently, if they have been treated rationally, the external organs, the limbs, as well as the senses, and the bodily mediators of all mental activity, the nerves, and their central organ, the brain, have reached a higher degree of development, and their physical powers have kept pace with such development, we may well expect a somewhat more extensive activity of the pupils so prepared, and be justified in presenting to them work requiring more skill and ingenuity than that of the previous Gifts.

And, in fact, the progress with these forms is apparently much greater than with the forms of life; because here the importance of each of the thirty-nine parts of the cube can be made more prominent. He who is not a stranger in mathematics knows that the number of combinations and permutations of thirty-nine different bodies does not count by hundreds, nor can be expressed by thousands, but that millions hardly suffice to exhaust all possible combinations.

Limitations are, therefore, necessary here; and these limitations are presented to us in the laws of beauty, according to which the whole structure is not only to be formed harmoniously in itself, but each main part of it must also answer the claims of symmetry. In order to comply with these conditions, it is sometimes necessary, during the process of building a Form of Beauty, to perform certain movements with various parts simultaneously. In such cases it appears advisable to divide the activity in its single parts, and allow the child's eye to rest on these transition figures, that it may become perfectly conscious of all changes and phases during the process of development of the form in question. This will render more intelligible to the young mind, that real beauty can only be produced when one opposite balances another, if the proportions of all parts are equally regulated by uniting them with one common center.

Another limitation we find in the fact, that each fundamental form from which we start is divided in two main parts—the internal and the external—and that if we begin the changes or mutations with one of these opposites, they are to be continued with it until a certain aim be reached. By this process certain small steps are created, which enable the child—and, still more, the teacher—to control the method according to which the perfect form is reached.

"Each definite beginning conditions a certain process of its own, and however much liberty in regard to changes may be allowed, they are always to be introduced within certain limits only."

Thus, the fundamental form conditions all the changes of the whole following series. All fundamental forms are distinct from each other by their different centers, which may be a square, (Fig. 65), a triangle, (Fig. 91), a hexagon, octagon, or circle.

Before the real formation of figures commences, the child should become acquainted with the combinations in which the new forms of the divided cubes can be brought with each other. It takes two half cubes, forms of them a whole, and, being guided by the law of opposites, arrives at the forms represented in Figs. 57-64, and perhaps at others of less significance.

The following series of Figs. 65-106 are all developed one from another, as the careful observer will easily detect. As it would lead too far to show the gradual growing of one from another, and all from a common fundamental form, we will show only the course of development of Figs. 65-70.

The fundamental form (Fig. 65) is a standing square, formed of nine cubes, and surrounded by four equilateral triangles.

The course of development starts from the center part. The four cubes *a* move externally, (Fig. 66), the four cubes *b* do the same, (Fig. 67), cubes *a* move farther to the corner of the triangles, (Fig. 68), cubes *b* move to the places where cubes *a* were previously, (Fig. 69). If all eight cubes continue their way in the same manner, we next obtain a

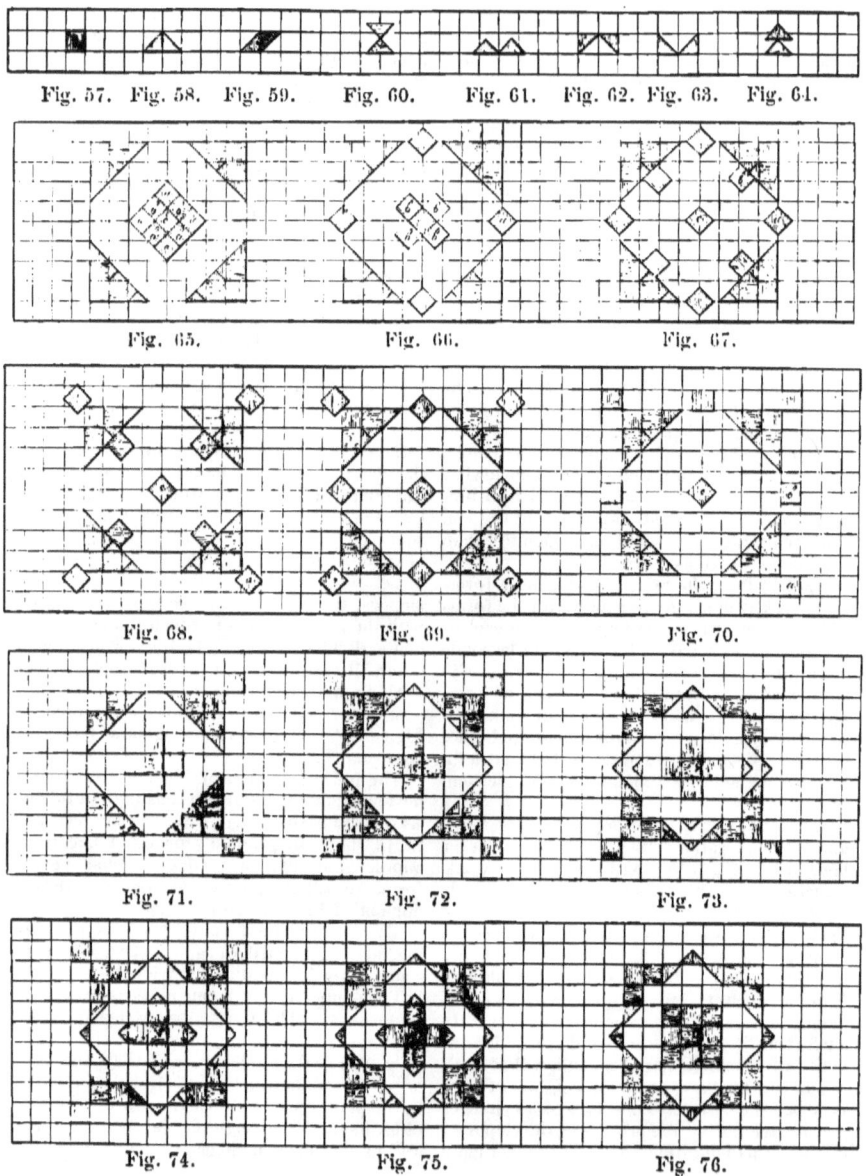

Fig. 57. Fig. 58. Fig. 59. Fig. 60. Fig. 61. Fig. 62. Fig. 63. Fig. 64.

Fig. 65. Fig. 66. Fig. 67.

Fig. 68. Fig. 69. Fig. 70.

Fig. 71. Fig. 72. Fig. 73.

Fig. 74. Fig. 75. Fig. 76.

PARADISE OF CHILDHOOD. 129

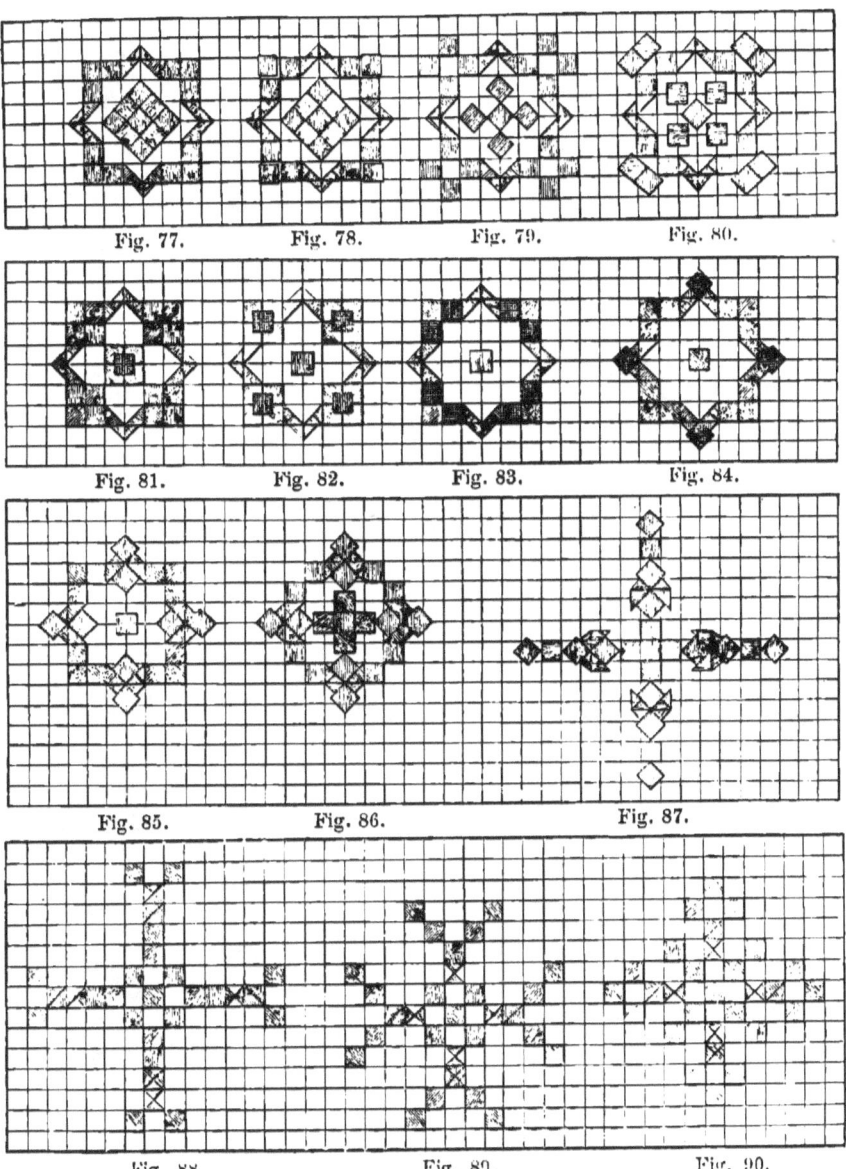

Fig. 77.   Fig. 78.   Fig. 79.   Fig. 80.

Fig. 81.   Fig. 82.   Fig. 83.   Fig. 84.

Fig. 85.   Fig. 86.   Fig. 87.

Fig. 88.   Fig. 89.   Fig. 90.

130 QUARTER CENTURY EDITION

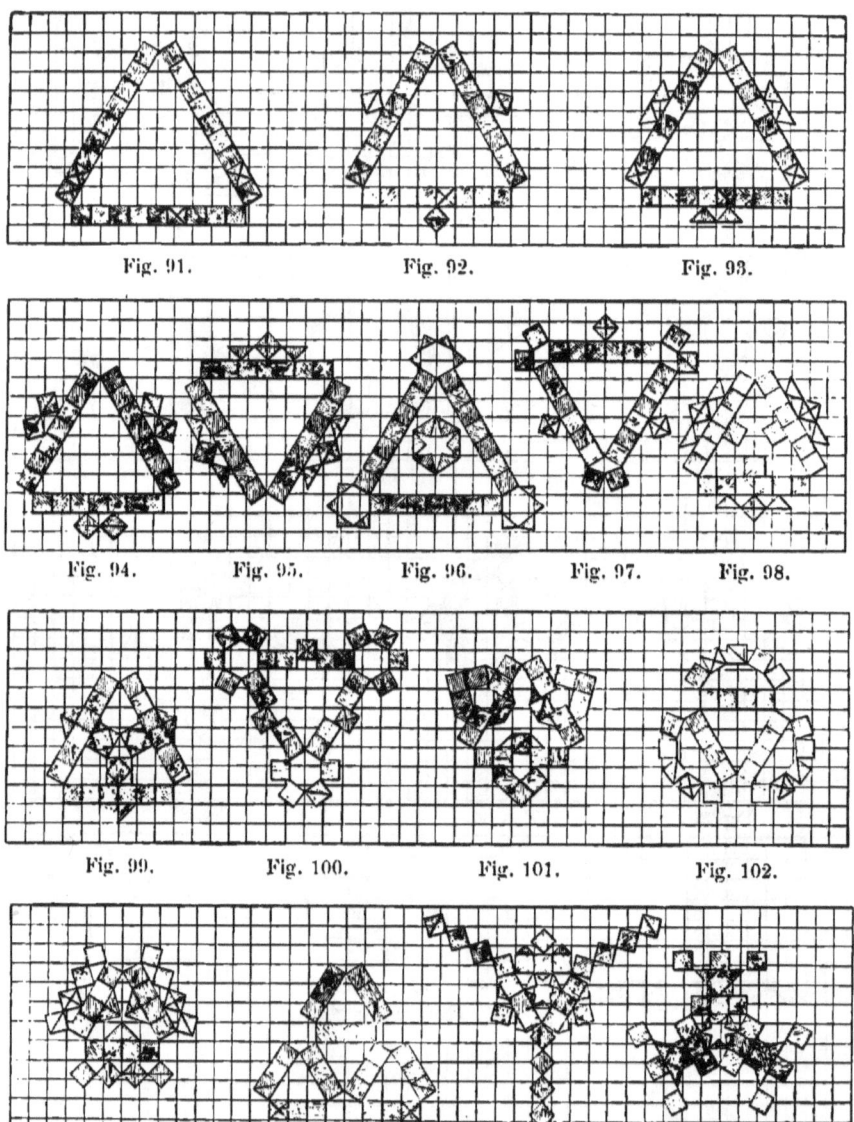

Fig. 91.   Fig. 92.   Fig. 93.
Fig. 94.   Fig. 95.   Fig. 96.   Fig. 97.   Fig. 98.
Fig. 99.   Fig. 100.   Fig. 101.   Fig. 102.
Fig. 103.   Fig. 104.   Fig. 105.   Fig. 106.

form in which a and b remain with their corners on the half of the catheti; then follows a figure like 69 different only in so far as a and b have exchanged positions; then, in like manner follow Figs. 68, 67, 66 and 65.

We therefore, discontinue the course. The internal cubes so far occupied positions that b and c turned corners, a and c sides toward each other. In Fig. 70 b shows the side and a the corner. In Fig. 71, we reach a new fundamental form. Here, not the cubes of the internal, but those of the external triangles furnish the material for changing the form.

It is not necessary that the teacher, by strictly adhering to the law of development, return to the adopted fundamental form. She may interrupt the course as we have done, and continue according to new conditions. But however useful it may be to leave free scope to the child's own fantasy, we should never lose sight of Froebel's principle, to lead to lawful action, to accustom to following a definite rule. Nor should we ever forget that the child can only derive benefit from its occupation, if we do not over-tax the measure of its strength and ability. The laws of formation should, therefore, always be as definite and distinct as simple. As soon as the child cannot trace back the way in which you have led him in developing any of the forms of life or beauty; if it can not discover how it arrived at a certain point, or how to proceed from it, the moment has arrived when the occupation not only ceases to be useful, but commences to be hurtful, and we should always studiously avoid that moment.

In order to facilitate the child's control of his activity, it is well to give the cubes, which are, so to say, the representatives of the law of development, instead of the letters a, b, c, names of some children present, or of friends of the pupils. This enlivens the interest in their movements, and the children follow them with much more attention.

EDITOR'S NOTES.

In the previous gifts only the vertical and horizontal lines have been introduced, but these require their intermediate. The slanting line was indicated in the forms of symmetry made with the third and fourth gifts, when edge and sides were brought to touch each other, but what was only indicated there, now becomes permanent by the bodily presence of the cube divided diagonally.

By this division of three cubes into halves and three into quarters, a new solid is presented—the triangular prism—which permits of a greater variety of forms, and gives an opportunity for the exercise of judgment in choosing the form which is best adapted for a certain purpose. This prism and its proper use in building constitute the chief characteristic of the gift.

Owing to its many parts this gift is much in advance of the previous ones, requiring greater dexterity and delicacy of touch, while it affords excellent training to the fingers. When first placed in the hands of the children, its greater quantity of material and variety of form is liable to confuse them; they are apt to become bewildered in the dictated exercise, and at a loss to know how to manage so much material in free play. Therefore the need of quantity should be felt that the material may not be wasted through misuse.

There are different ways of introducing this gift. Some kindergartners think it is best to present the triangular prism before the gift is offered to the child as a whole, by removing one or two cubes from the boxes of the third gift and substituting half cubes. Then, after the children have examined the form ask questions as to the number, the dimensions and shape of the faces, one of which they find is oblong, two square and two triangular. When they have become familiar with the form, then give the name triangular prism.

Have them place the halves according to dictation and combine them to form whole cubes. After this is done successfully substitute four quarters in place of two halves, and let the children study them in a similar way. They will notice the quarters are one-half as large as the half cubes, also that when two quarters are joined by their square faces they have a new square prism.

Direct one child to put four quarters together to make a cube, another to make a long triangular prism, another to make a square prism two inches high. It is well to let each child experiment for himself in building some form of life, as a locomotive, (Fig. 107), or a house with a roof, which helps the rain to run off quickly, (Fig. 108).

This small quantity of material will give the children facility in combining the new forms, and in placing them according to dictation without being bewildered and diverted. Having used these four small and two large triangular prisms successfully, the children will be better prepared for the manipulation of the whole gift.

Another plan is to present the gift as a whole, using only one, which stands on the kindergartner's table, for the first few lessons. Compare the gift as to size with the third and

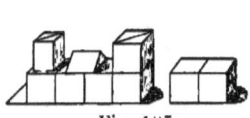

Fig. 107.

Fig. 108.

fourth, then bring out one of the half cubes, teach the different faces, dictate as to placing in different directions, give the name, etc. Proceed with the quarter cube in the same way, until the children are familiar with the form.

Let them use both half and quarter cubes with a single whole cube, combine the halves into a whole cube, make the quarters into cubes, square and triangular prisms. Then show the children the three ways of dividing the gift into thirds—right and left, front and back, up and down—letting them come forward to divide and combine it, using also other objects in illustration; afterward give one-third only to each child to work with, or give every third child the entire gift and assist him to divide the cube into thirds, giving one of these thirds to the neighbor on each side.

The top layer of each third should consist of one whole cube, one composed of halves and one of quarters. Familiarize the children with the new form by some play which will tend to disclose the relationship existing between the parts, and lead the children to find resemblances between the prism and familiar life forms. The following sequence shows the use of one-third of the gift.

FIRST SEQUENCE.

Mary's visit to her uncle, who is a lighthouse keeper in one of the small Atlantic towns. One-third of the gift with cubes running right and left, is placed before each child, Fig. 109.

STEPS AND BOATHOUSE.—(Near the landing where Mary took the small steamboat). Remove the two upper right-hand cubes and the top middle cube. Make a roof of the two half cubes by joining their square faces, and place on top of the two whole cubes, with the triangular faces front and back, Fig. 110.

Fig. 109.

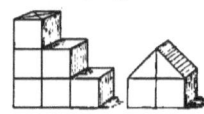

Fig. 110.

STEAMBOAT.—Combine the two halves which form the roof of the boathouse, into a cube, placing it at the left of the steps. Place one of the remaining cubes on top of the right-hand cube, and the other at the right. Remove the quartered cube, placing one of the quarters on top of the lower left-hand cube, with its oblong face against the upper left-hand cube, and its square face slanting to the left. Take another quarter and stand it on a triangular face at the left of the lower left-hand cube, touching it by its square face. Form the remaining two quarters into a square prism, and stand it on top of the upper left-hand cube, face front, Fig. 111.

FORT.—(Which is passed on the way). Of the two separated quarters, form a square prism and stand on top of the upper right-hand cube, face front. Lift the upper three cubes and prisms, placing them back of, and touching those they stand on, Fig. 112.

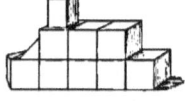

Fig. 111.

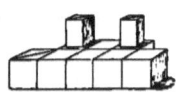

Fig. 112.

BOAT.—(Also passed on the way). Remove the two square prisms, and move the back row one inch back. Take the right-hand front cube and place in the center, connecting the two rows. Separate the left-hand front cube, and place over the front and back middle cubes, with the square faces slanting right and left. Stand one of the quarters on its triangular face, at each end of the four right and left cubes touching them by square faces, Fig. 113.

BOAT LANDING.—(Where Mary is met by her cousins). Remove the four quarters and combine into two square prisms. Combine the two halves into a whole cube and place at the right of the front row. Remove the center connecting cube and place at the right of the back row. Push the two rows together, and stand the two prisms on top of the right and left front cubes, faces front, these forming the posts to which the steamer is tied, Fig. 114.

 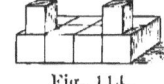

Fig. 113.   Fig. 114.

LIGHTHOUSE.—(Where she finds her uncle). Remove the square prisms and the divided cube. Lift the four back cubes and place in a standing position on top of the front left-hand cube. Place the right-hand cube on top of the cube to its left. Of the two half cubes make roofs, with the square faces slanting front and back. Lay one of the square prisms against the lower right-hand cube, and the other in front of the tower, touching by oblong faces, Fig. 115.

UNCLE'S HOUSE.—Lift the upper two cubes and roof of the tower and place against the left of the tower. Turn the half cubes with their square faces touching the center cube, the oblong faces slanting right and left. Remove the prism at the right and combine into a half cube, placing it on top of the middle cube, with the triangular face front, Fig. 116.

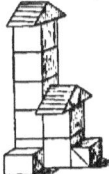 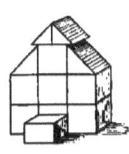

Fig. 115.   Fig. 116.

BARN, WAGON SHED AND WELL HOUSE.—Remove the steps. Lift the center cube and roof, and place in front of and against the lower left-hand cube, for the shed. Move the right-hand half cube over against the other half cube to form a roof. Move the two right-hand cubes two inches to the front, and one inch to the right. Join the quarter cubes which formed the steps into a half cube and place on top of these cubes with triangular face front, for the well house, Fig. 117.

CHURCH.—(Which they attended on the Sabbath). Remove the roof of the wagon shed and form into a square prism. Place the well house on top of the shed and move this tower to the left of the barn, roof slanting right and left. Lay the prism in front of the tower, touching by its oblong face, Fig. 118.

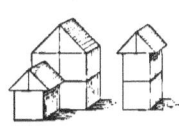 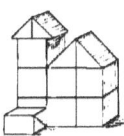

Fig. 117.   Fig. 118.

MARY'S HOME.—(Where she returns after spending many happy days). Remove the right-hand side of the church, and place it against the left of the tower. Turn the half cubes on their oblong faces for the roof, the square faces slanting front and back, Fig. 119.

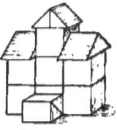

Fig. 119.

When the sequence is ended each child builds up his third of the cube, the three parts are pushed together and are ready to go into the boxes.

SECOND SEQUENCE.

This sequence shows how a third of the gift may be combined to produce one form.

COUNTRY HOME OF A WEALTHY LADY.—(Who loves little children). One third of the gift is placed before each child, the top layer removed and placed two inches in front. Take the two right-hand cubes and stand in front of the left-hand cubes. Combine the two half cubes and place on the back row of cubes for a roof, the oblong faces slanting right and left. Take the remaining whole cube, place one of the quarters on top, triangular face front, and stand at the right of the two front cubes. Combine two quarters into a square prism, with the remaining cube on top, triangular face front, and stand upon the left front cubes, Fig. 120.

BARN.—(Standing back of the house, where the cows and horses are kept, and where the children like to climb the haymow to hunt eggs, and watch Mrs. Puss and her kittens frolic and play). Move the back half two inches back, Fig. 121.

Fig. 120.

Fig. 121.

TENT.—(Where the hostess was obliged to shelter a number of "fresh air" children whom she entertained). Take the roof off the barn and place it one inch back. Take the upper two cubes of the barn and place in front of the lower two, Fig. 122.

COTTAGE.—(At a summer resort not far distant, where the daughter is stopping, and to which the children are driven behind Grey and Dapple for a day's pleasure). Remove the quarter cubes from the house, place the remaining three cubes in the center of the four back cubes, front and back, the two cubes to the front. Join the quarter cubes into two long triangular prisms, and place on their oblong faces at the right and left of the center cubes for a roof, the square faces slanting right and left. Place the two half-cubes on the front and back middle cubes for roofs, triangular faces front and back, Fig. 123.

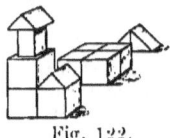
Fig. 122.

Fig. 123.

To combine the thirds:—

SUMMER HOTEL.—(Near the beach). Reverse the cottages so that the backs will face you. Let the child that divided the cube, remove the quarters from his cottage and form two square prisms, on which his neighbor on each side places the back half cube from his cottage, and stands this with triangular face front, on the back middle cube. The right and left cottages are then moved until they touch the middle one, Fig. 124.

These stories may be enlarged upon, and the sequences shortened or lengthened, according to the capacity of the children. At the close of the exercise the borrowed parts are returned, so that the thirds may be built up as they were at the beginning. Later on, the thirds may be divided by three different ways into nine, and those into twenty-seven parts; thus it will be seen that much mathematical knowledge may be gained through this gift.

Fig. 124.

If the entire gift is presented without any preliminary step, it should be used so simply that the child will feel delight in his material. Have the blocks arranged so that when taken from the box, the cubes will be uniform as to position and arrangement, the upper face showing the vertical, horizontal and slanting line, also three squares, six right isosceles triangles of one size and twelve smaller ones.

The children should become thoroughly acquainted with the number of whole and divided cubes, that they may be able to make free and full use of the gift, and they will readily learn to lift the upper face with its twenty-one pieces, and place it unbroken on the table.

Allow free scope to the childish imagination, and as with new material, free play directed by the kindergartner affords the best opportunity for self-activity, it is well to let the children build each his own form, the teacher connecting all their various creations by some little improvised story.

The combination of the cubes to form geometrical figures is full of interest, and the evolution of one form from another, important in developing the child. From a rectangular prism have the children develop the rhomboidal prism, from this the trapezoidal, then the pentagonal and hexagonal.

The educating power of this gift is wonderful, and there seems no limit to its constructive power. It gives a large number of the most varied and beautiful forms of symmetry, and a strong impression is made, that real beauty can only be produced when one opposite balances another, if all the parts are equally regulated by uniting them with one common center. The directions for forming these transition figures should be direct and simple, so that the child can return to the original form, by reversing the movements without taxing him too much.

The material is particularly adapted to architecture, and the forms of life come very near to reality on account of the prisms, which aid materially with their slanting surfaces to represent roofs, chimneys, towers, etc. The method followed in the handling of this material gives a sure guide for bringing order out of all manifoldness of form. The following sequence shows the use of the entire gift.

THIRD SEQUENCE.

Entire gift as placed before each child, Fig. 125.

TRIUMPHAL ARCH.—Move the back row of cubes two inches back and to the left. Remove the upper layer of half cubes, then separate into three columns, covering the right and left column with a half cube for a roof, and the center column with two halves joined by square faces. This forms three towers. Next move the front row of cubes to the right and on a line with what was the middle row, leaving a half-inch space between. Move the right-hand

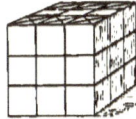

Fig. 125.

column half an inch to the right, and the left-hand column one half-inch to the left, and over these three openings stand the towers, with triangular faces front and back, the tower with the double roof being placed over the center opening. The two remaining halves place right and left of the outside towers, with the oblong faces slanting away from the towers, Fig. 126.

GATES OF A WALLED CITY.—Move the right-hand tower so it stands on the cubes at its left and the left-hand tower so it stands on the cubes at its right. Remove the right and left columns and of the right column make a base of two cubes with the third cube over the center, and on top of this place the half cube with triangular face front. Do the same with the left-hand column, then push these against the front of the double columns, Fig. 127.

Fig. 126.

CATHEDRAL.—Remove these two front pieces and the towers. Place the six left-hand cubes at the back of the six right-hand cubes, forming a square prism, three cubes high. Against the right and left of this prism, place the two front pieces so that the roofs slant front and back. Take the four halves from the towers and combine them into a roof for the top of the prism, the oblong faces slanting right and

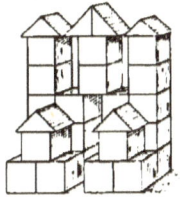 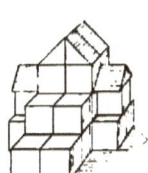

Fig. 127.   Fig. 128.

left. Place the two towers together and stand them in front of the square prism. Lay the remaining tower directly in front of these, for steps, Fig. 128.

From this form the children may easily return to the whole cube. In using the entire gift, each child might divide the gift into thirds using each third for a different form, making different buildings in a town.

FIFTH GIFT B.

This gift combines cylindrical with cubical forms and is in the line of the further development of the series of building blocks which Froebel evidently intended to carry out, as it is obvious that after the blocks containing straight forms derived from the cube have been presented, the round forms derived from the sphere and cylinder should follow.

This gift contains twelve whole cubes, three quartered cubes, eight hollowed cubes, and twelve half-cylinders. Like the fifth gift it is separated into three layers, one above the other.

The first layer consists of nine whole cubes, Fig. 1; the second layer presents three whole cubes, three quartered cubes, and three cylinders halved lengthwise, Fig. 2; the third and upper layer has eight hollowed cubes and six half-cylinders, Fig. 3.

Fig. 1.   Fig. 2.   Fig. 3.

In presenting this gift let the children find familiar forms first, and when they have become acquainted with the new elements in the gift, they may find the simple combination of these forms, one with another. They will recognize the cube and the triangular prism of the fifth gift, and the kindergartner should then call attention to the half-cylinder. Ask how many faces they find? How many are curved? how many are straight? They will notice that one face is a square like the face of the cube, that two are the form of a half-circle, Fig 4, and that the fourth is a curved surface.

Fig. 4.  Fig. 5.  Fig. 6.    Fig. 7. Fig. 8.

Ask how many edges the half cylinder has? Out of the six edges how many are straight? How many are curved? How many corners are there?

Let the children combine two half-cylinders and they will recognize their old friend the cylinder, Fig. 5. By comparing the cylinder and cube the children will find they are of the same dimensions.

Have them combine two half-cylinders with the cube and they have the oval, Fig. 6, and with four half-cylinders they obtain the double oval, Fig. 7.

Compare the half-cylinder with the triangular prism and combine the two by square faces, Fig. 8.

Place a half-cylinder and a triangular prism

 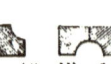
Fig. 9.   Fig. 10. Fig. 11. Fig. 12.  Fig. 13.

on opposite sides of the cube, joining it by square faces, so one end will be rounded and the opposite end pointed.

Bring out the peculiarities of the hollowed cube, Fig. 9. Call attention to the faces, which number seven; two of them are square like the face of the cube; two others are oblongs, just one half as large; one is a hollow curved surface, and the top and bottom faces are equal, being a square with a quarter circle removed from one corner, Fig. 10.

Ask how many edges they find on this form; how many are straight, how many are curved? What is the number of corners? Let the children combine two of these hollowed cubes by oblong faces and an arch is obtained, Fig. 11,

Fig. 14.   Fig. 15.   Fig. 16.

these forms being especially adapted to that purpose. A combination of three hollowed cubes, forms three quarters of a circle, Fig. 12, and by uniting four an entire circle is made, showing a hollow center into which the cylinder may be fitted, Fig. 13. By joining the square faces instead of the oblong we have Fig. 14, and by combining with the half-cylinder, we have the undulating curve, as seen in Figs. 15 and 16.

After the children have seen the gift as a whole and have become acquainted with the different forms, it is well to separate it into three layers, that the children may find the number of parts and the arrangement of each.

These exercises may be given gradually, the

kindergartner being careful that the child observes with clearness and decision, advancing him only as he is capable of making intelligent use of his materials.

FORMS OF LIFE.

style of architecture being prominent in the life forms of which the accompanying illustrations only serve as a hint to the possibilities of this

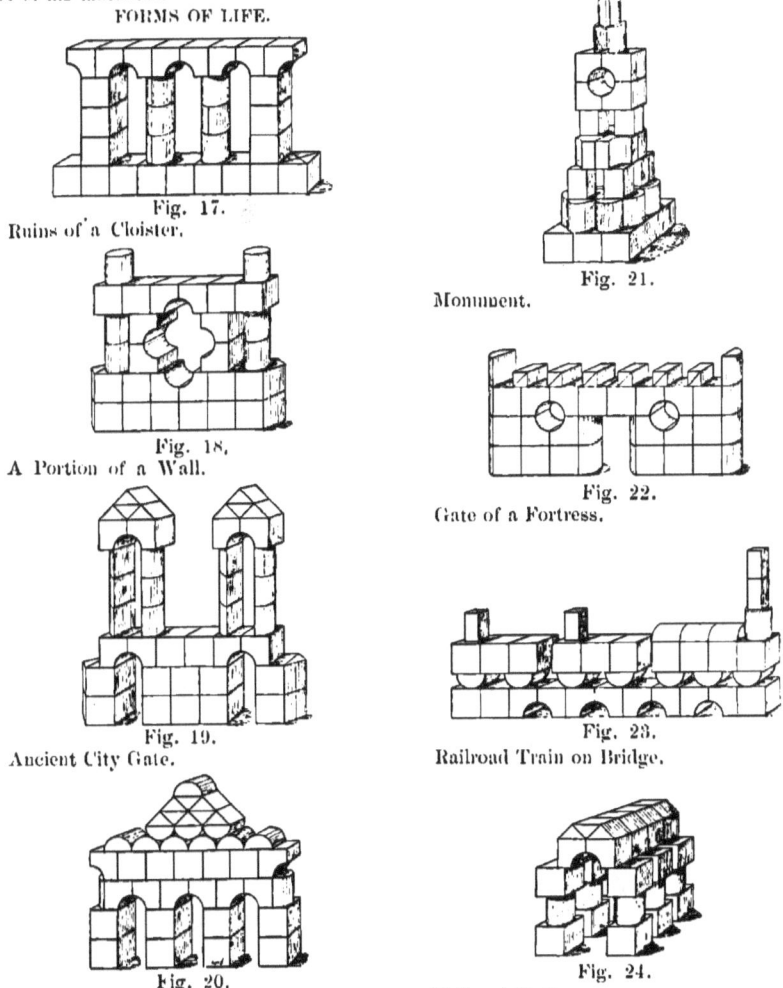

Fig. 17.
Ruins of a Cloister.

Fig. 18.
A Portion of a Wall.

Fig. 19.
Ancient City Gate.

Fig. 20.
Royal Archway.

Fig. 21.
Monument.

Fig. 22.
Gate of a Fortress.

Fig. 23.
Railroad Train on Bridge.

Fig. 24.
Railroad Station.

The curved line of this gift gives a special importance to the exercises. Arches and round columns may now be constructed, the Roman gift, which may be brought out under the skillful direction of the kindergartner and the full and careful attention of the children.

138   PARADISE OF CHILDHOOD.

Fig. 25.

Monument.

Fig. 26.

Portico.

FORMS OF SYMMETRY.

The forms of symmetry are treated in the same way as those of the previous gifts. Sequences may easily be developed and figures constructed which are varied and pleasing in design, the rounded forms of the gift giving a peculiar characteristic of their own.

Fig. 27.

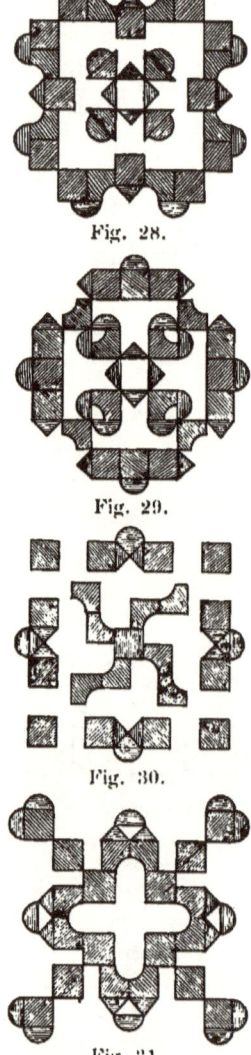

We give but a few illustrations, leaving the teacher free to follow her own ideas.

In the forms of knowledge, the child's attention should be directed to those which are the most simple, as Figs. 5, 6, 7, 11, 12 and 13, the children of the kindergarten being too young to grasp the special mathematical truths which may be derived by means of this gift.

THE SIXTH GIFT.

LARGE CUBE, CONSISTING OF DOUBLY DIVIDED OBLONG BLOCKS.

As the Third and Fifth Gifts form an especial sequence of development, so the Fourth and Sixth are intimately connected with each other. The latter is, so to say, a higher potence of the former, permitting the observation in greater clearness, of the qualities, relation, and laws, introduced previously.

The Gift contains twenty-seven oblong blocks of the same dimensions as those of the Fourth Gift. Of these twenty-seven blocks, eighteen are whole, six are divided breadthwise, each in two squares, and three by a lengthwise cut, each in two columns; altogether making thirty-six pieces.

The children soon become acquainted with this Gift, as the variety of forms is much less than in the preceding one, where by an oblique division of the cubes, an entirely new radical principle was introduced.

It is here, therefore, mainly the proportions of size of the oblong and square blocks, and columns contained in this Gift and the number of each kind of these bodies, about which the child has to become enlightened, before engaging in building—playing, creating—with this new material.

The cube is placed upon the table—all parts are disjoined—then equal parts collected into groups, and the child is then asked, "How many blocks have you altogether? How many oblong blocks? how many square blocks? how many columns? Compare the sides of the blocks with another, take an oblong block, how many square blocks do you need to cover it? how many columns?

Place the oblong block upon its long edge, now upon its shortest side—and state how many square blocks or columns you need in order to reach its height, in either case." Exercises of this kind will instruct the child sufficiently, to allow it to proceed, in a short time to the individual creating, or producing occupation with this new Gift.

FORMS OF LIFE.

It is the forms of life, particularly, for which this Gift provides material, far better fitted, than any previously used. The oblong blocks admit of a much larger extension of the plane, and allow the enclosure of a much more extensive hollow space, than was possible, for instance, with the cubes of the Fifth Gift. Innumerable forms can therefore be produced with this Gift, and the attention and interest of the pupil will be constantly increased.

This very variety, however, should induce the careful teacher to prevent the child's purely accidental production of forms. It is always necessary to act according to certain rules and laws, to reach a certain aim. The established principle, that one form should always be derived from another, can be carried out here only with great difficulty, owing to the peculiarity of the material. It is therefore frequently necessary, particularly with the more complicated structures, to lay an entirely new foundation for the building to be erected.

It is necessary, at all times, to follow the child in his operations—his questions should always be answered and suggestions made to enlarge the circle of ideas.

It affords an abundance of pleasure to a child to observe that we understand him and his work, it is, therefore, a great mistake in education to neglect to enter fully into the spirit of the pupil's sphere of thinking and acting; and if we ever should allow ourselves to go so far as to ridicule his productions instead of assisting him to improve on them, we would commit a most fatal error.

The selections of forms of life, nearly all of which are in the meantime forms of art and knowledge, because of their architectural fundamental forms and the mathematical proportions of their single parts, can, therefore, not fail to give nourishment to various powers of the mind.

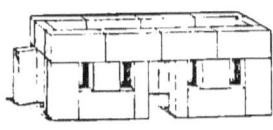

Fig. 1.

House Without Roof; back wall has no door.

Fig. 2.
Ground Plan for House.

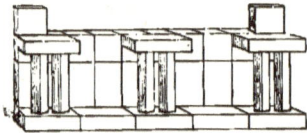

Fig. 3.

Colonnade. First row, five oblong blocks laid lengthwise, and back wall consisting of ten standing oblong blocks upon which are ten square blocks.

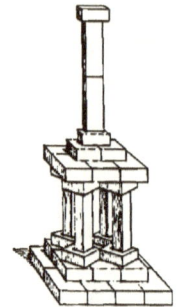

Fig. 7.

Monument in Honor of Some Fallen Hero. First row, eight oblong blocks; second, square of nine square blocks, partially constructed of oblong blocks; third, four single square blocks; then four columns, four single square blocks, square of four square blocks, etc.

Fig. 4.
Hall, with Columns.

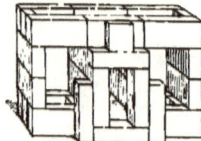

Fig. 5.
Summer House. Vestibule formed by six columns.

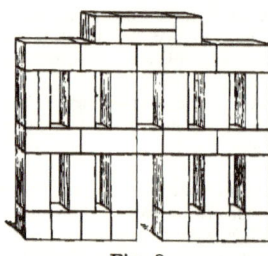

Fig. 8.
Facade of a Large House.

Fig. 6.
Memorial Column of the Three Friends.

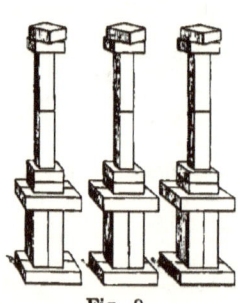

Fig. 9.
The Columns of the Three Heroes.

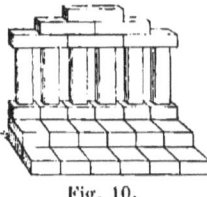

Fig. 10.

Entrance to Hall of Fame. First row, six square and six oblong blocks; second row, six oblong blocks; third row, six square blocks, etc.

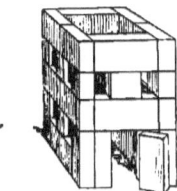

Fig. 11.

Two Story House.

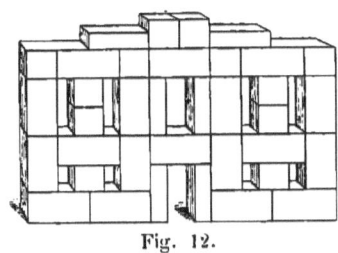

Fig. 12.

Facade.

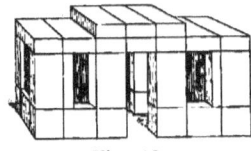

Fig. 13.

Covered Summer House.

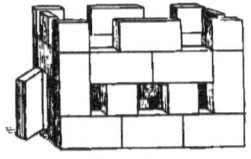

Fig. 14.

Front View of a Factory.

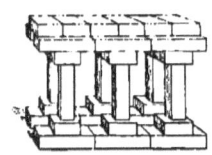

Fig. 15.

Double Colonnade.

Fig. 16.

An Altar.

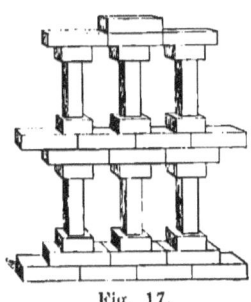

Fig. 17.

Monument.

Fig. 18.
Columns of Concord.

The fantasy of the child is inexhaustibly rich in inventing new forms. It creates gardens, yards, stables with horses and cattle, household furniture of all kinds, beds with sleeping brothers and sisters in them, tables, chairs, sofas, etc., etc.

If several children combine their individual building they produce large structures, perfect barnyards with all outbuildings in them, nay, whole villages and towns. The idea that in union there is strength, and that by co-operation great things may be accomplished, will thus early become manifest to the young mind.

FORMS OF KNOWLEDGE.

These also appear in much smaller numbers compared with the richness and multiplicity of the Fifth Gift. By the absence of oblique (obtuse and acute) angles, they are limited to the square and oblong, and exercises introduced with these previously, may be repeated here with advantage.

All Froebel's Gifts are remarkable for the peculiar feature that they can be rendered exceedingly instructive by frequently introducing repetitions under varied conditions and forms, by which means we are sure to avoid that dry and fatiguing monotony which must needs result from repeating the same thing in the same manner and form. And still more, the child, thereby, becomes accustomed to recognize like in unlike, similarity in dissimilarity, oneness in multiplicity, and connection in the apparently disconnected.

In Figs. 19-25 all squares that can be formed with the Sixth Gift are represented. In Fig. 26 we see a transition from the forms of knowledge to those of beauty.

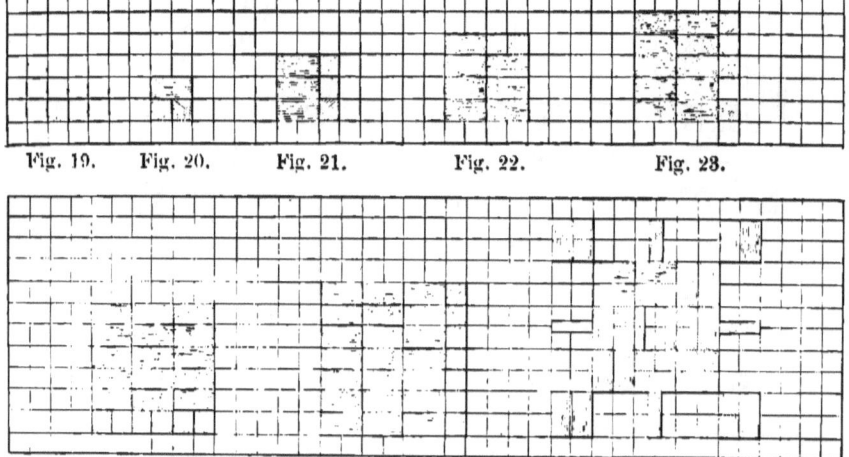

Fig. 19.   Fig. 20.   Fig. 21.   Fig. 22.   Fig. 23.

Fig. 24.   Fig. 25.   Fig. 26.

FORMS OF BEAUTY.

The forms of beauty of this Gift offer far less diversity than those of Gift No. 5; owing, however, to the peculiar proportions of the plane, they present sufficient opportunity for characteristic representations, not to be neglected.

We give in Figs. 27-41 a single succession of development of such forms. The progressive changes are easily recognized, as the oblong block, which needs to be moved to produce the following figure, is always marked by a letter. The center-piece always consists of two of the little columns, standing one upon another, and important modifications may be produced by using the oblong blocks in lying or standing positions. By employing the four little columns in various ways many pleasant changes can be produced by them.

With the Sixth Gift we reach the end of the two series of development given by Frœbel in the building blocks, whose aim is to acquaint the child with the general qualities of the solid body by his own observation and occupation with the same.

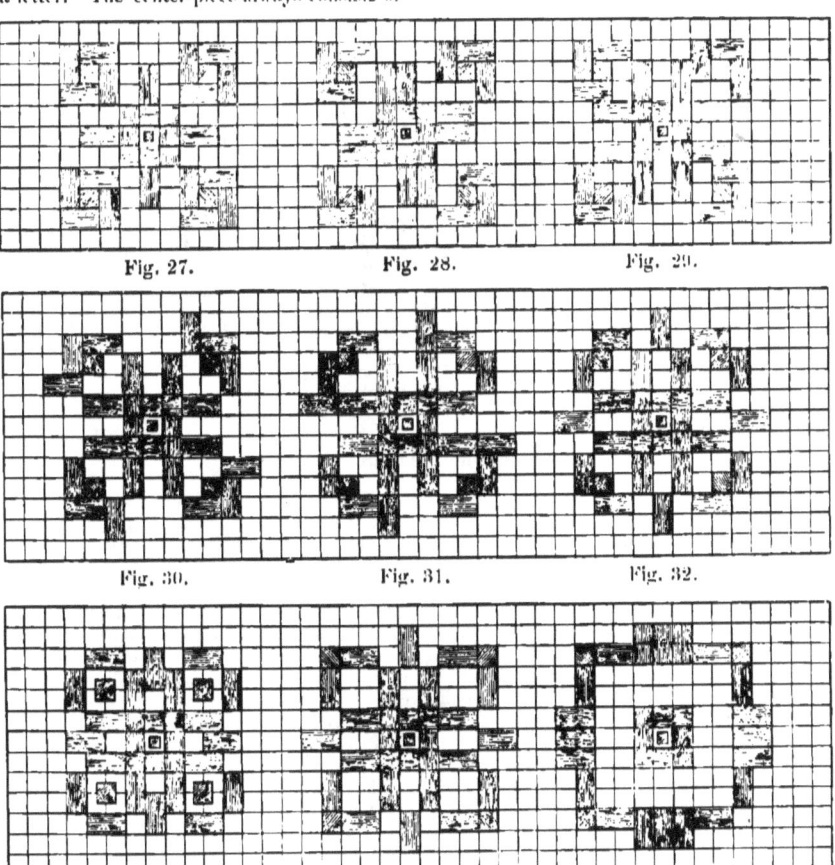

Fig. 27. Fig. 28. Fig. 29.

Fig. 30. Fig. 31. Fig. 32.

Fig. 33. Fig. 34. Fig. 35.

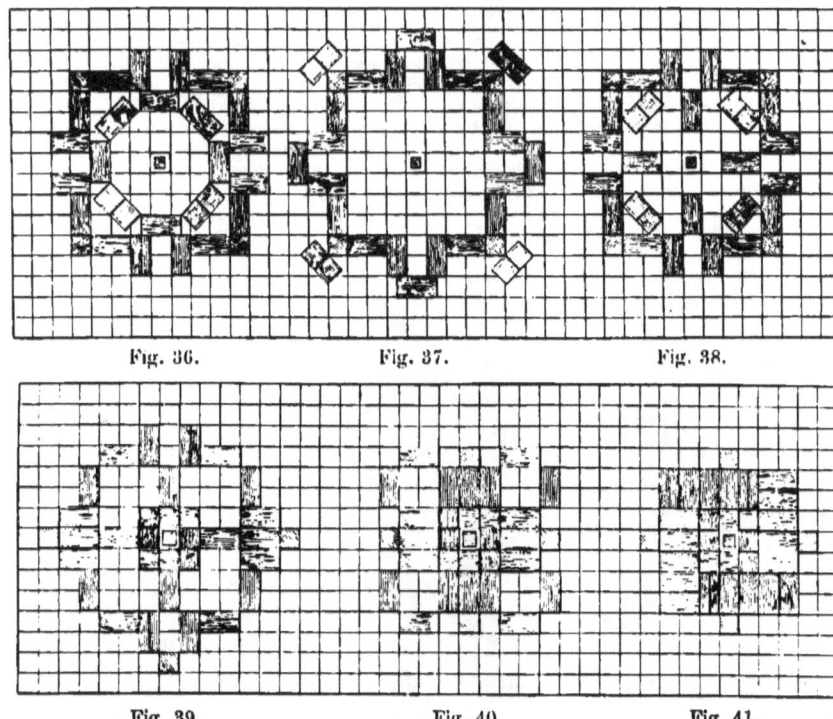

Fig. 36.   Fig. 37.   Fig. 38.
Fig. 39.   Fig. 40.   Fig. 41.

EDITOR'S NOTES.

While as a whole, this gift is more like the fifth it surpasses that gift in its constructive capacity, the forms built being more complete and finished, and requiring more delicacy of touch, as they are of a lighter and more graceful style of structure and more easily destroyed.

The column, which is the chief characteristic of the gift, and which was foreshadowed in the fifth gift when two quarters were joined by square faces, enables the children to build high structures resembling Grecian architecture, beside many other pleasing forms which are dependent upon it.

In its parts this gift most resembles the fourth gift, and the forms like the bricks of that gift, can stand, lie or sit; the different parts also serve in measuring length, breadth and heighth.

Although not so rich and varied in forms of symmetry and knowledge, this gift is more suitable for the construction of life forms than any of the previous ones, and the number is almost unlimited, the material being especially adapted for the forming of apertures. It allows the use of more forms of comparison than the other gifts, and emphasizes the proportion of different parts in respect to size, giving a clear idea of forms, their number and position.

In introducing this gift, let the children see if they can find any old friends among the forms, then count the edges, faces and corners of the brick, column and square plinth. Have them compare the column and brick, the square plinth and brick, and the column and square plinth. Lead them to see how the forms may vary in size and shape and yet be equal in volume.

Compare this gift with the fifth and point out the different ways of dividing each. By separating this gift into six layers the children may learn the number of bricks, columns and square plinths contained in it. The gift may be divided among three children by separating it into three groups, each consisting of two layers which they will see is one third of the gift. The laying out of the gift and the building of one form may constitute a lesson. Then these forms may be built and joined together; afterward these steps may all be retraced to the layer, or the gift may be built up direct from the last form.

Let the children experiment in finding and using the form which is best adapted for a certain purpose, and they will soon see how the column is fitted to meet certain needs. Give simple directions and let them work out the rest for themselves, having a definite purpose in view. Ask questions as to which form is best suited for their purpose, and lead them through the ideas of proportion and form to reach certain results, never losing sight of the idea of unity in any building the children may do. As soon as the children are able, let each child have a whole gift, then sequences may be given and connected by a story.

A LIFE SEQUENCE.

Separate the gift, (Fig. 42) into six layers, three of which shall each contain three bricks and three square plinths; the other three should consist of three bricks, two columns and one

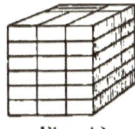

Fig. 42.

square plinth, which are placed one inch back of the former three layers, as in Fig. 43. The front and back right-hand layers form one third of the gift, with which we first build.

Take two square plinths and place in the center of the right and left bricks of the front layer. On each square plinth stand a column, face front, and place a square plinth on top of each column. Then lay a brick from right to left on its broad face, on top of the two square plinths just placed. Lay another brick on its broad face, in front and against the center of the base and the remaining brick on the one just placed so that its narrow face will touch the square plinths. These bricks form the steps. Make two similar figures with the remaining two thirds, as in Fig. 44.

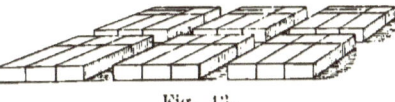

Fig. 43.

Place two of these thirds back to back so that the steps will face to the right and left; and against the front of this figure, place the steps from the remaining third, the upper brick

Fig. 44.

touching the square plinths, leaving the under brick one half inch from the base. Lift the remaining part of the third form with the exception of the three bricks which make the base, and stand on top of the other two thirds, with the columns right and left. On this stand one of the remaining three bricks, the narrow face front. Form steps of the other two bricks and place in the rear, as in Fig. 45.

Fig. 45.   Fig. 46.

Remove the standing brick, then lift the upper part of this form down to the square plinths which are on top of the lower columns, and put it one side, after having placed the removed brick between the two lower bricks to form a base of three bricks. Take away the steps and place four of the bricks on their broad faces, on top of the four square plinths, the sides running right and left. On these place the remaining four bricks on their broad faces, the sides running front and back. Then stand the form which was put one side in the center of these four bricks, the columns being on the right and left, Fig. 46.

Remove the top, including the base of three bricks, and place at the right of the figure, the bases touching by edges. Remove the remain-

Fig. 47.

ing two layers of bricks down to the square plinths on the columns and place two of the bricks with edges running front and back, on top of the center and left hand square plinths, forming a figure similar to that on the right hand. Place two bricks on their narrow faces above the opening at the right with the edges extending over it. Cover these with a brick placed on its broad face. Repeat this over the opening at the left, as in Fig. 47.

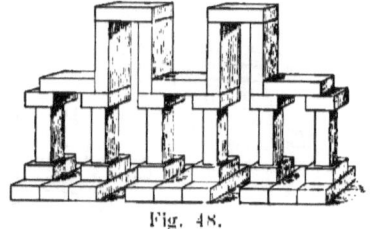

Fig. 48.

Remove the six bricks just placed on top, and then turn the three sections of the figure half-way round, placing them in a line running right and left, with an opening one inch wide between each section. Stand a brick with narrow face front, upon the exposed corners of the four center square plinths, and cover with the two remaining bricks placed on their broad faces, forming two archways, Fig. 48.

Of the two archways form steps for the three sections and we have the three original thirds, which the children may easily separate into layers, and then build up into the gift, the layers alternating.

A BEAUTY SEQUENCE.

The fundamental form is an enclosed hexagon made with all the bricks, three of them forming each side of the hexagon. Within the enclosed space is a hexagon formed with square plinths, the face of each plinth being directly opposite the central brick of the outer hexagon. In the spaces of the large hexagon is a square plinth touching adjacent sides by corners, and at the outer edge of the plinth is a column touching the center of each plinth by its square face, Fig. 49.

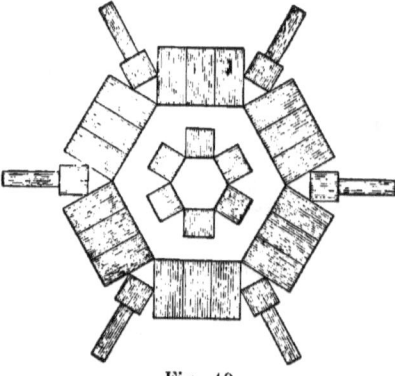

Fig. 49.

Push the center brick of each side of the hexagon toward the inner hexagon until their small faces meet, Fig. 50.

Remove the square plinths forming the inner hexagon to the space directly opposite on the outer hexagon. Form a new inner hexagon with the square faces of the columns, Fig. 51.

Push the bricks back to their original positions, Fig. 52.

Move the square plinths in the spaces out until two angles are in line with the angles of the adjacent bricks. Remove the columns from the center to the outside, and let them touch the plinths by their long faces, Fig. 53.

Push the center brick of each side of the hexagon toward the center of the form, the angles meeting and outlining a small hexagon, Fig. 54.

PARADISE OF CHILDHOOD. 147

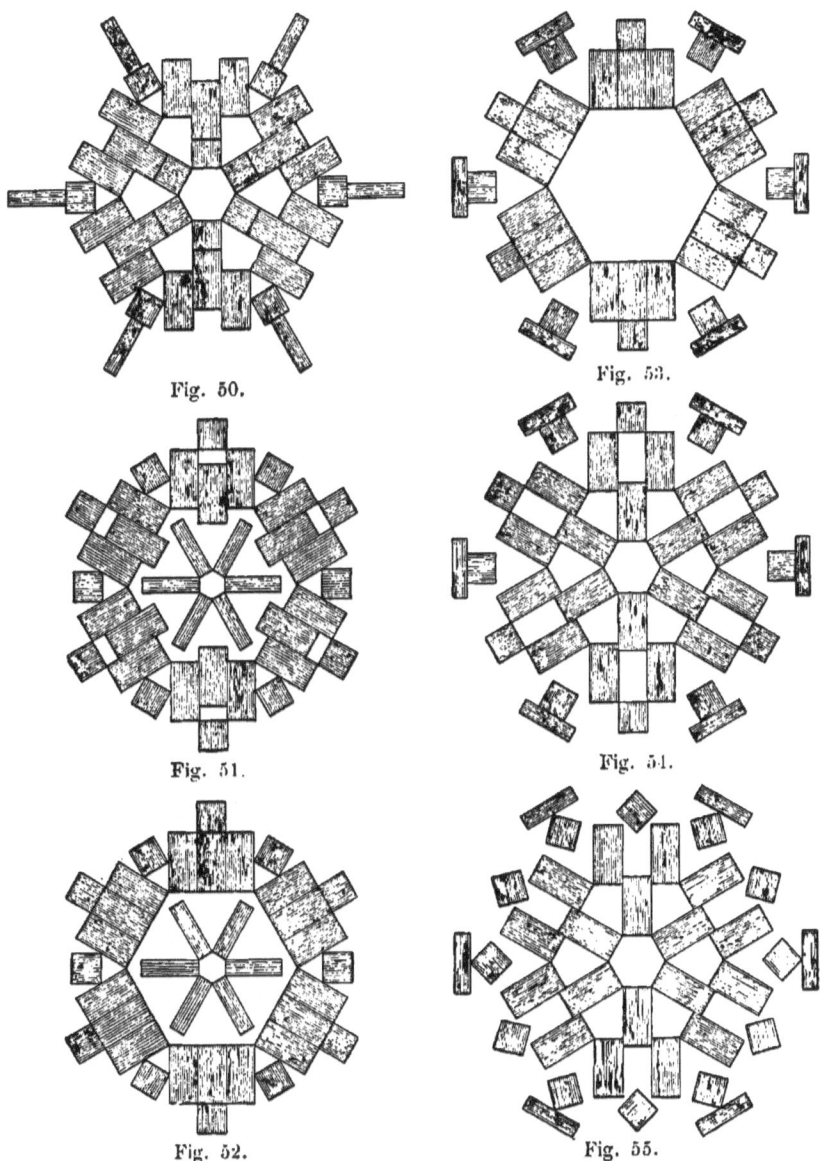

Fig. 50.

Fig. 53.

Fig. 51.

Fig. 54.

Fig. 52.

Fig. 55.

Turn the square plinths with one angle toward the center of the form, Fig. 55.

Move the columns along until they touch the outer angle of the plinth next to them by the center of their long faces. Move the remaining plinths to touch the columns on their outer faces by an angle, Fig. 56.

Move the plinths nearest the hexagon to the spaces of the hexagon. Move the center bricks back to their original positions, Fig. 57.

Change the columns so that they will touch the last plinths moved by their square faces. Place the remaining plinths in the center to from a small hexagon, and we have the original form.

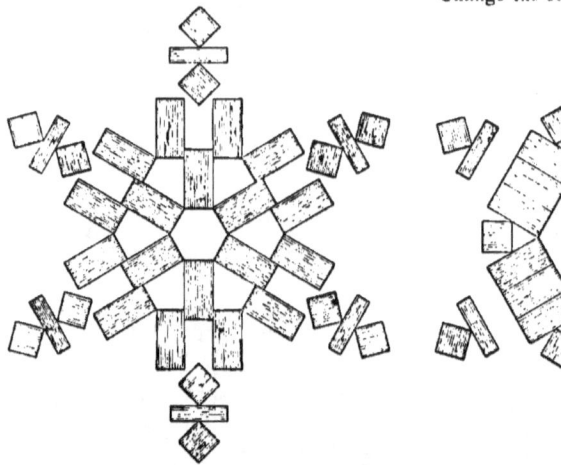

Fig. 56.

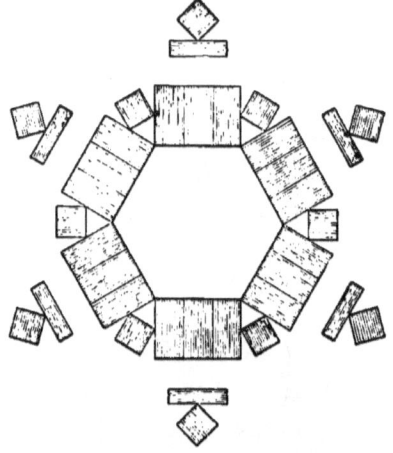

Fig. 57.

THE SEVENTH GIFT.

SQUARE AND TRIANGULAR TABLETS FOR LAYING OF FIGURES.

All mental development begins with concrete beings. The material world with its multiplicity of manifestations first attracts the senses and excites them to activity, thus causing the rudimentary operations of the mental powers. Gradually—only after many processes, little defined and explained by any science as yet, have taken place—man becomes enabled to proceed to higher mental activity, from the original impressions made upon his senses by the various surroundings in the material world.

The earliest impressions, it is true, if often repeated, leave behind them a lasting trace on the mind. But between this attained possibility to recall once-made observations to represent the object perceived by our senses, by mental image (imagination), and the real thinking or reasoning, the real pure abstraction, there is a very long step, and nothing in our whole system of education is more worthy of consideration than the sudden and abrupt transition from a life in the concrete, to a life of more or less abstract thinking to which our children are submitted when entering school from the parental house.

Froebel, by a long series of occupation material, has successfully bridged over this chasm which the child has to traverse, and the first place among it, the laying tablets of various forms occupy.

The series of tablets is contained in five boxes containing:—

A. Quadrangular square tablets.
B. Right angular (equal sides). } Triangular tablets.
C. Equilateral.
D. Obtuse angular (equal sides).
E. Right angular (unequal sides).

The child was heretofore engaged with solid bodies, and in the representation of real things. He produced a house, garden, sofa, etc. It is true the sofa was not a sofa as it is seen in reality; the one built by the child, was therefore, so to say, an image already, but it was a bodily image, so much so that the child could place upon it a little something representing his doll. The child considered it a real sofa, and so it was to the child, fulfilling, as it did, in his little world, the purposes of a real sofa in real life.

With the tablets the embodied planes, the child cannot represent a sofa, but a form similar to it; an image of the sofa can be produced by arranging the squares and triangles in a certain order.

We shall see, at some future time, how Froebel continues on this road, progressing from the plane to the line, from the line to the point and finally enables the child to draw the image of the object, with pencil or pen in his own little hand.

THE QUADRANGULAR LAYING TABLETS (Squares).

(See Figs. 1—15).

In a similar way as was done with the various building gifts, the child is led to an acquaintance with the various qualities of the new material, and to compare it, with other things, possessing similar qualities. It is advisable to let the child understand the connection existing between this and the previous gifts. The laying tablets are nothing but the embodied planes, or separated sides of the cube. Cover all the sides of a cube with square tablets and after the child has recognized the cube in the body thus formed, let it separate the tablets one by one, from the cube hidden by them.

The following, or similar questions are here to be introduced:—What is the form of this tablet? How many sides has it? How many angles? Look carefully at the sides. Are they alike or unlike each other? They are all alike. Now look at the corners. These also are all alike. Where have you seen similar figures? What are such figures called? Can you show me angles somewhere else? Where the two walls meet is an angle. Here, there and everywhere you find angles.

But all angles are not alike, and they are therefore differently named. All these different names you will learn successively, but now let us turn to our tablet. Place it right straight before you upon the table. Can you tell me now what direction these two sides have which form the angle? The one is horizontal, the other vertical. An angle which is formed if a vertical meets a horizontal line, is called a right angle. How many of such angles can you count on your tablet? Four. Show me such right angles somewhere else.

By the acquisition of this knowledge the child has made an important step forward. Looking for horizontal and vertical lines, and for right angles, he is led to investigate more deeply the relations of form, which he had heretofore observed only in regard to the size conditioned by it.

The child's attention should be drawn to the fact that, however the tablet may be placed the angles always remain right angles though the lines are horizontal and vertical only in four positions of the tablet, namely, those where the edges of the tablet are placed in the same direction with the lines on the table before the child. This will give occasion to lead the child to a general perception of the standing or hanging of objects according to the plummet.

But the tablet will force still another observation upon the child. The opposite sides have an equal direction; they are the same distance from each other in all their points; they never meet, however many tablets the child may add to each other to form the lines.

The child learns that such lines are called parallel lines. He has observed such lines frequently before this, but begins just now to understand their real being and meaning. He looks now with much more interest than ever before at surrounding tables, chairs, closets, houses, with their straight line ornaments, for now the little cosmopolitan does not only receive the impressions made by the surroundings upon his senses, but he already looks for something in them, an idea of which lives in his mind. Although unconscious of the fact that with the right angle and the parallel line, he received the elements of architecture, it will pleasantly incite him to new observations whenever he finds them again in another object which attracts his attention.

The teacher in remembrance of our oft-repeated hints, will proceed slowly, and carefully, according to the desire and need of the child. She repeats, explains, leads the child to make the same observations in the most different objects, and changing circumstances, or guides the child in laying other forms of knowledge, (lying or standing parallelograms Fig. 4 and 5), of life, (Steps, Fig. 6 and 8, double steps, Fig. 7 and 9, door, Fig. 10, sofa, Fig. 11, cross, Fig. 12), or forms of beauty. (Figs. 13, 14 and 15).

The number of these forms is on the whole only very limited. It is well now to augment the number of tablets in the hands of the pupil, by two, when a much larger number of forms can be produced. The various series of forms of beauty, introduced with the third Gift, can be repeated here and enlarged upon, according to the change in the material now at the disposal of the child.

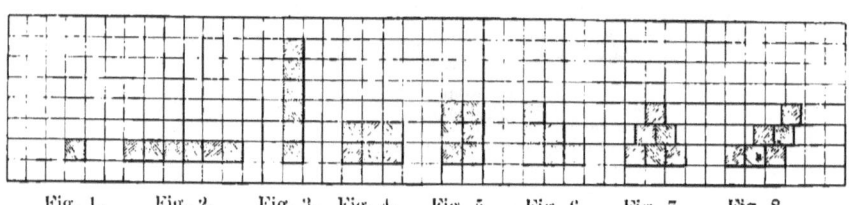

Fig. 1.   Fig. 2.   Fig. 3.   Fig. 4.   Fig. 5.   Fig. 6.   Fig. 7.   Fig. 8.

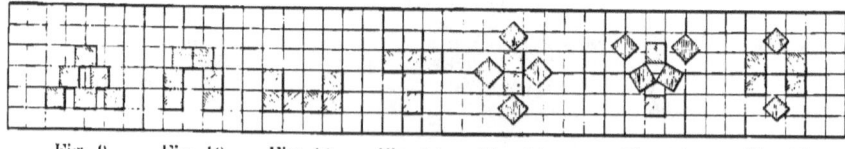

Fig. 9.   Fig. 10.   Fig. 11.   Fig. 12.   Fig. 13.   Fig. 14.   Fig. 15.

RIGHT-ANGLED TRIANGLES.

(SEE FIGS. 16—50.)

As from the whole cube, the divided cube was produced, so by division the triangle springs from the square. By dividing it diagonally in halves, we produce the rectangular triangle with two equal sides.

Although the form of the triangle was presented to the child in connection with the Fifth Gift, it here appears more independently, and it is not only on that account necessary to acquaint the child with the qualities and being of the new addition to his occupation material, but still more so because the forms of the triangles with which as a natural sequence he will have to do hereafter, will be entirely unknown to the pupil. The child places two triangles, joined to form a square upon the table.

What kind of a line divides your four-cornered tablet? An oblique or slanting line. In what direction does the line cut your square in two? From the right upper corner to the left lower corner. Such a line we call a diagonal.

Separate the two parts of the square, and look at each one separately. What do you call each of these parts? What did you call the whole? A square. How many corners or angles had the square? Four. How many corners or angles has the half of the square you are looking at? Three. This half, therefore, is called a triangle, because, as I have explained to you before, it has three angles. How many sides has your triangle? etc.

Looking at the sides more attentively, what do you observe? One side is long, the other two are shorter, and like each other. These latter are as large as the sides of the square, all sides of which were alike.

Now tell me what kind of angle it is, that is formed by these two equal sides? It is a right angle. Why? and what will you call the other two angles? How do the sides run which form these two angles? They run in such a way as to form a very sharp point, and these angles are, therefore called acute angles, which means sharp-pointed angles. Your triangle has then, how many different kinds of angles? Two; one right angle, and two acute angles.

It is not necessary to mention that the above is not to be taught in one lesson. It should be presented in various conversations, lest the acquired knowledge might not be retained by even the brightest child. The attention of the pupil may also be led, in subsequent conversations to the fact that the largest side is opposite the largest angle, and that the two angles are alike, etc. Sufficient opportunity for these and additional remarks will offer itself during the representations of forms of life, of knowledge, and of beauty, for which the child will employ his tablets, according to his own free will, and which are not necessarily to be separated, neither here nor in any other part of these occupations, although it is well to observe a certain order at any time.

Whenever it can be done, elementary knowledge may well be imparted, together with the representations of forms of life, and forms of beauty.

In order to invent, the child must have observed the various positions which a triangle may occupy. It will find these acting according to the laws of opposites, already familiar to the child.

The *right angle*, placed to the *right front*, (Fig. 17) will bring it into the opposite position to the *left back*, (Fig. 18) then into the mediative positions, to the *left front*, (Fig. 19) and to the *right back*, (Fig. 20). By turning, the right angle comes *back* of the long side, (Fig. 21) and in the opposite position it comes to the *front* of the Hypothenuse, (Fig. 22) then to the *right*, (Fig. 23) and finally to the *left* of it. (Fig. 24).

The various positions of two triangles are easily found by moving one of them around the other. Figs. 26-31 are produced from Fig. 25, by moving the back triangle, in six steps, around the other triangle, always keeping it in its original position.

In Figs. 32-37, the changes are produced, alternating regularly between a turn and a move of the back triangle. In Figs. 38-47, simply turning takes place.

After the child has become acquainted with the first elements from which its formations develop, it receives for a beginning four of the triangled tablets. It then places the right angles together, and thereby forms a standing full square. (Fig. 48).

By placing the tablets in an opposite position (turning the right angles from within to without, it produces a lying square with the hollow in the middle. (Fig. 49). This hollow space has the same shape and dimensions as Fig. 48. The child will fancy Fig. 48 into the place of this hollow space, and will thereby transfer the idea of a full square upon an empty or hollow one, and will consequently make the first step from the perception of the concrete to its idea, the abstraction.

The child will now easily find mediative forms between these two opposites. It places two right angles within and two without, (Figs. 58 and 59) two front and two back (Fig. 50) two to the right, and two to the left (Fig. 51).

So far, two tablets always remained connected with one another. By separating them we produce the new mediative forms, Figs. 52, 53, 54 and 55, in which again two and two are opposites. But instead of the right, the acute angle may meet in a point also, and thus Figs. 56 and 57 are produced, which are called rotation forms, because the isolated position of the right angle suggests, as it were, an inclination to fall, or turn, or rotate.

The mediation between these two opposite figures is given in Figs. 50 and 51—between them and Figs. 49 and 50 in Figs. 58 and 59; and it should be remarked in this connection, that these opposites are conditioned by the position of the right angle in all these cases.

All these exercises accustom the pupil to a methodic handling of all his material. They develop a correct use of his eye, because regular figures will only be produced when his tablets are placed correctly and exactly in their places shown by the network on the table. The precaution which must be exercised by the child not to disturb the easily movable tablets, and the care employed to keep each in its place, are of the greatest importance for future necessary dexterity of hand. In a still greater degree than by these simple elementary forms just described, this will be the case, when the pupil comes into possession of a larger number of tablets—up to sixty-four—for the formation of more complicated figures, according to the free exercise of his fantasy.

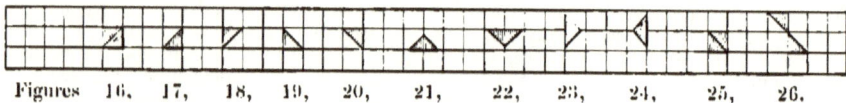

Figures 16, 17, 18, 19, 20, 21, 22, 23, 24, 25, 26.

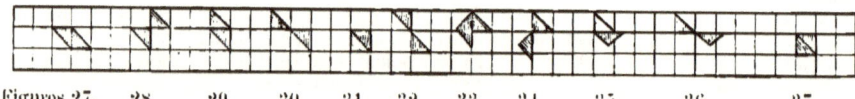

Figures 27, 28, 29, 30, 31, 32, 33, 34, 35, 36, 37.

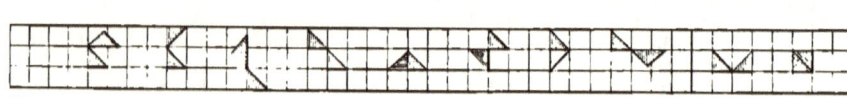

Figures 38, 39, 40, 41, 42, 43, 44, 45, 46, 47.

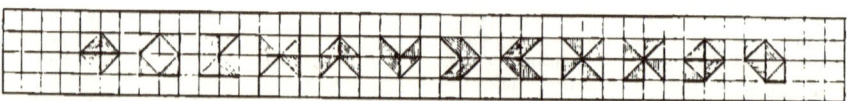

Figures 48, 49, 50, 51, 52, 53, 54, 55, 56, 57, 58, 59.

FORMS OF LIFE.
(SEE FIGS. 60—80.)

All hints given in connection with the building blocks, are also to be followed here, with this difference only, that we now produce images of objects, whereas, heretofore we united the objects themselves.

With four tablets the child forms Fig. 60, a flower pot. Fig. 61, a little garden-house. Fig. 62, a pigeon-house.

With eight tablets Fig. 63, a cottage. Fig. 64, a canoe or boat. Fig. 65, a covered goblet. Fig. 66, a lighthouse. Fig. 67, a clock.

With sixteen tablets Fig. 68, a bridge with two spans. Fig. 69, large gate. Fig. 70, a church. Fig. 71, a gate with belfry. Fig. 72, a fruit basket.

With thirty-two tablets Fig. 73, a peasant's house. Fig. 74, a forge with high chimney. Fig. 75, a coffee-mill. Fig. 76, a coffee-pot without handle.

With sixty-four tablets Fig. 77, a two-story house. Fig. 78, entrance to a railroad depot. Fig. 79, a steamboat.

In Fig. 80, we see the result of combined activity of many children. Although to some grown persons it may appear as if the images produced do not bear much resemblance to what they are intended to represent, it should be remembered that in most cases, the children themselves have given the names to the representations. Instructive conversation should also prevent this *drawing with planes*, as it were, from being a mere mechanical pastime; the entertaining, living word must infuse soul into the activity of the hand and its creations. Each representation, then, will speak to the child and each object in the world of nature and art will have a story to tell to the child in a language for which he will be well prepared.

We need not indicate how these conversations should be carried on, or what they should contain. Who would not think in connection with the pigeon-house, of the beautiful white birds themselves, and the nest they build; the white eggs they lay, the tender young pigeons coming from them, and the care with which the old ones treat the young ones, until they are able to take care of themselves? An application of these relations to those between parents and children, and, perhaps those between God and man, who, as His children enjoy His kindness and love every moment of their lives, may be made, according to circumstances—all depending on the development of the children. However, care should always be taken not to present to them, what might be called abstract morals which the young mind is unable to grasp, and which, if thus forced upon it cannot fail to be injurious to moral development. The aim of all education should be love of the good, beautiful, noble, and sublime; but nothing is more apt to kill this very love, ere it is born, than the monotony of dry, dull preaching of morals to young children. Words not so much as deeds—actual experiences in the life of the child, are its most natural teachers in this important branch of education.

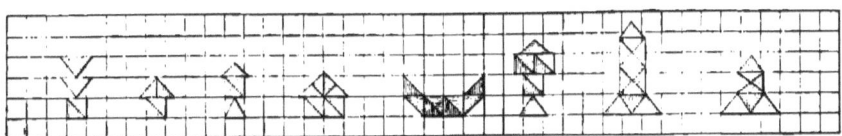

Fig. 60. Fig. 61. Fig. 62. Fig. 63. Fig. 64. Fig. 65. Fig. 66. Fig. 67.

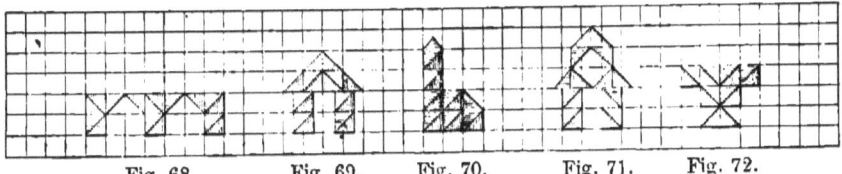

Fig. 68. Fig. 69. Fig. 70. Fig. 71. Fig. 72.

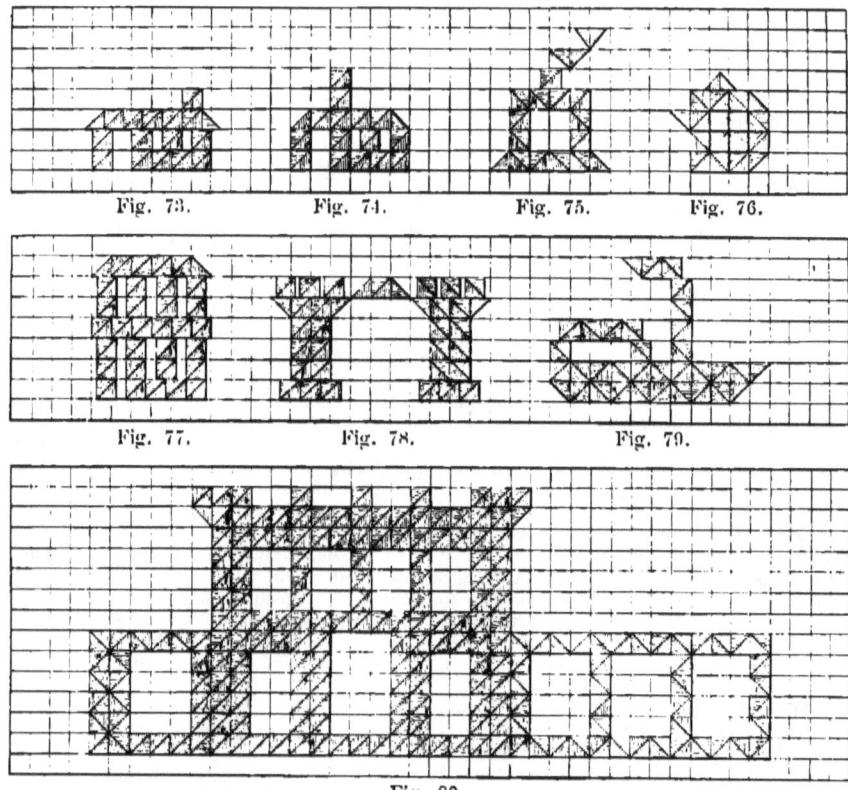

Fig. 73.   Fig. 74.   Fig. 75.   Fig. 76.

Fig. 77.   Fig. 78.   Fig. 79.

Fig. 80.

FORMS OF KNOWLEDGE.
(SEE FIGS. 81—94).

These tablets are, especially qualified to bring to the observation of the child different sizes of the same forms and equal sizes in different forms.

By joining two, four and eight tablets, we become acquainted with the regular figures which may be formed with them, as shown in Figs. 81-86. These with the exception of Fig. 81 are made from the four triangles arranged in different forms.

Figs. 87, 88 and 89 show triangles of which each is double the size of the previous one. In the squares shown in Figs. 90 and 91, the latter is double the size of the former. Figs. 92-94 show two triangles of the same size laid to produce different forms.

That the contemplation of these figures and the occupation with them, must tend to facilitate the understanding of geometrical axioms in the future, who can doubt? And who can gainsay that mathematical instruction, by means of Froebel's methods must needs be facilitated, and better results obtained? That such instruction, will be rendered more fruitful for practical life, is a fact which will be obvious to all, who simply glance at our figures, even without a thorough explanation. They contain demonstratively the larger number of the axioms in elementary geometry, which relate to the conditions of the plane in regular figures.

For the present purpose, it is sufficient if the child learns to distinguish the various kinds of angles, if he knows that the right angles are all equally large, the acute angles smaller, and the obtuse angles larger than a right angle, which the child will easily understand by putting one upon another. A deeper insight in the matter must be reserved for the primary department of instruction.

constantly touch one another. The opposite —long side touching short—we have in Fig. 117, and by traveling from right to left of half the triangles, Figs. 117-122 are obtained. We would have secured a much larger number of forms, if we had not interrupted progress by turning the triangles produced by Fig. 121.

In the fundamental forms Figs. 105 and 117, the sides touched one another. Fig. 123

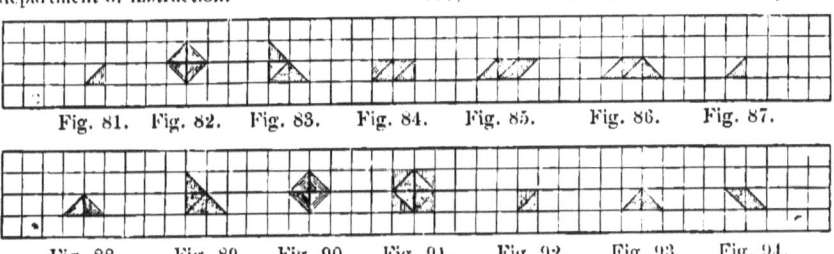

Fig. 81.   Fig. 82.   Fig. 83.   Fig. 84.   Fig. 85.   Fig. 86.   Fig. 87.

Fig. 88.   Fig. 89.   Fig. 90.   Fig. 91.   Fig. 92.   Fig. 93.   Fig. 94.

FORMS OF BEAUTY.

(SEE FIGS. 95—151).

Owing to the multiplicity of elementary forms to be made with the triangles, the number of Forms of Beauty is very large, and the great diversity and beauty of the forms produced by the triangle, square, rhomb, hexagon and octagon, lend a lasting charm to the child's occupation. His inventive power and desire, led by law, will find constant satisfaction, and to give satisfaction in the fullest measure should be a prominent feature of all systems of education.

FORMS BUILT WITH EIGHT TABLETS.

In working with this number we can illustrate the most varied principles. Figs. 95-104 are obtained by doubling the forms produced by four tablets, (Figs. 48-59). Figs. 105-116 start from the fundamental form Fig. 105, making one-half of the tablets move from left to right, the length of one side, with each move. New figures would be produced if we moved from right to left in a similar manner. In these figures, sides always touch sides, and corners touch corners—consequently, parts of the same kind.

The transition or mediation between these two opposites, the touching of corners and sides, would be produced by shortening the movement of the traveling triangle one-half, permitting it to proceed one-half side only.

But let us return to the fundamental form Fig. 105. In it, either long sides or short sides

shows that they may touch at the corners only. In this figure, the right angles are without; in Figs. 124 and 125, they are within. Fig. 125 is the mediation between Figs. 105 and 124, for in Fig. 105 four tablets touch with their sides and in Fig. 124 four with the corners. Fig. 126 is the opposite of Fig. 125, full center, (empty center), and mediation between Figs. 123 and 124—(four right angles without, as in Fig. 123 and four within, as in Fig. 124). It is already seen, from these indications, what a treasure of forms enfolds itself here.

FORMS BUILT WITH SIXTEEN TABLETS.

It would be impossible to exhaust them. Least of all, should it be the task of this work to do this, when it is only intended to show how the productive self-occupation of the pupil can fittingly be assisted. We believe, besides, that we have given a sufficient number of ways on which fantasy may travel, perfectly sure of finding constantly new, beautiful, eye and taste developing formations. We, therefore, add Figs. 127-141 which are produced by quadrupling some of the elementary forms given in Figs. 48-59, and also Figs. 142-144 which indicate how new series of forms of beauty may be developed from each of these forms. It must be evident, even to the casual observer, how here also the law of opposites, and their junction was observed. Opposites are Figs. 127 and 128; mediation Figs. 129

and 130; opposites, Figs. 131 and 132; mediation Figs. 133, 134 and 135; opposites, Figs. 136 and 137; mediation Fig. 138, etc.

FORMS BUILT WITH THIRTY-TWO TABLETS.

As heretofore, we proceed here, also, in the same manner, by multiplying the given elements, or by means of further development, according to the law of opposites. As an example, we give Figs. 145-148, the members of which are produced by a four-fold junction of the elements of Figs. 103 and 104. Figs. 145 and 146 are opposites; Figs. 147 and 148 are mediative forms.

FORMS BUILT WITH SIXTY-FOUR TABLETS.

Here, also, the combined activity of many children will result in forms most interesting. There is another feature of this combined activity not to be forgotten. The children are busy obeying the same law; the same aim unites them—one helps the other. Thus the conditions of human society—family, community, states, etc.,—are already here shown in their effects. A system of education which, so to speak, by mere play, leads the child to appreciate those requisites, by compliance with which it can successfully occupy its position as man in the future, certainly deserves the epithet of a natural and rational one.

Figs. 149, 150 and 151 are enlarged productions from Figs. 131 and 132. They are planned in such a way, as to admit of being continued in all directions, and thus serve to carry out the representation of a very large design.

After having acted so far, according to indications made here, it is now advisable to start from the fundamental forms presented in the Fifth Gift and to use them, with the necessary modifications, in farther occupying the pupils with the tablets.

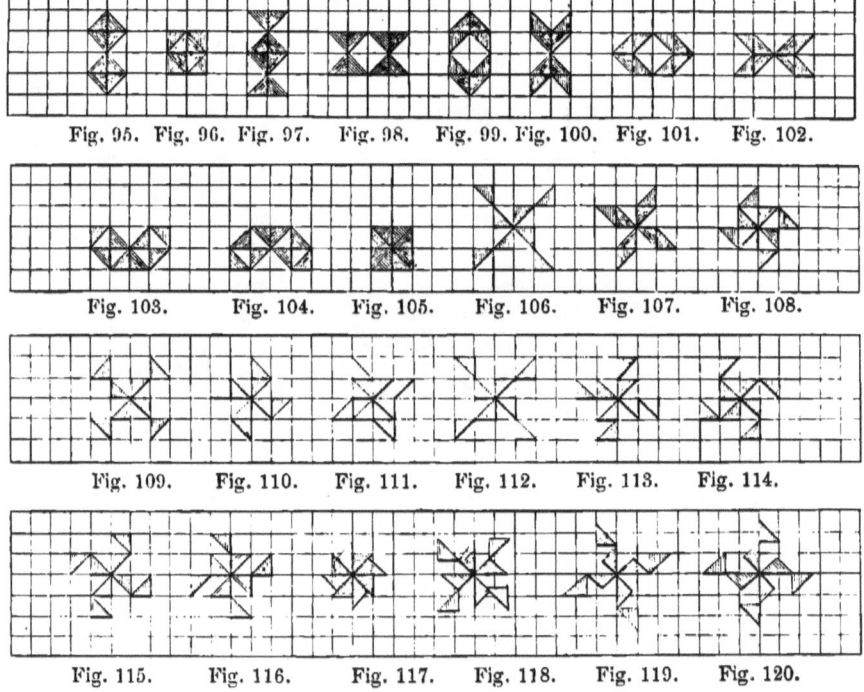

Fig. 95. Fig. 96. Fig. 97. Fig. 98. Fig. 99. Fig. 100. Fig. 101. Fig. 102.

Fig. 103. Fig. 104. Fig. 105. Fig. 106. Fig. 107. Fig. 108.

Fig. 109. Fig. 110. Fig. 111. Fig. 112. Fig. 113. Fig. 114.

Fig. 115. Fig. 116. Fig. 117. Fig. 118. Fig. 119. Fig. 120.

PARADISE OF CHILDHOOD.

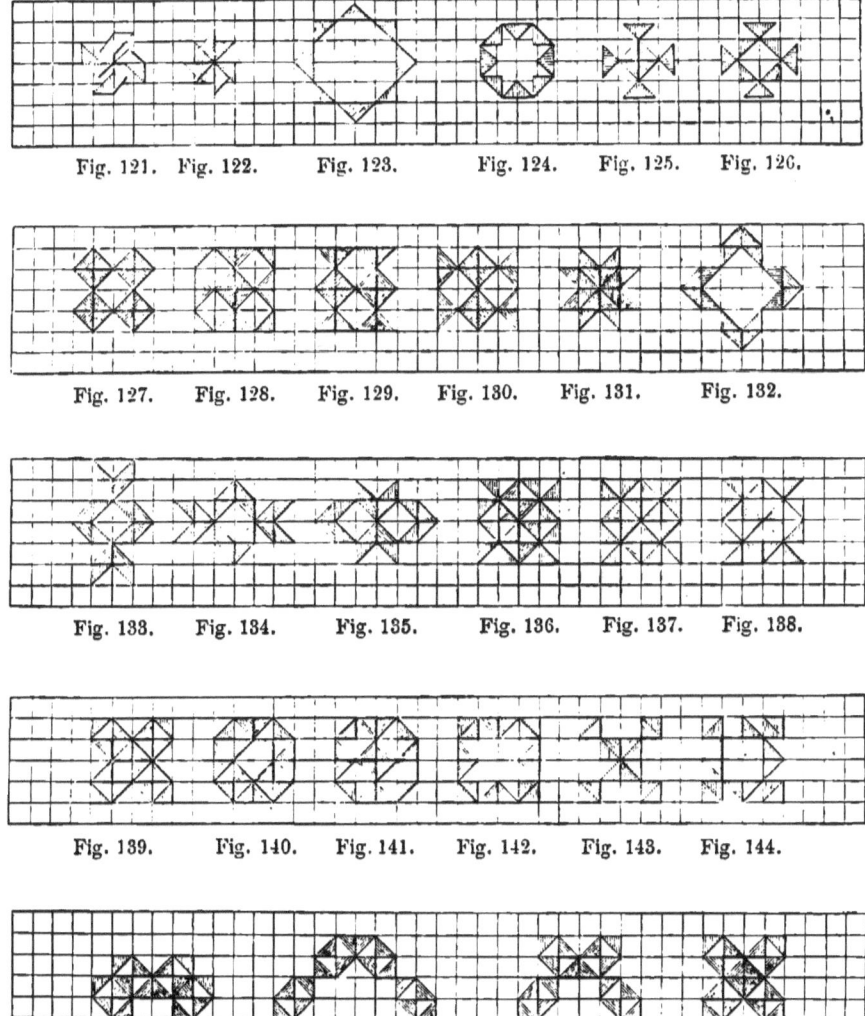

Fig. 121.　Fig. 122.　　Fig. 123.　　Fig. 124.　　Fig. 125.　　Fig. 126.

Fig. 127.　　Fig. 128.　　Fig. 129.　　Fig. 130.　　Fig. 131.　　Fig. 132.

Fig. 133.　　Fig. 134.　　Fig. 135.　　Fig. 136.　　Fig. 137.　　Fig. 138.

Fig. 139.　　Fig. 140.　　Fig. 141.　　Fig. 142.　　Fig. 143.　　Fig. 144.

Fig. 145.　　　Fig. 146.　　　Fig. 147.　　　Fig. 148.

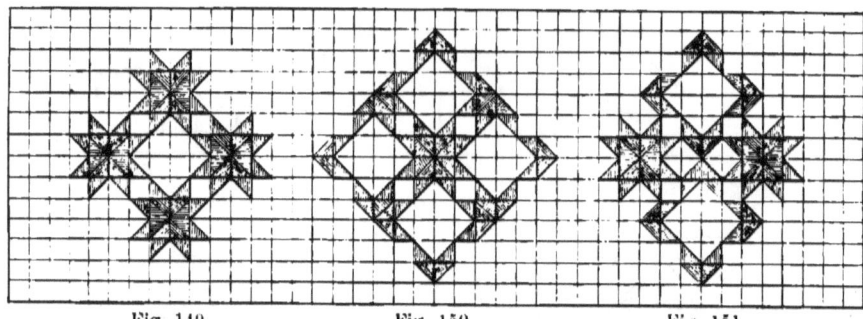

Fig. 149.   Fig. 150.   Fig. 151.

THE EQUILATERAL TRIANGLE.
(SEE FIGS. 154—227).

So far the right angle has predominated in the occupations with the tablets, and the acute angle only appeared in subordinate relations. Now it is the latter alone which governs the actions of the child in producing forms and figures.

The child will naturally compare the equilateral triangle, which he now receives with the isosceles, right-angled tablet already known to him. Both have three sides, both three angles, but on close observation not only their similarities, but also their dissimilarities will become apparent. The three angles of the new triangle are all smaller than a right angle, are acute angles and the three sides are just alike, hence the name—equilateral—meaning *"equal sided"* triangle.

Joining two of these equilateral tablets the child will discover that it cannot form a triangle, square or any of the regular figures previously produced. To undertake to produce forms of life with these tablets would prove very unsatisfactory.

FORMS OF KNOWLEDGE.

These are of particular interest because they present entirely new formations.

It has been mentioned before, that the previously introduced regular mathematical figures do not appear here as a whole. However, a triangle can be represented by four or nine tablets, a rhomboid by four, six or eight tablets, a trapezium by three, and manifold instructive remarks can be made and experiences gathered in the construction of these figures. But above all, it is the rhombus and hexagon, with which the pupil is to be made acquainted here. The child unites two triangles by joining side to side, and thus produces a rhombus.

The child compares the sides—are they alike? What is their direction? Are they parallel? Two and two have the same direction, and are therefore parallel.

The child now examines the angles and finds that two and two are of equal size. They are not right angles. Triangles, smaller than right angles, he knows, are called acute angles, and he hears now that the larger ones are called obtuse angles. The teacher may remark that the latter are twice the size of the former ones. By these remarks the pupil will gradually receive a correct idea of the rhombus and of the qualities by which it is distinguished from the quadrangle, right angle, trapezium and rhomboid.

In the same manner, the hexagon gives occasion for interesting and instructive questions and answers. How many sides has it? How many are parallel? How many angles does it contain? What kind of angles are they? How large are they as compared with the angles of the equal sided triangle? Twice as large.

The power of observation and the reasoning faculties are constantly developed by such conversation, and the results of such exercises are of more importance than all the knowledge that may be acquired in the meantime.

The greater part of this occupation, however, is not within the Kindergarten proper, but belongs to the realm of the Primary school department. If they are introduced in the former they are intended only to swell the sum of general experience in regard to the qualities of things, whereas in the latter, they serve as a foundation of real knowledge in the department of mathematics.

THE FORMS OF BEAUTY.

The child first receives *three tablets* and will find the various positions of the same toward one another according to the law of opposites and their combination.

Fig. 152.   Fig. 153.   Fig. 154.   Fig. 155.   Fig. 156.

Fig. 157.   Fig. 158.   Fig. 159.   Fig. 160.

SIX TABLETS.

The child will unite his tablets around one common center (Fig. 161), form the opposite (Fig. 162), and then arrive at the forms of mediation Figs. 163, 164, 165 and 166, or he unites three elementary forms each composed of two tablets as done in Fig. 167 and forms the opposite Fig. 168 and the mediations Figs. 169 and Fig. 170 or he starts from Fig. 161, turning first one, then two, then three tablets, outwardly. By turning one tablet Figs. 172 and 173, by turning two tablets Figs. 174, 175, 176, 177, 178, 179, and 180 are produced from Fig. 171. This may be continued with three, four and five tablets. All forms thus received give us elementary forms which may be employed as soon as a larger number of tablets are to be used.

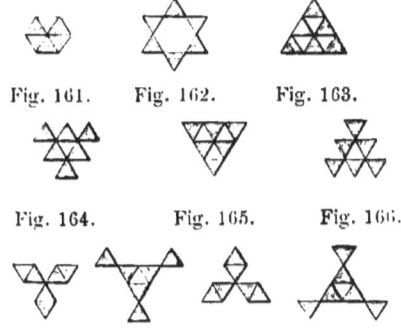

Fig. 161.   Fig. 162.   Fig. 163.
Fig. 164.   Fig. 165.   Fig. 166.
Fig. 167.   Fig. 168.   Fig. 169.   Fig. 170.

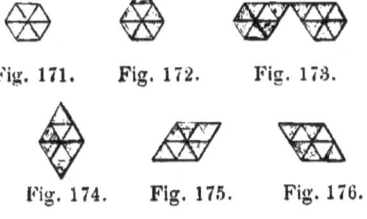

Fig. 171.   Fig. 172.   Fig. 173.
Fig. 174.   Fig. 175.   Fig. 176.
Fig. 177.   Fig. 178.   Fig. 179.   Fig. 180. 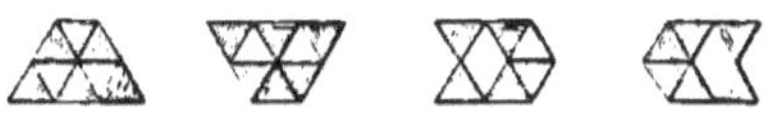

NINE TABLETS.

As with the right-angled triangle, small groups of tablets were combined to form larger figures, so we also do here. The elementary forms, Figs. 152-160 give us in three-fold combination the series as shown in Figs. 181-191 which in course of the occupation may be multiplied at will.

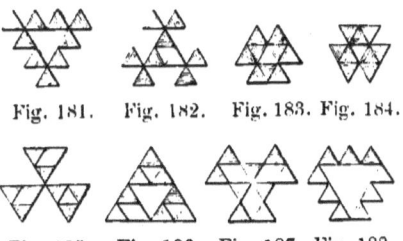

Fig. 181.   Fig. 182.   Fig. 183.   Fig. 184.
Fig. 185.   Fig. 186.   Fig. 187.   Fig. 188.

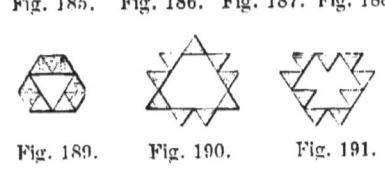

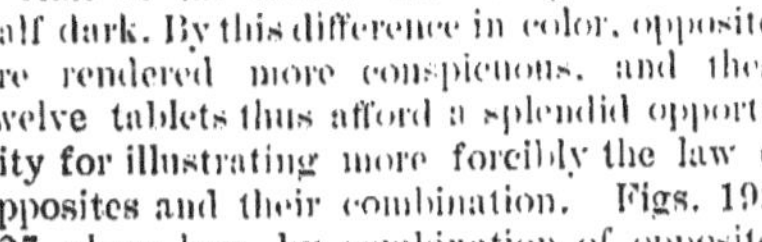

Fig. 189.   Fig. 190.   Fig. 191.

TWELVE TABLETS.

Half of the tablets are of light wood and half dark. By this difference in color, opposites are rendered more conspicuous, and these twelve tablets thus afford a splendid opportunity for illustrating more forcibly the law of opposites and their combination. Figs. 192-227, show how, by combination of opposites in the forms *a* and *b*, every time the star *c* is produced. Entirely new series of forms may be produced by employing a larger number of tablets, eighteen, twenty-four or thirty-six. We are, however, obliged to leave these representations to the combined inventive powers of teacher and pupil.

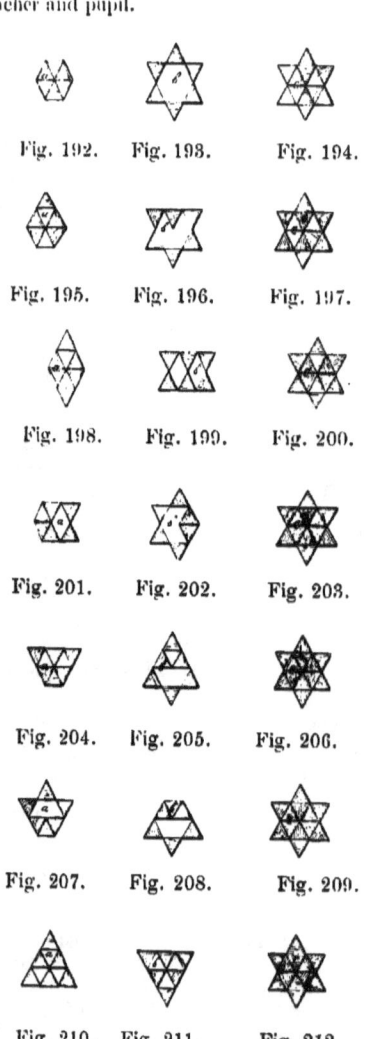

Fig. 192.   Fig. 193.   Fig. 194.

Fig. 195.   Fig. 196.   Fig. 197.

Fig. 198.   Fig. 199.   Fig. 200.

Fig. 201.   Fig. 202.   Fig. 203.

Fig. 204.   Fig. 205.   Fig. 206.

Fig. 207.   Fig. 208.   Fig. 209.

Fig. 210.   Fig. 211.   Fig. 212.

Fig. 213.    Fig. 214.    Fig. 215.

Fig. 216.    Fig. 217.    Fig. 218.

Fig. 219.   Fig. 220.    Fig. 221.

Fig. 222.   Fig. 223.    Fig. 224.

Fig. 225.    Fig 226.    Fig. 227.

THE OBTUSE-ANGLED TRIANGLE WITH TWO SIDES ALIKE.

(SEE FIGS. 228—250).

The child receives a box with sixty-four obtuse-angled tablets. He examines one of them and compares it with the right-angled triangle, with two sides alike. It has two sides alike, has also two acute angles, but the third angle is larger than the right angle; it is an obtuse-angle, and the tablet is, therefore, an obtuse-angled triangle with two sides alike.

The pupil then unites two and two tablets by laying them so that edges join edges, corners touch corners and edges join corners as shown in Figs. 228-236.

Fig. 228.   Fig. 229.

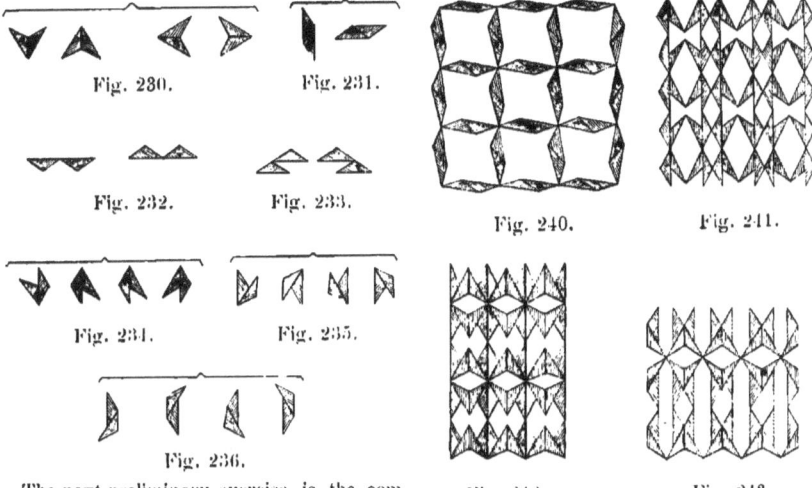

Fig. 230. Fig. 231.
Fig. 232. Fig. 233.
Fig. 234. Fig. 235.
Fig. 236.
Fig. 240. Fig. 241.
Fig. 242. Fig. 243.

The next preliminary exercise, is the combination by fours, of the elementary forms thus produced. Peculiarly beautiful, mosaic-like forms of beauty result from this process, such as Figs. 237-243, which are produced by the combination of two opposites or by mediative forms. Figs. 244-250 are samples of forms of life.

The forms of knowledge which may be produced, afford opportunity to repeat what has been taught and learned previously about proportion of form and size. In the Primary School the geometrical proportions are further introduced, by which means the knowledge of the pupils, in regard to angles, as to the position they occupy in the triangle, can be successfully developed by practical observation, without the necessity of ever dealing in mere abstractions.

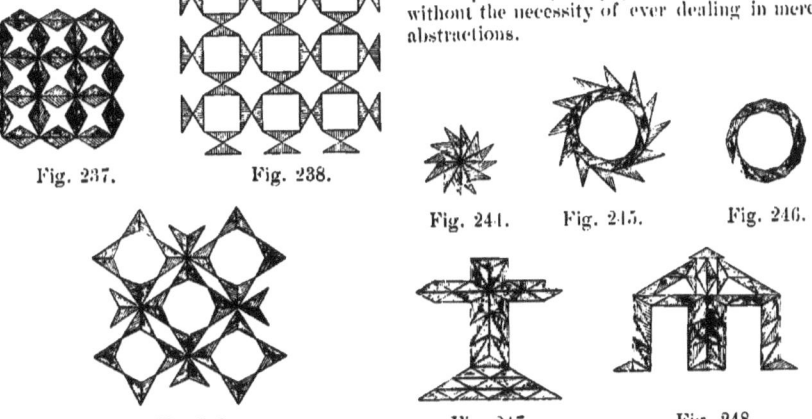

Fig. 237. Fig. 238.
Fig. 239.
Fig. 244. Fig. 245. Fig. 246.
Fig. 247. Fig. 248.

Fig. 249.

Fig. 250.

THE RIGHT-ANGLED TRIANGLE WITH NO EQUAL SIDES.

(SEE FIGS. 251—280).

The little box containing fifty-six tablets of the above description, each of which are in form like one-half of the obtuse-angled triangle, enables the child to represent a goodly number of forms of life, as shown in Figs. 251-264.

A comparison with the right-angled triangle with two equal sides will facilitate the matter greatly.

On the whole, however, the process of development may be pursued, as repeatedly indicated on previous occasions.

Fig. 253.

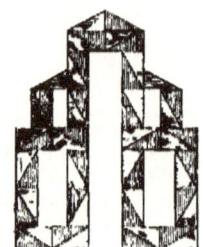

Fig. 254.

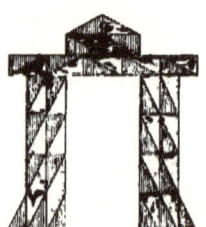

Fig. 251.

In producing them sufficient opportunities will present themselves to let the child find out the qualities of the new occupation material.

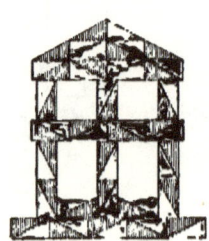

Fig. 255.

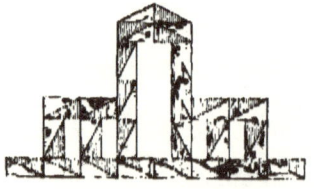

Fig. 252.

Fig. 256.

PARADISE OF CHILDHOOD. 163

Fig. 257.

Fig. 258.

Fig. 259.

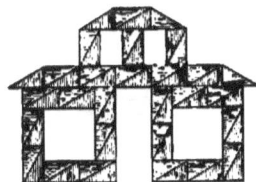
Fig. 260.

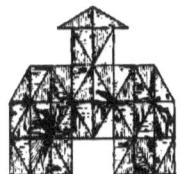
Fig. 261.

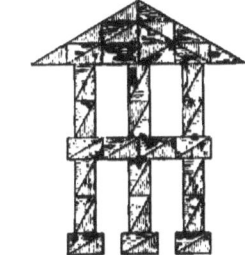
Fig. 262.

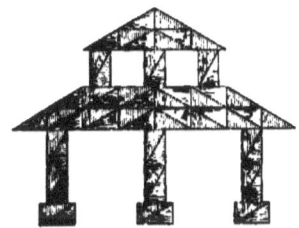
Fig. 263.

Fig. 264.

The variety of the forms of beauty to be laid with these tablets, is especially founded on their combination in twos. Figs. 265-270 show the forms produced by joining equal sides.

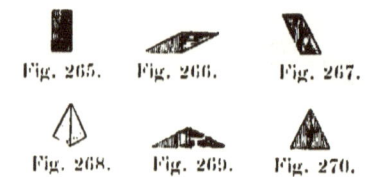

Fig. 265.   Fig. 266.   Fig. 267.
Fig. 268.   Fig. 269.   Fig. 270.

In similar manner, the child has to find out the forms which will be the result of joining unlike edges, like corners, unlike corners, and finally corners and edges.

By a fourfold combination of such elementary forms the child receives the material (Figs. 271-282), to produce a large number of forms of beauty similar to those given under Figs. 283-286.

For the purpose, also, of presenting to the child's observation, in a new shape, proportions of form and size, in the production of forms of knowledge, these tablets are very serviceable.

Like the previous tablets, these also, and a following set of similar tablets, are used in the Primary Department for enlivening the instruction in Geometry. It is believed that nothing has ever been invented to so facilitate, and render interesting to teacher and pupil, the instruction in this so important branch of education as the tablets forming the Seventh Gift of Froebel's Occupation Material, the use of which is commenced with the children when they have entered the second year of their Kindergarten discipline.

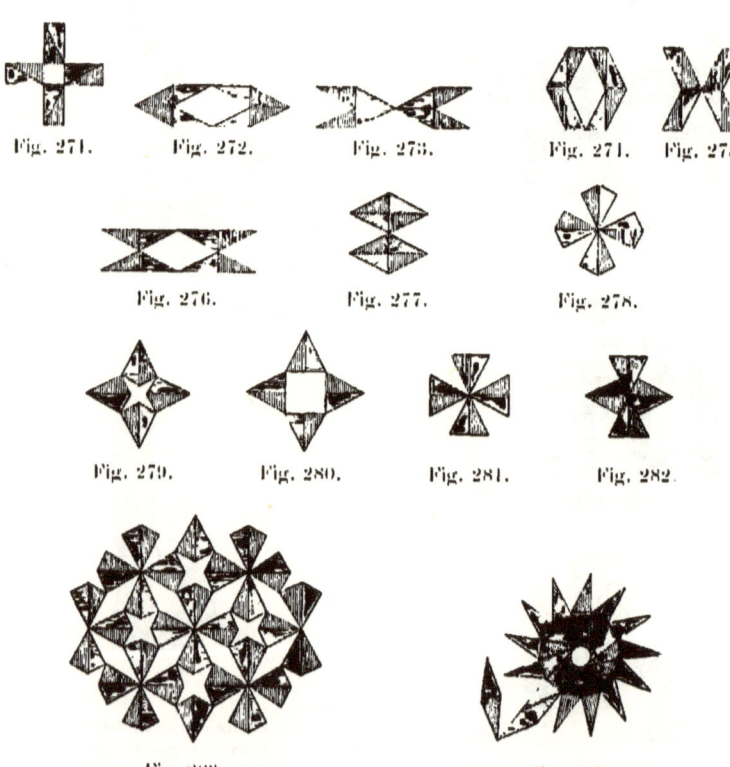

Fig. 271.   Fig. 272.   Fig. 273.   Fig. 274.   Fig. 275.
Fig. 276.   Fig. 277.   Fig. 278.
Fig. 279.   Fig. 280.   Fig. 281.   Fig. 282.
Fig. 283.   Fig. 284.

Fig. 285.

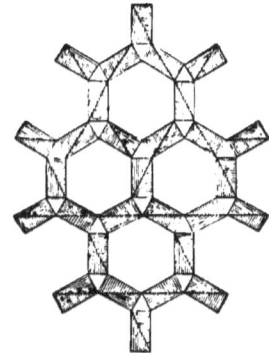

Fig. 286.

EDITOR'S NOTES.

As the tablets of the seventh gift represent surfaces instead of solids they at once become more ideal and serve as an introduction to the elements of drawing, or to the representation of solids by plane surfaces. These tablets, in fact, contain in concrete form the principles of plain geometry, and illustrate many of the problems in elementary industrial drawing. The natural foundation for a mathematical and scientific education which the kindergarten lays is an important element to aid in the production of more expert and accurate workmen in any manual occupation, and will tend to cultivate a more accurate and practical conception of every-day experiences. The manual training exhibit sent from Russia to Philadelphia in 1876 began the evolution of a practical system of manual training in this country, and the corresponding exhibition of the kindergarten work and material, with the first practical kindergarten guide in the English language, was equally a forerunner of the kindergarten in America, which to-day stands well in advance of the work in all other parts of the world, while its possibilities can as yet be only imagined. Twenty years ago America was at a great industrial disadvantage in comparison with older nations, because her artizans lacked the scientific and art education which was afforded the workmen of other countries. This defect is rapidly being overcome in the establishment of industrial schools, through the liberal donations of some of our capitalists and the general progress of our public school officials along the same lines. In laying the foundation of such education in the kindergarten the seventh gift has immense capabilities, but much of its force and value has been lost from lack of logical sequence in the derivation of the forms of the tablet, and the order of their use. In the original seventh gift tablets as imported from Germany there were five forms, namely, the square, half square, equilateral triangle, obtuse-angled triangle and scalene-triangle made by dividing diagonally an oblong of two squares. In this gift the absence of the circle and half circle seems to have been unfortunate, because the ball is the first solid, and correspondingly the circle should be the first surface form, and the general introduction of the circle and half circle by the leading kindergarteners of our day seems to particularly indorse this criticism.

Following the circle based on the sphere, should come the square which is one of the six equal faces of the cube, and the half square formed by a diagonal division of the square should follow. Next, we may have the equilateral triangle which is the type of three sided plane figures, as the square is the type of four-sided figures. If the equilateral triangle is divided by a line from one corner to the center of the opposite side, this line will be perpendicular to that side and one of these halves of the equilateral will be a scalene-triangle with two acute angles and one right angle. If these two triangles formed by dividing the equilateral triangle are placed base to base, we have an obtuse-angled triangle. These five forms are the same as in the original German gift, except the scalene triangle, and it is in the form and order of introduction of this tablet, that the objection to the old seventh gift is found. If the scalene-triangle is one-half of the equilateral it becomes a typical and valuable form, instead of a meaningless and useless one when it is a half of an oblong of two squares. In this new form the angles are ninety degrees, sixty degrees and thirty degrees, all of which are typical or in a sense standard angles, but if instead of this triangle we have the half of the oblong of two squares, the two acute angles become fractional and have

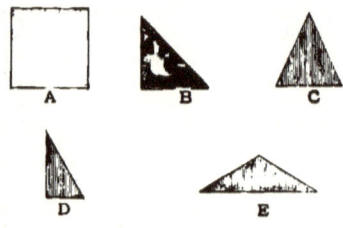

no value as standards and no logical relation to the other tablets. Two of them will not make an equilateral triangle, neither will they make the obtuse-angled triangle with which they must be associated, and no number of them will exactly fill a circle. In fact, the triangle is a constant source of error and false education to the eye, and in its use much of the practical value of this gift is sacrificed.

In the accompanying diagrams, A, B, C, D, E, the tablets of the seventh gift are shown in their proper order. The square A educates the eye to correctly estimate a right angle, one of the essential qualifications of a skilled artizan. The bisection of the square gives the forty-five degrees triangle B, thus training the eye to measure that universal angle, the miter, one-half of a right angle. These two angles are so common that the draftsman or the designer constantly uses a large "tablet B" in connection with the T square in his work. The angle of forty-five degrees is one eighth of the circle and this triangle is used in a very simple way for drawing the octagon, thus:—

Draw a circle and with the T square draw a tangent to the top and bottom of the circle. With the triangle sliding on the blade of the T

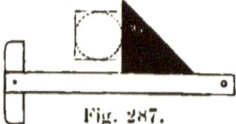

Fig. 287.

square draw the two tangents at opposite sides, Fig. 287. Then place the hypothenuse of the triangle on the T square and draw four diagonals tangent to the circle to complete the octagon, as in Fig. 288. This is but one of the many ways in which the forty-five degrees triangle is used by the draftsman. The equilateral triangle C has three angles of sixty de-

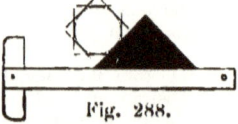

Fig. 288.

grees each, six of which form a complete circle. The divided equilateral or right-angled scalene triangle D has one angle of ninety degrees, one of sixty degrees and one of thirty degrees, and this tablet is another tool indispensable to the draftsman, and a constant companion of the forty-five degrees triangle and the T square. It is of the same service in drawing the hexagon that the forty-five degrees triangle is in

Fig. 289.

forming the octagon, as may be seen in Fig. 289, and Fig. 290, which following Figs. 287 and 288, will usually give the idea without further explanation. In case the matter is not perfectly clear these operations can be performed with the T square and triangles of the drawing kit of the elementary school. These two triangles represent all the angles which may be termed standards, namely, ninety degrees, forty-five degrees, sixty degrees and thirty degrees, and a child in the kindergarten should become as familiar with them as with the size of the squares on the table. The obtuse-angled triangle E, as made in the gifts, is in form like two of D, joined at the short sides, but for convenience the size is reduced one-half.

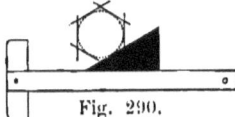

Fig. 290.

The only argument for the use of the scalene-triangle derived from the oblong of two squares, seems to be based on the fact that such a triangle is conveniently made on the netted drawing, but this certainly is not of sufficient importance to warrant the introduction of a mathematical monstrosity such as this triangle must be considered.

Among the seventh gift tablets for sale and in use in the kindergartens both forms of the scalene-triangles may be found. One is the half of an oblong of two squares and the other the half of a equilateral triangle. Some kindergartners are using either the one or the other with well settled convictions as to its superior value, while others have given little or no thought to the subject. The difference is so radical between the two geometrical forms that it should become a question of considerable importance in the mind of an intelligent kindergartner, which form she selects in her gifts. Having decided, she ought to be sure that she gets what she wants when ordering material. The argument in favor of the half equilateral has been briefly expressed above, because the experience of the editor in practical geometry and industrial drawing has convinced him of the truth of this position, but every kindergartner is entitled to the opposite opinion after having given careful thought to the subject.

In presenting this gift as the circle is the first plane to be given, a clay sphere may be modeled and by cutting through the center, the face of the hemisphere will show the circle thus proving to the children that it is derived from the ball.

Call attention to other circular objects and give simple lessons in direction and position; follow this by laying forms of symmetry with the circle, (Figs. 291-298), and half circle, (Figs. 299-304), also border patterns, (Fig. 305). Sequences may be derived by working by opposites, as shown in Figs. 306-310.

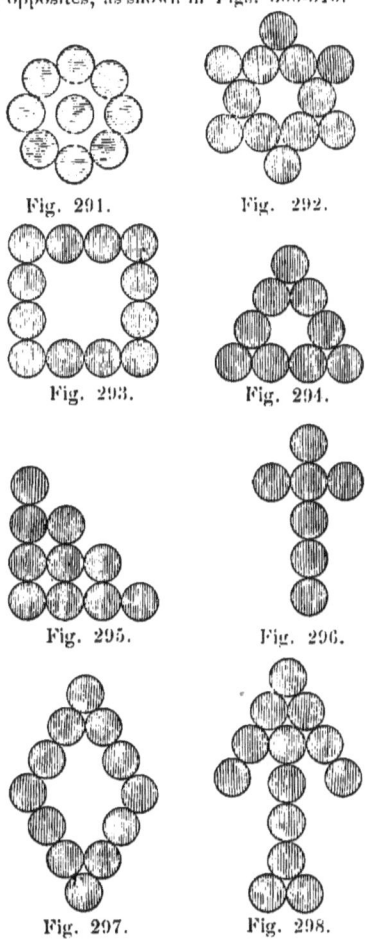

Fig. 291. Fig. 292.

Fig. 293. Fig. 294.

Fig. 295. Fig. 296.

Fig. 297. Fig. 298.

In considering the square let a piece of apple or bread be cut just the size and shape of the third gift, and then a slice cut from it to show how the square tablet is a representative of the surface of the cube. Most children would understand it, perhaps, without this, but something real is better and the fact that

168   PARADISE OF CHILDHOOD.

taking the slice from the cube has left only a part of a cube becomes more of a reality to in the tablets of this gift, it often gives him great pleasure to reproduce that design in permanent form by pasting colored papers cut

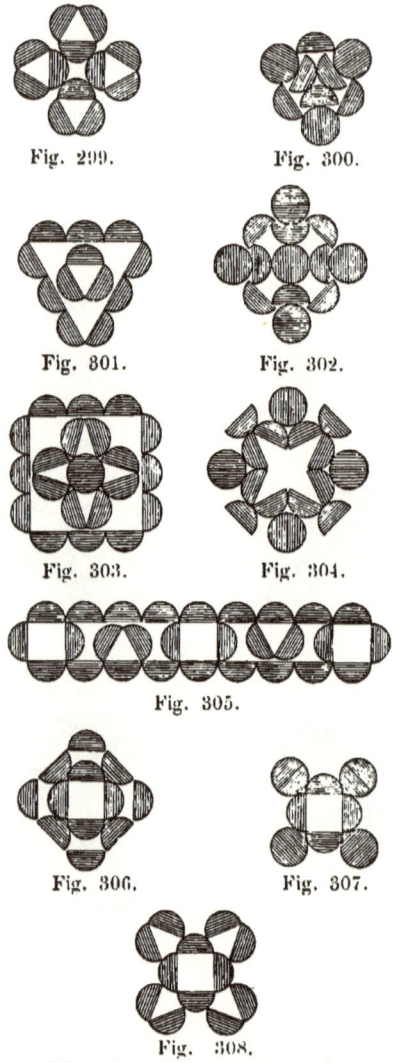

Fig. 299.   Fig. 300.

Fig. 301.   Fig. 302.

Fig. 303.   Fig. 304.

Fig. 305.

Fig. 306.   Fig. 307.

Fig. 309.

Fig. 310.

in shapes like the tablets on to a piece of card or heavy paper, which may be carried home as a souvenir. In this occupation which has been called "Parquetry," the element of color may be introduced while both the form instruction and manual training involved are invaluable. In some styles of the seventh gift the tablets are painted in a variety of colors, and while on first thought this feature may be very attractive, experience has seemed to demonstrate to the satisfaction of kindergartners in this country, that the tablets in light and dark woods, expressing tones rather than color are more valuable, educationally, than the colored tablets. Before the introduction of Parquetry papers the colored tablets were quite popular, but with the greatly improved expression of color sequences found in the modern educational colored paper, this feature seems open to many objections. No painted surfaces subject to constant use by the children and exposure to the light, can permanently retain their colors so as to have much educational value in color perception, and therefore the occupations are far better adapted to the teaching of color than the gifts. Also the consideration of the effects of light and shade in the designs as made with the tablets is as much as the child's mind is able to grasp at first, while increased interest is secured later by the addition of colors in the reproduction of the designs, by pasting papers selected from the great variety of colors in the modern educational colored papers. Parquetry not only delights the children but teaches accuracy of eye and hand in placing the small bits of paper, neatness in the gumming, and cultivates taste in the selection and combination of colors. It is distinctly an American occupation which has been generally accepted as a valuable addition to the earlier occupations of the kindergarten.

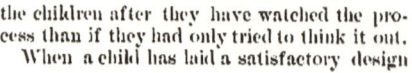
Fig. 308.

the children after they have watched the process than if they had only tried to think it out. When a child has laid a satisfactory design

THE EIGHTH GIFT.
STICKS FOR LAYING OF FIGURES.

As the *tablets* of the Seventh Gift are nothing but an embodiment of the *planes* surrounding or limiting the *cube*, and as these *planes*, limits of the cube, are nothing but the *representations* of the extension in *length, breadth and height*, already contained in the sphere and ball, so also the sticks are derived from the cube, forming as they do, and here bodily representing its *edges*. But they are also contained in the tablets, because the plane is thought of, as consisting of a continued or repeated line, and this may be illustrated by placing a sufficient number of one inch long sticks side by side, and close together, until a square is formed.

The sticks lead us another step farther, from the material, bodily, toward the realm of abstractions.

By means of the tablets, we were enabled to produce flat images of bodies; the slats, which, as previously mentioned, form a transition from plane to line, gave, it is true, the outlines of forms, but these outlines still retained a certain degree of the plane about them; in the sticks, however, we obtain the material to draw the outlines of objects, by bodily lines, as perfectly as it can possibly be done.

The laying of sticks is a favorite occupation with all children. Their fantasy sees in them the most different objects,—stick, yard measure, candle; in short, they are to them representatives of everything straight.

Our sticks are of the thickness of a line (one twelfth of an inch), and are cut in various lengths. The child, holding the stick in his hand, is asked: What do you hold in your hand? How do you hold it? Vertically. Can

Fig. 1.   Fig. 2.   Fig. 3.

you hold it in any other way? Yes! I can hold it horizontally. Still in another way? Slanting from left above, to right below, or from right above to left below. (Figs. 1-3).

Lay your stick upon the table. How does it lie? In what other direction can you place it?

The child receives a second stick. How many sticks have you now? Now try to form something. The child lays a standing cross. (Fig. 4). You certainly can lay many other and more beautiful things; but let us see what else we may produce of this cross, by moving the horizontal stick, by half its length, (Figs. 4 to 14).

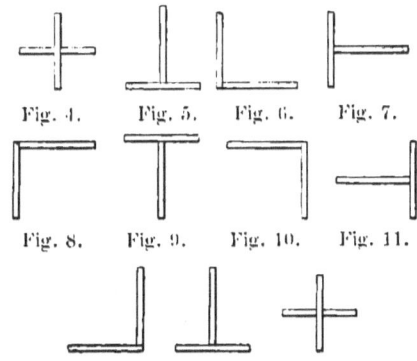

Fig. 4.   Fig. 5.   Fig. 6.   Fig. 7.

Fig. 8.   Fig. 9.   Fig. 10.   Fig. 11.

Fig. 12.   Fig. 13.   Fig. 14.

Starting from a lying cross, (Fig. 15) or from a pair of open tongs, (where two acute and two obtuse angles are formed by the crossing sticks), and proceeding similarly as with Figs. 4-14, we will produce all positions which two sticks can occupy, relative to one another, except the parallel, and this will give ample opportunity to refresh, and more deeply impress upon the pupil's mind, all that has been introduced so far, concerning vertical, horizontal and oblique lines, and of right, acute and obtuse angles. (Figs. 15-23).

Fig. 15.   Fig. 16.   Fig. 17.   Fig. 18.

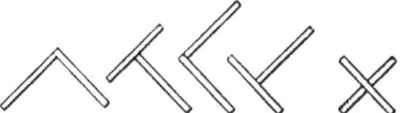

Fig. 19.   Fig. 20.   Fig. 21.   Fig. 22.   Fig. 23.

With two sticks, we can also form little figures, which show some slight resemblance with things around us. By them we enliven the power of recollection and imagination of the child, exercise his ability of comparison, increase his treasure of ideas, and develop in all these his power of perception and conception—the most indispensable requisites for disciplining the mind.

Following are given representations of objects made:—

With two sticks, Fig. 24, A Playing Table. Fig. 25, Pick Axe. Fig. 26, An Angle Measure. (Carpenter's square).

Fig. 24.   Fig. 25.   Fig. 26.

With three sticks, Fig. 27, A Flail. Fig. 28, A Small Flag. Fig. 29, A Star.

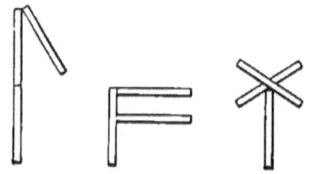

Fig. 27.   Fig. 28.   Fig. 29.

With four sticks, Fig. 30, A Wooden Chair. Fig. 31, A Wash bench. Fig. 32, A Crib. Fig. 33, Flower-pot.

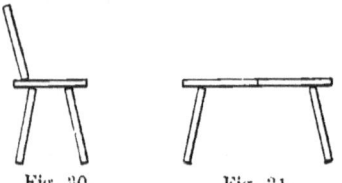

Fig. 30.   Fig. 31.

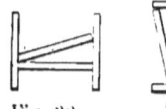

Fig. 32.   Fig. 33.

With five sticks, Fig. 34, Signal Flag of R. R. Guard. Fig. 35, A Cottage. Fig. 36, Sawhorse. Fig. 37, A Chair.

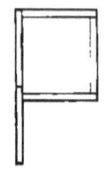

Fig. 34.   Fig. 35.

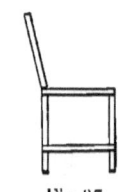

Fig. 36.   Fig. 37.

With six sticks, Fig. 38, A Flag. Fig. 39, A Boat. Fig. 40, A Reel. Fig. 41, A Small Tree.

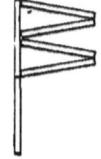
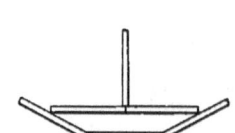

Fig. 38.   Fig. 39.

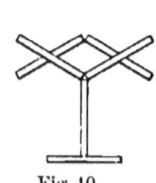

Fig. 40.   Fig. 41.

With seven sticks, Fig. 42, A Dwelling House. Fig. 43, A Bridge with Three Spans.

Fig. 44, Tombstone and Cross. Fig. 45, Rail Fence. With nine sticks, Fig. 51, Dwelling-house. Fig. 52, Sailboat. Fig. 53, Balance. Fig. 54, Coffee-mill. Fig. 55, Students Lamp.

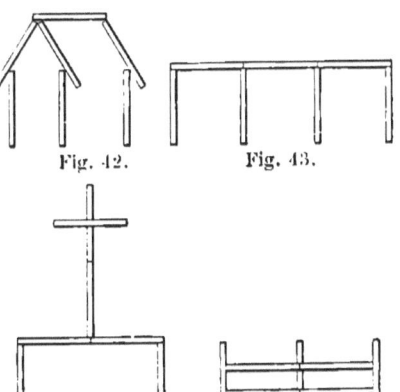

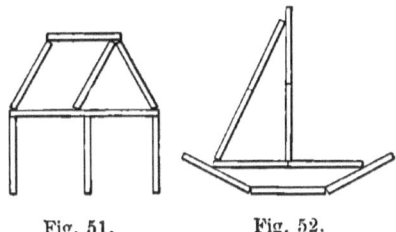

Fig. 51.   Fig. 52.

With eight sticks, Fig. 46, Church, with steeple. Fig. 47, Gas Lantern. Fig. 48, Corn-crib. Fig. 49, A Flower-pot. Fig. 50, A Piano forte.

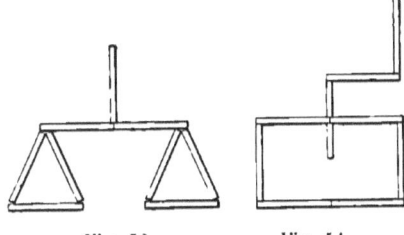

Fig. 53.   Fig. 54.

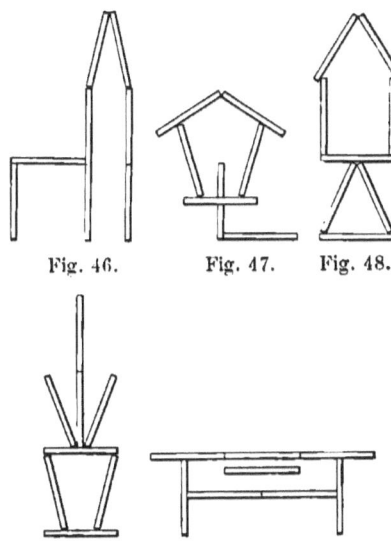

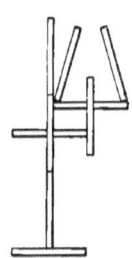

Fig. 55.

With ten sticks, Fig. 56, Graveyard Wall. Fig. 57, A Hall. Fig. 58, A Flower-pot. Fig. 59, A Bedstead. Fig. 60, A Flag.

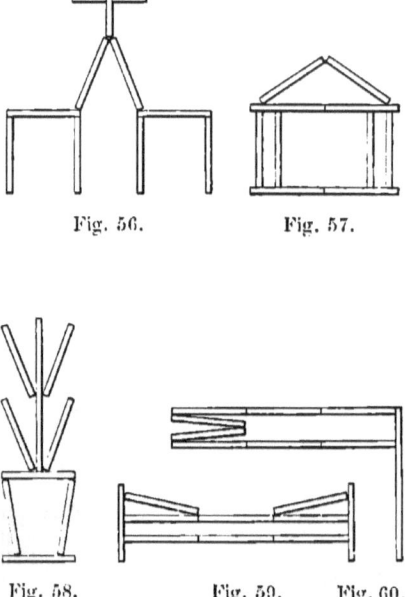

Fig. 56.   Fig. 57.

Fig. 63.

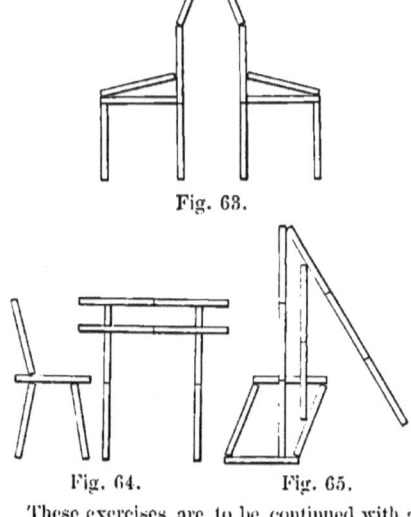

Fig. 64.   Fig. 65.

Fig. 58.   Fig. 59.   Fig. 60.

With eleven sticks, Fig. 61, A Kitchen Lamp. Fig. 62, Cup and Saucer.

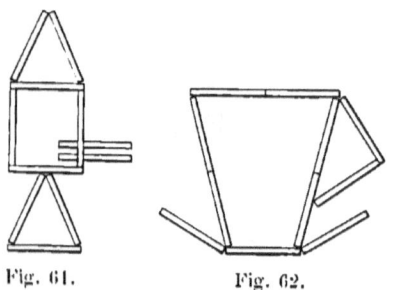

Fig. 61.   Fig. 62.

With twelve sticks, Fig. 63, A Church. Fig. 64, Chair and Table. Fig. 65, A Well with Sweep.

These exercises are to be continued with a larger number of sticks. The hints given above, will enable the teacher to conduct the laying of sticks in a manner interesting, as well as useful, for her pupils.

It is advisable to guide the activity of the child occasionally in another direction. The pupils may all be called upon to lay tables, which can be produced from two to ten sticks, or houses which can be laid with eighteen sticks.

Sticks are also employed for representing forms of beauty. The previous, or simultaneous occupation with the building blocks, and tablets, will assist the child in producing the same in great variety. Figs. 66-72 belong to this class of representations.

Combination of the occupation material of several, or all children taking part in the exercises, will lead to the production of larger forms of life, or beauty, which in the Primary Department, can even be extended to representing whole landscapes, in which the material is augmented by the introduction of sawdust to represent foliage, grass, land, moss, etc.

By means of combination, the children often produce forms which afford them great pleasure, and repay them for the careful perseverance and skill employed. They often express

PARADISE OF CHILDHOOD. 173

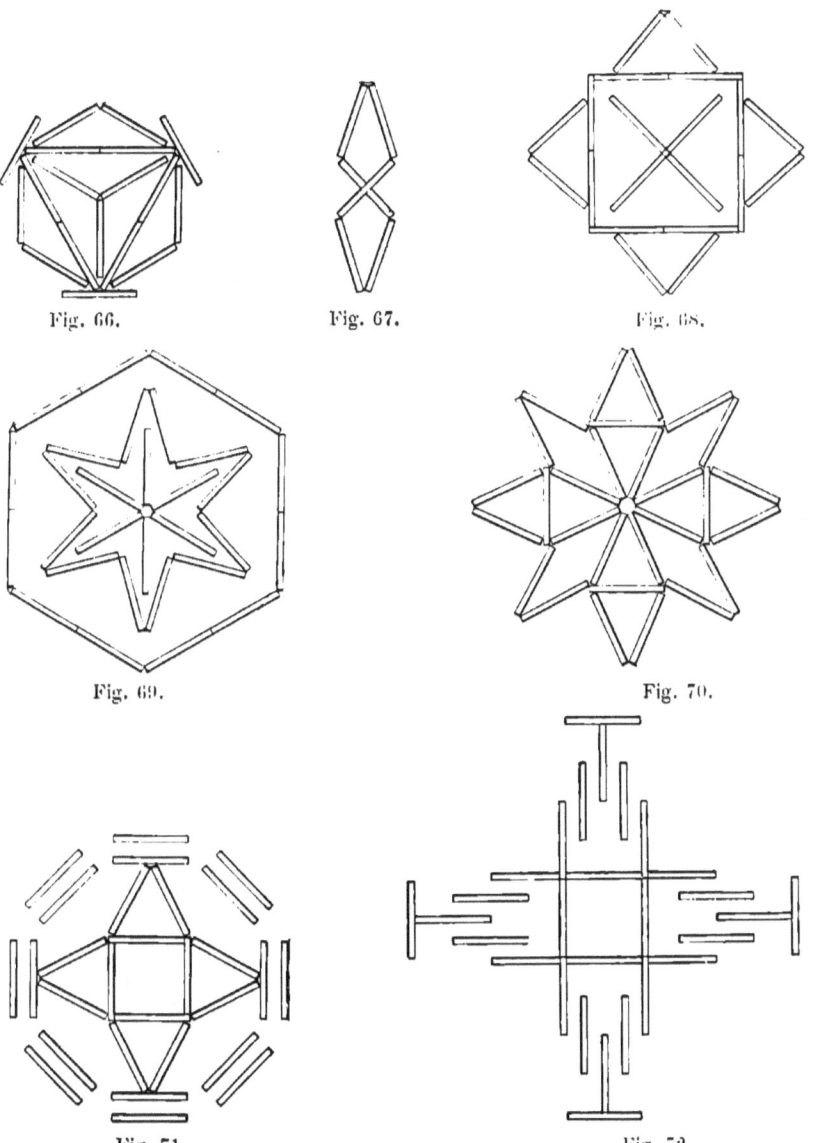

Fig. 66.   Fig. 67.   Fig. 68.

Fig. 69.   Fig. 70.

Fig. 71.   Fig. 72.

the wish that they might be able to show the production to father, or mother, or sister, or friend. But this they cannot do, as the sticks will separate when taken up.

We should assist the little ones in carrying out their desire of giving pleasure to others, by showing to, or presenting them with the result of their own industry, in portable form. By wetting the ends of the sticks with mucilage, or binding them together with needle and thread, or placing them on substantial paper, we can grant their desire, and make them happy, and be sure of their thanks for our efforts.

But we have another means of rendering these representations permanent, and it is by *drawing*, which, on its own account, is to be practiced in the most elementary manner. We begin the drawing, as will hereafter be shown, as a special branch of occupation, as soon as the child has reached its third or fourth year. The method of laying sticks is in general the same as applied for drawing, the latter, however, progresses less rapidly. It is advisable to combine sticks in regular figures, triangles and squares, and to find out in a small number of such figures all possible combinations according to the law of opposites.

All these occupations depend on the larger or smaller number of sticks employed; they therefore afford means for increasing and strengthening the knowledge of the child. The pupil, however, is much more decidedly introduced into the elements of ciphering, when the sticks are placed into his hands for this specific purpose. We do not hesitate to make the assertion that there is no material better fitted to teach the rudiments in figures, as also the more advanced steps in arithmetic, than Frœbel's sticks. A few packages of the sticks in the hands of the pupil is all that is needed in the Kindergarten proper, and the following Department of the Primary School.

The children receive a package with ten sticks each. Take one stick and lay it vertically on the table. Lay another at the side of it. How many sticks are now before you? Twice one makes two.

Lay still another stick upon the table. How many are there now? One and one and one—two and one are three.

Still another, etc., etc., until all ten sticks are placed in a similar manner upon the table. Now take away one stick. How many remain? Ten less nine leaves one. Take away another stick from these nine. How many are left? Nine less one leaves eight. Take another; this leaves seven———? etc., etc., until all the sticks are taken one by one from the table, and are in the child's hands again. Take two sticks and lay them upon the table, and place two others at some distance from them. (‖ ‖) How many are now on the table? Two and two are *four*. Lay two more sticks beside these four sticks. How many are there now? Four and two are *six*. Two more. How many are there now? Six and two are *eight*. And still another two. How many now? Eight and two are *ten*.

The child has learned to add sticks by twos. If we do the opposite, he will also learn to subtract by twos. In similar manner we proceed with *three*, *four* and *five*. After that we *alternate*, with addition and subtraction. For instance, we lay three times two sticks upon the table and take away twice two, adding again four times two. Finally we give up the equality of the number and alternate, by adding different numbers. We lay upon the table two and three sticks which equal five, adding two, which equal seven, adding three, which equal ten. This affords opportunity to introduce six and nine, as a whole, more frequently than was the case in previous exercises. In subtraction we observe the same method, and introduce exercises in which subtraction and addition alternate with unequal numbers. Lay six sticks upon the table, take two away, add four, take away one, add three and ask the child how many sticks are on the table, after each of these operations.

In like manner, as the child learned the figures from one to ten, and added and subtracted with them as far as the number of ten sticks admitted, it will now learn to use the tens up to one hundred. Packages of ten sticks are distributed. It treats each package as it did before the single stick. One is laid upon the table, and the child says, "Once ten;" add a second, "Twice ten;" a third, "Three times ten," etc. Subsequently he is told, that it is not customary to say twice, or two times ten, but twenty; not three times ten, but thirty, etc. This experience will take root so much the sooner, in his memory, and become knowledge, as all this is the result of his own activity.

As soon as the child has acquired sufficient ability in adding and subtracting by tens, the combination of units and tens is introduced.

The pupil receives two packages of ten sticks —places one of them upon the table, opens the second and adds its sticks one by one to the ten contained in the whole package. He learns ten and one equal eleven, ten and two equal twelve, ten and three equal thirteen, until ten and ten equal twenty sticks. Gathering the ten loose sticks, the child receives another package and places it beside the first whole package. Ten and ten equal twenty sticks. Then he adds one of the loose sticks and says twenty and one equal twenty-one, twenty and two equal twenty-two, etc. Another package of ten brings the number to thirty-one, etc., etc., up to ninety-one sticks. In this manner he learns twenty-two, thirty-two, up to ninety-two, twenty-three to ninety-three and one hundred, and to add and subtract within this limit. To be taught addition and subtraction in this manner, is to acquire sound knowledge, founded on self-activity and experience, and is far superior to any kind of mind-killing memorizing usually employed in this connection.

If addition and subtraction are each other's opposites, so addition and multiplication on the one hand, and subtraction and division on the other, are oppositionally equal, or, rather, multiplication and division are shortened addition and subtraction.

In addition, when using equal numbers of sticks, the child finds that by adding two and two, and two and two sticks he receives eight sticks and is told that this may also be expressed by saying four times two sticks are eight sticks. It will be easy to see how to proceed with division, after the hints given above.

Let none of our readers misunderstand us as intimating that all this should be accomplished in the Kindergarten proper.

Enough has been accomplished if the child in the Kindergarten by means of sticks and other material of occupation, has been enabled to have a clear understanding of figures in general.

This will be the basis for further development in addition, subtraction, multiplication and division in the Primary Department.

It now remains to add the necessary advice in regard to the introduction and representation with the sticks of the *numerals*. In order to make the children understand what *numerals* are, use the blackboard and show them that if we wish to mark down how many *sticks*, *blocks*, or other things each of the children have, we might make one line for each stick, block, etc. Write then *one* small vertical line on the blackboard, saying in writing, Charles has *one stick*; making *two* lines *below* the first, continue by saying Emma has *two blocks*; again, making *three lines*, Ernest has *three rubber balls*, and so on until you have written ten lines, always giving the name of the child and stating how many objects he has. Then write opposite each row of lines to the right, the *Arabic* figure expressing the number of lines, and remark that instead of using so many lines, we can also use these figures, which we call *numerals*.

After the children have learned that the figures which we use for marking down the *number of things* are called numerals, exercises of the following character may be introduced.

How many hands have each of you? Two. The numeral 2 is written on the board. How many fingers on each hand? Five. This is written also on the board—5. How many walls has this room? Four. Write this figure also on the board. How many days in the week are the children in the Kindergarten? Six days. The 6 is also written on the board.

Then repeat, and let the children repeat after you, as an exercise in speaking, and at the same time, for the purpose of recollecting the numerals:

Each child has 2 hands, on each hand are 5 fingers; this room has 4 walls,—always emphasizing the numerals, and pointing to them when they are named.

The children may then count the objects in the room or elsewhere, and then lay with their sticks, the numerals expressing the number they have found, speaking in the meantime, a sentence asserting the fact which they have stated.

As the occupation with laying sticks, is one of the earliest in the kindergarten, and is employed in teaching numerals, and reading and writing, and drawing also, it is evident how important a material of occupation was supplied by Frœbel, in introducing the sticks as one of his Kindergarten Gifts.

PARADISE OF CHILDHOOD.

EDITOR'S NOTES.

As this gift is used to represent the line, it takes the child one step farther, into the abstract world, teaching both direction and outlines.

It consists of sticks from one to five inches in length, which come in bundles or in a compartment box containing fifteen hundred sticks of the natural wood or of the six spectrum colors, which are more attractive to the children, and are helpful in color lessons and in representing familiar objects. In presenting this gift first hand one stick to each child, call attention to it by asking what it looks like and where it came from. Give a talk on trees, telling how they spring from the seed and grow, and how the wood is used for various purposes.

introduced, the teacher being careful to advance no faster than the child can follow.

With four sticks a square may be formed, or the sticks may be placed around a quadrangular tablet, and then removed, showing the outline.

The sticks are the foundation for outline drawing, and after the children have made simple objects with the sticks let them draw what they have made, on paper or the blackboard.

Give simple lessons in dictation, and in order to cultivate imagination and to draw out the inventive powers of the children, let them arrange short sequences in forms of life, adding interest by a story.

Give sticks of different lengths, as this enables the children to make a greater variety of figures. When using the two-inch stick lead them to see that it corresponds to the edge of the second gift cube.

This gift is useful in making angles and geometrical figures. In the geometrical figures the first to be outlined is the square, following the face of the second gift cube and the square tablet of the seventh gift.

Direct attention to the right angles and let the children point them out. Follow this with obtuse and acute angles. When the fifth gift and the triangle of the seventh gift have been used then lay the sticks to form triangles, oblongs, pentagons, etc.

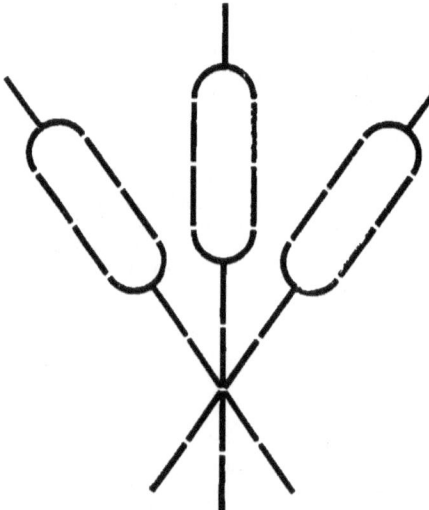

Fig. 73.

Fig. 74.

Ask for different articles that are made from wood and give the process by which the sticks are prepared for use, how they are dyed, etc.; then let the children place the sticks in different directions, the vertical, horizontal, and slanting. Give a second stick, place them parallel, in different directions; combine them and place them in all possible positions to each other. A number lesson in addition, subtraction and multiplication may be taught, and a third stick

A great variety of life forms can be shown and to some extent symmetrical forms. It is well to let the children unite their sticks or combine them with rings, especially in the life forms, (Figs. 73 and 74). In this way a house with interior furnishings may be made, or a house, yard and fence. The world of occupation furnished by this gift is a continual wonder to the kindergartner.

THE NINTH GIFT.
WHOLE AND HALF RINGS FOR LAYING FIGURES.

IMMEDIATELY connected with the sticks, or straight lines, Frœbel gives the representatives of the rounded, curved lines, in a box containing twenty-four whole and forty-eight half circles of two different sizes made of wire. The rings supply the means of representing a curved line perfectly, besides enabling us by their different sizes to show "the one within another."

This gift is introduced in the same way as all other previous gifts were introduced, and the rules by which this occupation is carried on must be clear to every one who has followed us in our "Guide" to this point.

The child receives one whole ring and two half rings of the larger size. Looking at the whole ring the children observe that there is neither beginning nor end in the ring—that it represents the circle, in which there is neither beginning nor end. (Fig. 1). With the half

Fig. 1.   Fig. 2.

ring, they have two ends; half rings, like half circles and all other parts of the circle or curved lines, have two ends. Two of the half rings form one whole ring or circle, and the children are asked to show this by experiment. Various observations can be made by the children, accompanied by remarks on the part of the teacher. Whenever the child combined two cubes, two tablets, sticks or slats with one another, in all cases where corners and angles and ends were concerned in this combination,

Fig. 3.

corners and angles were again produced. The two half rings or half circles, however, do not form any angles. Neither could closed space be produced by two bodies, planes, nor lines. The two half circles, however, close tightly up to each other so that no opening remains.

The child now places the two half circles in opposite directions. (Fig. 2). Before, the ends touched one another, now the middle of the half circles; previously a closed space was formed, now both half circles are open, and where they touch one another, angles appear.

Mediation is formed in Fig. 3, where both half circles touch each other at one end and re-

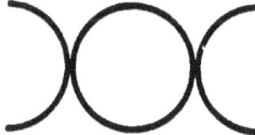

Fig. 4.

main open or as indicated by the dotted line, join at end and middle, thereby enclosing a

Fig. 5.   Fig. 6.

small plane and forming angles in the meantime. Two more half circles are presented. The

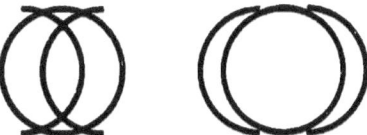

Fig. 7.   Fig. 8.

child forms Fig. 4, and develops by moving the half circles in the direction from without to within. (Figs. 5-8).

All these forms are, owing to the nature of the circular line, forms of *beauty* or beautiful forms of life, and, therefore, the occupation with these rings is of such importance. The child produces forms of beauty with other material, it is true, but the curved line suggests to him in a higher degree than anything else ideas of the beautiful, and the simplest combinations of a small number of half and whole circles, also bear in themselves the stamp of beauty. (Figs. 9-12).

Fig. 9.

Fig. 10.

If the fact cannot be refuted, that merely looking at the beautiful favorably impresses the mind of the grown person in regard to direction of its development, enabling him to more fully appreciate the good and true, and noble, and sublime, this influence upon the tender and pliable soul of the child, must needs be greater and more lasting. Without believing in the doctrine of two inimical natures in

Fig. 11.

man said to be in constant conflict with each other, we do believe that the talents and disposition in human nature are subject to the possibility of being developed in two opposite directions. It is this possibility which conditions the necessity of education, the necessity of employing every means to give the dormant inclinations and tastes in the child, a direction toward the true, and good, and beautiful,—in one word, toward the ideal. Among these means stands pre-eminently a rational and

Fig. 12.

timely development of the sense of beauty, upon which Fræbel lays so much stress.

Showing the young child objects of art which are far beyond the sphere of his appreciation, however, will assist this development, much less than to carefully guard that his surroundings contain, and show the fundamental requisites of beauty, viz.: Order, cleanliness, simplicity and harmony of form, and giving assistance to the child in the active representation to the beautiful in a manner adapted to the state of development in the child himself.

Like forms laid with sticks, those represented with rings and half rings also are imitated by the children by drawing them on slate or paper.

EDITOR'S NOTES.

This gift now consists of twelve whole, eighteen half and twelve quarter wire rings, for laying figures which involve circles. It is a continuation of the eighth gift and preparatory to drawing and designing, being used to represent an outline of a surface.

The rings are made of steel, and come in three different sizes of one inch, one and one-half inch and two inches in diameter. In introducing this gift the largest ring should be given first, and attention called to its form and properties. A talk on iron, its uses, how it is dug out of the ground by miners, a description of the mines, of the process the ore passes through, how it is melted and molded into useful machines and articles, how it is changed into steel, is both interesting and instructive to the children. Ask for different things that are made of iron and steel, and draw from the children the reason why steel is valuable for knives, axes and other cutting utensils. A second tions, the number and size of rings being increased gradually.

When a third ring is given, let the children suggest ways of laying them. If they are of the same size, they may be placed side by side,

Fig. 13.

Fig. 16.

in a group, in the form of a triangle, etc. If the different sizes are used, they may be placed

Fig. 14.

Fig. 17.

one within the other, so that they are parallel, or they may touch at some point. Forms of

Fig. 15.

Fig. 18.

ring may be added and an exercise given in placing the rings in different ways and positions, symmetry may be developed by several of these grouped together, as in Fig. 9.

The exercises with the half-rings are more

interesting and instructive, as the forms are more varied and change at every step. Have the children place the half-rings in different positions. Give each child the same quantity of material and let them lay a design. Fig. 10 shows a combination of the half-rings. Sequences involving both half and whole rings may be given, as shown in Figs. 13-17.

When the quarter-ring is given, let the children compare it with the half-ring and combine the two in different sizes. Figs. 18 and 19 are the smallest half and quarter-rings combined, and Fig. 20, shows the largest size of each.

Figs. 21 and 22 give pretty border patterns which may be embellished.

As the curved line is the line of beauty, this gift is better adapted for beautiful forms than any of the others. Forms of life, especially in flower designs, are developed with the quarter-rings as shown in Fig. 23, while Figs. 24 and 25 show a combination of the whole, half and quarter-rings.

Fig. 26, shows a combination of the three smallest sizes of each, Fig. 27, of the second size, and Fig. 28 of the largest. Fig. 29 is a combination of the whole, half and quarter-rings in the three different sizes.

The rings of this Gift and the sticks of the eighth may be combined with pleasing and profitable results as shown in Figs. 30-38 of which Figs. 34-38 are a sequence.

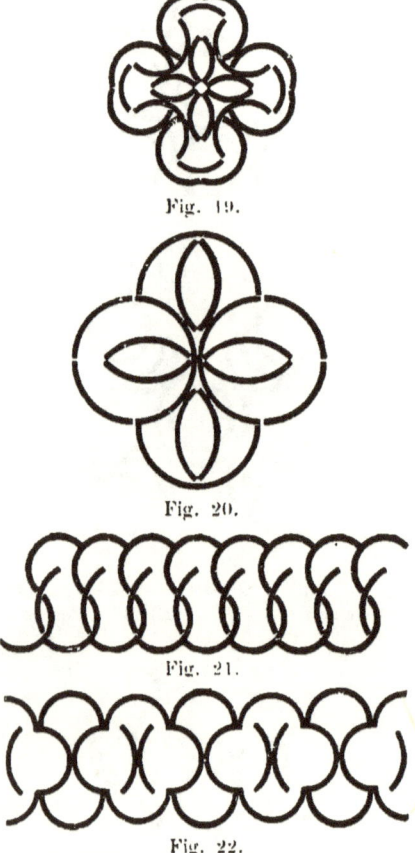

Fig. 19.

Fig. 20.

Fig. 21.

Fig. 22.

Fig. 23.

Fig. 24.

Fig. 25.
Fig. 26.
Fig. 27.
Fig. 28.
Fig. 29.
Fig. 30.

182 PARADISE OF CHILDHOOD.

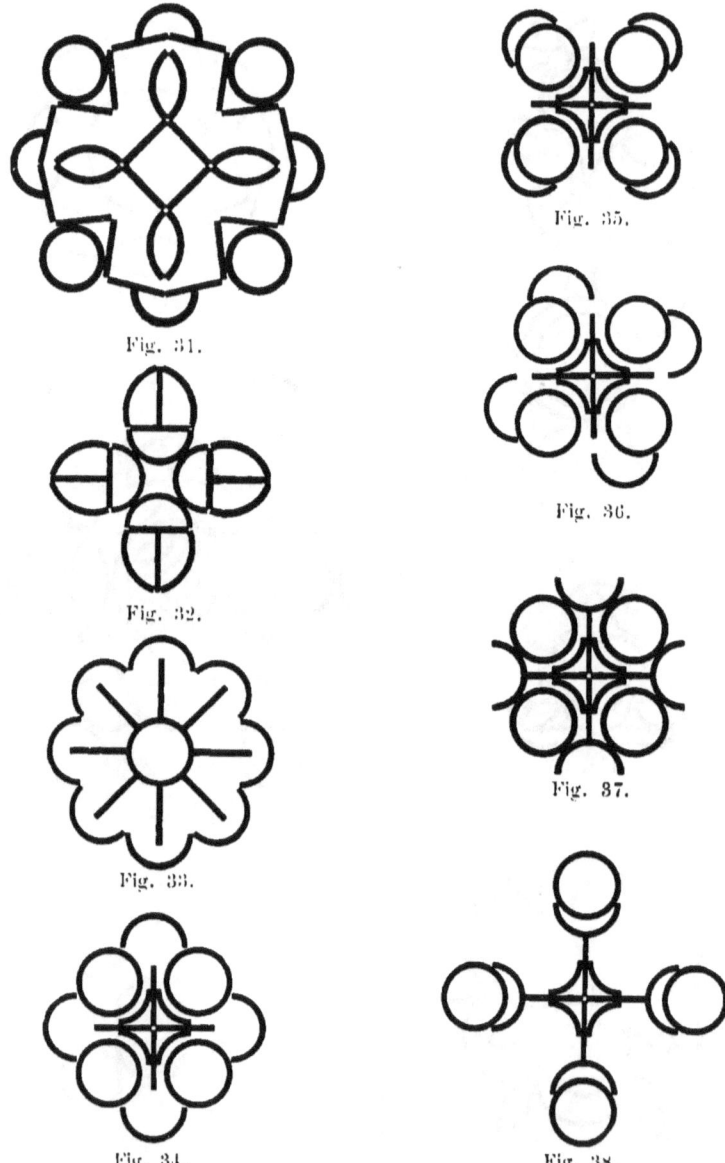

Fig. 31.

Fig. 32.

Fig. 33.

Fig. 34.

Fig. 35.

Fig. 36.

Fig. 37.

Fig. 38.

THE TENTH GIFT.
THE MATERIAL FOR DRAWING.

One of the earliest occupations of the child should be methodical drawing. Froebel's opinion and conviction on this subject, deviates from those of other educators, as much as in other respects. Froebel, however does not advocate drawing, as it is usually practiced, which on the whole, is nothing else but a more or less thoughtless mechanical copying. The method advanced by Froebel, is invented by him, and perfected in accordance with his general educational principles.

The pedagogical effect of the customary method of instruction in drawing, rests in many cases simply in the amount of trouble caused the pupil in surmounting technical difficulties. Just for that reason it should be abandoned entirely for the youngest pupils, for the difficulties in many cases are too great for the child to cope with. It is a work of Sisyphus, *labor without result*, naturally tending to extirpate the pleasure of the child in his occupation, and the unavoidable consequence is that the majority of people will never reach the point where they can enjoy the fruits of their endeavors.

If we acknowledge that Froebel's educational principles are correct, namely, that all manifestations of the child's life are manifestations of an innate instinctive desire for development, and therefore should be fostered and developed by a rational education in accordance with the laws of nature, drawing should be commenced with the third year; nay, its preparatory principles should be introduced at a still earlier period.

With all the gifts, hitherto introduced, the children were able to study and represent forms and figures. Thus they have been occupied as it were, in *drawing with bodies*. This developed their fantasy and taste, giving them in the meantime correct ideas of the solid, plane, and the embodied line.

A desire soon awakes in the child, to represent by *drawing* these lines and planes, these forms and objects. He is desirous of representation when he requests the mother to tell him a story, explain a picture. He is occupied in representation when breathing against the window-pane, and scrawling on it with his finger, or when trying to make figures in the sand with a little stick. Each child is delighted to show what he can make, and should be assisted in every way to regulate this desire.

Drawing not only develops the power of representing things the mind has perceived, but affords the best means for testing how far they have been perceived correctly.

It was Froebel's task to invent a method adapted to the tender age of the child, and his slight dexterity of hand, and in the meantime to satisfy the claim of all his occupations, *i.e.*, that the child should not simply imitate, but proceed self-actingly, to perform work which enables him to reflect, reason, and finally to invent himself.

Both claims have been most ingeniously satisfied by Froebel. He gives the three years' old child a slate, one side of which is covered by a net-work of engraved lines (one-fourth of an inch apart), and he gives him in addition, thereto, the law of opposites and their mediation as a rule for his activity.

The lines of the net-work guide the child in moving the pencil, they assist him in measuring and comparing situation and position, size and relative center, and sides of objects. This facilitates the work greatly, and in consequence of this important assistance the child's desire for work is materially increased; whereas obstacles in the earliest attempts at all kinds of work must necessarily discourage the beginner.

Drawing on the slate, with slate pencil is followed by drawing on paper with lead pencil. The paper of the drawing books is ruled like the slates. It is advisable to begin and continue the exercises in drawing on paper, in like manner as those on the slate were begun and continued, with this difference only, that owing to the progress made and skill obtained by the child, less repetitions may be needed to bring the pupil to perfection here, as was necessary in the use of the slate.

It has been repeatedly suggested, that whenever a new material for occupation is introduced, the teacher should comment upon, or enter into conversation with the children, about the same; the difference between drawing on the slate and on paper, and the material used for both may give rise to many remarks and instructive conversation.

It may be mentioned that the slate is first used, because the children can easily correct mistakes by wiping out what they have made, and that they should be much more careful in drawing on paper, as their productions can not appear perfectly clean and neat if it should be necessary to use the rubber often.

Slate and slate pencil are of the same material; paper and lead pencil are two very different things. On the slate the lines and figures drawn, appear white on darker ground. On the paper, lines and figures appear black on white ground.

More advanced pupils use colored lead pencils instead of the common black lead pencils. This adds greatly to the appearance of the figures, and also enables the child to combine colors tastefully and fittingly. For the development of their sense of color, and of taste, these colored mosaic like figures are excellent practice.

Drawing, as such, requires observation, attention, conception of the whole and its parts, the recollection of all, power of invention and combination of thought. Thus, by it, mind and fantasy are enriched with clear ideas and true and beautiful pictures. For a free and active development of the senses, especially eye and feeling, drawing can be made of incalculable benefit to the child, when its natural instinct for it is correctly guided at its very awakening. The child is first occupied by

THE VERTICAL LINE.
(See Figs. 1—42).

The teacher draws on the slate a vertical line of a single length (one fourth of an inch), saying while so doing, I draw a line of a single length downward. She then (leaving the line on the slate, or wiping it out) requires the child to do the same. (Fig. 1). She should show that

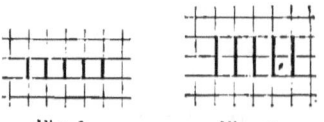

Fig. 1.   Fig. 2.

the line she made commenced exactly at the crossing point of two lines of the net-work, and also ended at such a point.

Care should be exercised that the child hold the pencil properly, not press too much or too little on the slate, that the lines drawn be as equally heavy as possible, and that each single line be produced by one single stroke of the pencil. The teacher should occasionally ask: What are you doing? or, what have you done?

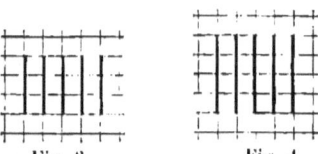

Fig. 3.   Fig. 4.

and the child should always answer in a complete sentence, showing that he works understandingly. Soon the lines may be drawn up-

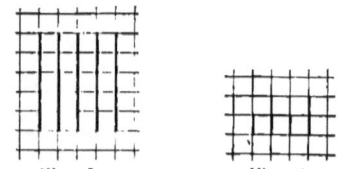

Fig. 5.   Fig. 6.

wards also, and then they may be made alternately up and down over the entire slates until the child has acquired a certain degree of ability in handling the pencil.

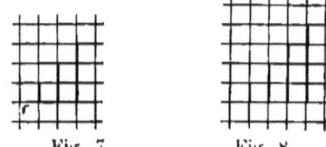

Fig. 7.   Fig. 8.

The child is then required to draw a vertical line of two lengths, and advances slowly to lines of three, four and five lengths, (Figs. 2-5).

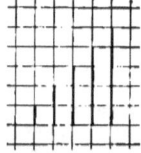

Fig. 9.

With the number five Froebel stops on this step. One to five are known, even to the child three years old, by the number on his fingers.

The productions thus far accomplished are now combined. The child draws, side by side

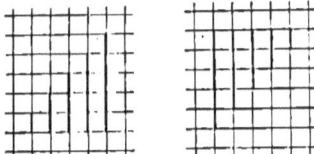

Fig. 10.   Fig. 11.

of one another, lines of one and two lengths (Fig. 6), of one, two and three lengths (Fig. 7), of one two, three and four lengths (Fig. 8), and finally lines of one, two, three, four and five lengths (Fig. 9). It always forms

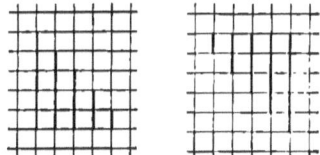

Fig 12.   Fig. 13.

by so doing a right-angled triangle. We have noticed already, in using the tablets, that

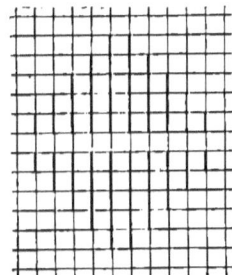

Fig. 14.

right-angled triangles may lie in many different ways. The triangle (Figs. 9 and 10) can also assume various positions. In Fig. 10 the five lines stand on the base line—the smallest is the first, the largest the last, the right angle is to the right below. In Fig. 11 the opposite is found—the five lines hang on the base-line, the largest comes first, the smallest last, and the right angle is to the left above. Figs. 12 and 13 are forms of mediation of Figs. 10 and 11.

The child should be induced to find Figs. 11-13 himself. Leading him to understand the points of Fig. 10 exactly, he will have no difficulty in representing the opposite. Instead

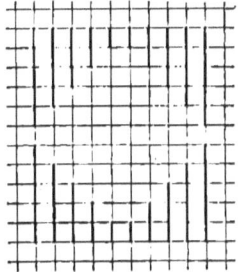

Fig. 15.

of drawing the smallest line first, he will draw the longest; instead of drawing it downward, he will move his pencil upward, or at least be-

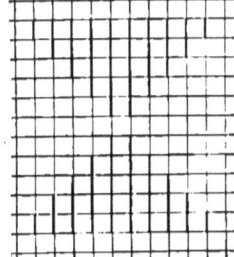

Fig. 16.

gin to draw on the line which is bounded above and thus reach Fig. 11. By continued reflec-

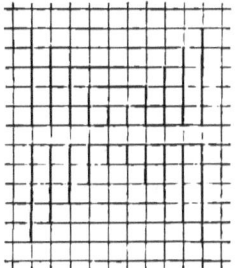

Fig. 17.

tion entirely within the limits of his capabilities he will succeed in producing Figs. 12 and 13.

Thus by a different way of combination of five vertical lines, four forms have been produced, consisting of equal parts being, however, unlike, and therefore oppositionally alike.

Each of these figures is a whole in itself. But as everything is always part of a large whole, so also, these figures serve as elements for more extensive formations.

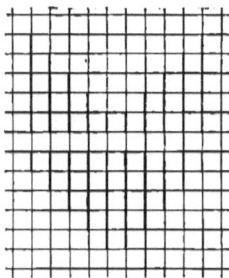

Fig. 18.

In this feature of Fræbel's drawing method in which we progress from the simple to the more complicated in the most natural and logical manner, unite parts to a whole and recognize the former as members of the latter, dis-

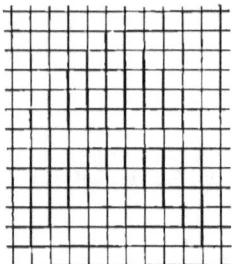

Fig. 19.

cover the like in opposites, and the mediation of the latter, unquestionable guarantee is given that the delight of the child will be renewed and increased, throughout the whole course of instruction. Let Figs. 10-13 be so united that the right angles connect in the center (Fig. 14), and again unite them so that all right angles are on the outside (Fig. 15). Figs. 14 and 15 are opposites. Fig. 14 is a square with filled inside and standing on one corner. Fig. 15 one resting on its base, with hollow middle.

In Fig. 14 the right angles are just in the middle; in Fig. 15 they are the most outward corners. In the forms of mediation (Figs. 16 and 17), they are, it is true, on the middle line; but in the meantime on the outlines of the figures formed. In the other forms of mediation. (Fig. 18, 19, etc.,) they lie together on the middle line; but two in the middle, and two in the limits of the figure.

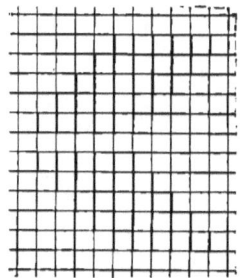

Fig. 20.

Thus we have again, in Fig. 18-22, four forms consisting of exactly the same parts, which therefore are equal and still have qualities of opposites. In the meantime, they are fit to be used as simple elements of following formations. In Fig. 22, they are combined into a star with filled middle. Numerous forms of mediation may be produced, but we will work at present with our simple elements.

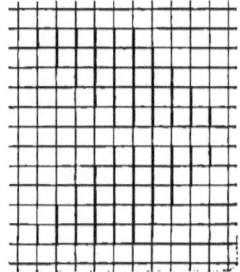

Fig. 21.

Owing to the similarity in the method of drawing to that employed in the laying of the right angled, isosceles triangle, it is natural that we should here also arrive at the so-called rotation figures, by grouping our triangles with their acute angles toward the middle (Figs. 23

and 24), or arrange them around a hollow square (Figs. 25 and 26).

Figs. 27 and 28 are forms of mediation between Figs. 23 and 24 and at the same time between Figs. 14 and 15.

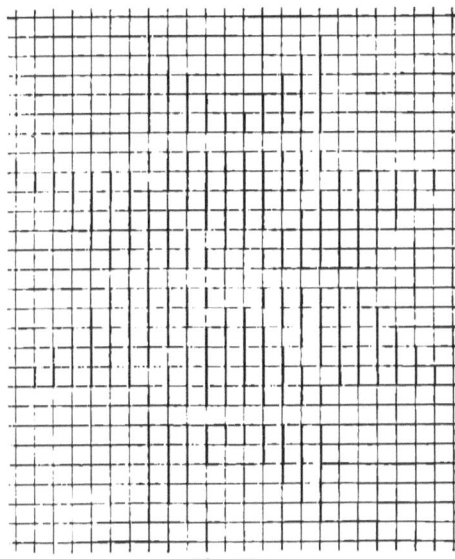

Fig. 22.

All these forms again serve as material for new inventions. As an example, we produce Fig. 29 composed of Figs. 27 and 28.

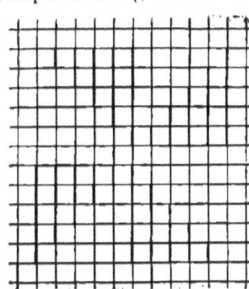

Fig. 23.

The number of positions in which our original elements (Figs. 10-13) can be placed by one another, is herewith not exhausted by far, as the initiated will observe.

As previously remarked, the slate is exchanged for a drawing book as soon as the progress of the child warrants this change. It affords a peculiar charm to the pupil to see his productions assume a certain durability and

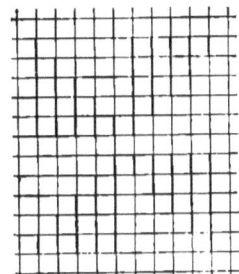

Fig. 24.

permanency enabling him to measure, by them, the progress of growing strength and ability.

So far the triangles produced by co-arrangement of our five lines were right-angled. Other triangles, however, can be produced also. This however, requires more practice and security in handling the pencil.

Figs. 30 and 31 show an arrangement of the five lines of acute angled (equilateral) triangles, and are opposites. Their

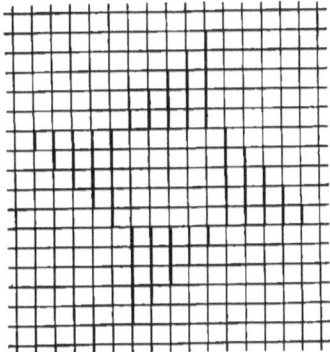

Fig. 25.

union gives the opposites Figs. 32 and 33; finally, the combination of these two, Fig 34.

In the last three figures we also meet now

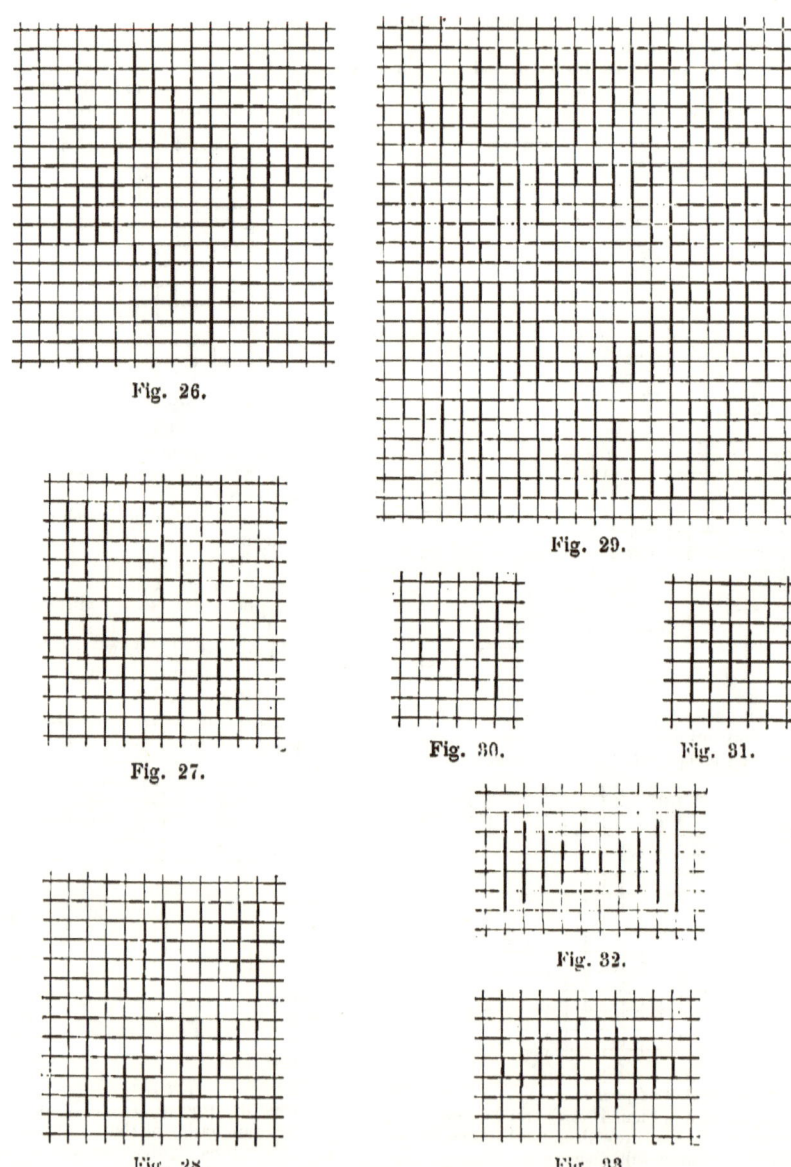

Fig. 26.

Fig. 27.

Fig. 28.

Fig. 29.

Fig. 30.

Fig. 31.

Fig. 32.

Fig. 33.

PARADISE OF CHILDHOOD.

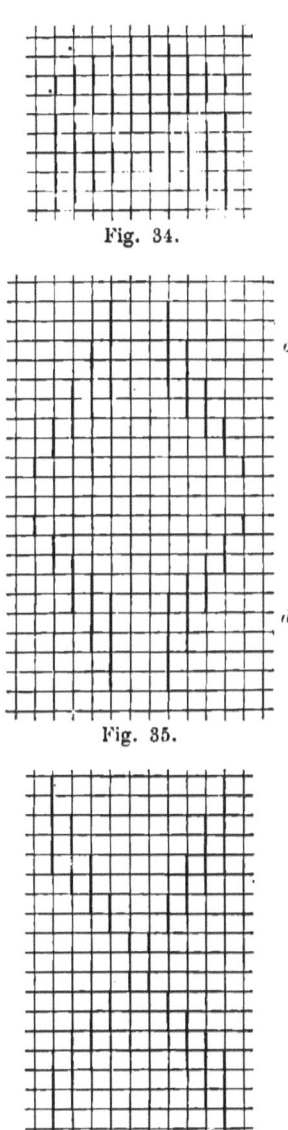

Fig. 34.

Fig. 35.

Fig. 36.

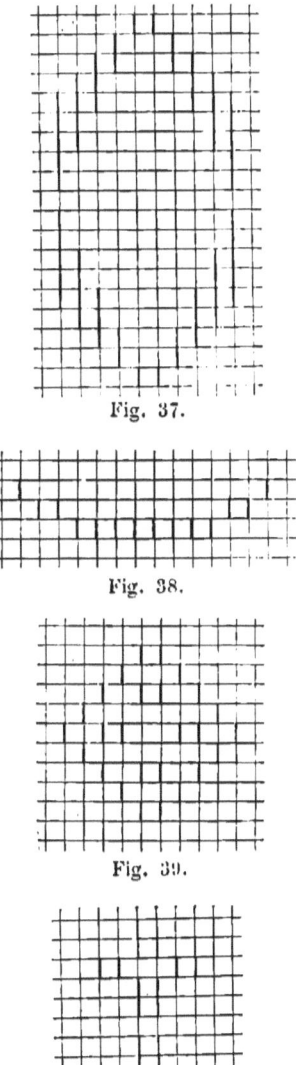

Fig. 37.

Fig. 38.

Fig. 39.

Fig. 40.

the obtuse angle. This finds its separate representation in *a* of Fig. 35; opposition according to position is given in *b*; mediation in *c* and *d* and the combination of these four elements in one rhomboid forming Fig. 35. The four obtuse angles are turned inwardly. Fig. 37, the

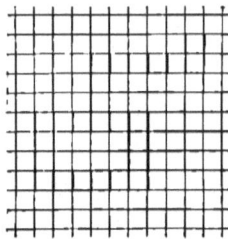

Fig. 41.

opposite of Fig. 35, is produced by arranging the triangles in such a manner that the obtuse angles are turned outwardly. Fig. 36 presents the form of mediation.

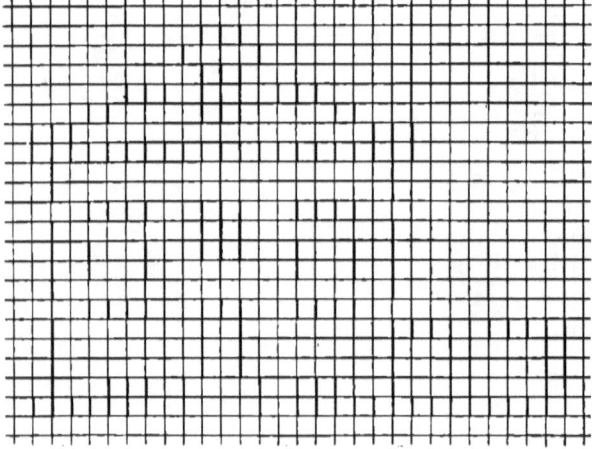

Fig. 42.

It is evident that with obtuse angled triangles as with right angled triangles, combinations can be produced. Indeed, the pupil who has grown into the systematic plan of development and combination will soon be enabled to unite given elements in manifold ways; he will produce stars with filled and hollow middle, rotation forms, etc., and his mental and physical power and capacity will be developed and strengthened by such inventive exercises.

Side by side with invention of forms of beauty and knowledge, the representation of forms of life, take place, in free individual activity. The child forms, of lines of one length, a plate, (Fig. 38), or a star, (Fig. 39), of lines of one and two lengths a cross, (Fig. 40), of lines up to four lengths he represents a coffee-mill, Fig. 41), and employs the whole material of vertical lines at his command in the construction of a large building with part of wall connected with it. (Fig. 42). Equal consideration, however, is to be bestowed upon the opposite of the vertical.

THE HORIZONTAL LINE.

Figs. 43—63.

The child learns to draw lines of a single length below each other, then lines of two, three, four and five lengths, (Figs. 43-47). He arranges them also beside each other, (Figs. 48-50), unites lines of one and two lengths, (Fig. 51), of one, two and three lengths, (Fig. 52), of one to four lengths, (Fig. 53), finally of one to five lengths, thereby producing the right angled triangle, Fig. 54, its opposite, Fig. 55, and forms of mediation, Figs. 56 and 57. The pupil arranges the elements into a square with filled middle, (Fig. 58), with hollow middle, (Fig. 59), produces the forms of mediation, (Fig. 60), and continues to treat the horizontal line just as he has been taught to do with the vertical. Rotation forms, larger figures, acute and obtuse angled triangles can be formed; forms of beauty, knowledge and life are also invented here, (Fig. 61, adjustable lamp; Fig. 62, key; Fig. 63, pigeon-house); and after the child has accomplished all this, he arrives finally, in a most natural way, at the combination of vertical and horizontal lines.

PARADISE OF CHILDHOOD. 191

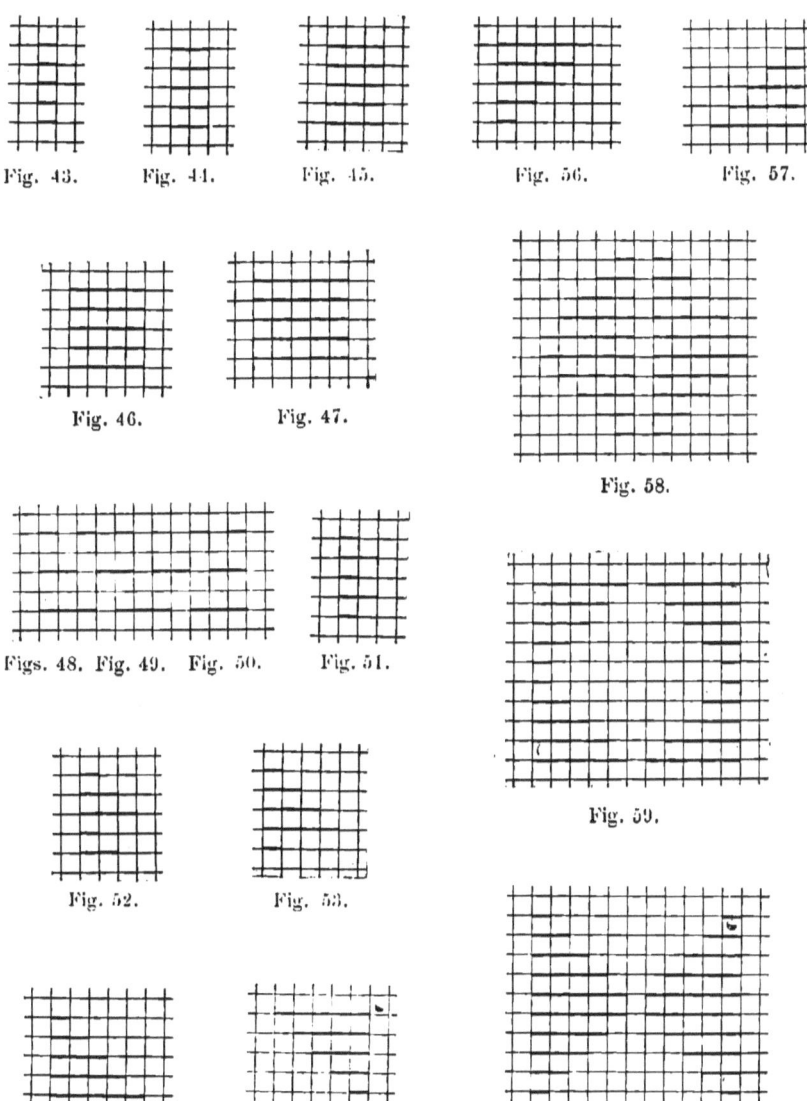

Fig. 43.   Fig. 44.   Fig. 45.   Fig. 56.   Fig. 57.

Fig. 46.   Fig. 47.

Fig. 58.

Figs. 48. Fig. 49. Fig. 50.   Fig. 51.

Fig. 59.

Fig. 52.   Fig. 53.

Fig. 54.   Fig. 55.   Fig. 60.

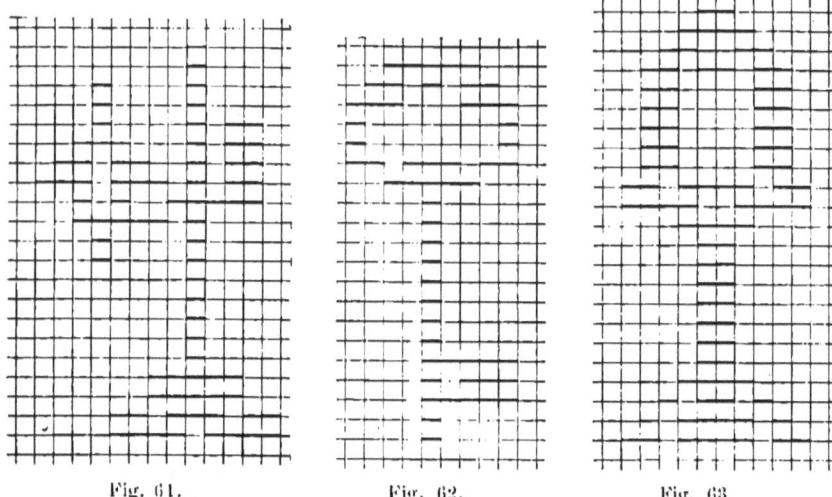

Fig. 61.   Fig. 62.   Fig. 63.

COMBINATION OF VERTICAL AND HORIZONTAL LINES.

Figs. 64—92.

First, lines of one single length are combined; we already have four forms different as to position, (Fig. 64). Then follow the combination of two, three, four, five-fold lengths.

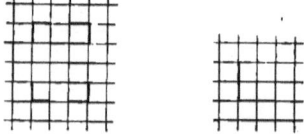

Fig. 64.   Fig. 65.

(Figs. 65-68) with each of which four opposites as to position are possible. As previously,

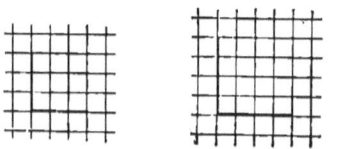

Fig. 66.   Fig. 67.

lines of one to five-fold lengths are united to triangles, so now the angles are united and

Fig. 69 is produced. Its opposite Fig. 70 and the forms of mediation, can be easily found. A union of these four elements appears in the square, Fig. 71; opposite Fig. 72. In Fig. 71, the right angles are turned toward the middle,

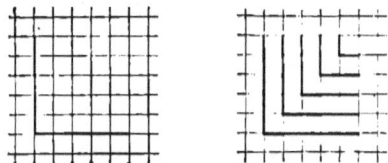

Fig. 68.   Fig. 69.

and the middle is full. In Fig. 71 the reverse is the case. Forms of mediation easily found.

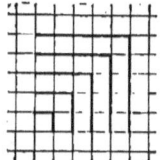

Fig. 70.

If vertical and horizontal lines can be united only to form right angles, we have previously seen that vertical as well as horizontal lines

PARADISE OF CHILDHOOD.   193

may be combined to obtuse and acute-angled triangles. The same is possible, if they are united. Fig. 73 gives us an example.

As in Fig. 73, the vertical lines form an obtuse-angled triangle, so the horizontal lines, and finally both kinds of lines can at the same time be arranged into obtuse-angled triangles.

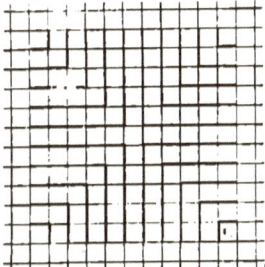

Fig. 71.

Thus a series of new elements is produced, whose systematic employment the teacher should take care to facilitate.

So far we have only formed angles of lines equal in length; but lines of unequal lengths

known manner. Figs. 73 and 75 are such fundamental forms; the development of which to other figures will give rise to many instruc-

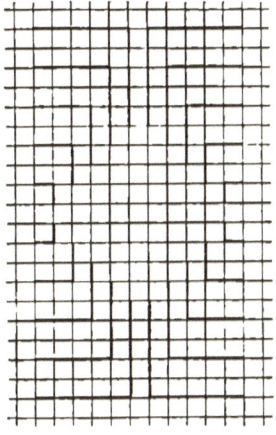

Fig. 73.

tive remarks. These figures show us that for such formations the horizontal as well as the

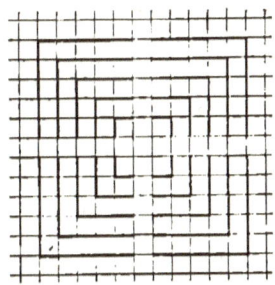

Fig. 72.

may be combined for this purpose. Exactly in the same manner as lines of a single length were treated, the child now combines the line of a single length with that of two lengths, then, in the same way, the line of two lengths with that of four lengths, that of three with that of six, that of four with that of eight, and finally, the line of five lengths with that of ten. The combination of these angles affords new elements with which the pupil can continue to form interesting figures in the already well-

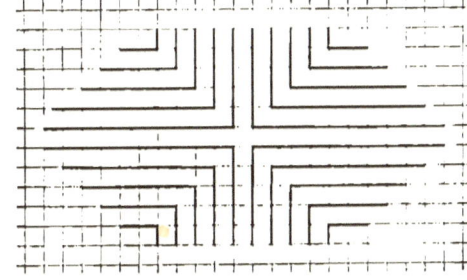

Fig. 74.

vertical line may have the double length. Fig. 74 shows the horizontal lines combined in such a way as if to form an acute-angled triangle. They, however, form a right-angled triangle, only the right angle is not, as heretofore, at the end of the longest line, but where? An acute-angled triangle would result, if the horizontal lines were all two net-squares distant from each other. Then, however, the vertical lines would form an obtuse-angled triangle.

Important progress is made, when we com-

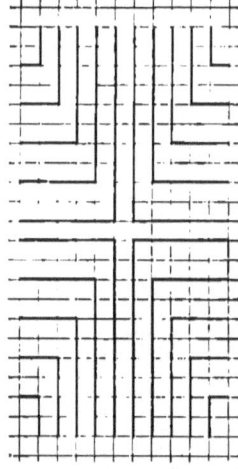

Fig. 75.
bine horizontal and vertical lines in such a way that by touching in two points they form closed figures, squares and oblongs.

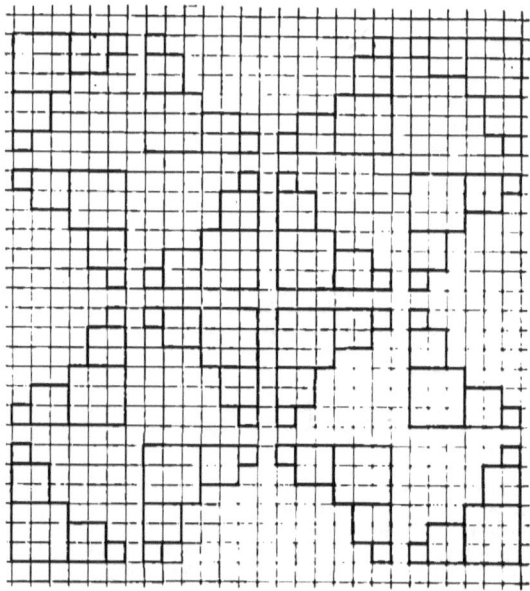

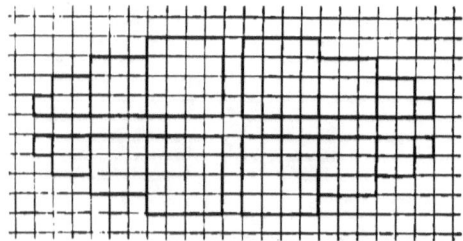

Fig. 76.

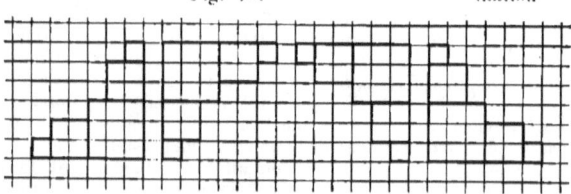

Fig. 77.

First, the child draws squares of one-length's dimension, then of two-lengths, of three, four,

Fig. 78.

and five lines. These are combined then as vertical lines were combined also 1^2 with 2^2, the 1^2, 2^2, and 3^2, etc. These combinations can be carried out in a vertical direction, when the squares will stand over or under each other; or in a horizontal, when the squares will stand side by side; or, finally, these two opposites may be combined with one another.

Fig. 76, shows as an example a combination of four squares in a horizontal direction, its opposite, and forms of mediation

In Fig. 77, squares of the first, second and third sizes are combined, vertically and horizontally, f o r m i n g a right angle to the right below; then comes the opposite, (angle left above) and the forms of mediation. The same rule is followed here as with the right angle formed by single lines. The simple elements are combined with each other into a square with

PARADISE OF CHILDHOOD. 195

hollow middle, etc.; and from the new elements thus produced larger figures are again created, as the example Fig. 78, illustrates. Squares of

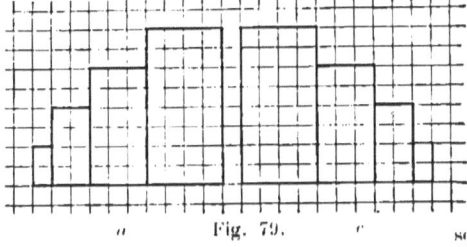

Fig. 79.

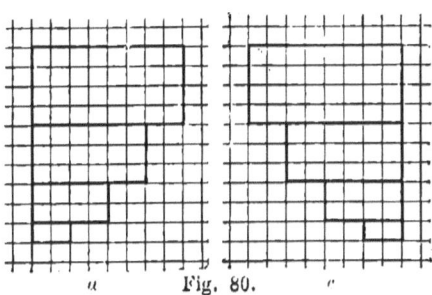

Fig. 80.

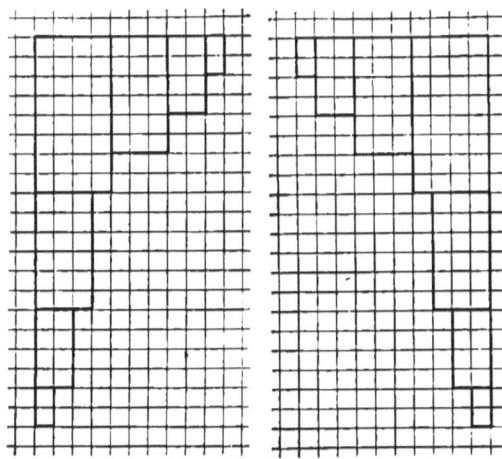

Fig. 81.

from one to five length lines of course admit of being combined in similar manner. Each essen-tially new element should give rise to a number of exercises, conditioned only by the individual ability of the child. It must be left to the faithful teacher, by an earnest observation and study of her pupils, to find the right extent, here as every where in their occupations. Indiscriminate skipping is not allowed, neither to pupil nor teacher; each following production must, under all circumstances be derived from the preceding one.

As the square was the result of angles formed of lines of equal length, so also with the oblong. Here, too, the child begins with the simplest. He forms oblongs, the base of which is a single line, the height of which is a line of double length. He reverses the case then. Base line two, height single length. Retaining the same proportions, he progresses to larger oblongs, the height of which is double the size of its base, and vice versa, until he has reached the numbers five and ten.

It is but natural that these oblongs, standing or lying, should also be united in vertical and horizontal directions. Each form thus produced again assumes four different positions, and the four elements are again united to new formations, according to the rules previously explained. Fig. 79 a, shows an arangement of standing oblongs, in horizontal directions. The opposite would contain the right angle, at a to the right below—to the left above; Fig. 79 c would be one form of mediation, a second one, (opposite of Fig. 79 c) would have its right angle to the right above.

Fig. 80, shows a combination of lying oblongs, in a vertical direction. Fig. 81, shows oblongs in vertical and horizontal directions. Fig. 82, a combination of standing and lying oblongs, the former being arranged vertically, the latter, horizontally.

In Fig. 83, we find standing oblongs so combined that the form represents an acute angled triangle; a and c are the only possible opposites in the same.

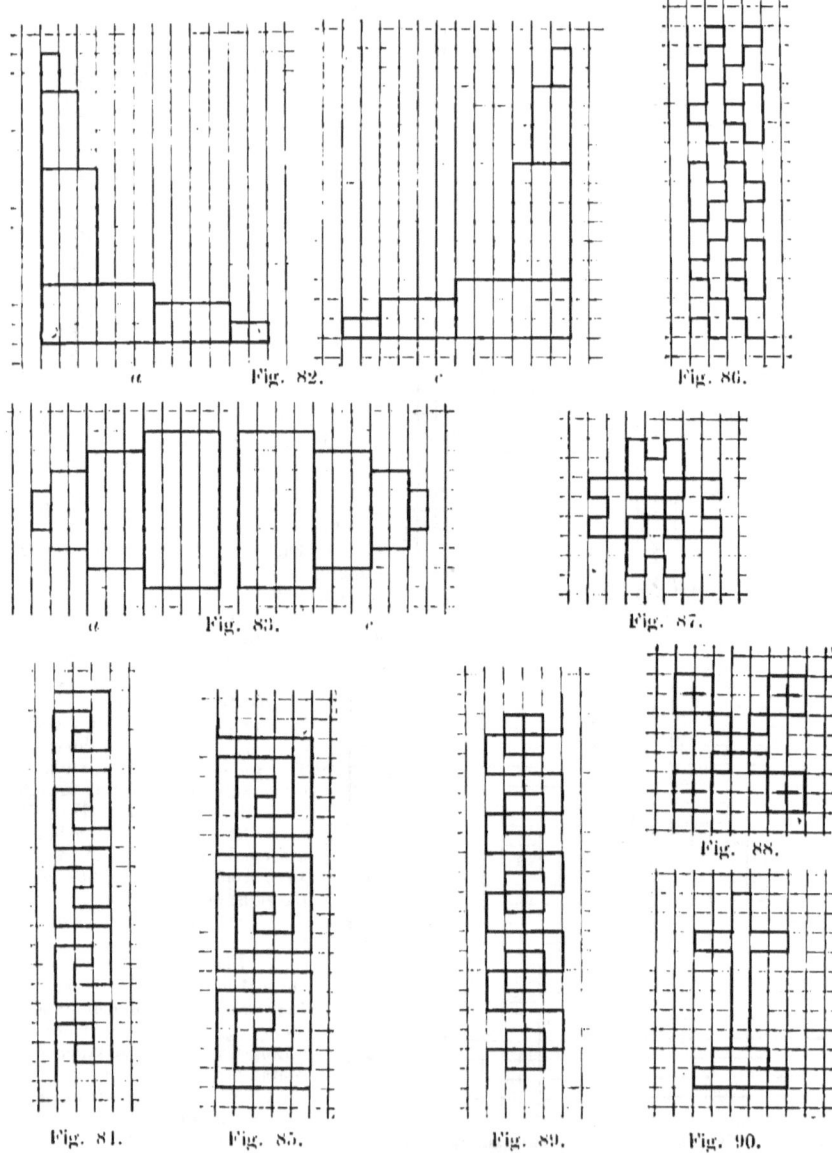

Fig. 82. Fig. 86. Fig. 83. Fig. 87. Fig. 84. Fig. 85. Fig. 89. Fig. 88. Fig. 90.

PARADISE OF CHILDHOOD.

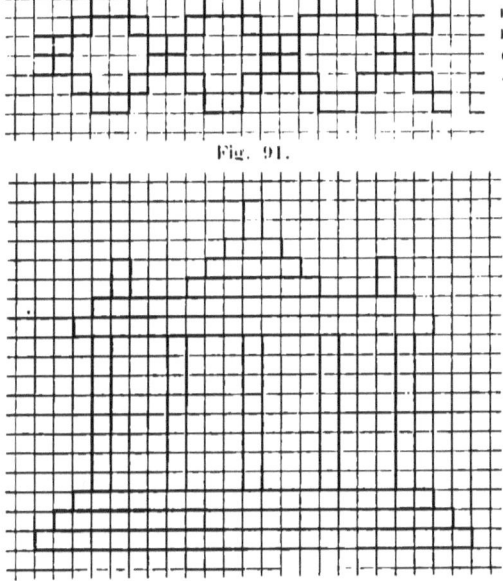

Fig. 91.

Fig. 92.

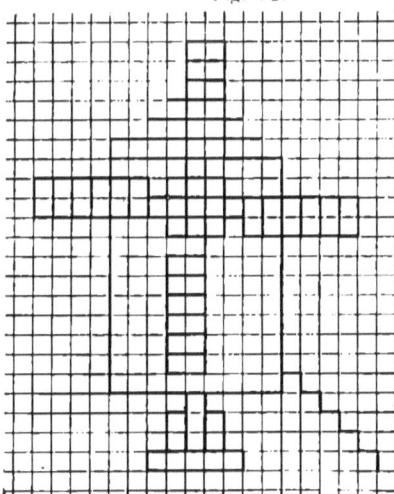

Fig. 93.

These few examples may suffice to indicate the abundance of forms which may be constructed with such simple material as the horizontal and vertical lines, from one to five lengths, (and double).

It is the task of the educator to lead the learner to detect the elements, logically, in order to produce with them, new forms in unlimited numbers, within the boundaries of the laws laid down for this purpose.

But even without using these elements, the child will be able, owing to continued practice, to represent manifold forms of life and beauty, partly by his own free invention, partly by imitating the objects he has seen before. As samples of the former, Fig. 90 shows a cross, Fig. 92 a triumphal gate, Fig. 93 a windmill; of the latter, Figs. 84–86, 89 and 91 show samples of borders. Figs. 87 and 88 show other simple embellishments. As the vertical line conditioned its opposite, the horizontal line, both again condition their mediation.

OBLIQUE LINES.

(Figs. 94—134).

Our remarks here can be brief as the operations are nothing but a repetition of those in connection with the vertical line.

The child practices the drawing of lines from one to five lengths, (Figs 94–98) and combines these, receiving thereby four oppositionally equal right-angled triangles, (Fig. 99–102), of which it produces a square, (Fig. 103), its opposite, (Fig. 104), forms of mediation, (Fig. 105), and finally large figures.

Then the lines are arranged into obtuse angles, and the same process gone through with them.

With these, as in Fig. 106, its opposite Fig. 109, and its forms of mediation, Figs. 107 and 108, the obtuse angles will be found at the vertical middle line, or as in Fig. 110, at the horizontal middle line. By a combination of Figs. 108 and 110 we produce a star, Fig. 112. Finally we have also, reached here the formation of the acute angled triangle, (Fig. 111). The oblique line presents particular richness in forms, as it may be a line of various degrees of inclination. It is an oblique of the first degree whenever it appears as the diagonal of a

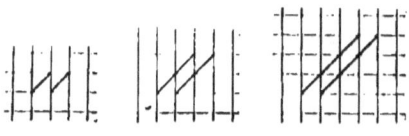

Fig. 94.   Fig. 95.   Fig. 96.

square, as in Figs. 94-112. When it appears as the diagonal of an oblong, it is either an

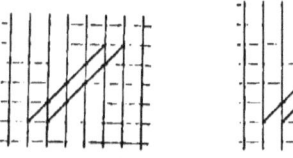

Fig. 97.   Fig. 98.

oblique of the second, third, fourth or fifth degree, according to the proportions of the base line and height of the oblong, one to two, one to three, one to four, one to five.

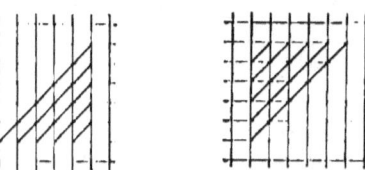

Fig. 99.   Fig. 100.

The upper left hand corner of Fig. 113, shows obliques of the second degree united to a right-angled triangle; the lower right hand

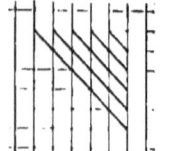

Fig. 101.   Fig. 102.

its opposite; and the remaining two corners form mediations.

In Fig. 114, the same lines are united in an obtuse angled triangle. In Fig. 115, they finally form an acute angle.

In all these cases, the obliques were diagonals of standing oblongs. They may just as well be diagonals of lying oblongs. Fig. 116,

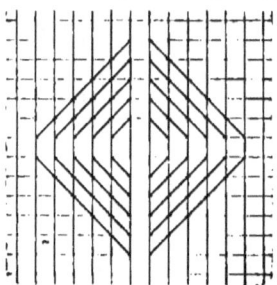

Fig. 103.

in which obliques from the first to the fifth degree are united, will illustrate this. The obliques are here arranged one above the other.

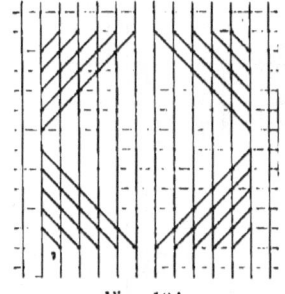

Fig. 104.

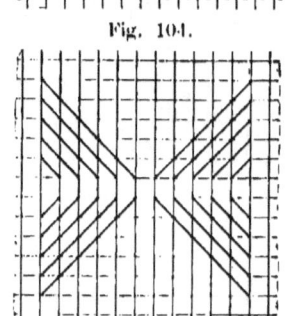

Fig. 105.

In Fig. 117, the right and left sides show a similar combination; the obliques, however, are arranged beside one another; the upper and

PARADISE OF CHILDHOOD. 199

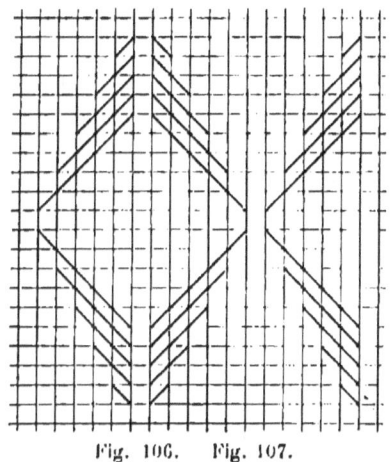

Fig. 106.   Fig. 107.

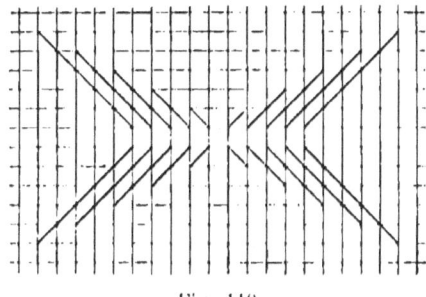

Fig. 110.

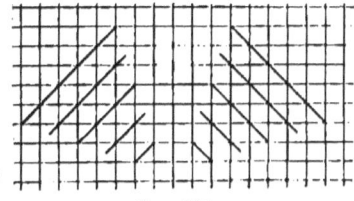

Fig. 111.

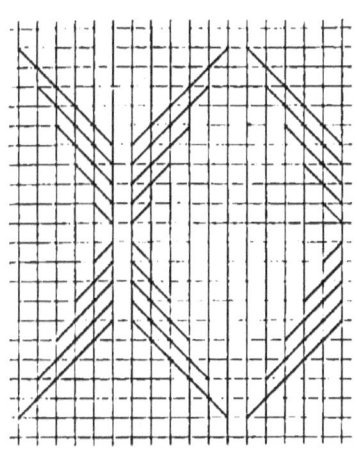

Fig. 108.   Fig. 109.

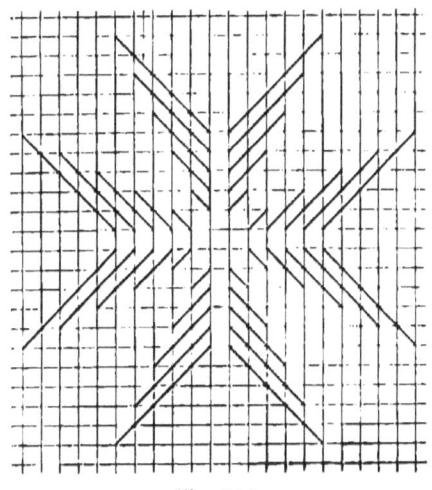

Fig. 112.

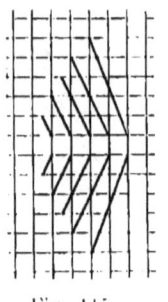

Fig. 115.

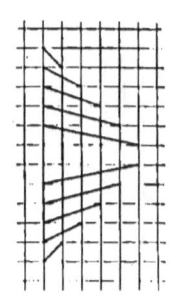

Fig. 116.

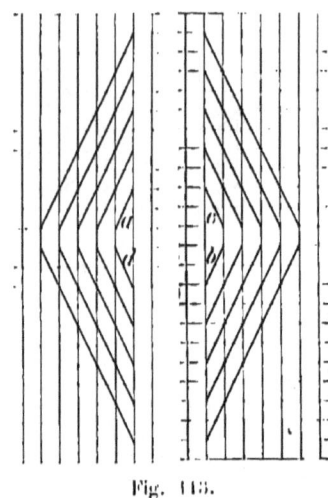

Fig. 113.

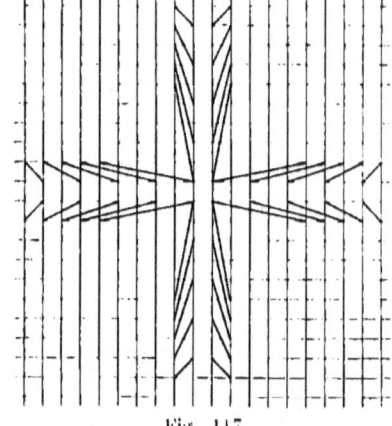

Fig. 117.

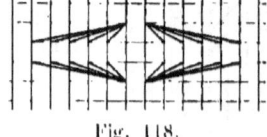

Fig. 118.

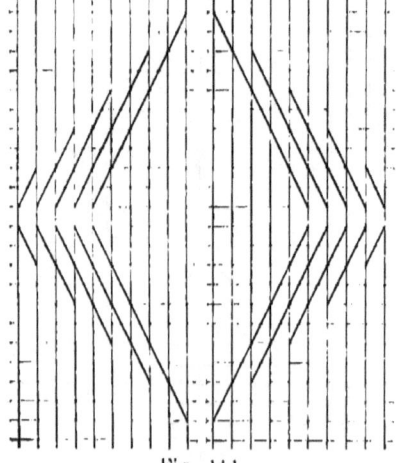

Fig. 114.

Fig. 119.

PARADISE OF CHILDHOOD.

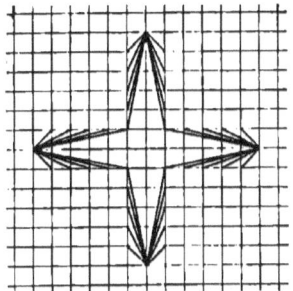

Fig. 120.

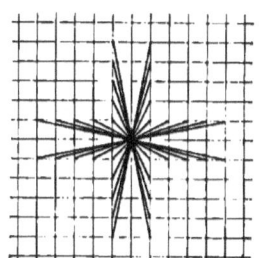

Fig. 121.

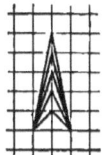

Fig. 122.

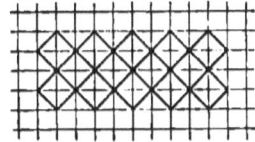

Fig. 123.

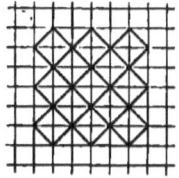

Fig. 124.

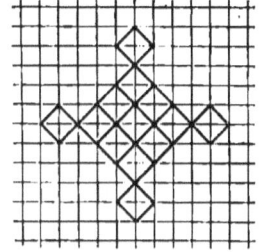

Fig. 125.

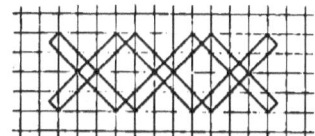

Fig. 126.

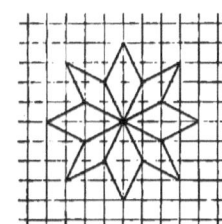

Fig. 127.

Fig. 128.

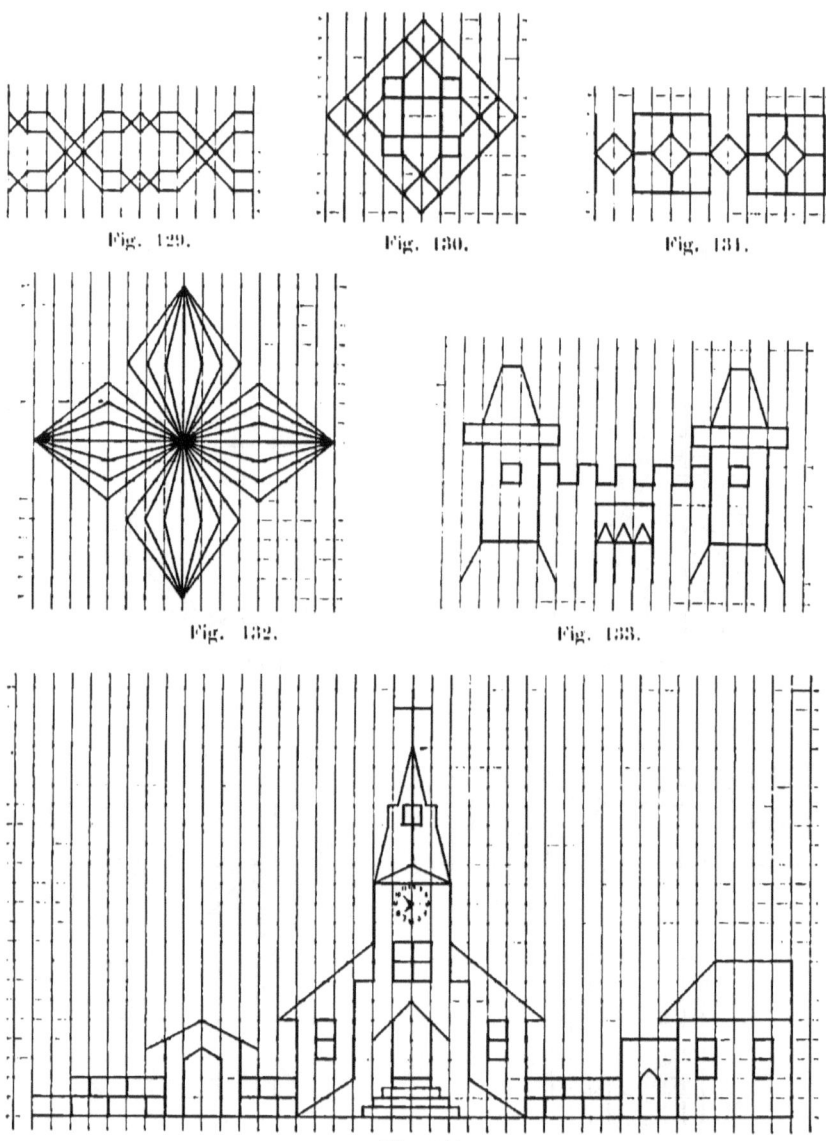

Fig. 129.　　　　Fig. 130.　　　　Fig. 131.

Fig. 132.　　　　Fig. 133.

Fig. 134.

lower members are formed of diagonals of standing oblongs.

Obliques of various grades can be united with one point as in Fig. 118, beside which the form of mediation would appear as Fig. 119.

As in this case, lying figures are produced, standing ones can be produced likewise. Each two of the elements thus received may be united so that all obliques issue from one point, as in Fig. 120, and in its opposite, Fig. 121.

An oppositional combination can also take place, so that each two lines of the same grade meet, (Fig. 122). The combination of obliques with obliques to angles, to squares and oblongs now follow, analogous to the method of combining oblongs, vertical and horizontal lines. Finally the combination of vertical and oblique, horizontal and oblique lines to angles, rhombus and rhomboid is introduced.

With these, the child tries his skill in producing forms of life: Fig. 133, gate of a fortress; Fig. 134, church with a schoolhouse and cemetery wall, and forms of beauty: Figs. 123-132. The task of the Kindergarten and the teacher has been accomplished, if the child has learned to manage oblique lines of the first and second degree skillfully. All given instruction which aimed at something beyond this was intended for the study of the teacher and the primary department, which is still more the case in regard to the curved line.

THE CURVED LINE.

(Figs. 135—147.)

Simply to indicate the progress, and to give Froebel's system of instruction in drawing complete, we add the following, and Figs. 135-147 in illustration of it.

First, the child has to acquire the ability to draw a curved line. The simplest curved line is the circle, from which all others may be derived.

However, it is difficult to draw a circle, and the net on slate and paper do not afford sufficient help and guide for so doing. But on the other hand, the child has been enabled to draw squares, straight and oblique lines, and with the assistance of these it is not difficult to find a number of points which lie on the periphery of a circle of given size.

It is known that all corners of a quadrangle (square or oblong) lie in the periphery of a circle whose diameter is the diagonal of the quadrangle. In the same manner all other right angles constructed over the diameter, are periphery angles, affording a point of the desired circular line. It is therefore necessary to construct such right angles, and this can be done very readily with the assistance of obliques of various grades.

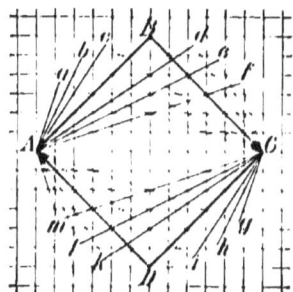

Fig. 135.

Suppose we draw from point *a* (Fig. 135), an oblique of the third degree, as the diagonal of a standing oblong; draw then, starting from point *c*, an oblong of the third degree, as diagonal of a lying oblong, and continue both these lines. They will meet in point *a*, and there form a right angle.

All obliques of the same degree, drawn from opposite points, will do the same as soon as the one approaches the vertical in the same proportion in which the other comes near the horizontal, or as soon as the one is the diagonal of a standing, the other of a lying oblong.

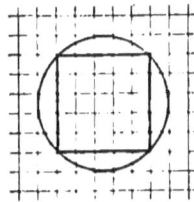

Fig. 136.

The lines *Aa* and *Ca* are obliques of the third, *Ab* and *Cb* of the second, *Af* and *Cf* of the third degree, etc., etc. In this manner it is easy to find a number of points, all of which are points in the circular line, intended to be drawn. Two or three of them over each side, will suffice to facilitate the drawing of the circumscribing circle (Fig. 136). In like manner the inscribing circle, will be obtained by drawing the middle transversals of the square, (Fig. 137), and constructing from their endpoints angles in the previously described manner.

After the pupil has obtained a correct idea of the size and form of the circle, whose radius may be of from one to five lengths, he

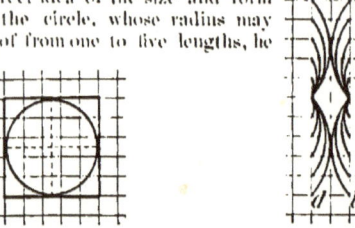

Fig. 137. Fig. 138.

will divide the same in half and quarter circles, producing thereby the elements for his farther activity.

Fig. 139.

The course of instruction is here again the same as that in connection with the vertical line. The pupil begins with quarter circles, radius of which is of a single length. Then follow quarter circles with a radius of from two to five lengths. By arrangement of these five

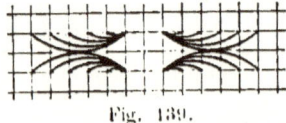

Fig. 140. Fig. 141.

quarter circles, four elements are produced, which are treated in the same manner as the triangles produced by arrangement of five straight lines. The segments may be parallel and the arrangement may take place in vertical and horizontal direction, (Figs. 138 and 139), or they may, like the obliques of various degrees, meet in one point, as in Fig. 142, of which Figs. 138 and 139 are examples.

Fig. 140, represents the combination of the elements a and d as a new element; Fig. 141, the combination of d and c. In Fig. 142, the arrangement finally takes place in oblique direction, and all lines meet in one point.

The quarter circle is followed by the half

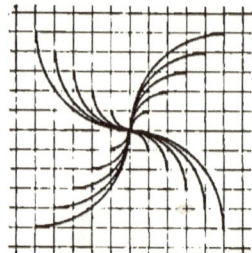

Fig. 142.

circle, Figs. 143–145; then the three fourths circle, (Fig. 146), and the whole circle, as shown in Fig. 147.

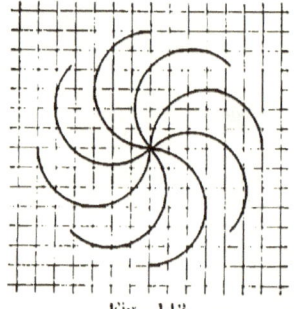

Fig. 143.

With the introduction of each new line, the same manner of proceeding is observed.

Notwithstanding the brevity with which we

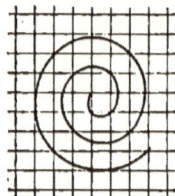

Fig. 144.

have treated the subject, we nevertheless believe we have presented the course of instruction in drawing sufficiently clear and forcible, and hope that by it we have made evident:—

1. That the method described here is perfectly adapted to the child's abilities, and fit to develop them in the most logical manner.

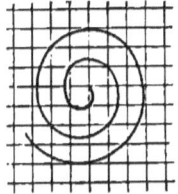
Fig. 115.

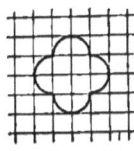
Fig. 146.

2. That the abundance of mathematical perceptions offered with it, and the constant necessity for combining according to certain laws, cannot fail to surely exert a wholesome influence in the mental development of the pupil.

3. That the child thus prepared for future instruction in drawing, will derive from such instruction more benefit than a child prepared by any other method.

Whosoever acknowledges the importance of drawing for the future life of the pupil—may he be led therein by its significance for indus-

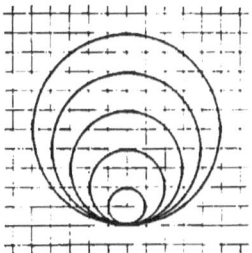
Fig. 117.

trial purposes, or æsthetic enjoyment, which latter it may afford even the poorest!—will be unanimous with us in advocating an early commencement of this branch of instruction with the child.

If there be any skeptics on this point, let them try the experiment, and we are sure they will be won over to our side of the question.

EDITOR'S NOTES.

The system of drawing based on netted slates and paper, as recommended by Froebel has been freely criticised in recent years, and by some kindergartners entirely discarded. The drawing exercises which have been already given were devised either by Froebel or his early followers in accordance with the principles which he is supposed to have held. If Froebel had received in his youth the instruction in drawing which is enjoyed by the children of the present time he probably would have developed a system of drawing for the kindergarten somewhat different from that which bears his name, and yet it is safe for his followers to hesitate before they entirely discard his suggestions on this subject. It is well in this connection to consider how much of his work has come to be recognized as of great value, after having been neglected and practically ignored by our best educators for a generation, and we should give careful attention to the claims made for the netted drawing, adopt as much of it as seems to be of value and then go on with the more modern methods which have been proved to be desirable, during the last twenty-five years of progress in art and industrial education. In free-hand drawing Froebel has practically left us no suggestions. He was a surveyor and a mathematical draftsman with no training in artistic free-hand drawing. Prof. Wiebe seems to have quite clearly set forth the principal features of value in the system of drawing used by Froebel and developed by his followers for twenty-five years after his death. The editor prefers in this edition of Prof. Wiebe's book to treat of netted drawing as it was advocated by Froebel, without addition to the original text or argument for its valuable qualities.

In addition to the exercises thus recommended there is undoubtedly some educational profit in copying on netted paper the designs laid on the kindergarten table with sticks, and whatever of value there is in this work may be secured by using sticks from one to four inches long to form the designs on the table, and netted paper with one quarter to one half inch squares for copying the figures. A habit of accuracy is cultivated and some ability in imitating is developed in such work, which must be of value in almost any phase of industrial art. The reproduction of this school of netted drawing, with such prominence as it here assumes in comparison with all else that is shown of drawing in this book, is not intended to indicate its relative importance at the present time, but to avoid losing sight of Froebel's recommendations. Little space is here devoted to the modern methods of instruction in drawing because these are constantly before the teachers and are also fully explained by competent writers in various publications relating to the subject. For the use of slates, either in the kindergarten or the school, there is no excuse at the present day. The one argument of economy is offset a hundred fold by hygienic and other objections which are patent to all who have given thought to the question.

Before drawing can be intelligently taught in any kindergarten the teacher must know so much of the subject as to be able to select from the various systems of primary drawing the peculiar features best adapted to the kindergarten. A child in his second kindergarten year ought to be better prepared to undertake any phase of drawing than a pupil in the second year of the primary school without any previous kindergarten experience, because of the superior training in form perception and manual dexterity which the kindergarten affords in the first year.

Drawing is a universal language by which communication may be held between all classes of the human race. The Hieroglyphics of the ancient nations and the rude drawings of the American Indians are the means by which ideas were transmitted from one age to another and by which we are to learn much of life in the past. Careful observation must precede drawing, and any drawing which represents in a reasonable degree the leading truths regarding the form of objects, is legitimate and not without value. The most progressive methods of teaching drawing in our schools to-day are founded on form study and model drawing, and therefore the children of the kindergarten have a great advantage over others in learning to draw, because the instruction of the kindergarten includes so much of form study that the pupils learn to perceive more clearly than other children the fundamental forms in the objects around them.

Educationally, elementary drawing may be divided into three general classes: Illustrative drawing; mathematical or instrumental drawing, which is often termed mechanical drawing; and free-hand objective drawing, or drawing from models. In this order illustrative drawing is placed first because it is the first attempt of the savage and the child to express ideas by pictorial illustration. This must also be considered again after all others, because it is the highest achievement of the artist to express ideals surpassing in beauty all nature. If properly encouraged, the child from the earliest age at which he can hold a pencil is delighted to draw rude representations of his pets and toys. He will often see in his drawing a likeness to an object which does not appear to the more mature perceptions, because the child grasps the general forms or more striking features without observing the minor details. In this faculty the infant possesses naturally that which the older student must acquire before he can become an expert artist. Therefore the kindergarten child should have free access at proper times to the blackboard, or be furnished with cheap paper and pencil for illustrating in his own way the stories which are told to him or which he may be led to tell of his own experience. In such drawings it is not expected that any of the truths of perspective will be very accurately expressed. It may be that a cat, a chicken, a house or a tree will be drawn, and if the resemblance which is attempted is approximated in the result it should receive such approval as will furnish encouragement to further effort. This idea was not popular fifty years ago and the noontime efforts of the district school pupils to decorate the blackboards, schoolroom walls and desk tops with samples of elementary art and "knife work" were frowned upon in such a practical manner as to destroy all ambition for excellence in graphic expression as well as manual training. The kindergarten may be the means for developing many an artist as well as an artizan who would otherwise never show any talent in these directions.

If the teacher has given such attention to the simplest elements of illustrative drawing as

PARADISE OF CHILDHOOD.

Fig. 148.

Fig. 152.

Fig. 149.

Fig. 153.

Fig. 150.

Fig. 151.

Fig. 154.

will enable her to produce such blackboard sketches as are suggested by the simple outlines shown in Figs. 148-154, the frequent use of this faculty will give the children samples that may stimulate them to accomplish the same results in the expression of their own ideas, and if they should merely imitate the work of the teacher no harm can result as the work will afford the best possible training in finger and arm movements.

Instrumental drawing which is suggested as the second division of the general subject, includes all drawing made to a scale, such as a map which is the plan of a section of country, or a square which is a drawing of one face of a cube. In all such drawings no representation of solidity by means of perspective is attempted, and they are made either the exact size of the object or of some definite proportion as one half size, one quarter size, etc., and therefore by the use of a suitable "scale" may be measured and the actual size of the object determined so that it can be correctly reproduced from the drawing. Such drawings are often called "working drawings." In the kindergarten only "full size" drawings should be attempted and for this purpose the forms found in the kindergarten material cannot be surpassed as models. Because the ball is a circle from whatever position it is viewed, this fact regarding its form is easily perceived by the child and thus if he lays the round tablet of the seventh gift on his paper and marks around it, he will have a circle which is an outline of a ball and may be finished to represent a first-gift ball by adding a line for the string. If the square tablet is used as a pattern to be marked around, it will represent the face of a third-gift cube. So also the other tablets may serve as patterns for drawing representations of the faces of the other gift blocks.

In the four inch folding paper we have one of the most valuable drawing models for this class of work. For example let the pupil lay a four-inch square folding paper on a sheet of plain drawing paper, make a dot at each corner, remove the paper and with a ruler for a guide draw the four straight lines connecting the dots and forming a square. This square is a complete mathematical drawing of the folding paper, because the paper practically has no thickness and therefore has but two dimensions, both of which are shown in the drawing. Now fold the paper accurately, one edge to the opposite edge, unfold and carefully lay the paper on the drawing of the square already outlined, and make a dot at each end of the crease procured by the fold. Remove the paper and with the aid of the ruler draw a line connecting the dots and representing the

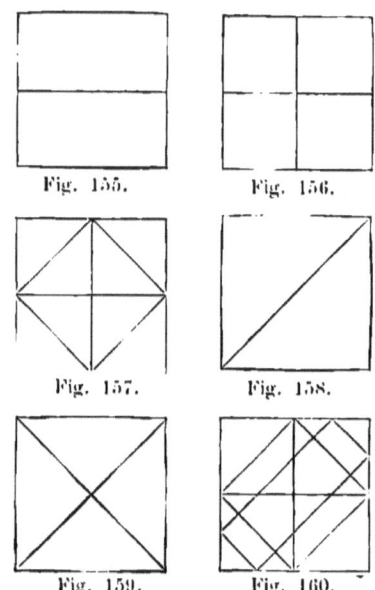

Fig. 155.   Fig. 156.

Fig. 157.   Fig. 158.

Fig. 159.   Fig. 160.

creases made by the fold, as in Fig. 155. Fold the other two opposite edges together in the same way and draw the line representing the second crease at right angles to the first, forming Fig. 156. Now fold the four corners to the center, unfold and draw lines representing the four new creases as indicated in Fig. 157. Another simple sequence is shown in Figs. 158, 159, and 160, while many others may be devised. As geometrical drawing in the higher grades develops the power of exact observation and manual performance, so the netted drawing of Froebel and the previously described practice with the tablets and folding papers as models are equally useful in cultivating the same qualities in the kindergarten. The teacher must constantly have in mind the fact that all exercises with the children which require accuracy and close attention must be used for only a very few minutes at one sitting. But because this restriction is necessary it must not be inferred that all exercises requiring any degree of exactness must be abolished or forbidden in the kindergarten. It is not necessary to especially impress upon a competent kindergartner the necessity for accuracy when accuracy is required, as it is a fundamental principle of her profession, but it is well for her to know also that it is not ignored by the best artists, although too often neglected by pseudo-artists who pose as authority. In these days of practical ideas an artist enhances his commercial value and does not lose caste professionally because he can produce a design correct in drawing, and, if occasion requires, within given dimensions.

It is well to remember that a sharp distinction must be made between mechanical or instrumental drawing and free-hand drawing. One is as valuable as the other in its own place, and it is no more creditable to be an expert in free-hand than in mechanical drawing. There are occasions when the free-hand drawing must be as accurate as the instrumental drawing, although the quality of the required lines may be quite different in the two classes of work. Therefore inasmuch as accuracy must be observed when it is called for, the pupil should be required to know what it means and how to secure it if necessary, which is more frequent than the practice of some professional artists would seem to indicate.

We now come to our third division of the subject, free-hand drawing, which is the broadest and most practical for school instruction and may be encouraged in the kindergarten as an aid to illustrative drawing, the first section in our division of the subject. If the boy can draw the cube and cylinder of the second gift in perspective approximately correct, he has the fundamental experience for many of the forms in his future work, and with the addition of some of the fifth-gift forms very many of the principal outlines of architectural construction may be represented. The accompanying sketches suggest some of the applications of the gift-block forms to nature drawing.

Figs. 161-165 represent objects embodying the spherical form; Figs. 166-169 embody the form of the cube; Figs. 170-177 illustrate modifications of the cylinder; Figs. 178-183 represent the fourth gift, while Figs. 184-186 embody the triangular prism of the fifth gift; Figs. 178, 183 and 184 may be considered a combination of the fourth and fifth gifts.

It is neither necessary nor desirable to attempt in the brief space of a Kindergarten Hand Book to make further suggestions in this line, because so many simple and practical books on the subject, have been published which apply as well to the higher grades of the kindergarten as to the lower school grades for which they were written. Form perception and manual training, which are such prominent features in the kindergarten, are the chief factors in correct drawing, and correct drawing is absolutely necessary to good art, as well as to mechanical construction. A well-known teacher and writer on the subject of art instruction has said: "The geometric figures enter into the subject of

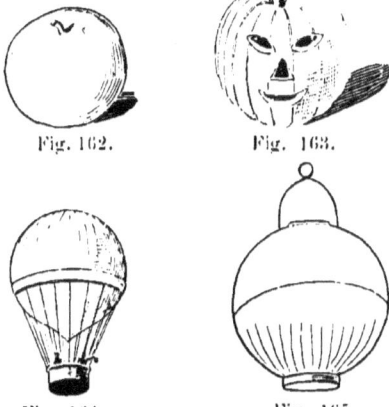

Fig. 161.

Fig. 162.   Fig. 163.

Fig. 164.   Fig. 165.

all forms, natural and artificial, and their application is of absorbing interest when traced through object and ornament, through architecture and painting, through snow-flake and crystal, flower and fruit, shell and insect, and

210　QUARTER CENTURY EDITION

Fig. 166.　　Fig. 167.
　　　　　　　　　　　　Fig. 172.　　Fig. 173.
Fig. 168.　　Fig. 169.
　　　　　　　　　　　　Fig. 174.　　Fig. 175.
　　　　　　　　　　　　Fig. 176.　　Fig. 177.
Fig. 170.
Fig. 171.　　　　Fig. 178.　　Fig. 179.

PARADISE OF CHILDHOOD. 211

all higher forms of life. These should be illustrated. Working drawings of cylinders and cubes are but the beginning; they have new meaning when seen as the first types which prefigure the steam-cylinder, the railway car, the soldiers' monument and the mausoleum, the Tower of Pisa and the Grand Opera of Paris." No kindergartner can do her best until she has a good knowledge of elementary geometry and some ability at illustration and free-hand drawing. One who has not experienced it cannot imagine the pleasure of being able, even though quite imperfectly, to make a hasty pencil sketch for future reference. A series of note sketch books kept for years become a constant source of pleasure and there is a personality in the sketches which never can pertain to the results of the snap-shot with the camera.

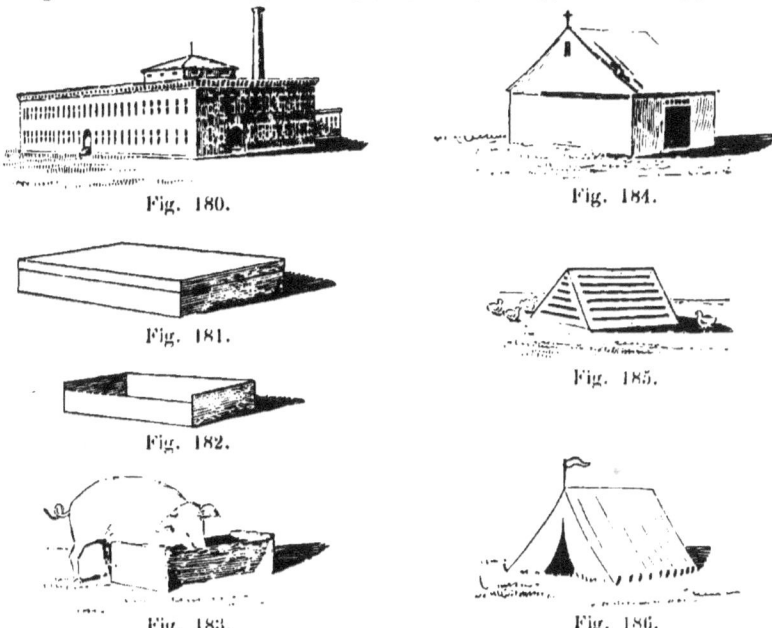

Fig. 180.

Fig. 181.

Fig. 182.

Fig. 183.

Fig. 184.

Fig. 185.

Fig. 186.

THE ELEVENTH AND TWELFTH GIFTS.
MATERIAL FOR PERFORATING AND EMBROIDERING.

It is claimed by us that all occupation material presented by Froebel, in the Gifts of the Kindergarten, are, in some respects, related to each other, complementing one another. What logical connection is there between the occupation of perforating and embroidering, introduced with the present and the use of the previously introduced Gifts of the Kindergarten? This question may be asked by some superficial enquirer. Him we answer thus: In the first Gifts of the Kindergarten, the *solid mass of bodies* prevailed; in the following ones the *plane*; then the *embodied line* was followed by

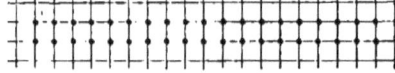

Fig. 1.

the *drawn* line, and the occupation here introduced brings us down to the *point*. With the introduction of the perforating paper and pricking needle, we have descended to the *smallest part of the whole*—the *extreme limit of mathematical divisibility*; and in a playing manner, the child followed us unwittingly, on this, in an abstract sense, difficult journey.

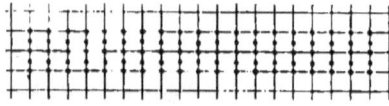

Fig. 2.

The material for these occupations is a piece of net paper, which is placed upon some layers of soft blotting paper. The pricking or perforating tool is a rather strong sewing needle,

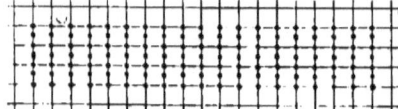

Fig. 3.

fastened in a holder so as to project about one fourth of an inch. Aim of the occupation is the production of the beautiful, not only by the child's own activity, but by his own invention.

Steadiness of the eye and hand are the visible results of the occupation which directly prepares the pupil for various kinds of manual labor. The perforating, accompanied by the use of the needle and silk, or worsted, in the way embroidery is done, it is evident in what direction the faculty of the pupil may be developed.

The method pursued with this occupation is analogous to that employed in the drawing department. Starting from the single point, the child is gradually led through all the various grades of difficulty; and from step to step his

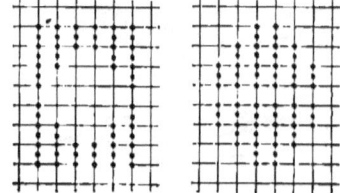

Fig. 4. Fig. 5.

interest in the work will increase, especially as the various colors of the embroidered figures add much to their liveliness, as do the colored pencils in the drawing department.

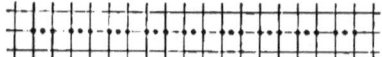

Fig. 6.

The child first pricks vertical lines of two and three lengths, then of four and five lengths, (Figs. 2 and 3). They are united to a triangle, opposites and forms of mediation are found, and these again are united into squares with hollow and filled middle, (Figs. 4 and 5). The horizontal line follows, (Figs. 6–8), then the

Fig. 7.

combination of vertical and horizontal to a right angle in its four oppositionally equal positions, (Figs. 9–12). The combination of the four elements present a vast number of small figures. If the external point of the angle of Figs. 9 and 10 touch one another, the cross (Fig. 13) is produced; if the end points of the legs of these figures touch, the square is made, (Fig. 14). By repeatedly uniting Figs. 9 and 12,Fig. 15 is produced, and by the combination of all four angles, Figs. 16 and 17. According to the rules followed in laying figures with tablets of Gift Seven, and in drawing, or by a simple application of the law of opposites, the child will produce a large number of other figures.

The combination of lines of one and two lengths is then introduced, and standing and lying oblongs are formed, (Figs. 18 and 19), etc. The school of perforating, *per se* has to consider still simple squares and lying and standing oblongs, consisting of lines of from two to five lengths. In order not to repeat the same form too often, we introduce in Figs. 21–31 a series less simple; containing, however, the fundamental forms, showing in the meantime the combination of lines of various dimensions.

In a similar way, the oblique line is now introduced and employed. The child pricks it in various directions, commencing with a one length line, (Figs. 32–35), combines it to angles, (Figs. 36–39), the combination of which will again result in many beautiful forms. Then follows the perforating of oblique lines of from two to five lengths, (a single length containing up to seven points), which are employed for the representation of borders, corner ornaments,etc., (Figs. 42–45, 61). The oblique of the second degree is also introduced, as shown in Figs. 46 and 47, and the peculiar formations in Figs. 48–51.

Finally, the combination of the oblique with the vertical line, (Figs. 52 and 54), and with the horizontal, (Figs. 53 and 55), or with both at the same time, (Figs. 56–60), takes place.

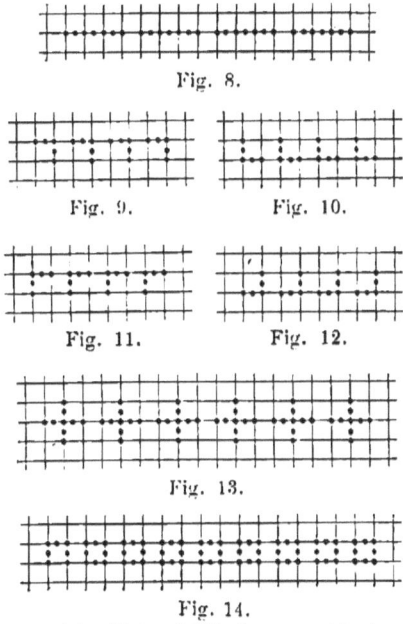

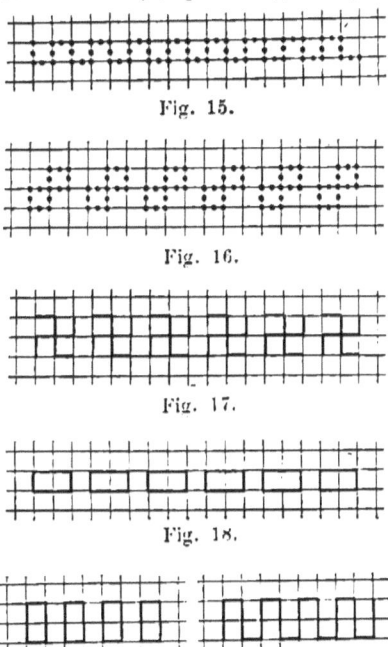

All these elements may be combined in the most manifold manner, and the inventive activity of the pupil will find a large field in pro-

214 QUARTER CENTURY EDITION

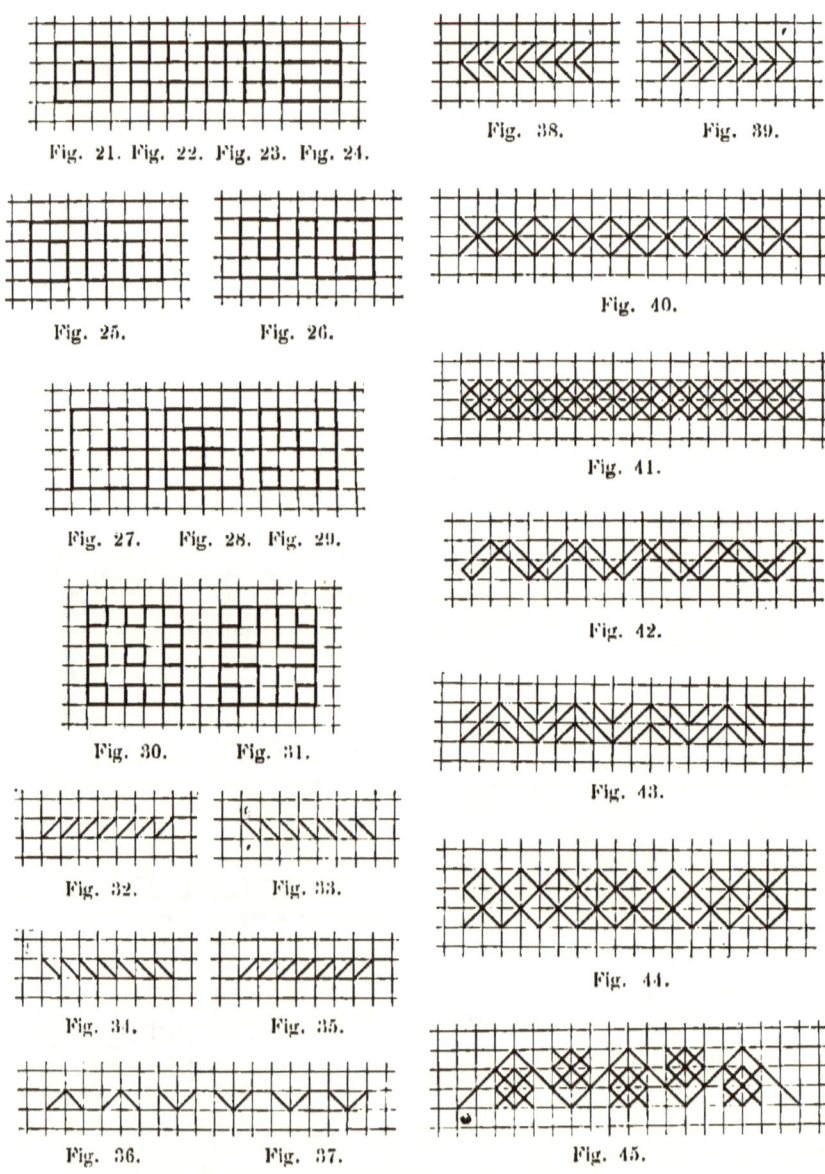

Fig. 21. Fig. 22. Fig. 23. Fig. 24.
Fig. 25. Fig. 26.
Fig. 27. Fig. 28. Fig. 29.
Fig. 30. Fig. 31.
Fig. 32. Fig. 33.
Fig. 34. Fig. 35.
Fig. 36. Fig. 37.
Fig. 38. Fig. 39.
Fig. 40.
Fig. 41.
Fig. 42.
Fig. 43.
Fig. 44.
Fig. 45.

PARADISE OF CHILDHOOD.

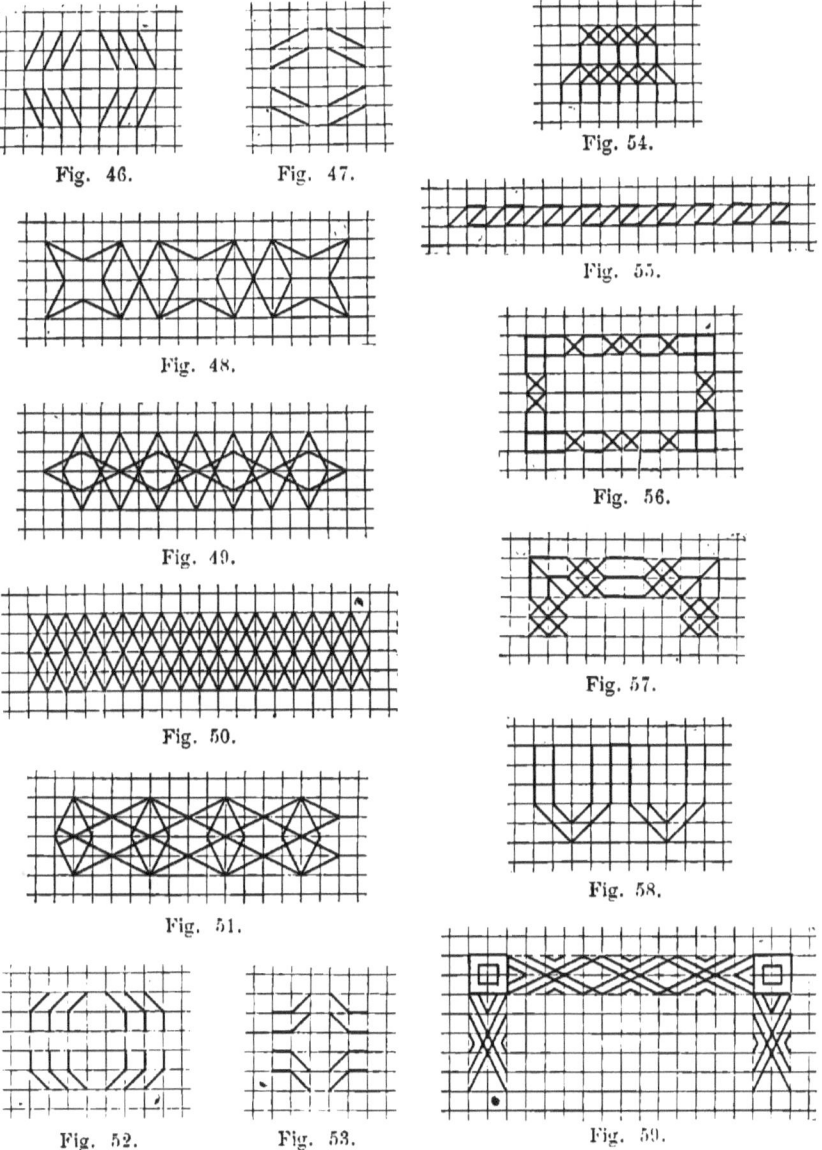

Fig. 46. Fig. 47. Fig. 54. Fig. 48. Fig. 55. Fig. 49. Fig. 56. Fig. 50. Fig. 57. Fig. 51. Fig. 58. Fig. 52. Fig. 53. Fig. 59.

ducing samples of borders, corner pieces, frames, reading marks, etc., etc.

When it is intended to produce anything of a more complicated nature, the pattern should be drafted by pupil or teacher upon the net paper previous to pricking. In such cases, it is advisable and productive of pleasure to the pupils, if beneath the perforating paper another one doubly folded is laid, to have the pattern transferred by perforation upon this paper in various copies. Such little productions may

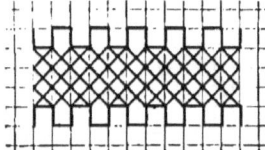

Fig. 60.

be used for various purposes, and be presented by the children to their friends on many occasions. To assist the pupils in this respect, it is recommended that simple drawings be placed in the hands of the pupils, which, owing to their little ability, they certainly could not yet produce by drawing, but which they can well trace with their perforating tool. These

Fig. 61.

drawings should represent objects from the animal and vegetable kingdoms, and may thus be of great service to the mental development of the children. The slowly and carefully perforated forms and figures will undoubtedly be more lastingly impressed upon the mind and longer retained by the memory, than if they were only described or hurriedly looked at. It should be mentioned that the embroidering does not begin simultaneously with the perforating, but only after the children have acquired considerable skill in the last named occupation. For purposes of

EMBROIDERING.

The same net paper which was used for exercises in perforating may be employed, by filling out the intervals between the holes with threads of colored silk or worsted. It will be sufficient for this purpose to combine the points of one net square only, because otherwise the stitches would become too short to be made with the embroidery needle in the hands of children yet unskilled. For work, to be prepared for a special purpose, the perforated pattern should be transferred upon stiff paper or bristol-board.

Fig. 62.   Fig. 63.

Course of instruction just the same as with perforating.

Experience will show that of the figures given, some are more fit for perforating, others better adapted for embroidering. Either occupation leads to peculiar results. Figures in which strongly rounded lines predominate may

Fig. 64.

be easily perforated, but with difficulty, or not at all be embroidered. By the process of embroidering, however, plain forms, as stars, and rosettes, are easily produced, which could hardly be represented, or, at best, very imperfectly only, by the perforating needle. Figs. 62–67, are examples of this kind.

To develop the sense of color in the children, the paper on which they embroider, should be of all the various shades and hues,

means of education and in Froebel's institution it occupies a prominent place; it should approach the child in various ways; not only in *form*, but in *color*, and *tone* also. To insure

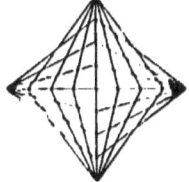

Fig. 66.

the desired result in this direction, we begin in the Kindergarten, where we can much more readily make impressions upon the blank mind of children, than at a later period when other influences have polluted their tastes.

Fig. 65.

through the whole scale of colors. If the paper is gray, blue, black, or green, let the worsted or silk be of a rose color, white, or ange or red, and if the pupil is far enough advanced to represent objects of nature, as fruit, leaves, plants, or animals, it will be very proper to use in embroidering, the colors shown by these natural objects. Much can thereby be accomplished toward an early development of appreciation and knowledge of color, in which grown people in all countries are often sadly deficient. It has appeared to some, as if this occupation is less useful than pleasurable. Let them consider that the ordinary seeing of objects already is a difficult matter, nay, really an art, needing long practice. Much more difficult and requiring much more careful exercise, is a true and correct perception of color.

If the *beautiful* is introduced at all as a

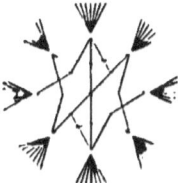

Fig. 67.

For this reason, we go still another step further, and give the more developed pupil a box of colors, showing him their use, in covering the perforated outlines of objects with the paint. Children like to occupy themselves in this manner, and show an increased interest, if they first produce the drawings and are subsequently allowed to use the brush for further beautifying their work.

The perforating and embroidering are begun with the children in the Kindergarten when they have become sufficiently prepared for the perfection of forms by the use of their building blocks and sticks.

profitable. In the same general class may be included the perforating of outlines by making a succession of holes very close together without the intention of subsequent sewing; and also such designs for sewing as involve intricate patterns with very short stitches. Neither is the pricking of holes with exactness at the printed dots or at the crossing of lines on netted paper believed to be good practice for small fingers and young eyes, and when many of these are quite near together the whole occupation is not to be encouraged. On the other hand such condemnation of cardboard sewing of all kinds for the children as has emanated from some sources indicates a reaction as unreasonable as was the sanction of the most extreme practice of the raised surface perforating.

But this criticism of line perforating has been of great value, because it has brought into general use for the youngest children a series of ready-pricked cards in simple designs with large holes, long stitches, and coarse needles and thread. For earliest sewing, such designs on small cards not more than four by five inches in size are most suitable, and in order to secure holes large enough for the large needles and coarse thread required at this stage it seems quite desirable that each perforation be made by punching out a minute disk of the card, thus producing a smooth, round hole of suitable size to be easily seen on both sides of the card and to receive the thread without wear and unnecessary friction.

The following figures represent a series of such cards, which are technically called "Perforated Cards," in distinction from Pricked Cards, which are punctured with pointed needles. These cards retain their numbers as found in the catalogue of Bradley's kindergarten material.

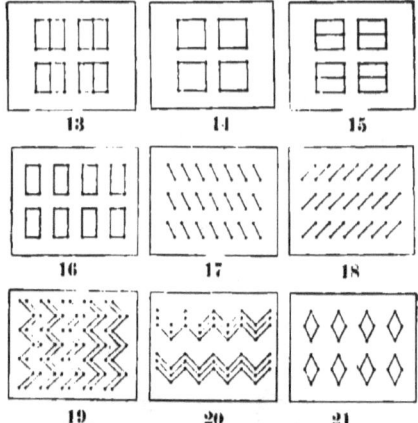

Nos. 1, 2, 3, 10, 11, etc., to 21, show the principal or first intention of the several arrangements of holes in these cards, and 1a, 1b, 1c, 2a, 2b, 2c, etc., represent some of the modifications or inventions which may be sewed with the cards.

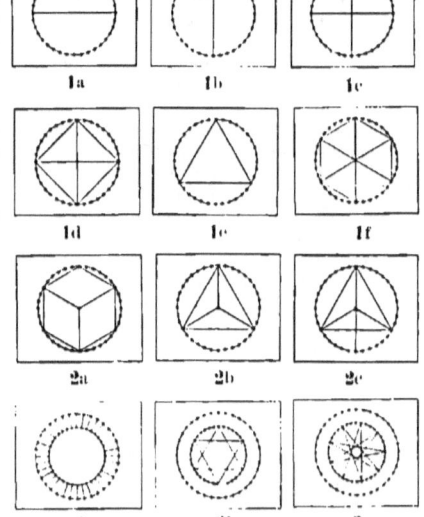

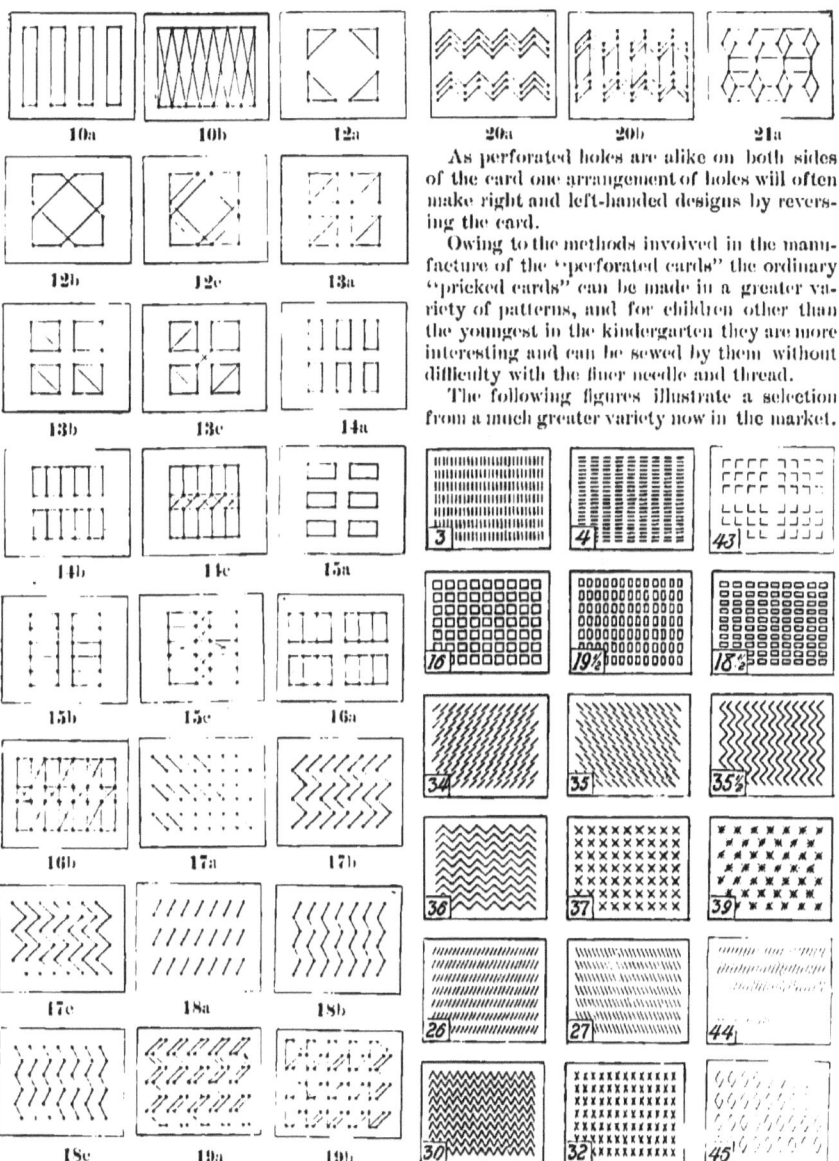

As perforated holes are alike on both sides of the card one arrangement of holes will often make right and left-handed designs by reversing the card.

Owing to the methods involved in the manufacture of the "perforated cards" the ordinary "pricked cards" can be made in a greater variety of patterns, and for children other than the youngest in the kindergarten they are more interesting and can be sewed by them without difficulty with the finer needle and thread.

The following figures illustrate a selection from a much greater variety now in the market.

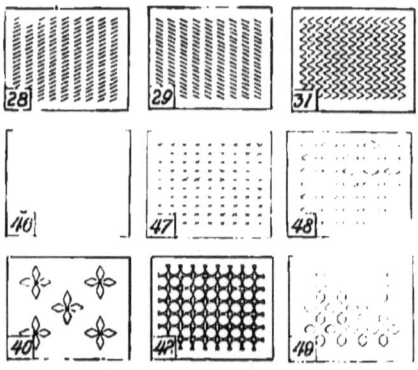

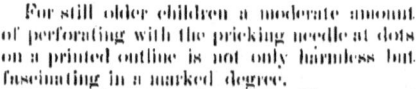
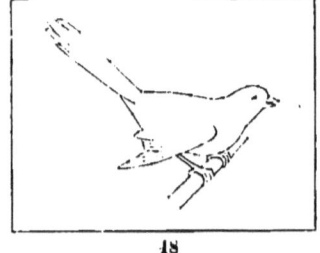

For still older children a moderate amount of perforating with the pricking needle at dots on a printed outline is not only harmless but fascinating in a marked degree.

In this class of work a much wider range of designs extending into life forms can be introduced, because of the difference in process in the manufacture of cards which are for sale for this purpose.

Also in this work original designs may be prepared by the teacher or even by the pupils as they may be traced from prints and transferred to cards by the use of impression paper.

The foregoing figures show examples of this class of designs.

In cardboard pricking and sewing as in all other kindergarten occupations the adjustment of the grade of work to the age and condition of each child must be left to the judgment of the trained kindergartner, and fortunately this may safely be trusted to the corps of competent teachers now in the work and to those being prepared by the normal kindergarten schools in this country.

ELEMENTARY COLOR TEACHING.

THE educational phase of color has assumed such importance within the past decade that it must receive more than passing notice in any treatise on the kindergarten gifts and occupations, taken as a whole. As the color question presents itself quite prominently in the selection of the threads for embroidering and still more in the use of colored papers, the editor feels that this is the proper place to introduce certain special suggestions on that subject.

There is a fascination about the study of color which increases as we become more and more familiar with the subject. We meet it at every turn in the natural world. It makes the loftiest hilltops radiant in early morning and paints its hues in wondrous brilliancy on the evening sky.

Art revels in color, and praise as we may the chisel of the sculptor and the cunning of the engraver, we find only cool comfort in colorless art. Consequently we are always seeking the best color effects. We want them in the arrangement of our lawns, the decoration of our houses, both within and without, in our clothing, in public and private, wherever we admit color. Indeed a knowledge of color and its skillful use in all the affairs of life ministers more effectively to our best equipment and our enjoyment than does a knowledge of form. Nevertheless all attempts to place color study on a practical footing have failed until recently, because of the universal opinion among artists that art in color would be degraded by contact with scientific truths.

And yet from Euclid down to the present generation of students the mathematicians have been occupied in discovering and perfecting instruments and a language of form by which the graceful outlines of architecture and ornament may be analyzed and recorded. But those who have labored in the kingdom of color have found it as impossible to accurately describe any given hue or tone of color in an accepted nomenclature as it was when the Queen of Sheba brought her royal gifts to Solomon. When Froebel prepared his material for the kindergarten, color was for the first time introduced into a system of elementary instruction disconnected from drawing and painting, and it is worthy of note that the only system by which colors can now be intelligently designated without actual samples was originated and developed in response to the demands of the kindergartners of America for better material.

In the kindergarten material first imported from Germany to the United States the first-gift balls were fairly good examples of red, orange, yellow, green, blue and purple or violet. But the colored papers used in the occupation material of that time were selected without order, scientific knowledge or fine color perceptions. The result was that the American kindergartners began to complain of the colors found in the papers and to suggest other colors either in addition to those in use or in place of them. While many colors already in the market were added and some made to order in response to such criticisms and requests, no material advance was made in producing a logical assortment of colors in the papers for a number of years. But the difficulties thus early encountered induced the editor of these notes to begin a series of experiments which has resulted, by the aid and cordial co-operation of many of his friends among scientists, artists and kindergartners, in the scheme of color instruction now known as the Bradley System of Color Education. As this is quite fully set forth in other publications it is unnecessary to use sufficient space here to explain it in detail, and therefore only a brief outline of the fundamental principles on which it is based is presented.

In form, the constant companion of color in material objects, we have the foot or meter by which we measure lengths and breadths, and the divided circle by which the directions of lines may be noted, and with these two accepted standards of measurements all surfaces and solids can be described. If all material forms were destroyed to-day any one of them could be reconstructed from suitable records preserved in terms of these standards, but this has not been true regarding color, because of the lack of standards and means for measuring and recording color effects. In the solar spectrum we have the only known source to which we may look for permanent standards of color. In music we have certain standards of tones and a language accepted by general agreement which render it possible to transmit musical compositions from one country to another and from generation to generation. Every tone produced by a musical instrument is due to a given number of vibrations or waves in some substance, which vibrations are ordinarily conveyed to the ear by waves in the air; and by a record of these tones in terms of their vibrations musical compositions are transmitted from age to age.

It is supposed that light and color are transmitted by vibrations or waves in an unknown something which we call ether and that different wave lengths produce various effects in the eye which are conveyed to the brain as colors. Therefore when we select in the solar spectrum certain standards of color and determine the wave length of each, we have a series of definitely located "Spectrum Standards" which are absolutely permanent. If we then produce the best possible imitation of these colors in pigments or other substances, we shall have standard Material Colors. The Material Colors will be very inferior to the Spectrum Colors in purity and brilliancy, but if they are to be used as standards each must be the same kind of color as the Spectrum Color which it represents; for instance, the "orange" must be neither more red nor more yellow than the location in the spectrum which has been accepted as the standard orange. The training and habits of a good kindergartner will especially enable her to appreciate this necessity for exact standards in a color nomenclature as much as in form study.

For example, the third-gift cube is a solid which has six plane faces, each of which is a quadrilateral having four right angles and four straight sides, each one inch long. Therefore a somewhat similar solid in which the angles are not right angles and the sides are unequal is not a cube. So it is necessary that there be definite terms regarding color in which accurate statements can be made and recorded before there can be any language on which to base intelligent discussion regarding the questions involved in the consideration of color and its best uses. The Bradley Color Scheme is based on the determination of these standards in the solar spectrum and the best material imitations of them to serve as Pigmentary Standards.

Having selected these pigmentary or material standards there must be secured some means by which they can be combined in definitely expressed proportions to produce all other colors, so that we may have an exact but simple and easily-understood nomenclature. There is but one device known at present which fulfills these conditions, and that is the "Maxwell Disks." If a live coal on the end of a stick is rapidly whirled in a circle, a ring of light is seen, because the light-impression which is made on the retina of the eye remains fixed while the stick is moving through an entire circle. On this principle, if a disk of cardboard is divided by a diameter and one of the semi-circles covered with white paper and the other with black paper, and the disk rapidly whirled on a pin at its center, the two half circles will no longer appear as distinctively white and black, but the whole surface will assume a uniform gray color. If the amount of white surface is increased to three quarters of the whole the gray will be much lighter, and if the black is increased the resulting color will be darker. So, also, if instead of the white and black semi-circles two standard colors, as red and orange, are combined in the same way, a new color between red and orange will result.

As it is quite inconvenient to paste up a colored disk for each experiment, a celebrated English scientist named Maxwell conceived the idea of slitting each of two disks, from circumference to center, so that they could be joined, and by a movement on each other around the common center made to show any required amount of the surface of each. If two disks are joined in this way and laid on to a slightly-larger disk which is divided at the circumference into one hundred parts the amount of surface of each color which is exposed may be measured and recorded. Thus if the red and orange disks are joined so as to show three quarters red and one quarter orange, the color resulting by rotation would be recorded as Red 75, Orange 25, or using the initials of the colors, R. 75, O. 25, which becomes the definite symbol of that particular orange hue of red. This brief explanation may serve to convey an idea of the scope of such a system of color study.

On this scientific foundation a line of colored papers has been prepared for the kindergarten. In the spectrum colors of the educational papers two hues between each two standards are provided, making eighteen of these full spectrum colors. If a color is in strong sunlight it becomes much lighter and is a tint of the color; if in shadow it is darker and is called a shade. These two effects may be secured with the rotating disks by using a white disk with the color disk for the tints, and a black disk with the color for the shades.

Thus these papers furnish a systematic line of scales or families of colors for color instruction. A line of grays and another of broken or gray colors is added, so that there is no reasonable demand in primary education for other colors in papers. For class instruction the color wheel or color mixer is very valuable, but if such apparatus is not available a simple modification of the larger apparatus in the form of a color-top furnishes much instruction and amusement.

Some educators who have not fully understood this subject have believed that the color-wheel and color top are too advanced in scientific principles to be profitable in the primary school grades, and necessarily from the same standpoint much less useful in the kindergarten. But actual test is better than theories, and a large number of kindergartners are already prepared to certify to the great value of the color wheel and color tops in their work. The following is but a simple illustration of many lines in which color instruction can be imparted and color interest excited. In one of our large public kindergartens, as the teacher entered the room one morning, she saw an admiring group of children gathered around Bessie, whom she noticed had on a new dress. As the kindergartner approached, one child exclaimed excitedly, "See what a pretty dress Bessie has on. What color is it?" After various guesses, many of which were somewhat wild, as it was early in the year, some one made a reasonably good guess, and the teacher said, "Let us see what the color-wheel says. If Bessie will come and stand by it we will see if we can make a color like her dress by whirling the color disks."

The children were interested at once, and as Bessie stood by the color wheel, they were allowed to suggest their objections to the color made by the rotating disks. Mary said that it was too blue, and after a change had been made, Willie thought it was too green; but at last a good result was obtained, as the happy exclamations of the little ones testified, and as the disks ceased rotating a complete chart of the true color was before the children. If a color wheel is not available the same exercises may be tried with a color top.

In many of the gifts and occupations of the kindergarten, color is prominent, but it is specially so in all the work in papers. If colored papers are to be used they should not only be selected so as to do no harm, but the Modern Educational Colored Papers may be so used as to afford much instruction at the same time that manual exercises are being enjoyed.

With colored papers, in the established standards and their modifications in their hues and tones, the kindergartners and primary school teachers are well equipped for color teaching, but with the addition of a color wheel or color mixer and a few color charts, which can be made from the paper at small cost, color teaching becomes simply a recreation to both teacher and pupils. The fact that there is so much color material used in the kindergarten insures constant attention on the part of the children, and where there is interested attention there is rapid advance, so a child that has had two years in a true kindergarten and one year in a connecting school will require very little more of colored papers, blocks and sticks of any kind, but will be amply able to proceed with the more abstract consideration of subjects brought to his attention. It is not expedient to present the subject of color teaching in detail within the reasonable limits of this book, and hence the editor ventures to note the contents of two books which he has prepared to explain his system of color instruction.

"Color in the Kindergarten," is a book of about sixty pages in paper covers which gives a somewhat detailed statement of the subject, under two principal heads: First, "The Theory of Color," and second, "Color Materials in the Kindergarten." In the first of these divisions the following sub-heads occur: The Theory of Sir David Brewster; The Young-Helmholtz Theory; The Standards must be Chosen from the Solar Spectrum; The Use of the Color Wheel; The Old Theories Tested by the Wheel; Concerning the Complementary Colors; How to Secure a Color Nomenclature; Tints and Shades; Scales of Color; Classification of Harmonies; Broken Colors; The So-called Tertiary Colors; How the Grays are Classified; Simultaneous Contrast; A Review of the Bradley Color Scheme; Some Color Definitions. The second section, Color Material, contains the following divisions: The Prismatic Spectrum; The Colored Papers; The Rainy Day Spectrum; Value of the Color Wheel; Spectrum Hues; Tints and Shades of Hues; The First Gift; Sewing; Weaving; Intertwining; Parquetry; Paper Cutting; Paper Folding; Concerning Water Colors; Color Blindness.

A book entitled "Elementary Color" contains one hundred and thirty pages freely illustrated and a miniature color chart in pasted papers showing "Pure Spectrum Scales" and "Broken Spectrum Scales." This has an introduction by Prof. Henry Lefavour of Williams College and completely sets forth the Bradley system of color instruction under the following principal heads: The Theory of Color; Color Definitions; Practical Experiments Illustrating the Theory of Color; Color Teaching in the Schoolroom; Outline of Course in Color Instruction.

Under this last head the following divisions are very briefly treated: The Solar Spectrum; Pigmentary Spectrum Colors; Study of Tones; Broken Colors; Complete Chart of Pure Spectrum Scales in Five Tones; Advanced Study of Harmonies.

This system of color instruction has been criticised as mechanical, scientific and inartistic by many artists of reputation who seem to agree that because definite formulas cannot be given for producing works of the highest rank in art all standards and facts regarding color are debasing to the artistic instincts. If this claim is admitted to be sound in regard to color may we not also urge that the study of geometry is to be ignored because of its degrading effect on art in form, and that English grammar is out of date because it is not especially conducive to highest flights in poetry? But it is the belief of one who has known the kindergartners of America intimately for a quarter of a century that they will not disparage the value of the exact and methodical elements that are introduced by this color scheme into a most important feature of elementary work, in place of the entirely indefinite methods of the past.

THE THIRTEENTH GIFT.

MATERIAL FOR CUTTING PAPER AND MOUNTING PIECES TO PRODUCE FIGURES AND FORMS.

The labor, or occupation alphabet presented by Froebel in his system of education, cannot spare the occupation, now introduced—the cutting of paper—the transmutation of the material by division of its parts, notwithstanding the many apparently well-founded doubts, whether scissors should be placed in the hands of the child at such an early age. It will be well for such doubters to consider: Firstly, that the scissors which the children use have no sharp points, but are rounded at their ends, by which the possibilities of doing harm with them are greatly reduced. Secondly, it is expected that the teacher employs all possible means to watch and superintend the children with the utmost care during their occupation with the scissors. Thirdly, as it can never be prevented, that, at least, at times the child produces, by cutting according to certain laws, highly interesting and beautiful forms, their desire of destroying with the scissors will soon die out, and they, as well as their parents, will be spared many an unpleasant experience, incident upon this childish instinct, if it were left entirely unguided.

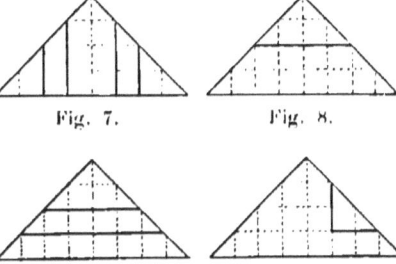

Fig. 7.   Fig. 8.

Fig. 9.   Fig. 10.

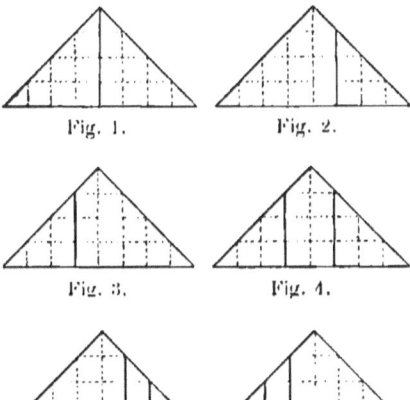

Fig. 1.   Fig. 2.

Fig. 3.   Fig. 4.

Fig. 5.   Fig. 6.

scissors, knives and similar dangerous objects may fall into the hands of children, it is of great importance to accustom them to such, by a regular course of instruction in their use, which, it may be expected, will certainly do something to prevent them from illegitimately applying them for mischievous purposes.

By placing material before them from which

As material for the cutting, we employ a square piece of paper of the size of one-sixteenth sheet, similar to the folding sheet. Such a sheet is broken diagonally, the right acute angle placed upon the left, so as to produce four triangles resting one upon another. Repeating the same proceeding, so that by so doing the two upper triangles will be folded upwards, the lower ones downwards in the halving line, eight triangles resting one upon another, will be produced, which we use as our

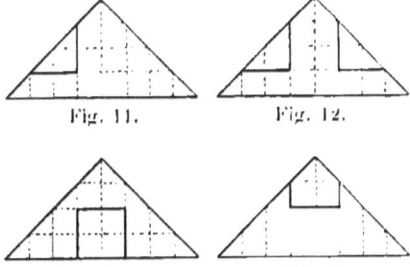

Fig. 11.   Fig. 12.

Fig. 13.   Fig. 14.

first fundamental form. *This fundamental form is held, in all exercises, so that the open* side, where no plane connects with another is always turned toward the left.

In order to accomplish a sufficient exactness in cutting, the uppermost triangle contains, (or if it does not, is to be provided with) a kind of net as a guide in cutting. Dotted lines on the figures indicate this net work.

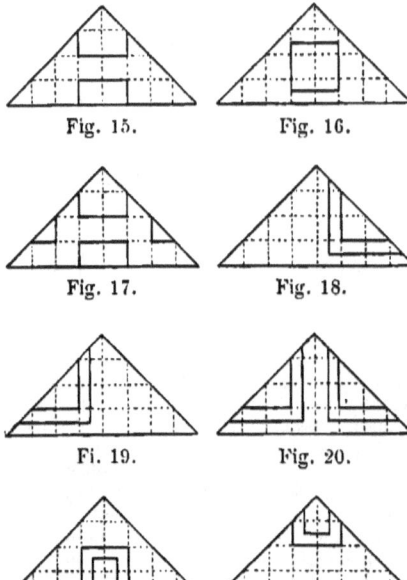

Fig. 15.   Fig. 16.
Fig. 17.   Fig. 18.
Fi. 19.   Fig. 20.
Fig. 21.   Fig. 22.

The activity itself is regulated according to the law of opposites. We commence with the vertical cut, come to its opposite, the horizontal and finally to the mediation of both, the oblique.

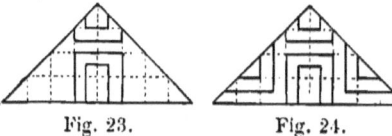

Fig. 23.   Fig. 24.

Figs. 1–132 indicate the abundance of cuts which may be developed according to this method, and it is advisable to arrange for the child a selection of the simpler elements into a school of cutting.

The following selection presents, almost always, two opposites and their combination, or leaves out one of the former, as is the case with the horizontal cut, wherever it does not produce anything essentially new.

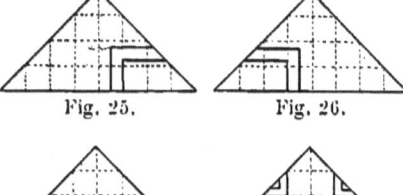

Fig. 25.   Fig. 26.

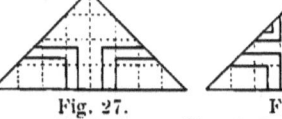

Fig. 27.   Fig. 28.

a. Vertical cuts, Figs. 2, 3, 4–5, 6, 7.
b. Horizontal cuts, Figs. 8, 9—(above, and below).
c. Vertical and horizontal, Figs. 18, 19, 20—21, 22, 23.
d. Oblique cuts, Figs. 34, 35—36, 37, 38.
e. Oblique and vertical, Figs. 51, 52, 53, —54, 55, 56,—58, 59, 60.

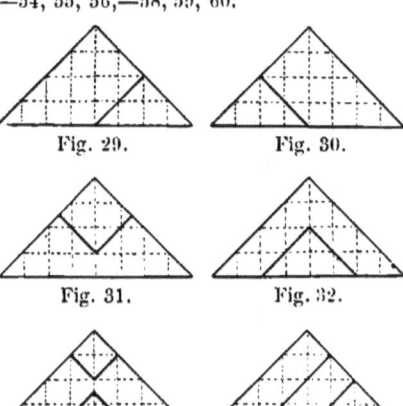

Fig. 29.   Fig. 30.
Fig. 31.   Fig. 32.
Fig. 33.   Fig. 34.

f. Oblique and horizontal, Figs. 65, 66, 67.
g. Half oblong cuts, where the diagonals of standing and lying oblongs, formed of two net squares serve as guides—Figs. 117, 118, 119—121, 122, 123—125, 126, 127.

Here ends the school of cutting, *per se*, for

PARADISE OF CHILDHOOD. 227

the first fundamental form, the right-angled triangle. The given elements may be combined in the most manifold manner, as this has been sufficiently carried out in the forms given.

The fundamental form used for Figs. 133–167 is a *six fold equilateral triangle*. It also is

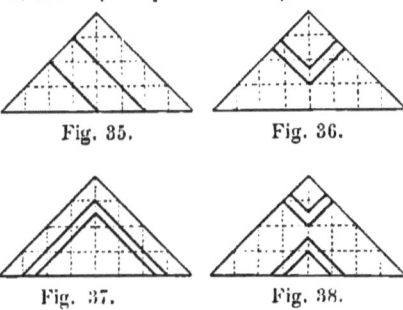

Fig. 35.   Fig. 36.

Fig. 37.   Fig. 38.

produced from the folding sheet, by breaking it diagonally, halving the middle of the diagonal, dividing again in three equal parts the angle situated on this point of halving. The angles thus produced will be angles of sixty degrees. The leaf is folded in the legs of these angles by bending the one acute angle of the original triangle upwards, the other downwards. By cutting the protruding corners, we shall have the desired form of the six fold equilateral triangle, in which the entirely open side serves

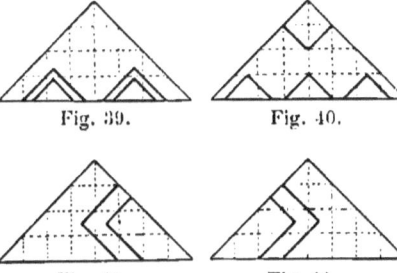

Fig. 39.   Fig. 40.

Fig. 41.   Fig. 42.

as basis of the triangle. The net for guidance is formed by division of each side in four equal parts, uniting the points of division of the base, by parallel lines with the sides, and drawing of a vertical from the upper point of the triangle upon its base. It is the oblique line, particularly which is introduced here. The designs and patterns from Figs. 133–145, will suffice for this purpose. The same fundamental form is used for practicing and performing the circular cuts, although the right angular funda-

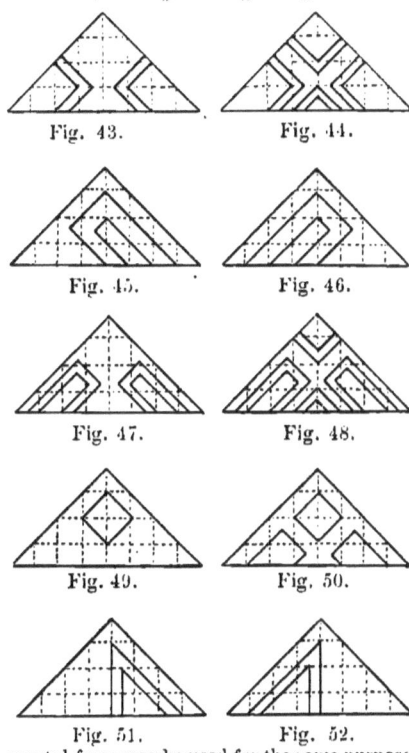

Fig. 43.   Fig. 44.

Fig. 45.   Fig. 46.

Fig. 47.   Fig. 48.

Fig. 49.   Fig. 50.

Fig. 51.   Fig. 52.

mental form may be used for the same purpose. Both find their application subsequently, in a sphere of development only, after the child by means of the use of the half and whole rings, and drawing, has become more familiar with the curved line. These exercises require great facility in handling the scissors besides, and are, therefore, only to be introduced with children who have been occupied in this department quite a while. For such it is a capital employment, and they will find a rich field for operation, and produce many an interesting and beautiful form in connection with it. The course of development is indicated in Figs. 163–167.

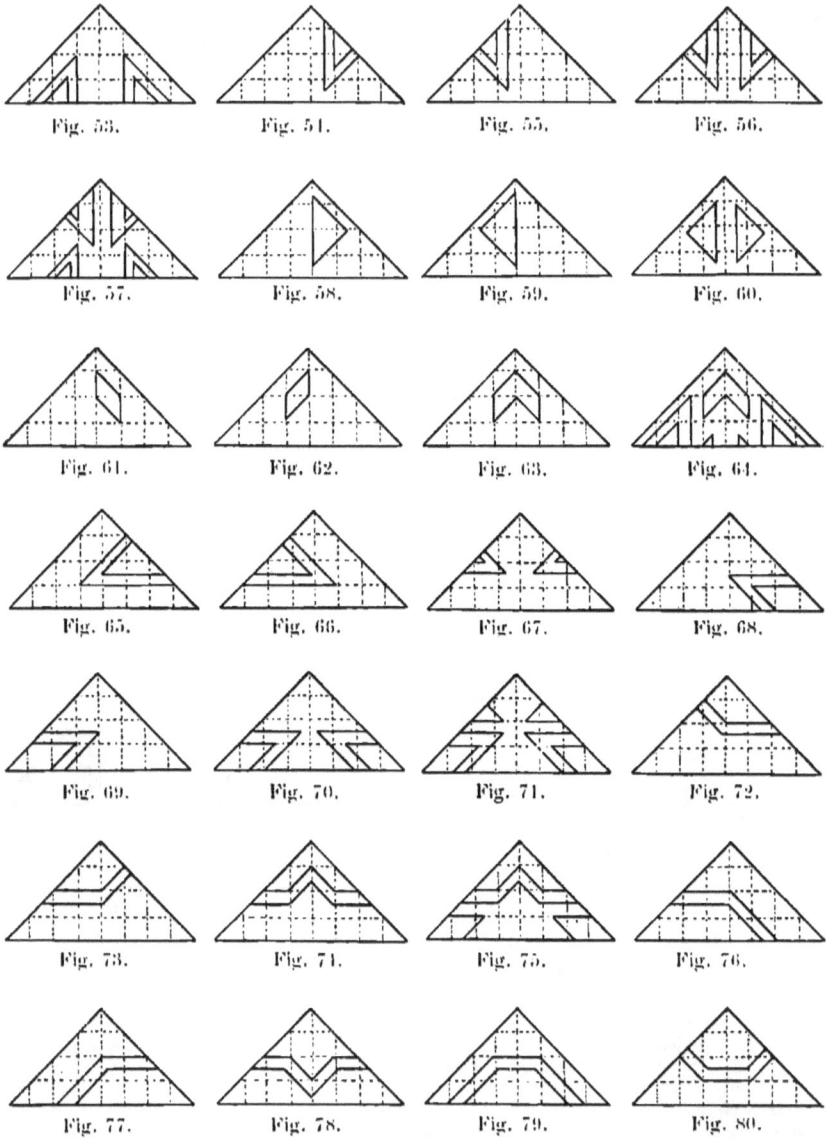

PARADISE OF CHILDHOOD.   229

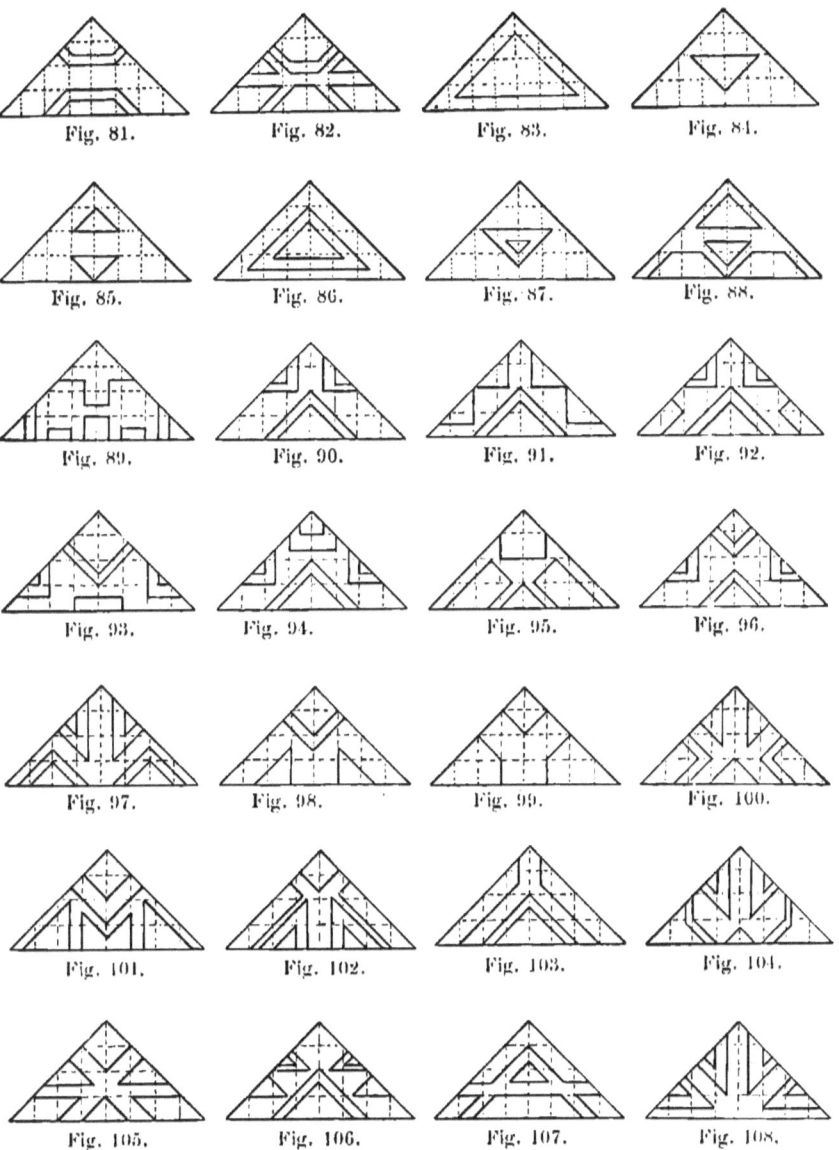

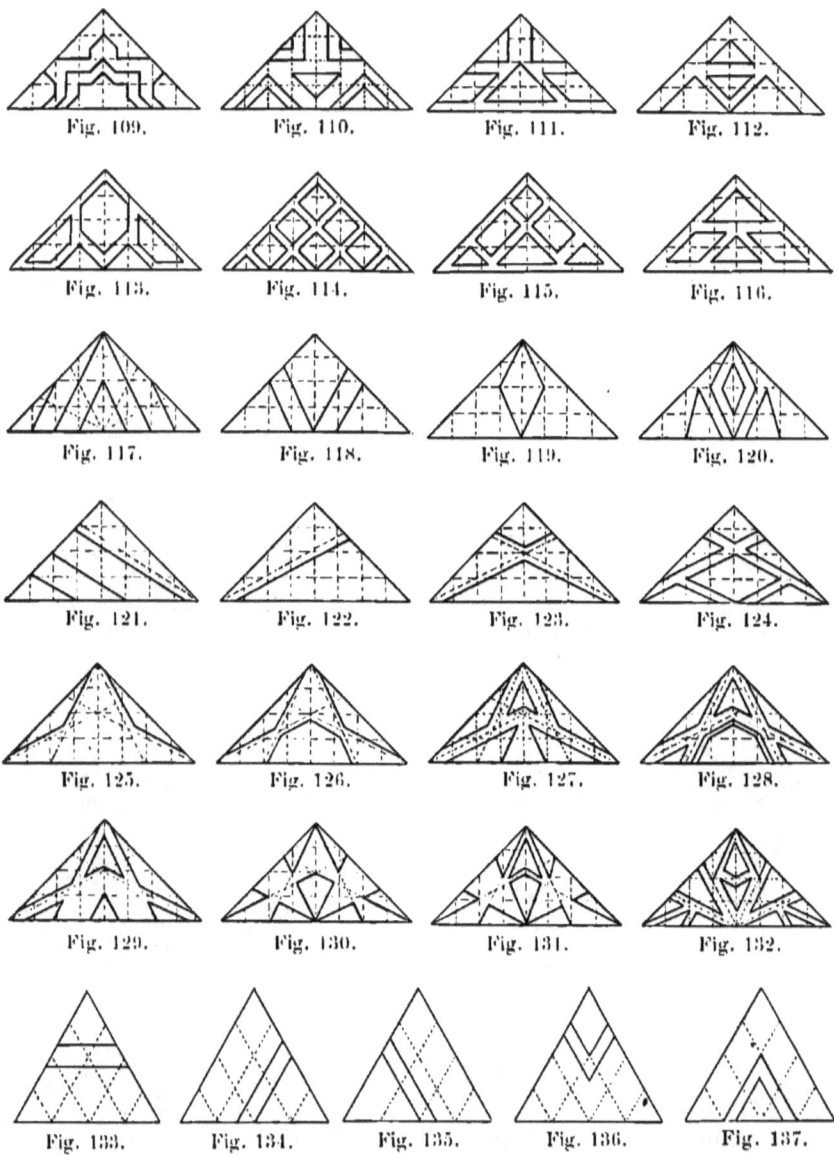

PARADISE OF CHILDHOOD. 231

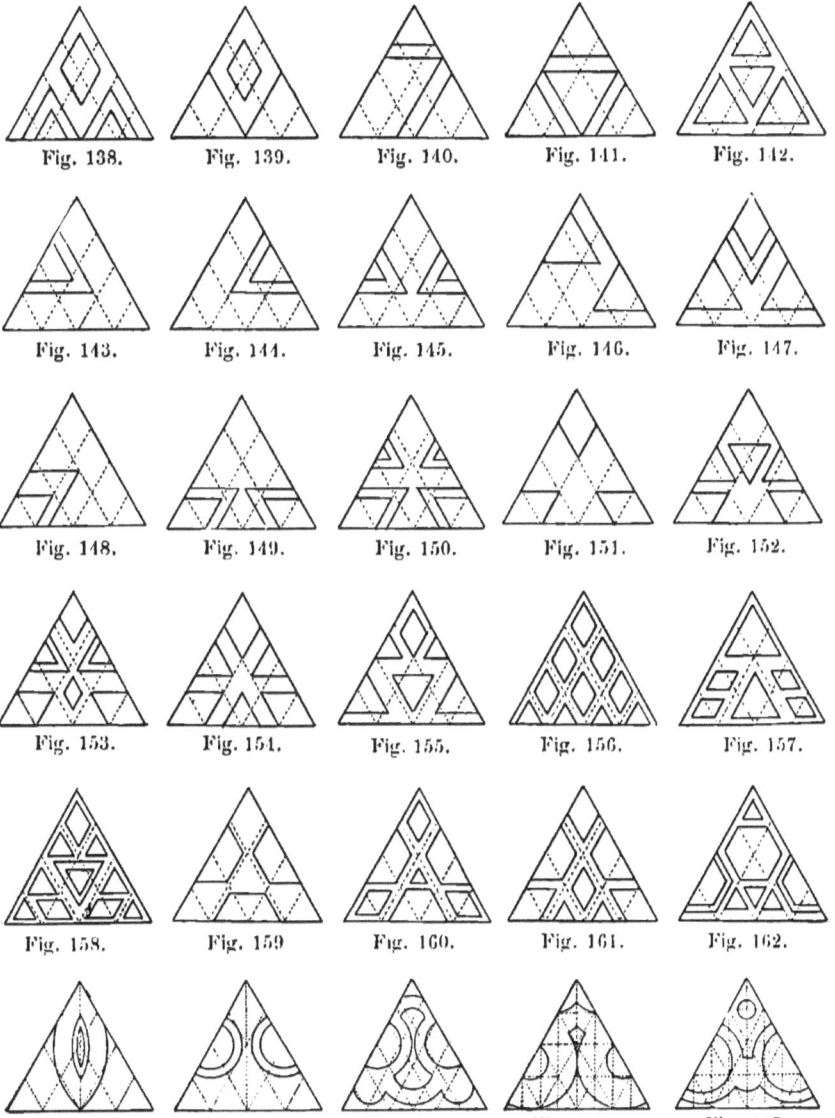

After the child has been sufficiently introduced into the cutting school, in the manner indicated, after his fantasy has found a definite guidance in the ever-repeated application of the law, which protects him against unbounded option and choice, it will be an easy task to him, and a profitable one to pass over to free invention, and to find in it a fountain of enjoyment, ever new, and inexhaustibly overflowing. To let the child, entirely without a guide, be the master of his own free will, and to keep all discipline out of his way, is one of the most dangerous and most foolish principles to which a misunderstood love of children, alone could bring us. This absolute freedom condemns the children, too soon, to the most insupportable annoyance. All that is in the child should be brought out, by means of external influence. To limit this influence as much as possible is not to suspend it. Frœbel has limited it, in a most admirable way by placing this guidance into the child as early as possible; that from one single incitement issues a number of others, within the child, by accustoming him to a lawful and regulated activity from his earliest youth.

With the first vertical cut, which we made into the sheet, (Fig. 1), the whole course of development, as indicated in the series of figures up to Fig. 132 is given, and all subsequent inventions are but simple, natural combinations of the element presented in the "school." Thus a logical connection prevails in these formations, as among all other means of education, hardly any but mathematics may afford.

Whereas, the activity of the cutting itself, and the logical progress in it produces a most beneficial influence upon the intellect of the pupil, the results of it will awaken his sense of beauty, his taste for the symmetrical, and his appreciation of harmony in no less degree. The simplest cut already yields an abundance of various figures. If we make as in Fig. 5, two vertical cuts, and unfold all single parts we shall have a square with hollow middle, a small square, and finally the frame of a square. If we cut according to Fig. 6, we produce a large octagon, four small triangles, four strips of paper of a trapezium form, nine figures altogether.

All these parts are now symmetrically arranged according to the law: union of opposites —here effected by the position or direction of the parts relative to the center—and after they have been arranged in this manner, the pupils will often express the desire to preserve them in this arrangement. This natural desire finds its gratification by

MOUNTING THE FIGURES.

As separation always requires its opposite, uniting, so the cutting requires mounting. The following figures present examples of the manner in which the cutting is mounted: Fig. 5 a is Fig. 5 cut and mounted; Fig. 9 a corresponds to Fig. 9, and so on. With the simpler cuts, the clippings should be used, but

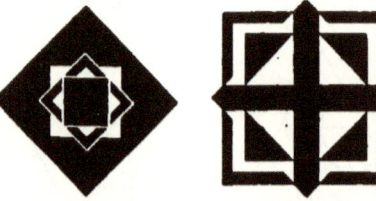

Fig. 5 a.   Fig. 9 a.

if a main figure is complete and symmetrical in itself, the addition of the clippings would not be necessary.

This occupation also, can be made subservient to influence the intellectual development of the child by requiring him to point out different ways in which these forms may be arranged and put together, (Fig. 37 a).

Fig. 12 a.   Fig. 20 a.

In order to increase the interest of the children, to give a larger scope to their inventive power, and at the same time, to satisfy their taste and sense of color, they may have paper of various colors and be allowed to exchange their productions among one another.

Both these occupations, cutting and mounting, are for the Kindergarten as well as higher grades of schools. For older pupils, the cut-

ting out of animals, plants and other forms of life will be of interest, and silhouettes even may be prepared by the most expert.

It is evident that not only as a simple means of occupation for the children, during their early life, but as a preparation for many an occupation in real life, the cutting of paper and mounting the parts to figures, as introduced here, are of undeniable benefit.

The main object, however, is here, as in all other occupations in the Kindergarten, development of the sense of beauty, as a preparation for subsequent performance in and enjoyment of art.

EDITOR'S NOTES.

This occupation emphasizes color and develops the artistic sense of the child by the symmetrical forms which he produces in beautiful colors. For the first series of cuts the six spectrum colors should be chosen, as a knowledge of pure colors and normal tones must precede color combinations.

The cutting may be given as a class exercise, the children doing the folding, cutting, arranging and pasting all together.

The square is taken as a basis for all the simplest designs, and out of it the child clips a house, barn, church, etc., with the consciousness of possessing a power over this little sheet of paper which is really creative and with which he is able to produce a great variety of forms and designs. The work requires accuracy and delicate handling, being easy or difficult according to the skill of the worker.

Outlines of objects, animals, leaves, forms of beauty and geometric forms may be cut, by leading the child in logical succession from the vertical cut to the horizontal, and, after combining these two, proceeding to the oblique cut and its combinations, the cuts being made upon the square, equilateral triangle, oblong and circle.

Beginning with the straight lines the child may gradually advance to intricate circular cuts, though the curved line should not be given until the child has gained dexterity in handling the scissors.

On the plain, unruled paper the marking or folding should be on the upper triangle only; the cutting through them all. At first the line may be lightly traced with a pencil before cutting, but this practice should not continue long enough to make the child dependent upon it.

For the sake of obtaining sufficient accuracy in the cutting, the ruled cutting papers are manufactured, which have a network on the upper triangle and are exactly in the line of Froebel's method, because they assist the child to accurately draw from dictation his own patterns for cutting.

The child must be led to free creation by first imitating, and when he learns obedience through dictation, and also gains in manual dexterity, after a few cuts inventions may be called for, each child being allowed to choose the form and color he prefers for his invention from among the forms previously made, thus encouraging his will-power in making a selection and adding interest and variety to the occupation. Sequences should be used in order to develop continuity of thought and to illustrate the idea of growth, the value of the sequence depending upon the form produced and upon the color used.

When the forms are made they should be pasted on one side of the mounting sheet and the several sheets belonging to each child may be kept loose until the whole number is completed and then put in book form. As only one design is seen at a time the standard colors may be used in succession without unpleasant effects. The same cut can be mounted in different ways and various results produced. A house with furnishings may be cut and many lessons in good housekeeping taught. Border patterns are easily cut. Delicate lace-like patterns make decorations for sachet bags, lamp screens, box covers, needle books or the lining for a box or basket. Cut upon larger squares they furnish pretty designs for outline stitching or braiding.

As this occupation is fully treated in books written on the subject, it is inexpedient to give in this connection more than a few hints as to its possibilities.

"Paper and Scissors in the Schoolroom," by Emily A. Weaver gives a practical and systematic course in paper cutting and folding, the third chapter being devoted to cutting the geometric figures and useful and ornamental forms based on them.

THE FOURTEENTH GIFT.

MATERIAL FOR BRAIDING OR WEAVING.

Braiding is a favorite occupation of children. The child instinctively, as it were, likes everything contributing to his mental and bodily development, and few occupations may claim to accomplish both, better than the occupation now introduced. It requires great care, but the three year old child may already see the result of such care, whereas even from twelve to fourteen years old pupils, often have to combine all their ingenuity and perseverance to perform certain more complicated tasks in the braiding or weaving department. It does not develop the right hand alone, the left also finds itself busy most of the time. It satisfies the taste of color, because to each piece of braiding, strips of at least two different colors belong. It excites the sense of beauty because beautiful, i. e., symmetrical, forms are produced; at least their production is the aim of this occupation. The sense and appreciation of number are constantly nourished, nay it may be asserted, that there is hardly a better means of affording perceptions of numerical conditions, so thorough, founded on individual experience and rendered more distinct by diversity in form and color, than "*braiding*." The products of the child's activity, besides, are readily made useful in practical life, affording thereby capital opportunities for expression of his love and gratitude, by presents prepared by his own hand.

The material used for this occupation are sheets of paper cut into strips which are left joined at the ends, as shown in Fig. 1, and the braiding needle, as represented in Fig. 2.

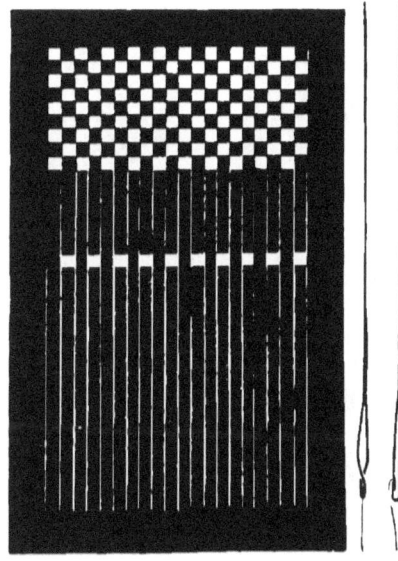

Fig. 1. Fig. 2.

Fig. 3. Fig. 4.

A braid work is produced by drawing with the needle a loose strip (white) through the strips of the braiding sheet (green), so that a number of the latter will appear over, another under the loose strip. These numbers are conditioned by the form the work is to assume. As there are but two possible ways in which to proceed, either lifting up, or pressing down

Fig. 5. Fig. 6.

the strips of the braiding sheet, the course to be taken by the loose strip is easily expressed in a simple formula. All varieties of patterns are expressible in such formulas and therefore easily preserved and communicated.

The simplest formula of course, is when one strip is raised and the next pressed down.

We express this formula by 1 u (up), 1 d (down). All such formulas in which only two figures occur, are called simple formulas; combination formulas, however, are such as contain a combination of two or more such simple formulas.

But with a single one of such formulas, no braid work can yet be constructed. If we should, for instance, repeat with a second, third, and fourth strip, 1 u, 1 d, the loose strips would slip over one another at the slightest

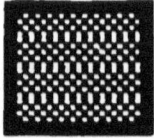 

Fig. 7. Fig. 8.

handling, and the strips of the braiding sheet and the whole work, drops to pieces if we should cut from it the margin. In doing the latter, we have, even with the most perfect

 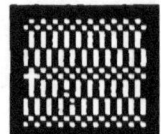

Fig. 9. Fig. 10.

braidwork, to employ great care; but it is only then a braid or weaving work exists—when all strips are joined to the whole by other strips, and none remain entirely detached.

Fig. 11. Fig. 12.

To produce a braid work, we need at least two formulas, which are introduced alternately. Proceeding according to the same fundamental law which has led us thus far in all our work, we combine first with 1 u, 1 d, its opposite 1 d, 1 u. Such a combination of braiding formulas by which not merely a single strip, but the whole braid work, is governed, is a *braiding scheme*.

Braiding formulas, according to which the single strip moves, are easily invented. Even if one would limit one's self to take up or press down no more than five strips, (and such a limitation is necessary, because otherwise the braiding would become too loose), the following thirty formulas would be the result:—

1, 1u 1d	9, 3u 1d	17, 4u 2d	24, 5d 1u
2, 1d 1u	10, 3d 1u	18, 4d 2u	25, 5u 2d
3, 2u 2d	11, 3u 2d	19, 4u 3d	26, 5d 2u
4, 2d 2u	12, 3d 2u	20, 4d 3u	27, 5u 3d
5, 2u 1d	13, 1u 1d	21, 5u 5d	28, 5d 3u
6, 2d 1u	14, 4d 4u	22, 5d 5u	29, 5u 4d
7, 3u 3d	15, 4u 1d	23, 5u 1d	30, 5d 4u
8, 3d 3u	16, 4d 1u		

Fig. 13. Fig. 14.

From these thirty formulas, among which are always two oppositionally alike, as for instance, 1 and 2, 9 and 10, 25 and 26, hundreds of combined, or combination formulas can be formed by simply uniting two of them. In the beginning it is advisable to combine such as

Fig. 15. Fig. 16.

contain equally named numbers either even or odd. The following are some examples:—

Formulas	1 and 3,	1u 1d, 2u 2d.
"	1 and 5,	1u 1d, 2u 1d.
"	1 and 7,	1u 1d, 3u 3d.
"	1 and 9,	1u 1d, 3u 1d.
"	1 and 11,	1u 1d, 3u 2d.
"	1 and 13,	1u 1d, 4u 4d.
"	1 and 15,	1u 1d, 4u 1d.
"	1 and 17,	1u 1d, 4u 2d.
"	1 and 19,	1u 1d, 4u 3d.
"	1 and 21,	1u 1d, 5u 5d.
"	1 and 23,	1u 1d, 5u 1d.
"	1 and 25,	1u 1d, 5u 2d.
"	1 and 27,	1u 1d, 5u 3d.
"	1 and 29,	1u 1d, 5u 4d.

If we also add the formulas under the even numbers in the given thirty, we have to read them inversely. Thus:—

PARADISE OF CHILDHOOD.

Formulas 1 and 6, 1u 1d, 1u 2d.
"   1 and 10, 1u 1d, 1u 3d.
"   1 and 12, 1u 1d, 2u 3d.
"   1 and 16, 1u 1d, 1u 4d.
"   1 and 18, 1u 1d, 2u 4d.
"   1 and 20, 1u 1d, 3u 4d.
"   1 and 24, 1u 1d, 1u 5d.
"   1 and 26, 1u 1d, 2u 5d.
"   1 and 28, 1u 1d, 3u 5d.
"   1 and 30, 1u 1d, 4u 5d.

By a combination of one single formula with

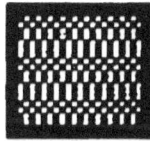

Fig. 17.   Fig. 18.

the twenty-four others, we receive new combination formulas and see that inventing formulas is a simple mathematical operation, regulated by the laws of combination.

Much more difficult it is to invent *braiding schemes*. Not to dwell too long on this point,

Fig. 19.   Fig. 20.

we introduce the reader to the course shown in the following figures, which are arranged so systematically that either as a whole or with some omissions, it may be worked through with children from three to six years, as a *braiding school*. It begins with simple formulas and by

Fig. 21.   Fig. 22.

means of the law of opposites is carried out to the most beautiful figures.

Formula 1, 1u 1d, (Fig. 3), is first introduced; opposite in regard to number is 2u 2d, (Fig. 4). In Fig. 5 the numbers one and two are combined; Fig. 6 is a combination of Figs. 3 and 4; Fig. 7 a combination of Figs. 3 and 5 by combining the simple formulas. If we examine Fig. 7 the number three makes itself prominent in the strips running obliquely. In Fig. 8 it occurs independently as opposite

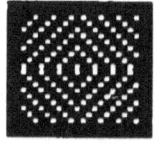
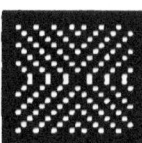

Fig. 23.   Fig. 24.

to one and two and then follows in Figs. 9–17 a series of mediative forms all uniting the opposites in regard to number. In all these patterns the squares or oblongs produced are arranged vertically under, or horizontally

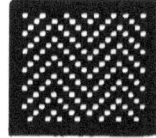

Fig. 25.   Fig. 26.

beside, one another. Except in Fig. 3, the oblique line appears already beside the horizontal and vertical. Thus, this given opposite *of form* is prevailing in Figs. 18–32, and we apply here the same formulas in Figs. 3–17, with the difference, however, that we need only

Fig. 27.   Fig. 28.

one formula, which in the second, third strip, etc., always begins one strip later or earlier. Thus in Fig. 18, the formula 2u 2d (as in Fig. 4) is carried out. The dark and light strips of the pattern run here from right above, to left below. Opposite of position to Fig. 18 is shown in Fig. 19 where both run the opposite way. Fig. 20 shows combination, and Fig. 21 double combination. In opposition to the connected oblique lines, the broken line appears in Fig. 22. As the formula 2u 2d has furnished us five patterns, so the formula of Fig. 5, in 2d, furnishes the series, Figs. 23-27. Figs. 23 and 24 are opposites as to direction. Fig. 25 shows the combination of these opposites. Figs. 26

Fig. 29. Fig. 30.

and 27, opposites to one another, are forms of mediation between Figs. 23 and 24. With them for the first time a middle presents itself.

While in Figs. 23–28 the dark color is prevailing, Figs. 28–30 show us predominantly, the light strip, consequently the opposite *in*

Fig. 31. Fig. 32.

color. In Figs. 31-33, formulas from Figs. 5-7 are employed. Fig. 31 requires an opposite of *direction*, a pattern in which the strips run from left above to right below. Fig. 32 gives the combination of both directions and Figs. 33 and 34 are at the same time opposites as to direction and color.

 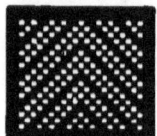

Fig. 33. Fig. 34.

It is obvious that each single formula can be used for a whole series of divers patterns, and the invention of these patterns is so easy that it will suffice if we introduce each new formula very briefly.

Fig. 35 is a form of mediation for the formula 3u 3d; Fig. 36 shows a different application of the same formula. In Fig. 37 the broken line appears again, but in opposition to Fig. 22 it changes its direction with each break. In Figs. 38–42 the formulas of Figs. 9, 10, 12, 13, and 15 are carried out. The braiding school, *per se*, is here concluded. Whoever may think it too extensive may select from it Figs. 3, 4, 5, 8, 9, 12, 18, 19, 20, 23, 26, 27, 28, 35 and 36.

Fig. 35. Fig. 36.

But if any one would like still to enlarge upon it, she may do so by working out, for each single formula, the forms or patterns 18, 19, 20, 21, 16 and 27, and continue the school to the number 5. The number of patterns will be made, thereby, ten times larger.

Another change and enlargement of the

Fig. 37. Fig. 38.

school may be introduced by cutting the braiding strips, as well as those of the braiding sheet of different widths. We can thereby represent quite a number of patterns after the same formula, which are, however, essentially different. This is particularly to be recom-

Fig. 39. Fig. 40.

mended with very small children, who necessarily will have to be occupied longer with the simple formula 1u 1d. But for more developed braiders, such change is of interest, because,

PARADISE OF CHILDHOOD.

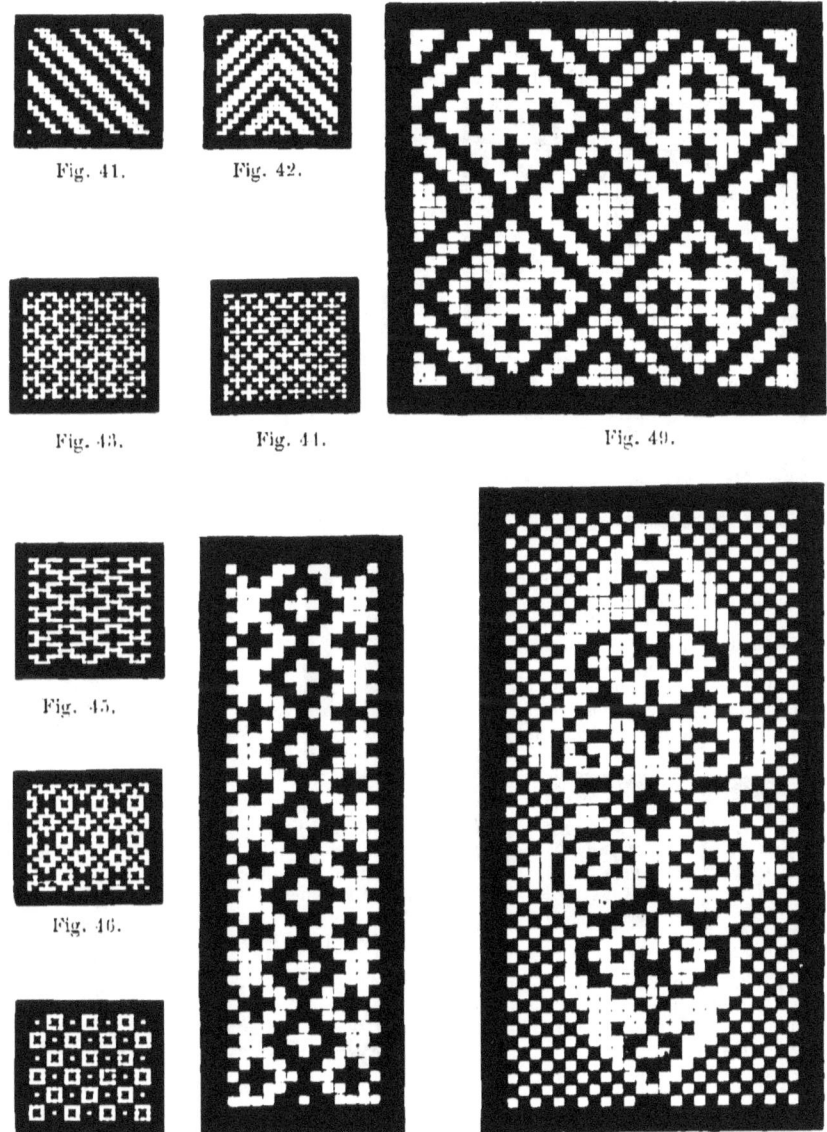

Fig. 41. Fig. 42. Fig. 49.

Fig. 43. Fig. 44.

Fig. 45.

Fig. 46.

Fig. 47. Fig. 48. Fig. 50.

by it a variety of forms may be produced which may be rendered still more attractive, by a variety of colors in the loose braiding strips.

With patterns that have a middle, as Figs. 26

Fig. 51.

and 30 it is advisable to let the braiding begin with the middle strip, and then to insert always one strip above, and one below it.

It is not unavoidably necessary that the school should be finished from beginning to end, as given here. The pupil, having successfully produced some patterns, may be afforded an opportunity for developing his skill by his own

Fig. 52. Fig. 53. Fig. 54.

invention, in trying to form, by braiding a cross, with hollow middle, (Fig. 43), a standing oblong, (Fig. 44), a long cross, (Fig. 45), a small window, (Fig. 47), etc.

Figs. 48–51, present some patterns which may be used for wall-baskets, lamp tidies, bookmarks, etc.

Finally, Figs. 52–54, obliquely intertwined strips, representing the so-called free braiding,

the braiding without braiding sheet. This is done as follows: Cut two or more long strips (Fig. 55), of a quarter sheet of colored paper, (green) and fold to half their length, (Fig. 56) cut then, of differently colored paper, (white), shorter strips, also fold these to half their length. Put the green strips, side by side of one another, as shown in Fig. 58, so that the closed end of one strip lies above and that of the other below, (Fig. 58cc). Then take the white strip bend it around strip 1, and lead it through strip 2, (Fig. 59). The second strip is applied in an opposite way, laying it around 2, and

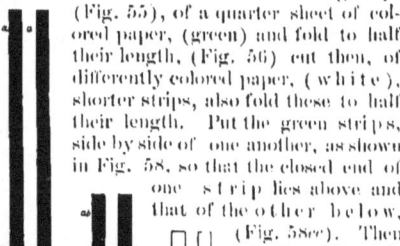

Fig. 55. Fig. 56. Fig. 57.

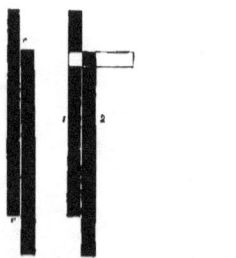 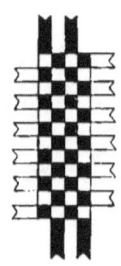

Fig. 58. Fig. 59. Fig. 60.

leading it through 1. Employing four instead of two green strips, the bookmark, Fig. 60, will be the result. The protruding ends are either cut or scolloped.

By introducing strips of different widths, a variety of patterns can be produced.

Fig. 61. Fig. 62. Fig. 63.

Instead of paper, glazed muslin, leather, silk or ribbon, straw and the like may be used as material for braiding.

EDITOR'S NOTES.

The occupation of mat weaving is fully explained in the foregoing pages, and the variety of material now prepared and for sale in the market is so great that almost anything which a teacher may require can be obtained without the "special cutting" which formerly was oftentimes deemed necessary. With the weaving material prepared in the modern educational colored papers the best possible exercises in color combinations are introduced, and by judicious selections of mats and fringes on the part of the teacher the child may be accustomed to harmonious combinations of colors, and thus never acquire the preference for gaudy combinations which is usually attributed to children and savages. Bright pure colors do not necessarily make "loud" combinations, and muddy colors are not essential to artistic effects.

For youngest children a mat four inches square with a cut surface of three inches is very desirable, because little hands can manipulate such mats to better advantage than the larger sizes. These small mats are cut with various numbers of strips from five to ten, thus providing for much practical use of numbers and a great variety of designs in the patterns of the weaving. The very elaborate and intricate weaving designs which are possible with large mats and narrow strips are not adapted to younger children, and those who are experienced enough to do this grade of work can be profitably employed in more advanced work, which may be less intricate and fatiguing and more educational.

Free braiding is developed quite extensively by some teachers, while others make comparatively little of it, but it is capable of varied and beautiful results.

THE FIFTEENTH GIFT.

THE INTERLACING SLATS.

FRŒBEL in his Gifts of the Kindergarten, does not present anything perfectly new. All his means of occupation are the result of careful observation of the playful child. But he has united them in one corresponding whole; he has invented a method, and by this method presented the possibility of producing an exhaustless treasure of formations which, each influencing the mind of the pupil in its peculiar way, effect a development most harmonious and thorough of all the mental faculties. The use of slats for interlacing is an occupation already known to our ancestors, and who has not practiced it to some extent in the days of childhood? But who has ever succeeded in producing more than five or six figures with them? Who has ever derived, from such occupation, the least degree of that manual dexterity and mental development, inventive power and talent of combination, which it affords the pupils of the Kindergarten since Frœbel's method has been applied to the material?

Our slats, ten inches long, one-fourth of an inch broad and one-sixteenth of an inch thick,

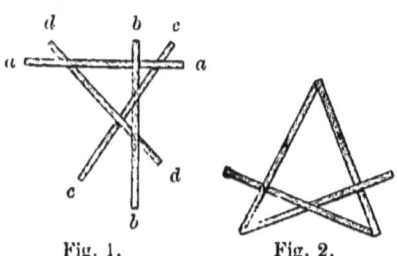

Fig. 1.   Fig. 2.

are made of birch or any tough wood, and a dozen of them are sufficient to produce quite a variety of figures. They form, as it were the transition from the plane of the tablet to the line of the sticks, (Ninth Gift) differing, however, from both, in the fact that forms produced by them are not bound to the plane, but contain in themselves a sufficient hold to be separated from it.

The child first receives *one single slat*. Examining, it he perceives that it is flexible, that its length surpasses its breadth many times and again that its thickness is many times less than its breadth.

Can the pupil name some objects between which and the slat, there is any similarity?

The rafters under the roof of a house, and in the arms of a wind mill, and the laths of which fences, and certain kinds of gates and lattice work are made, are similar to the slat.

The child ascertains that the slat has two long plane sides and two ends. He finds its

Fig. 3.

middle or center point, can indicate the upper and lower side of the slat, its upper and lower end, and its right and left side. After these preliminaries, a second slat is given the child. On comparison the child finds them perfectly alike, and he is then led to find the positions which the two slats may occupy to each other. They can be laid parallel with each other, so as to touch one another with the whole length of their sides, or they may not touch at all.

They can be placed in such positions that their ends touch in various ways, and can be laid crosswise, over or under one another.

With an *additional* slat, the child now continues these experiments. He can lay various figures with them, but there is no binding or connecting hold. Therefore, as soon as he attempts to lift his work from the table, it falls to pieces.

By the use of *four* slats, he becomes enabled to produce something of a connected whole, but this only is done, when each single slat *comes in contact with at least three other slats.* Two of these should be on one side, the third or middle one should rest on the other side of the connecting slat, so that here again the law of opposites and their mediation is followed and practically demonstrated in every figure.

It is not easy to apply this law constantly in the most appropriate manner. But this very necessity of painstaking, and the reasoning, without which little success will be attained, is productive of rich fruit in the development of the pupil.

The child now places the slat *aa*, horizontally upon the table. *Bb*, is placed across it in a vertical direction; *cc*, in a slanting direction under *a* and *b*, and *dd*, is shoved under *aa*, and over *bb*, and under *cc*, as shown in Fig. 1.

This gives a connected form, which will not

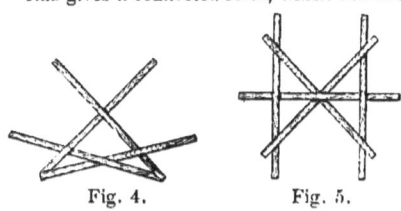

Fig. 4. Fig. 5.

easily drop apart. The child investigates how each single slat is held and supported—he indicates the angles, which were created, and the figures which are bounded by the various parts of the slats.

To show how rich and manifold the material for observation and instruction given in this one figure is, we will mention that it contains twenty-four angles, of which eight are right,

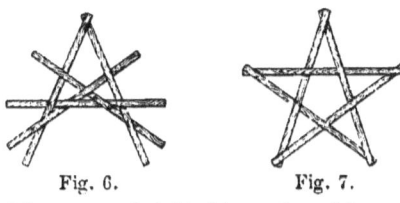

Fig. 6. Fig. 7.

eight acute, and eight obtuse—formed by one vertical slat, *bb*, one horizontal *aa*, one slanting from left above to right below, *cc*, and another slanting from right above to left below, *dd*.

Each single slat touches each other slat once; two of them, *aa* and *bb*, pass over two and under one, and the others, *cc* and *dd*, pass under two and over one of the other slats, by which interlacing, three small figures are

formed within the large figure, one of which is a figure with two right, one obtuse and one acute angle, and four unequal sides, and two others, one of which is a right-angled triangle with two equal sides, and the other is a right angled triangle with no equal sides.

By drawing the slats of Fig. 1 apart, Fig. 2, an acute-angled triangle is produced—by drawing them together, Fig. 3 results, from which

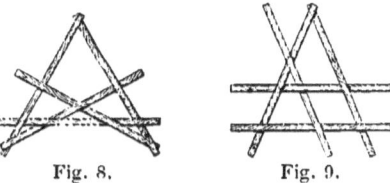

Fig. 8. Fig. 9.

the acute-angled triangle, Fig. 4, can again be easily formed. Each of these figures presents abundant matter for investigation and instructive conversation, as shown in connection with Fig. 1.

The child now receives a *fifth* slat. Suppose we have Fig. 2, consisting of four slats — ready before us—we can, by adding the fifth slat, easily produce Fig. 8.

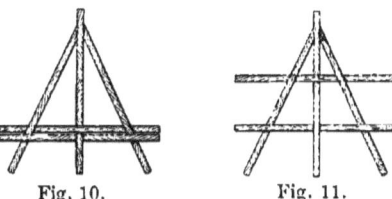

Fig. 10. Fig. 11.

If the five slats are disconnected, the child may lay two, vertically at some distance from each other, a third in a slanting position over them from right above to left below, and a fourth in an opposite direction, when the two latter will cross each other in their middle. By means of the fifth slat the interlacing then is carried out, by sliding it from right to left under the vertical over the crossing two, and again under the other vertical slat, and thereby the Fig. 5 made firm.

By bending the vertical slats together, Fig. 6 is produced; when the horizontal slat assumes a higher position, a five-angled figure appears—one of the slanting slats, however,

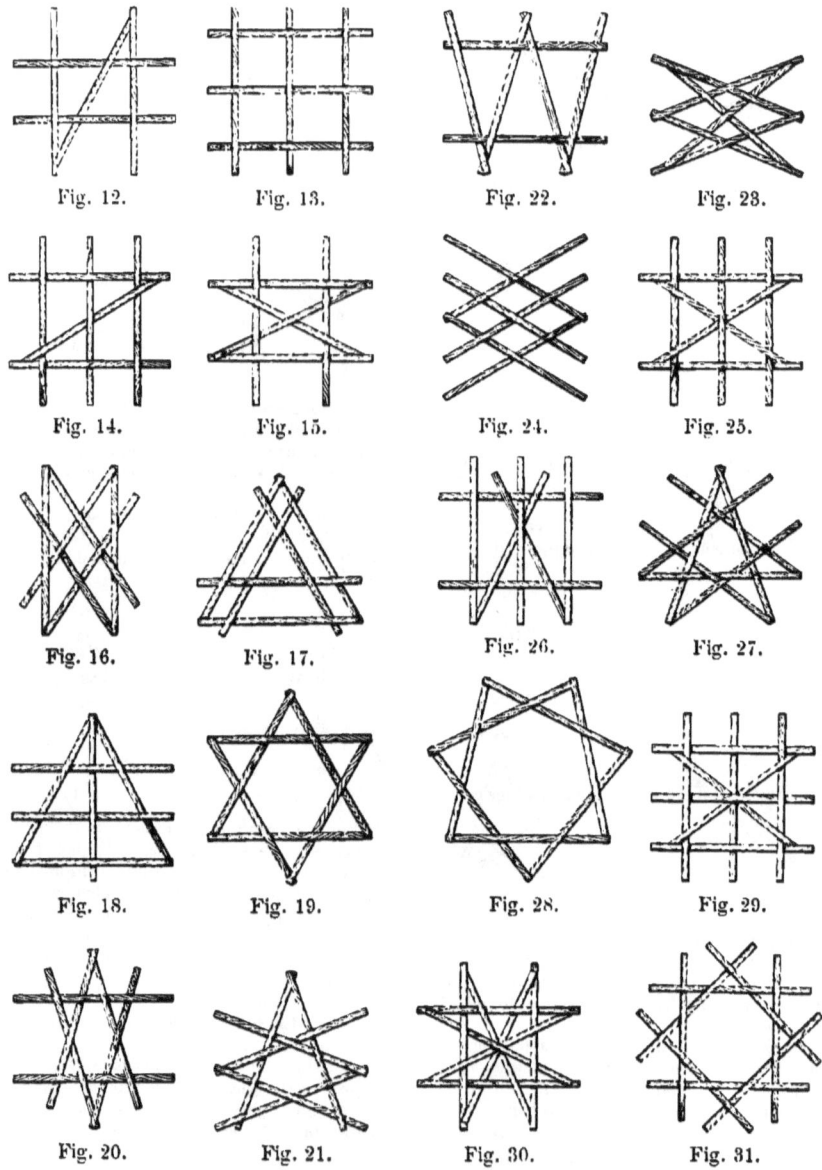

PARADISE OF CHILDHOOD.

has to change its position also, as shown in Fig. 7. In Fig. 8, the horizontal slat is moved downward. In Fig. 9, the original position of the crossing slats is changed; in the triangle, Fig. 10, still more, and in Figs. 11 and 12, other changes of these slats are introduced.

The addition of a sixth slat enables us still

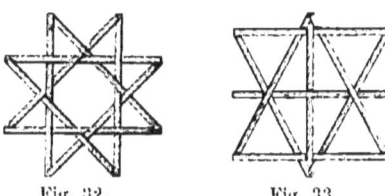

Fig. 32.   Fig. 33.

further to form other figures from the previous ones—Fig. 17 can be produced from Fig. 9, Fig. 18 from Figs. 10 or 11, Fig. 22 from Fig. 12, and then a following series can be obtained by drawing apart and shoving together as heretofore.

Let us begin thus: The child lays (Fig. 13)

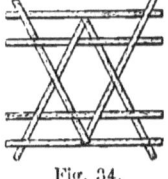 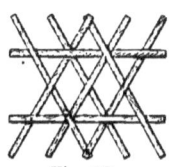

Fig. 34.   Fig. 35.

two slats horizontally upon the table—two slats vertically over them; a large square is produced. A fifth slat horizontally across the middle of the two vertical slats, gives two parallelograms, and by connecting the sixth slat

 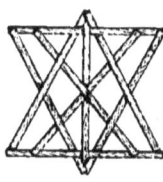

Fig. 36.   Fig. 37.

from above to below with the three horizontal slats so that the middle one is under and the two outside slats over it, the child will have formed four small squares, of equal size.

The Figs. 17 and 18, (triangles) and Figs. 19 and 23, (hexagons), deserve particular attention, because they afford valuable means for mathematical observations.

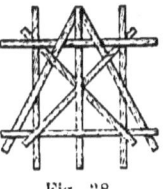 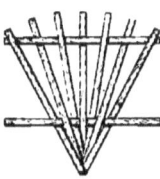

Fig. 38.   Fig. 39.

We find some few examples of seven intertwined slats, in (Figs. 25-28), of eight slats, (Figs. 29-36), of nine slats, (Figs. 37-40), and of ten slats, (Figs. 41-43).

All we have given in the above are mere hints to enable the teacher and pupil to find

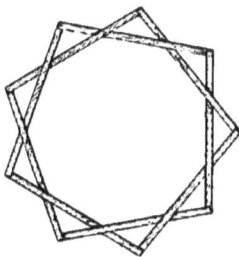

Fig. 40.

more readily by individual application, the richness of figures to be formed with this occupation material.

It is particularly mathematical forms, reg-

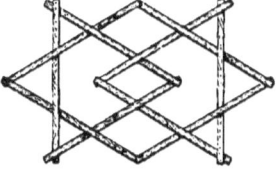

Fig. 41.

ular polygons, (Figs. 28, 31, 40, 42), contemplation of divisions, produced by diagonals, etc., planes and proportions of form, which, in *forms of knowledge*, are brought before the eye of the pupil, with great clearness and distinctness, by the interlacing slats.

In the meantime, it will afford pleasure to behold the *forms of beauty*, as given in Figs. 30, 33, 37; nor should the *forms of life* be forgotten, as they are easily produced by a larger number of slats, (Fig. 39—a fan; Figs. 35 and 36—fences), by combining the work of several pupils.

The occupation with this material will frequently prove perplexing and troublesome to the pupil; oftentimes he will try in vain to represent the object in his mind.

Having almost successfully accomplished the task, one of the slats will glide out from his structure, and the whole will be a mass of ruins. It was the *one slat*, which, owing to its dereliction in performing its duty, destroyed the figure, and prevented all the others from performing theirs.

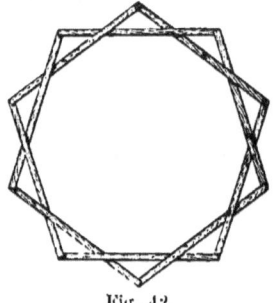

Fig. 42.

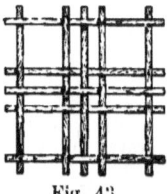

Fig. 43.

The figures are not simply to be constructed and to be changed to others, but each of them is to be submitted to a careful investigation by the child, as to its angles, its constituent parts, and their qualities, and the service each individual slat performs in the figure, as indicated with Fig. 1.

It will not be difficult for the thinking teacher to derive from such an occurrence, the opportunity to make an application to other conditions in life, even within the sphere of the young child, and his companions in and out of school. The character of this occupation does not admit of its introduction before the pupils have spent a considerable time in the Kindergarten, in which it is only begun, and continued in the primary department.

THE SIXTEENTH GIFT.
THE SLAT WITH MANY LINKS.

This occupation material, which may be used at almost any grade of development in the Kindergarten, the primary and higher school departments, is rich in its application, and may be employed in representing various kinds of lines and angles.

In making simple geometrical figures the gift is invaluable and the forms of life and beauty which may be produced with it offer profitable exercise for the inventive powers of the child. A few figures here given may suggest the possibilities of this gift in the several classes of outlines to which it is adapted.

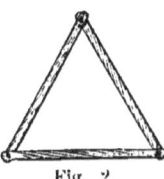

Fig. 1.   Fig. 2.

We have slats with four, six, eight and sixteen links, which are introduced one after the other when opportunities offer. In putting the first in the hand of the child we would ask him to unfold all the links of the slat, and to place it upon the table so as to represent a vertical, horizontal and then an oblique line.

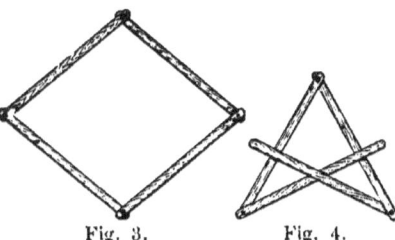

Fig. 3.   Fig. 4.

By bending two of the links vertically and the two others horizontally we form a right angle. Bending one of the links of the angle toward or from the other, we receive the acute and obtuse angles, which grow smaller or larger, the nearer or farther the links are brought to, or from each other, until we reduce the angles to either a vertical line of two links' length, or a horizontal line of the length of four links.

We may then form a square, Fig. 1. Pushing two opposite corners of it toward each other, and bending the first link so as to cover

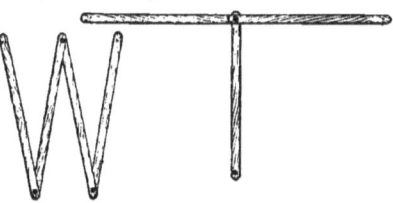

Fig. 5.   Fig. 6.

with it the second, and, then joining the end of the fourth link to where the first and second are united, we shall form an equilateral triangle, Fig. 2. (Which other triangle can be formed with this slat, and how?)

The capital letters V, W, N, M, Z, and the

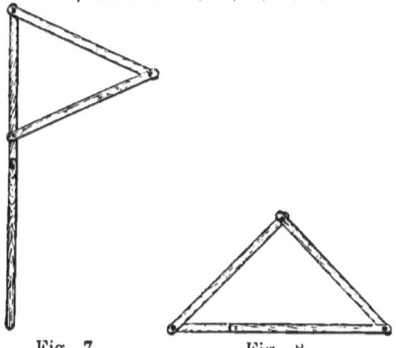

Fig. 7.   Fig. 8.

figure four can be easily produced by the children, and many figures constructed by the teacher in which the pupils may designate the number and kinds of angles, which they contain, as is done with the movable slats on other occasions.

Fig. 1-8 are examples given with the four

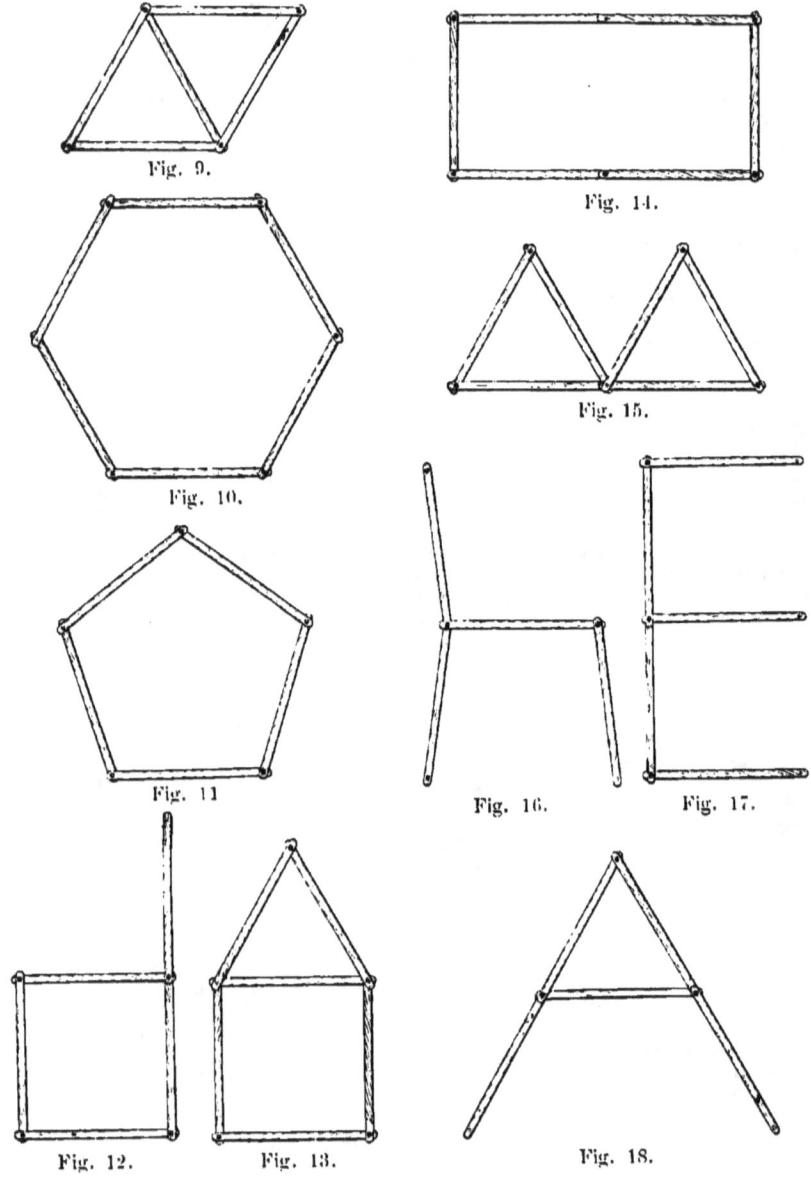

PARADISE OF CHILDHOOD.

links. The slats with six links are introduced next, from which the oblong be made. Figs. 9-21 furnish examples of six links. to the pupils. A combination of the different forms of knowledge may be made, as two equilaterals, Fig. 15; a square and triangle, Fig. 21; a square and pentagon, Fig 35; oblong

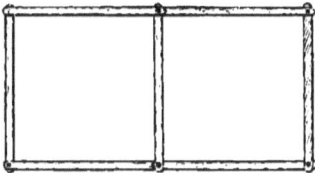

Fig. 23.

and rhombus, Fig. 36, etc. Figs. 22-35 are figures made with the eight links and Figs. 36-45 with the sixteen links.

The ingenuity and inventive power of the children will find a large field in the occupation

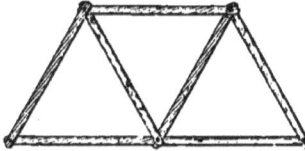

Fig. 24.

with this material, if, at times, they are allowed to produce figures themselves, of which the more advanced pupils may make drawings and give a description of each orally.

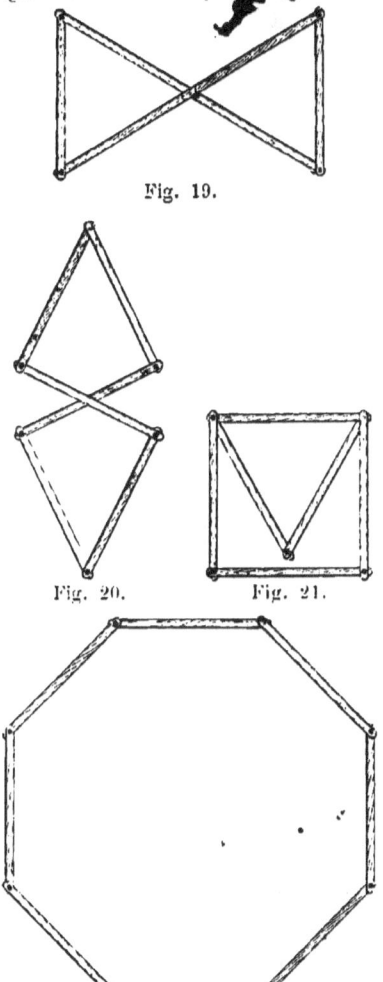

Fig. 19.

Fig. 20.   Fig. 21.

Fig. 22.

Then come the eight and sixteen links, which if used in the manner here indicated can be rendered exceedingly interesting and instructive

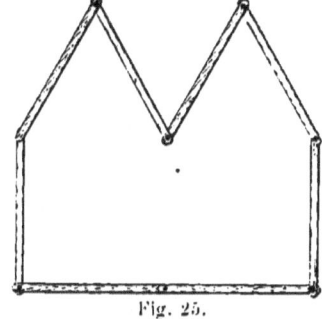

Fig. 25.

It would be needless to enlarge here upon the richness of material afforded by this gift, as half an hour's study of and practice with it will convince each thinking teacher fully of the treasure in her hand and certainly make her admire it on account of the simplicity of its application for educational purposes in school and family.

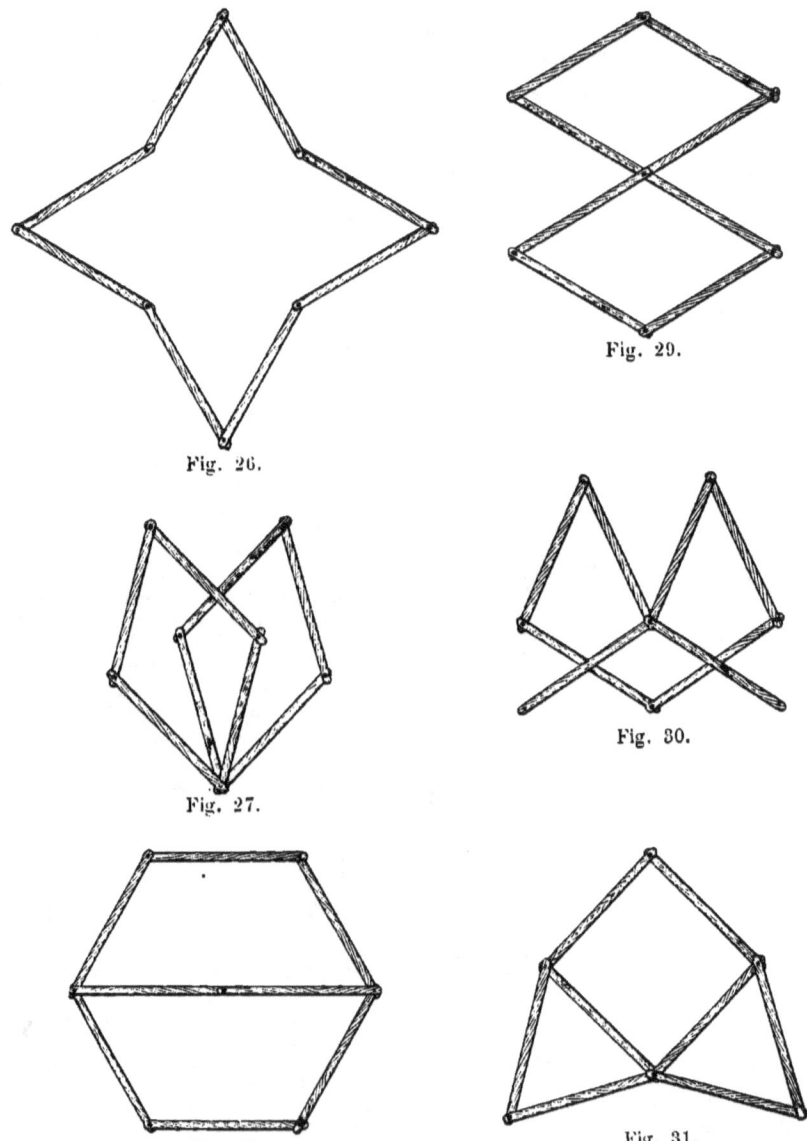

Fig. 26.
Fig. 27.
Fig. 28.
Fig. 29.
Fig. 30.
Fig. 31.

PARADISE OF CHILDHOOD. 251

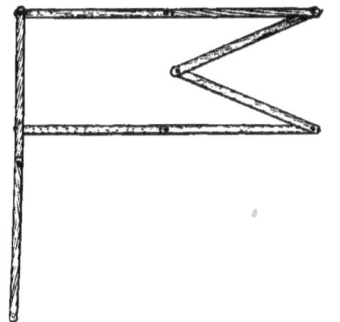

Fig. 32.

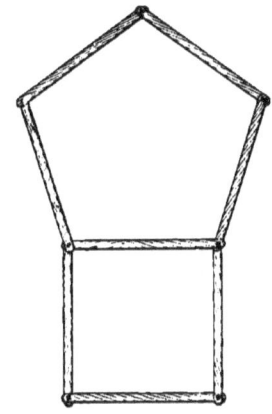

Fig. 35.

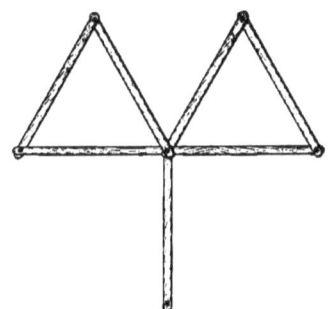

Fig. 33.

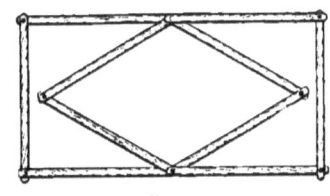

Fig. 36.

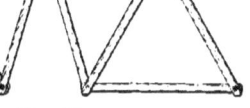

Fig. 34.

Fig. 37.

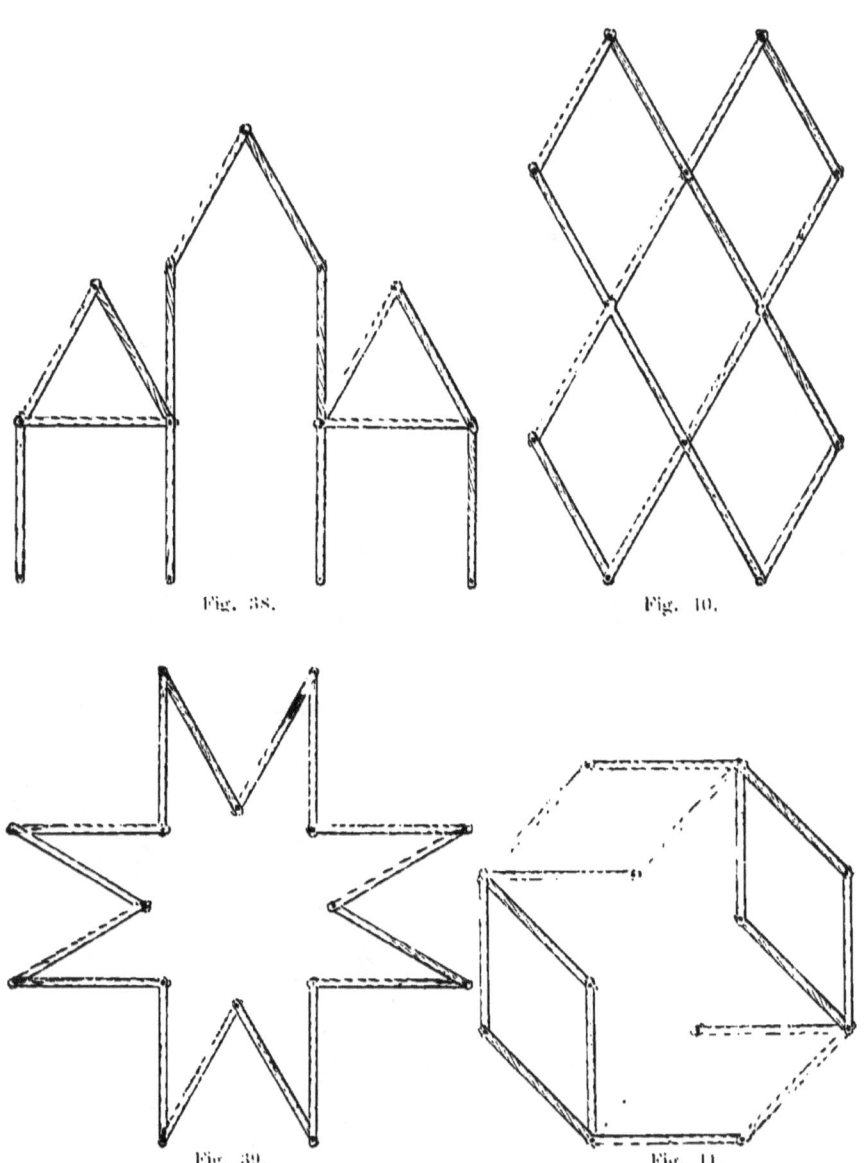

Fig. 38.   Fig. 40.

Fig. 39.   Fig. 41.

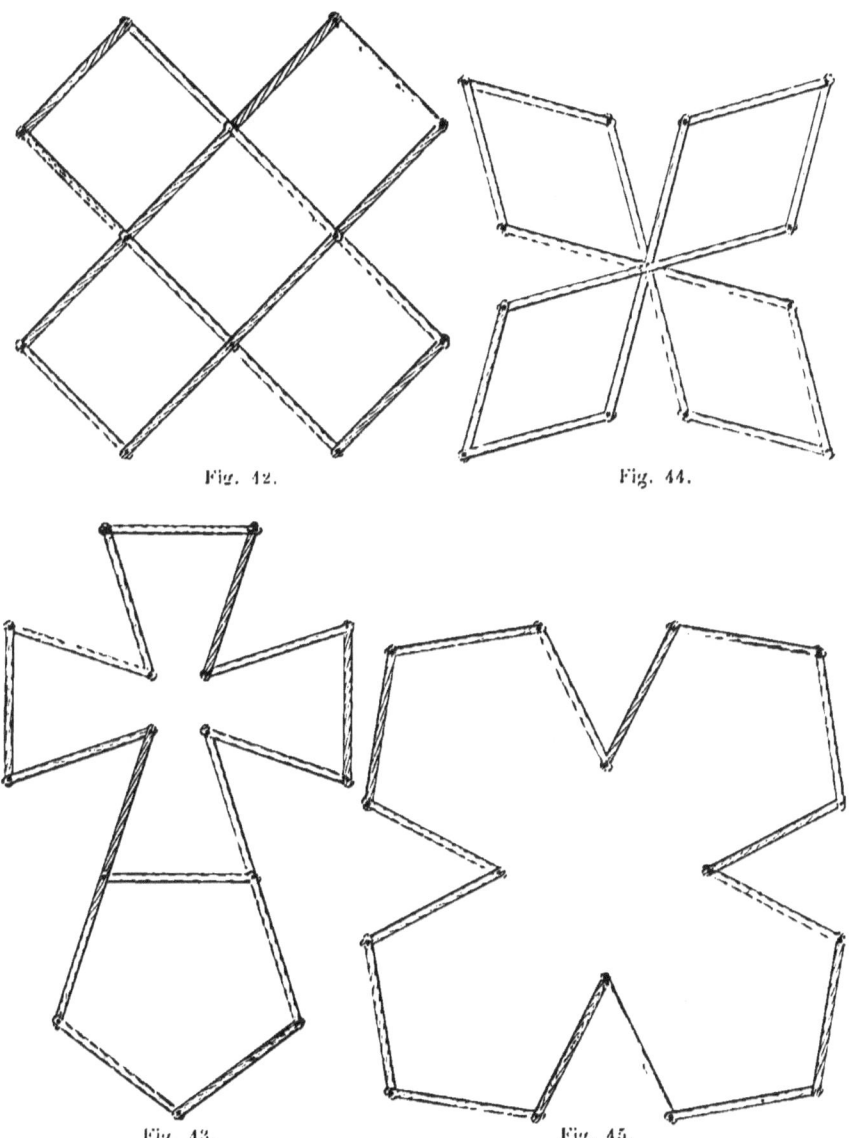

Fig. 42. Fig. 44.

Fig. 43. Fig. 45.

THE SEVENTEENTH GIFT.
MATERIAL FOR INTERTWINING.

Intertwining is an occupation similar to that of interlacing. Aim of both is representation of plane—outlines. In the occupation with the interlacing slats we produced forms, whose peculiarities, at least, had to be changed to produce something new; here, we produce permanent results. There, the material was in every respect a ready one; here, the pupil has to prepare it himself. There, hard slats of little flexibility; here, soft paper, easily changed. There, production of purely mathematical forms by carefully employing a given material; here, production of similar forms by changing the material, which forms, however, are forms of beauty.

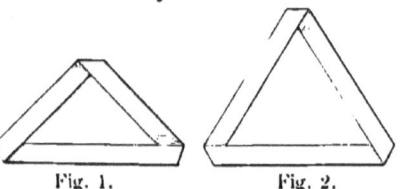

Fig. 1.   Fig. 2.

The paper strips, not used when preparing the folding sheets, are used as material, adapted for the present occupation. They are strips of white or colored paper, twenty inches long and varying in breadth. Each strip is subdivided in smaller strips, which by folding their long sides are transformed to threefold strips of eight to ten inches long and one-quarter of an inch wide.

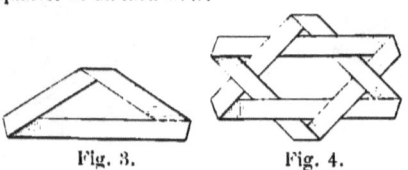

Fig. 3.   Fig. 4.

The children will not succeed well, in forming regular figures from these strips at first. As the main object of this occupation is to accustom the child to a clean, neat and correct performance of his task, some of the tablets of Gift Seven are given him as patterns to assist him; or the child is led to draw three, four, or many cornered forms, and to intertwine his paper strips according to these.

First, a right-angled isosceles triangle is used for laying around it one of these strips so as to enclose it entirely. We begin with the left cathetus, put the tablet upon the strip, folding it toward the right over the right angle. The

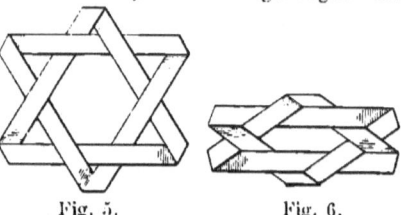

Fig. 5.   Fig. 6.

break of the paper is well to be pressed down, and then the strip is again folded around the acute angle toward the left. Where the hypotenuse (large side) touches the left cathetus

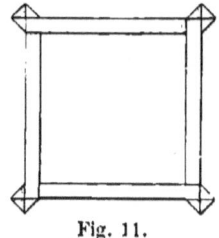

Fig. 7. Fig. 8. Fig. 9.   Fig. 10.

(small side), the strip is cut and the ends of the figure there closed by gluing them together by some clean adhesive matter. Care should

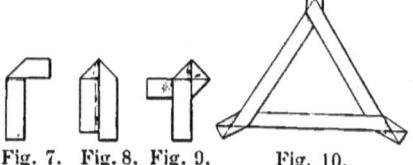

Fig. 11.

be taken that the one end of each side be under, the other over, that of the other.

Thus the various kinds of triangles, (Figs. 1–3), squares, rhombus, rhomboids, etc., are produced.

Two like figures are combined, as shown in

PARADISE OF CHILDHOOD. 255

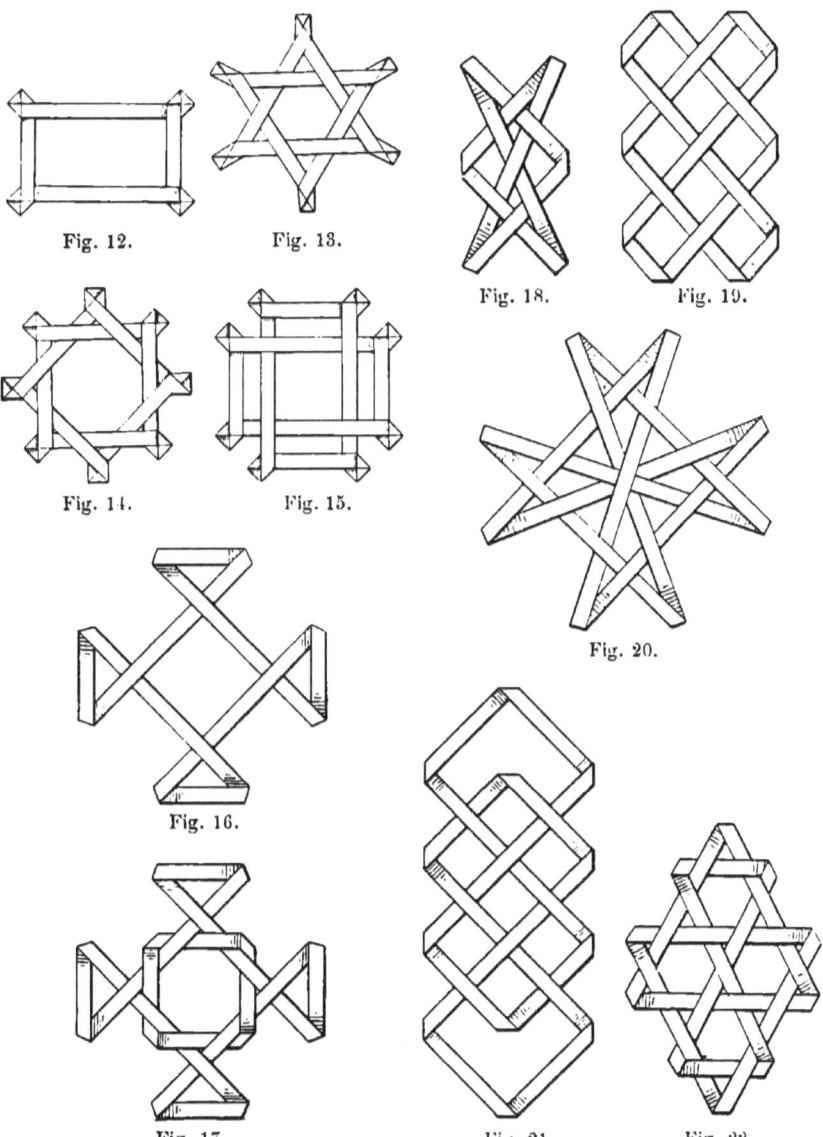

Fig. 12. Fig. 13. Fig. 18. Fig. 19.

Fig. 14. Fig. 15.

Fig. 20.

Fig. 16.

Fig. 17. Fig. 21. Fig. 22.

Figs. 4–6. If strips prove to be too short the child is shown how to glue them together, to procure material for larger and more complicated forms. Thus, it produces with one long strip, Figs. 16, 18, 19, 20; with two long strips, Figs. 17, 21. Fig. 22 shows the natural size; all others are drawn on a somewhat reduced scale. It cannot be difficult to produce a great variety of similar figures, if one will act according to the motives obtained with and derived from the occupation with the interlacing slats.

two like figures combined, and finally more complicated figures produced. (Compare examples given in Figs. 10–15).

Whatever issues from the child's hand sufficiently neat and clean and carefully wrought, may be mounted on stiff paper or bristol board and disposed of in many ways.

The occupation of intertwining shows plainly how by combination of simple mathematical forms, forms of beauty may be produced. These latter should predominate in the Kinder-

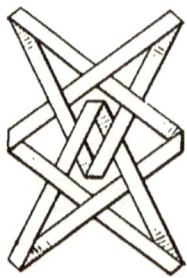

Fig. 23.

Fig. 24.

This occupation admits of still another and very beautiful modification, by not only pinching and pressing the strip where it forms angles, but by folding it to a rosette. This process is illustrated in Figs. 7–9. The strip is first pinched toward the right, (Fig. 7), then follows the second pinch downwards, (Fig. 8), then a third toward the left, when the one end of the strip is pushed through under the other. (Fig. 9).

Here, also, simple triangles, squares, pentagons and hexagons are to be formed, then

garten, and the mathematical are of importance as they present the elements for their construction. The mathematical element of all our occupations is in so far of significance, as the child receives from it impressions of form; but of much more importance is the development of the child's taste for the beautiful, because with it, the idea of the good is developed in the meantime.

As the various performances of this occupation, cutting, folding and mounting, require a somewhat skilled hand, it is introduced in the upper section of the Kindergarten only.

EDITOR'S NOTES.

PREFACE the work of intertwining by a division of the strip, which may be folded to different widths according to the design required. Exercises in position are interesting. Any object that can be represented by a flat outline can be made with the strips, in forms of life, knowledge and beauty, and then mounted on sheets of bristol board for safe keeping. In the geometrical forms the square, oblong, right isosceles and equilateral triangles, and the hexagon and octagon, give fundamental forms for a large number of designs.

This gift, however, is better adapted for older children than are found in the kindergarten,

as it requires greater dexterity and accuracy than the little ones have at their command. The simplest work for them is the making of paper chains from strips about three inches long. Make a chain by joining the ends and fastening them with paste. Put a new strip of paper through the last ring made, each time before joining the ends. Alternate rings of two harmonizing colors may be used with a pretty effect. The two colors may be mixed and given to the children to sort, before beginning to paste. Rings, bracelets, necklaces, and long chains make a pleasant variety and teach the children neatness in pasting and harmony in color.

THE EIGHTEENTH GIFT.
MATERIAL FOR PAPER FOLDING.

FRŒBEL's sheet of paper for folding, the simplest and cheapest of all materials of occupation, contains within it a great multitude of instructive and interesting forms. Almost every feature of mathematical perceptions, obtained by means of previous occupations, we again find in the occupation of paper folding. It is indeed a compendium of elementary mathematics, and has, therefore, very justly and judiciously been recommended as a useful help in the teaching of this science in public schools.

Fig. 1.

Lines, angles, figures and forms of all varieties appear before us, after a few moments' occupation with this material. The multitude of impressions, however, should not misguide us; and we should always, and more particularly in this work, be careful to accompany the work of the children with necessary conversation and pleasant entertainment, for the relief of their young minds.

The child should be accustomed to the strictest care and cleanliness in the folding. This is necessary, because paper carelessly

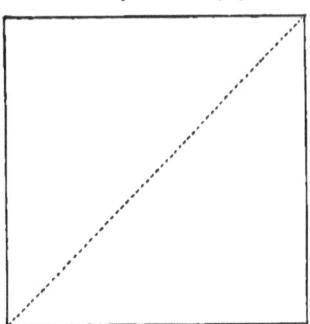

Fig. 3.

folded and cut, will not only render more difficult every following task, nay, make impossible every satisfactory result; especially should this be the case, because, we do not intend simply to while away our own and the

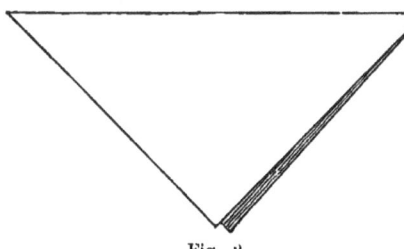

Fig. 2.

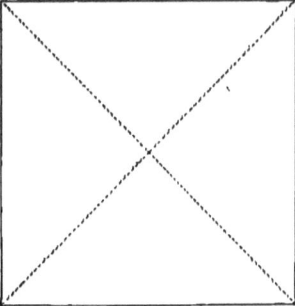

Fig. 4.

child's precious time, but are engaged in an occupation whose final aim is acquisition of ability to work, and to work well—one of the most important claims human society is entitled to make upon each individual.

The fundamental forms are produced by a series of regular changes of folding and creasing, from which sequels of forms of life and beauty are subsequently developed, by means of the law of opposites.

Fold again on the other diagonal, and when unfolded we find a square divided by two diagonals into four right-angled isosceles triangles, (Fig. 4). Now the lower and right hand corners are folded over to the left, making two oblong halves by a transversal as in Fig. 5.

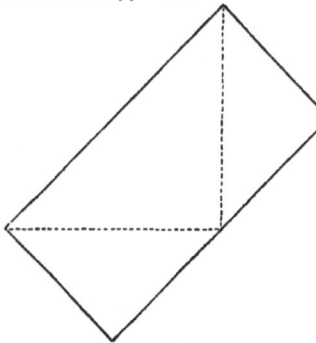

Fig. 5.

On the road to this goal, a surprising number of forms of knowledge present themselves.

In beginning lessons in paper folding give each child a piece of paper four inches square, (Fig. 1), and have him place it on the table

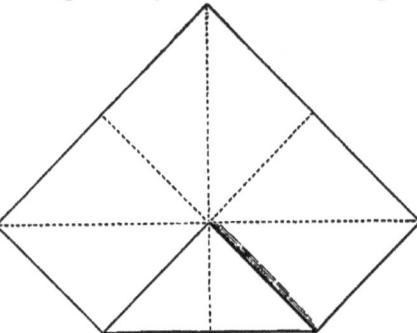

Fig. 7.

The same is done to the opposite transversal and when unfolded we have Fig. 6, which affords a multitude of mathematical object perceptions. With the square placed cornerwise, fold the lower corner to the center of the paper and the pentagon, Fig. 7, will be the result. We fold the opposite corner in like manner and produce the hexagon, (Fig. 8), and finally with the two remaining corners, Fig. 9 is formed, containing four triangles, touching one another with their free sides, each of them again showing a line halving them in two equal triangles.

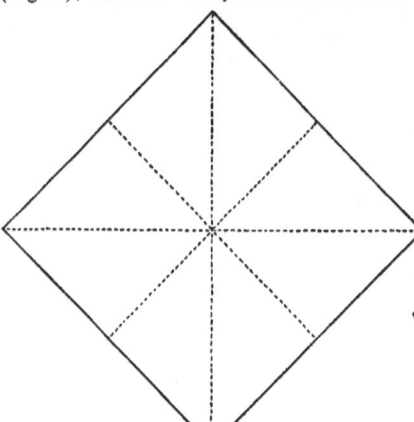

Fig. 6.

with the corner toward him. Fold the upper corner over to meet the lower corner, as shown in Fig. 2. This when unfolded will show the division of the square in two right-angled isosceles triangles, (Fig. 3).

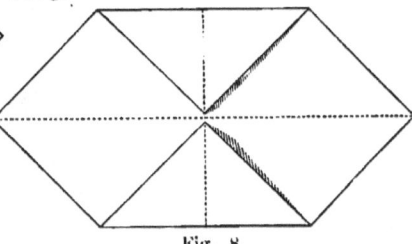

Fig. 8.

If we invert Fig. 9, we have Fig. 10, a connected square in which the outlines of eight congruent triangles appear. If Fig. 9 is unfolded we shall see beside a multiplication of previous forms, parallelograms also. If we start from Fig. 9, and fold the corners toward the middle as in Fig. 11, we shall receive a form consisting of four thickness of paper, and showing four triangles, under which again, four separate squares are found. (Fig. 12). This is the fundamental form for a series of forms of life.

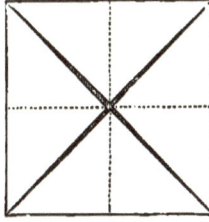

Fig. 9.

It is utterly impossible to give a minute description how forms of life may be produced from this fundamental form. Practical attempts and occasional observation in the Kin-

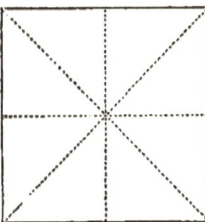

Fig. 10.

dergarten will be of more assistance than the most detailed illustrations and descriptions. Froebel's Manual mentions, among others, the

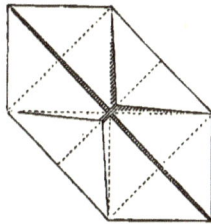

Fig. 11.

following objects: A table-cloth with four hanging corners, Fig. 13. A sailboat, Fig. 14. A double canoe, Fig. 15. A little work-

basket, Fig. 16. Cup and saucer, Fig. 17. Crown, Fig. 18. Still richer become the forms of life, if we bend the corners of the described fundamental form, once more toward the middle. In connection with this, the manual mentions the following forms: The knitting-pouch, the chest of drawers, the boots, the hat, the cross, the pantaloons, the frame, the gondola, etc. But the simple fundamental form

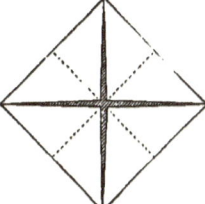

Fig. 12.

for the forms of life, (Fig. 12), is also the fundamental form for the forms of beauty. Unfold the fundamental form and press the middle of the upper and lower sides, then the

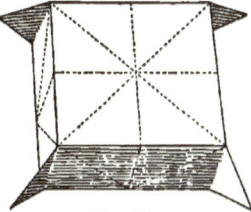

Fig. 13.

remaining two sides to the center of the square, as in Fig. 19. Fold each of the over reaching triangles to the left, Fig. 20, then back to the center of the square, Fig. 21.

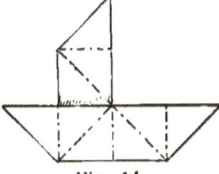

Fig. 14.

Once more fold back to the outer corner, Fig. 22. This forms a small triangle, which when pressed open will form a small square. Fig. 23. Turning each corner of this square

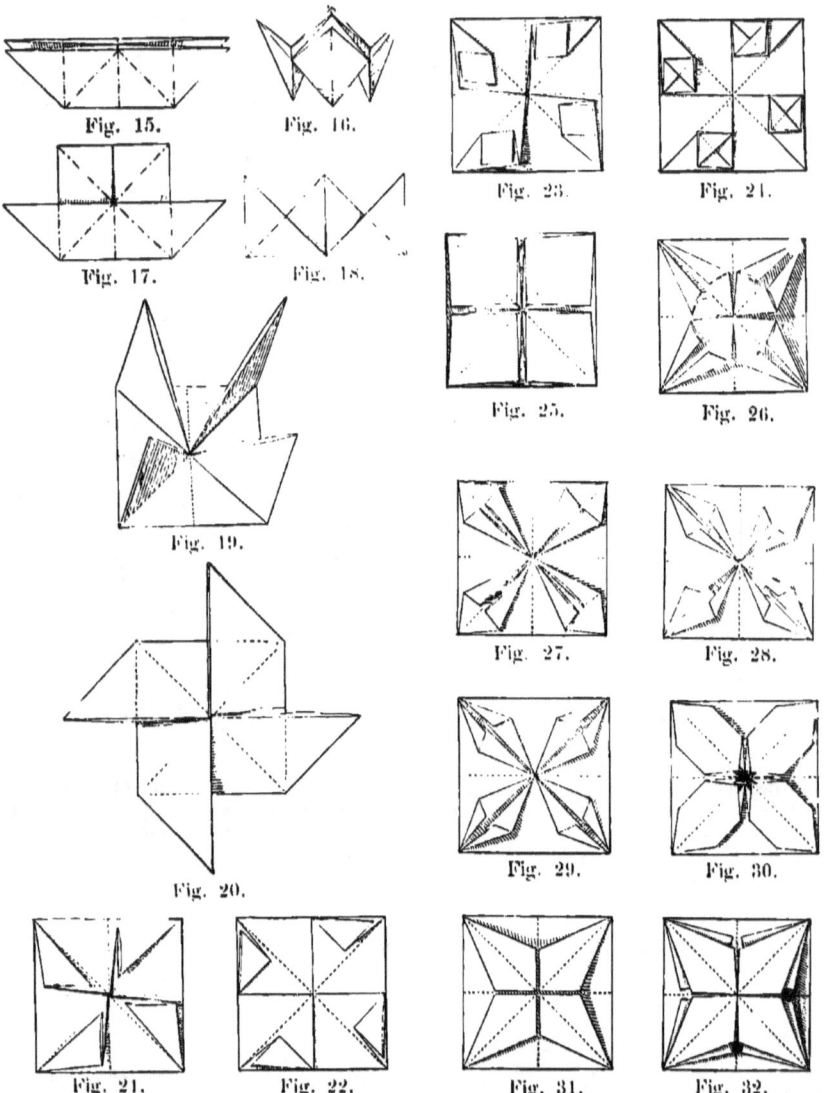

Fig. 15. Fig. 16. Fig. 17. Fig. 18. Fig. 19. Fig. 20. Fig. 21. Fig. 22. Fig. 23. Fig. 24. Fig. 25. Fig. 26. Fig. 27. Fig. 28. Fig. 29. Fig. 30. Fig. 31. Fig. 32.

back half way to its opposite corner we have Fig. 24. From a similar fundamental form the series of Figs. 26-34 originate. To make this form take the paper as in Fig. 19, open and press each corner to the center making four small squares as in Fig. 25. From this form the sequence is easily produced. If we finally take the paper as represented in Fig. 10, fold the lower right corner toward the middle, also the left upper, then the two remaining corners, we shall have four triangles consisting of a double layer of paper, Fig. 35, which may be lifted up from the square ground and the upper layer again divided in triangles.

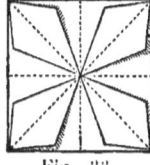
Fig. 33.
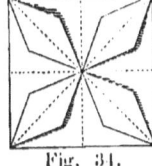
Fig. 34.

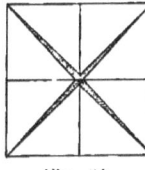
Fig. 35.
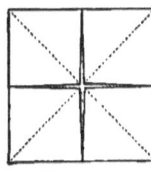
Fig. 36.

Invert this figure and you will have four single squares, as shown in Fig. 36, which is the fundamental form of a series of forms of beauty, shown in Figs. 37–46, the latter easily derived from this former under the guidance of the well-known law of opposites.

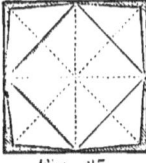
Fig. 37.
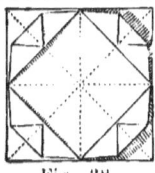
Fig. 38.

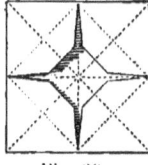
Fig. 39.
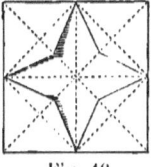
Fig. 40.

The hints given in the above might be augmented to a considerable extent and still not exhaust the matter. They are given especially to stimulate teacher and child to individual, practical attempts in producing forms by folding.

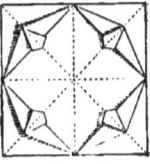
Fig. 41.
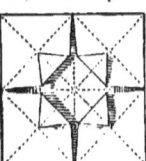
Fig. 42.

The best results of their activity can be improved by cutting out or coloring, which adds a new and interesting change to this occupation. A change of the fundamental form in three directions yields various series of forms of beauty, which may be multiplied *ad infini-*

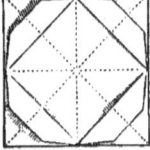
Fig. 43.
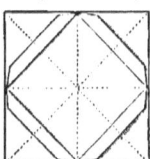
Fig. 44.

tum. Thereby, not only the idea of sequel in representations is given, but also the understanding unlocked for the various orders in nature.

Furthermore, this occupation gives the pupil such manual dexterity as scarcely any other does, and prepares the way to various female occupations, besides being immediately preparatory to all plastic work. Early training

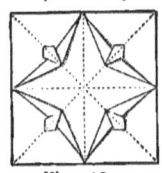
Fig. 45.
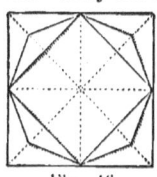
Fig. 46.

in cleanliness and care is also one of the results of a protracted use of the folding paper. It is evident that only those children who have been a good while in the Kindergarten, can be employed in this department of occupation. The peculiar fitness of the folding paper for mathematical instruction beyond the Kindergarten, must be apparent after we have shown how useful it can be made in this institution.

EDITOR'S NOTES.

THE material for paper folding consists of square, rectangular, triangular and circular pieces of various colors. Begin the lessons with a talk on the material, telling the process by which paper is made, and asking the children to name different articles which are made from it, and different things for which it is used. When the papers are given to the children and placed in the position directed, have them quietly wait until all are ready to begin work. See that they thoroughly understand the different positions, as front, back, right, left, front-right, back-left, front-left, and back-right. Bring out the ideas of edge, corner, vertical, horizontal and diagonal lines. In giving dictations see that the children work by opposites, and that they do not lift or turn the paper, as they should learn to fold in all directions equally well. Let them name and use

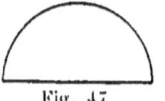
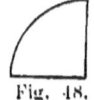

Fig. 47. Fig. 48.

the forms they make, taking a fresh square for each object. The folds are repeated every time, but each additional fold makes a new object, which, if named, helps the children to remember the order of succession, especially if a story is added, and they can use the object. Arrange the folding according to the season of the year and the special subject of the week, and yet follow a sequence that the children may see the development of one form from another.

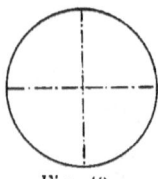
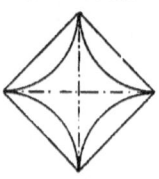

Fig. 49. Fig. 50.

By the means of paper folding we are able to trace the evolution of the seventh gift tablets from the circular folding paper. As the ball is the most elementary form among solids, so the circle is the primary form in surfaces with its single dimension, the diameter. From the circle the several elementary forms in plain geometry can be evolved and this fact is pleasingly brought out in this occupation. For these exercises the four-inch paper is most convenient and a single fold on a diameter gives the semicircle shown in Fig. 47. Fold again bringing the two ends of the diameter together, and the quarter circle shown in Fig. 48 is the result. Unfold and Fig. 49 shows the circle divided into four equal parts by two creases perpendicular to each other. Fold the edge of the circle over towards the center so as to make a crease joining the ends of two diameters, and repeat four times to produce Fig. 50. Unfold, and Fig. 51

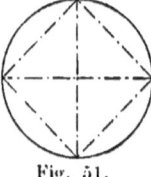

Fig. 51. Fig. 52.

is the result, showing by the creases a complete square with two diagonals. In these we have the square and half square, which is again divided into two other similar forms each one half the size of the first. Take another paper circle and again fold on one diameter, as in Fig. 47.

The next operation is somewhat more difficult than any which have preceded it and is shown in Fig. 52. This operation consists in folding the semi-circumference of the once folded circle into three equal parts, Fig. 52, and then, while

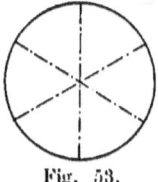
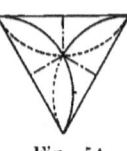

Fig. 53. Fig. 54.

holding the circumference edges together closely making the folds to the center of the circle. In this operation accuracy may be facilitated by first folding the semi-circumference into halves as though the paper were to be folded into quarters as in Fig. 48 and then, instead of completing the radial fold, just pinch the fold at the center of the circle and thus indicate the common point of meeting for the two folds in completing Fig. 52. Having completed Fig. 52, unfold, and Fig. 53 is the result. Now fold the

Fig. 55.

segments of the circle towards the center as was done in making the square but instead of having the fold subtend ninety degrees let it subtend one hundred and twenty degrees so that three folds will form a triangle as in Fig. 54. Unfold, and Fig. 55 is is result. In this we have the equilateral triangle a, b, c. The obtuse angle a, b, x, the scalene-triangle a, b, d, or the smaller one b, x, d.

The above evolution of the seventh gift forms from the circle, is the result of thought along this line by kindergarteners in America, and has been extended to the evolution of solid forms from the sphere, which it is not in the province of these notes to discuss. This occupation is one of the best for busy work in the primary department because of its practical application to form and number. Modern suggestions may be found in Paper and Scissors in the Schoolroom by Emily A. Weaver, and also in other books.

THE NINETEENTH GIFT.

MATERIAL FOR PEAS-WORK.

We have already tried, in connection with the Eighth Gift, (the laying sticks), to render permanent the productions of the pupils by stitching or pasting them to stiff paper. We satisfied by so doing a desire of the child,

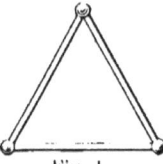 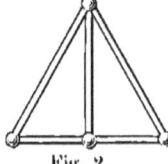

Fig. 1.   Fig. 2.

which grows stronger as the child grows older, the desire to produce by his own activity certain lasting results. It is no longer the incipient instinct of activity which governs the

 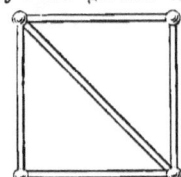

Fig. 3.   Fig. 4.

child, the instinct which prompted him apparently without aim, to destroy everything and to reconstruct in order to again destroy.

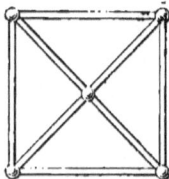 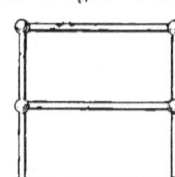

Fig. 5.   Fig. 6.

A higher pleasure of production has taken its place; not satisfied by mere doing, but requiring for his satisfaction also, delight in the created object—if even unconsciously—the delight of progress, which manifests itself in the production, and which can be observed only in and by the permanency of the object which enables us to compare it with objects previously produced.

To satisfy the claims of the pupils in this direction in a high degree, the working with peas is eminently fitted, although considerable

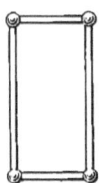 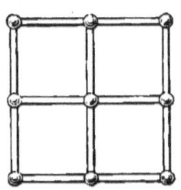

Fig. 7.   Fig. 8.

manual skill is required for it, not to be expected in any child before the fifth year. The material consists of pieces of wire of the thickness of a hair-pin, of various sizes in length,

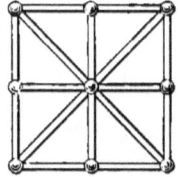 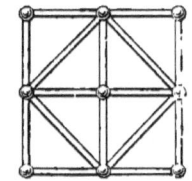

Fig. 9.   Fig. 10.

and pointed at the ends. They again represent lines. As means of combination, as embodied points of junction, peas are used, soaked about twelve hours in water and dried

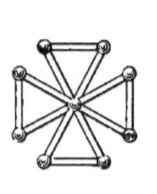 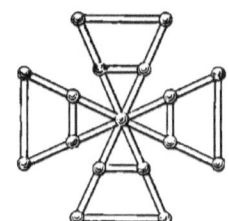

Fig. 11.   Fig. 12.

one hour previous to being used. They are then just soft enough to allow the child to introduce the points of the wires into them and also hard enough to afford a sufficient hold to the latter.

The first exercise is to combine two wires, by means of one pea, into a straight line, an obtuse, right and acute angle. What has been said in regard to laying of sticks in connection with Figs. 1-23 sticks of that gift will serve here also.

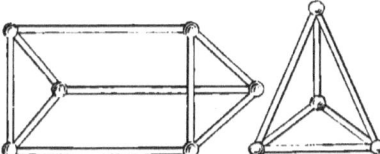

Fig. 13. Fig. 14.

Of three wires, a longer line is formed; angles, with one long, and one short side. The three wires are introduced into one pea,

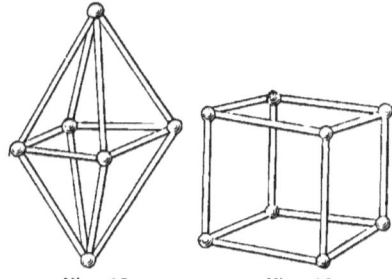

Fig. 15. Fig. 16.

so that they meet in one point; two parallel lines may be continued by a third; finally the equilateral triangle is produced.

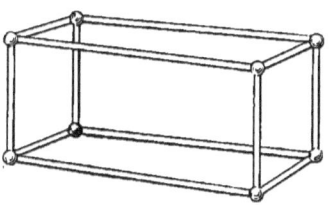

Fig. 17.

Then follows the square, parallelogram, rhomboid; diagonals may be drawn and the forms shown in Figs. 1-10 be produced. The possibility of representing the most manifold forms of knowledge, of life and of beauty is reached, and the forms produced may be used for other purposes. The child may produce six triangles of equal size, and repeat with them all the exercises, gone through with the tablets, and may enlarge upon them.

Or the child may prepare four, eight, sixteen right-angled triangles, or obtuse-angled, or acute-angled triangles and lay with them Figs. 1-12 for the course of drawing, and carry them out still further.

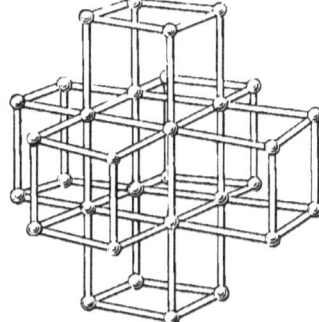

Fig. 18.

After these hints it seems impossible not to occupy the child in an interesting and instructive manner; for the condition attached to each new gift of the Kindergarten is some special progress in its course.

We produced outlines of many objects with the sticks; all formations, however, remained planes, whose sides were represented by sticks.

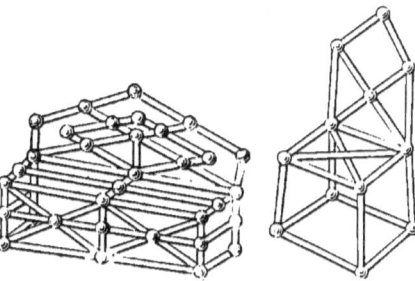

Fig. 19. Fig. 20.

In the working with peas, the wires represent edges, the peas serve as corners, and these skeleton bodies are so much more instructive, as they allow the observation of the outer forms in their outlines and the inner structure and being of the body, at the same time.

The child unites two equilateral triangles by

three equally long wires, and forms thereby a prism, (Fig. 13); four equilateral triangles, give the three-sided pyramid; eight of them, the octahedron. (Figs. 14 and 15).

From two equal squares, united by four wires of the length of the sides, the skeleton cube, Fig. 16, is formed; if the uniting wires are longer than the sides of the square, the four-sided column (Fig. 17); if one of the squares is larger than the other, a topless pyramid will be produced, etc. Fig. 18, shows a combination of cubes.

It is hardly possible that pupils of the Kindergarten should make any further progress

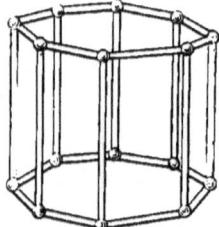

Fig. 21.

in the formation of these mathematical forms of crystallization, as the representation of the many-sided bodies, and especially this development of one from another, requires greater care and skill than should be expected at such an early period of life. It will be reserved for the primary, and even a higher grade of school, to proceed farther on the road indicated, and in this manner prepare the pupil for a clear understanding of regular bodies.

This, however, does not exclude the construction by the more advanced pupils of the kindergarten, of simple objects, in their surroundings, such as benches, (Fig. 19), chairs, (Fig. 20), baskets, etc., or to try to invent other objects.

Whoever has himself tried peas-work, will be convinced of its utility. Great care, and much patience, are needed to produce a somewhat complicated object; but a successful structure repays the child for all painstaking and perseverance. By this exercise, the pupils improve in readiness of construction, and this is an important preparation for organization.

More advanced pupils try also, successfully, to construct letters and numerals, with the material of this gift.

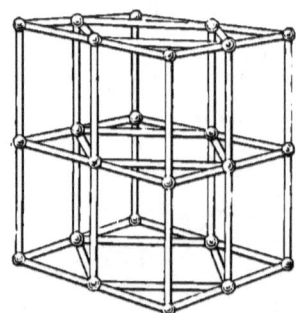

Fig. 22.

The bodies produced by peas work may be used as models in the modeling department. The one occupation is the complement of the other. The skeleton cube allows the observation of the qualities of the solid cube, in greater distinctness. The image of the body becomes in this manner more perfect and clear, and above all, the child is led upon the road, on which alone he is enabled to come into possession of a true knowledge and correct estimate of things; the road on which he learns, not only to observe the external appearance of things, but in the meantime, and always to look at their internal being.

EDITOR'S NOTES.

The outline solids made in the peas work are merely the forerunners of the wire models now so highly prized by all teachers of drawing, in illustrating the elementary principles of perception. As the more elaborate forms can only be made by the more advanced pupils of the kindergarten, they may be rendered valuable in imparting these same principles to the kindergarten pupils in their drawing exercises, even though these pupils are not able to very correctly represent the forms in their drawing.

Various substitutes for soaked peas have been suggested and tried, as cork cubes and clay pellets used while soft, but still good peas are usually preferred.

Instead of wire, thin, round sticks are used,

which, when sharpened at the ends, are not so liable to split the peas.

In the first lesson give one dry pea and ask the children to tell you of other things which are of the same shape. Lead them back to the ball and develop various exercises which will recall the ideas of movability, smoothness, hardness, roundness and dryness, then give each child a pea which has been soaked in water, and lead the class to a comparison of size and hardness.

Call attention to the crease which divides the pea into halves, and show how readily the outer covering may be taken off. Give a talk on peas, how they are planted, how they sleep, are fed and watered, how they are awakened, drawing out the ideas of the children by various questions. Have them lay designs with peas in the sand or on the peg boards. Let them outline walks and flower beds, with stars crosses and crescents in them.

After the pea has been carefully studied give the children a stick and let them put a pea on one end of it, telling what they have made, then one on the other end, letting them always name and use what they make.

When the children are ready add more sticks and peas, and as nearly all things made are built on geometric forms it is well that the pupils should first learn to make the square, oblong and triangle, then they will be able to construct many objects.

Numberless life forms may be built from this gift, as a garden with the various implements, or a house and many pieces of furniture, the children feeling amply rewarded in the results for the care and patience needed to construct these articles.

THE TWENTIETH GIFT.
MATERIAL FOR MODELING.

Modeling, or working in clay, held in high estimation by Fræbel, as an essential part of the whole of his means of education is, strange to say, much neglected in the Kindergarten. As the main objection to it named is that the children even with the greatest care, cannot prevent occasionally soiling their hands and their clothes. Others, again believe that an occupation, directly preparing for art, very rarely can be continued in life. They call it therefore, aimless pastime without favorable consequences, either for internal development or external happiness.

If it must be admitted that the soiling of the hands and clothing cannot always be avoided, we hold that for this very reason, this occupation is a capital one, for it will give an opportunity to accustom the children to care, order and cleanliness, provided the teacher herself takes care to develop the sense of the pupils, for these virtues, in connection with this occupation; as on all other occasions, she should strive to excite the sense of cleanliness as well as purity. Certainly, parts of the adhesive clay will stick to the little fingers and nails of the children, and their wooden knives, but, pray, what harm can grow out of this? The child may learn even from this fact. It may be remarked in connection with it, that the callous hand of the husbandman, the dirty blouse of the mechanic, only show the occupation, and cannot take aught from the inner worth of a man. As regards the objection to this occupation as aimless and without result, it should be considered that occupation with the beautiful, even in its crudest beginnings, always bears good fruit, because it prepares the individual for a true appreciation and noble enjoyment of the same. Just in this the significance of Fræbel's educational idea partly rests, that it strives to open every human heart for the beautiful and good —that it particularly is intended to elevate the social position of the laboring classes, by means of education not only in regard to knowledge and skill, but also, in regard to development of refinement and feeling.

Representing, imitating, creating, or transforming in general, is the child's greatest enjoyment. Bread-crumbs are modeled by him into balls, or objects of more complicated form, and even when biting bits from his cooky, it is the child's desire to produce *form*. If a piece of wax, putty or other pliable matter, falls into his hands, it is kneaded until it assumes a form, of which they may assert that it represents a baby,—the dog Roamer, or what not! Wet sand, they press into their little cooking utensils, when playing "housekeeping," and pass off the forms as puddings, tarts, etc.; in one word most children are born sculptors. Could this fact have escaped Fræbel's keen observation? He has provided the means to satisfy this desire of the child, to develop also this talent in its very awakening.

According to Fræbel's principle, the first exercises in modeling are representation of the fourteen stereometric fundamental forms of crystallization, which he presents in a box, by themselves, as models. Starting from the *cube* the *cylinder* follows—then the *sphere*, *pyramid* with three, four and six *sides*, the *prism* in its various formations of planes, the *octahedron* or *decahedron* and *cosahedron*, or bodies with eight, twelve and twenty equal sides or faces, etc. However interesting and instructive this course may be, we prefer to begin with somewhat simpler performances, leaving this branch of this department for future time.

The child receives a small quantity of clay, (wax may also be used), a wooden knife, a small board, and a piece of oiled paper, on which he performs the work. If clay is used, this material should be kept in wet rags, in a cool place, and the object formed of it, dried in the sun, or in a mildly-heated stove, and then coated with gum arabic, or varnish, which gives them the appearance of crockery.

First the child forms a sphere, from which he may produce many objects. If he attaches a stem to it, it is a cherry; if he adds depressions and elevations, which represent the dried calyx, it will look like an apple; from it the pear, nut, potato, a head, may be molded, etc. Many small balls made to adhere to one another, may produce a bunch of grapes, (Figs. 1-5).

From the ball or sphere, a cylindrical body

may be formed, (Fig. 6), by rolling on the board, usually called by the children a loaf of bread, a candle, loaf of sugar, etc.

A bottle, (Fig. 8), a bag, (Fig. 9), filled with flour or something else, can also easily be produced.

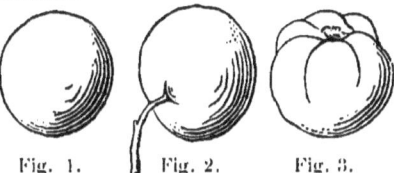

Fig. 1.   Fig. 2.   Fig. 3.

Very soon the child will present the cube, (Fig. 11), an old acquaintance and playmate. From it, he produces a house, a box, a coffee mill and similar things. Soon other forms of life will grow into existence, as plates, dishes,

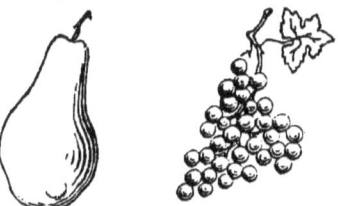

Fig. 4.   Fig. 5.

animals and human beings, houses, churches, birds' nests, etc. If this occupation is intended to be more than mere entertainment, it is necessary to guide the activity of the child in a definite direction.

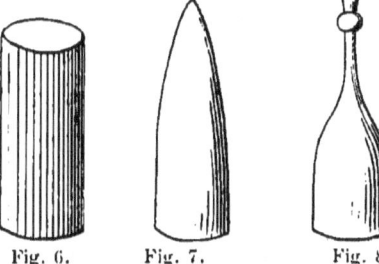

Fig. 6.   Fig. 7.   Fig. 8.

The best direction to be followed in Freebel's occupations is that for the development of regular forms of bodies. The fundamental form, of course, is the sphere. The child represents it easily, if perhaps not exactly true.

By pressing and assisted by his knife, the one plane of the sphere is changed to several planes, corners, and edges, which produces the cube. If the child changes its corners to planes (indicated in Fig. 12), a form of fourteen sides is produced. If this process is continued so that the planes of the cube are

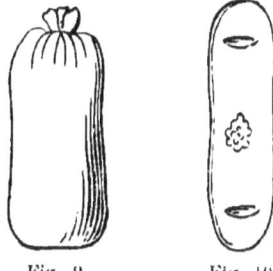

Fig. 9.   Fig. 10.

changed to corners, the octahedron is the result. (Fig. 13). By continued change of edges to planes and of planes to corners, the most important regular forms of crystallization will be produced, which occupation, however, as mentioned before, belongs rather to a higher grade of school, and is, therefore, better postponed until after the Kindergarten training.

Some regular bodies are more easily formed from the cylinder, the mediation between the

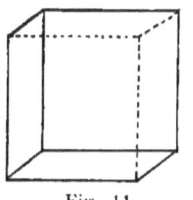

Fig. 11.

sphere and cube. By a pressure of the hand, or by means of his knife, the child changes the one round plane to three or four planes, and as many edges, producing thereby the prism and the four-sided column.

If we reduce the circular surface of one end of the cylinder to a point at its center, and connect this point with the circumference of the other end with a curved surface, we have a cone. If we change this new conical surface to a number of plane triangles we shall have for a base a polygon and the curved surface reduced to several triangles. If we act in the same manner with the other end of the cylinder, we may form a double cone, and from it we may produce a double pyramid. If again we take the cylinder and change its circular edges to a definite number of planes, we again have the sphere.

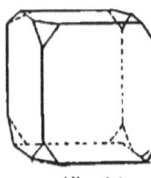   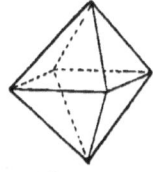

Fig. 12.   Fig. 13.

Well formed specimens may, to acquire greater durability, be treated as indicated previously. The production of forms and figures from soft and pliable material belongs, undoubtedly, to the earliest and most natural occupations of the human race, and has served all plastic arts as a starting-point. The occupation of modeling, then, is eminently fit to carry into practice Fræbel's idea that children, in their occupations, have to pass through all the general grades of development of human culture in a diminished scale. The natural talent of the future architect or sculptor, lying dormant in the child, must needs be called forth and developed by this occupation, as by a self-acting and inventing construction and formation, all innate talents of the child are made to grow into visible reality.

If we now cast a retrospective look upon the means of occupation in the Kindergarten we find that the material progresses from the *solid* and *whole*, in gradual steps to its *parts*, until it arrives at the *image* upon the *plane*, and its conditions as to *line* and *point*. For the heavy material, fit only to be placed upon the table in unchanged form (the building blocks), a more flexible one is substituted in the following occupations: *Wood* is replaced by *paper*. The paper *plane* of the folding occupation, is replaced by the paper *strip* of the weaving occupation, as *line*. The wooden *stick*, or very thin *wire*, is then introduced for the purpose of executing permanent figures in connection with *peas*, representing the *point*. In place of this material the *drawn line* then appears, to which *colors* are added. Perforating and embroidering introduces another addition to the material to create the images of fantasy, which, in the paper cutting and mounting, again receive new elements.

The *modeling* in clay, or wax, affords the immediate plastic artistic occupation, with the most pliable material for the hand of the child. *Song* introduces into the realm of sound, when *movement plays*, *gymnastics* and *dancing*, help to educate the body, and insure a harmonious development of all its parts. In practicing the technical manual performances of the mechanic, such as boring, piercing, cutting, measuring, uniting, forming, drawing, painting and modeling, a foundation of all future occupation of artisan and artist—synonymous in past centuries—is laid. For ornamentation especially, all elements are found in the occupations of the Kindergarten. The forms of beauty in the paper-folding, serve as series of rosettes and ornaments in relief, as architecture might employ them, without change. The productions in the braiding department contain all conditions of artistic weaving, nor does the cutting of figures fail to afford richest material for ornamentation of various kinds.

For every talent in man means of development are provided in the Kindergarten material, opportunity for practice is constantly given, and each direction of the mind finds its starting-point in *concrete* things. No more complete satisfaction, therefore can be given to the claim of modern pedagogism, that all ideas should be founded on previous perception derived from real objects, than is done in the genuine Kindergarten.

Whosoever has acquired even a superficial idea only of the significance of Fræbel's means of occupation in the Kindergarten, will be ready to admit that the ordinary playthings of children cannot, by any means, as regards their usefulness, be compared with the occupation material in the Kindergarten. That the former may, in a certain degree, be made helpful in the development of children, is not denied; occasional good results with them, however, most always will be found to be owing to the child's own instinct rather than to the nature of the toy. Planless playing, without guidance and supervision, cannot prepare a child for the earnest side of life as well as for the enjoyment of its harmless amusements and pleasures. Like the plant, which, in the wilderness even, draws from the soil its nutrition, so the child's mind draws from its surroundings and the means, placed at its command, its educational food. But the rosebush, nursed and cared for in the garden by the skillful horticulturist produces flowers, far more perfect and beautiful than the wild growing sweet briar. Without care neither mind nor body of the child can be expected to prosper. As the latter cannot, for a healthful development, use all kinds of food without careful selection, so the mind for its higher cultivation requires a still more careful choice of the means for its development. The child's free choice is limited only in so far as it is necessary to limit the amount of occupation material in order to fit him for systematic application. The child will find instinctively all that is requisite for his mental growth, if the proper material only be presented and a guiding mind indicate its most appropriate use in accordance with a certain law.

Froebel's genius has admirably succeeded in inventing the proper material as well as in pointing out its most successful application to prepare the child for all situations in future life, for all branches of occupation in the useful pursuits of mankind.

When the Kindergarten was first established by him, it was prohibited in its original form and its inventor driven from place to place in his fatherland on account of his liberal educational principles, which he wanted to have carried out in the Kindergarten. The keen eye of monarchial government officials quickly saw that such institutions could not turn out willing subjects to tyrannical oppression, and the rulers "*by the grace of God*," tolerated the Kindergarten, only when public opinion declared too strongly in its favor.

In pleading the cause of the Kindergarten on the soil of republican America, is it asking too much that all may help in extending to the future generation the benefits which may be derived from an institution so eminently fit to educate free citizens of a free country?

EDITOR'S NOTES.

In accordance with the general scheme of this book the few simple illustrations accompanying the text of the original edition are reproduced. Owing to the influence of the kindergarten the advance in educational thought in America during the past thirty-five years, has been so great that no argument is now necessary to convince progressive teachers that clay modeling should have a prominent place in primary instruction, and with the promotion of this occupation to the high place which it holds in the modern kindergarten, has come the publication of suggestions and instructions for this work which are of great value, and are given more in detail than the space in this book will allow. Among these excellent hand-books perhaps none holds a higher place than "Clay Modeling in the Schoolroom" by Ellen Stephen Hildreth, who is a practical kindergartner and therefore handles her subject strictly according to kindergarten principles, although the work is carried somewhat further than may be possible during the kindergarten years. The methods of this author, as shown in an exhibit of kindergarten work sent from St. Louis to the Paris Exposition and afterward presented to Madam Marenholtz Von Bulow, received her unqualified endorsement which was expressed in a letter to Mrs. Hildreth at the time. In the opening sentences of the first chapter of "Clay Modeling in the Schoolroom" the author says:—

"Modeling in clay is valuable educationally because it enables us to comprehend and re-

Fig. 14.

produce ideas of form. With such knowledge we convert raw material to our use. It is also valuable as a stimulus to observation, developing through reproduction the faculties of classification and generalization. The art of modeling deals with universal types of form, modified, blended and combined. These types are the curved solids, and in the following pages a definite method is given by which educators may utilize modeling in the discipline of the mind, at an age when sense impressions are strongest."

Fig. 15.

In accordance with a definite scheme the lessons are based on seven geometrical forms, the Sphere, Oblate Spheroid, Prolate Spheroid,

Fig. 16.

Ovoid, Cone, Cylinder, and Cube in the order named, which are designated as Normal Types. This general classification is subdivided into

Fig. 17.

several series, one for each Normal Type. In the first series, the first Normal Type is the Sphere, and the typical objects are sugar-bowl, Fig. 14, lunch-basket Fig. 15, and globe fish, Fig. 16.

The second Normal Type in this series is the Hemisphere. Typical objects, toadstool, Fig. 17, Nelly Bly cap, Fig. 18.

The third Normal Type, is a Circle. Typical objects, sewing-basket, Fig. 19, bird's-nest, Fig. 20.

A similar series is based on each of the above-named seven geometrical forms, and explicit instructions given for the treatment of

Fig. 18.

each subject, with illustrations so that other forms and other typical objects can be handled intelligently from the directions furnished. For material the best artist's clay is most desirable and can be obtained from all dealers in kindergarten material or from potteries, if near at

Fig. 19.

hand. In such case ask for unmixed, washed clay. Clay prepared for firing is usually unfit for modeling. Mrs. Hildreth's instructions for preparing the clay are as follows:—

"If the clay is dry, in lumps or powder, tie it up in a large cloth, as if it were a pudding. Place the cloth full of clay in a vessel, and pour

Fig. 20.

in water enough to cover the clay. After one or two hour's immersion take out the cloth full of clay, and, without untying, knead thoroughly until the mass seems plastic, and perfectly free from lumps. Open the cloth and examine it from time to time while kneading it. If too wet allow it to dry off, if too dry return to the water. When properly kneaded it will have a springy feeling under the fingers, and when rubbed smooth will glisten as if oily. It must not be wet enough to be sticky, or dry enough to feel hard to the touch. A little practice will enable the teacher to tell when it is just right. When worked into an elastic mass, replace in the empty pail the clay which is still in the cloth, and cover with several other folds of wet

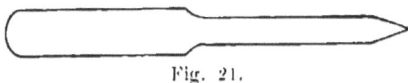

Fig. 21.

cloth. This keeps it in good condition. After each exercise any remnants or broken objects from previous exercises may be thoroughly wet and replaced in the cloth, at one side, in order that they may be softened and re-kneaded. In this way no clay is wasted."

The clay as sold is usually in five pound, dry or six pound moist bricks, or in a powder. The most convenient form is dust-tight paper boxes of powder containing five pounds each.

Artists in plastic materials use a great variety of fine box-wood modeling tools, but these are not necessary for elementary work, although a few simple tools or knives are quite desirable, and Figs. 21 and 22 illustrate two which seem to cover in very simple forms the principal requisites.

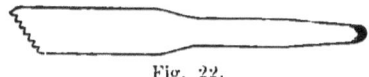

Fig. 22.

Fig. 21 is a spatula or knife with a blade sharpened on both edges and rounded on the end, and a handle terminating in a point which is very useful in many operations.

Fig. 22 is somewhat similar in shape but provided at the blade-end with a serrated edge for leveling down a flat surface of clay when it is required for a base or other purpose.

In this tool the end of the handle is formed to a blunt rounded point which is very useful in many cases. Each of these tools is about six inches long and with them a very large variety of work can be done successfully

THE KINDERGATEN GAMES.

In the whole world of nature nothing develops without activity, consequently play or the exercising of the child's activity is the first means of development of the human mind, the means by which the child is to become acquainted with the outer world and his own powers of body and mind. Watching the play of children Fræbel found it was a spontaneous God-given activity, by which they were surely but unconsciously educating themselves, getting their first knowledge of duty and the truths of life through play. The games which are the organized plays, and the very life of the kindergarten, give the child the means of expression through the activities of the body, so that he can reproduce his individual life, for while in the occupations and gifts the children reproduce with their hands, in the games they enter into the life and act out what they wish to represent and for the time being are really these things, whether it be birds, trees, flowers, stars or water, thus developing and cultivating the imagination.

Every way which exists of expressing the inner life through the outer enriches us, and in the games the child gives forth freely all which he has taken in, and having thus made the unity which he sees and comprehends he becomes fully conscious of it, and his whole life, inner and outer, is lifted to a higher plane. By means of the directed games the surplus energy of the child may be guided, the basis for study laid and the foundation principles in chemistry, physics, geometry, construction and design furnished, thus utilizing his activities for an educational purpose.

The community spirit is fostered as the child finds he is only one of many, and that each one has his part to do to make the many happy and useful. It is also an aid to self-government, for through play he learns that certain effects follow certain causes, and in all that he does the child feels constant freedom under law and soon finds the closer he follows the law the more freedom he has. Thus the will of the child is guided and strengthened, and principles of justice, honesty and kindness are inculcated.

The games representing the trades show ideas of labor and trade and our dependence upon them. The child is in turn a shoemaker, a farmer, a baker, a blacksmith, and is thus brought into relations with the universal activities of the race and gains a respect for those who do in reality what he does in play. Such play broadens a child's view of life and creates an intelligent interest in the lives of many classes of workers, as he sees the skill, patience, and perseverance required on the part of these workers. Thus the intellectual nature is strengthened and developed and also the physical, as the games exercise and give more perfect control of the body, as well as grace and directness of movement. The physical being is brought into activity, different sets of muscles being constantly used, until all parts of the body are engaged in active play. Children need to be free in thought and action, and as the child imitates the activities about him his environment cannot be overrated. We should gain the same freedom in our bodies to express clearly and simply the more mature ideas in our minds, so that we may always meet the little child on his own plane and from there lead him step by step to clearer sight and appreciation of the laws we wish to teach.

Through the dramatic representation of sun, moon and stars and all plant and animal life the child is brought into sympathy and acquaintance with nature, and what he imitates he learns to understand and love. Thus nature grows dearer and the child's conception of all these newly-made friends more beautiful and vivid, awakening in him a spiritual truth which leads him to trace all life back to its source, making this the means of spiritual culture. There is nothing that cannot be made real to the child through games, and any truth may be impressed upon him that is a vital and necessary one.

When the time for the games arrives the children sit with folded hands listening for a chord from the piano, which is a signal to stand. Another chord is struck and the children see how quietly they can put their chairs up to the table. Still another chord, and they turn and form in marching line, singing a simple melody, as :—

"We'll march and march and march around,
And marching gaily sing," etc.,

until they are in good line, then joining hands sing :—

"This is the way that we form our ring,
Tra la la la tra la la la.
Working together we gaily sing,
Tra la la la la la.
Each little pair of children's feet
May help us to make our ring complete.
So this is the way that we form our ring,
Tra la la la la la."
—*Song Stories in the Kindergarten.*

Thus an unbroken circle is formed which has its ethical significance in the fact that no individual is more prominent than another, is but a part of a perfect whole, yet is responsible in himself for that whole. This song may be followed by another, as :—

"See the children on our ring.
Joining in our song;
They together form our ring,
Standing straight and strong."
—*Song Stories in the Kindergarten.*

Then the kindergartner advances to the center of the circle, or bows to some child to do so, while all sing :—

"Let us look at ———
So happy and gay,
Let us look at ———
What does she now play?"

The child in the center then imitates by gesture the game she desires to play, and at the close of the play she chooses another child to take her place in the center of the circle, and so on, each new leader upon her entrance to the center being greeted with the above song.

This is but a simple illustration of one way of opening the games and should not be followed literally, but be subject to the individuality of the teacher. The games should reflect the prevailing thought of the day or week or season of the year, and the children should be made familiar with the life and work of the things they represent by means of pictures and talks and they will readily give spontaneous expression to their conceptions of the subject. At the indication of the slightest disturbing element, a chord from the piano will instantly change the children into animals, birds, or a running stream, thus expressing nature and restoring harmony at once.

Let the games be spontaneous, merely allow and guide the play spirit, keeping the child unconscious by making the thing he does prominent and not the child. If the child does not choose wisely, by questioning and careful suggestions the kindergartner can usually get him to select a more suitable game, and all the games played can be woven into a whole which gives a feeling of unity and completeness.

www.ingramcontent.com/pod-product-compliance
Lightning Source LLC
Chambersburg PA
CBHW032111230426
43672CB00009B/1698